Women Who Would Be Rabbis

Women Who Would Be Rabbis

A HISTORY OF WOMEN'S ORDINATION, 1889–1985

Pamela S. Nadell

Beacon Press

Boston

Beacon Press

25 Beacon Street

Boston, Massachusetts 02108-2892

www.beacon.org

Beacon Press books
are published under the auspices of
the Unitarian Universalist Association of Congregations.

03 02 01 00 99 98   8 7 6 5 4 3 2 1

This book is printed on recycled acid-free paper that contains at
least 20 percent postconsumer waste and meets the uncoated paper
ANSI/NISO specifications for permanence as revised in 1992.

Text design by Margaret M. Wagner
Composition by Wilsted & Taylor Publishing Services

Library of Congress Cataloging-in-Publication Data
Nadell, Pamela Susan.
Women who would be rabbis : a history of women's ordination,
1889–1985 / Pamela S. Nadell.
p.   cm.
ISBN 0-8070-3648-X
1. Ordination of women—Judaism—History.
2. Women rabbis—United States—History.
3. Women in Judaism.   I. Title.
BM652.N33   1998
296.6′1′082—DC21   98-7321

For Yoni and Orly

Contents

Introduction

In the mid-1970s, a reporter for the Jewish press, with aplomb characteristic of the media, proclaimed: "With the ordination of Rabbi Sally Priesand in 1972, Judaism learned that a great religious debate over women in the pulpit had been settled before it began."[1] This book counters that conceit, revealing, to the contrary, that for more than a century Judaism and Jews argued the question of "women in the pulpit," a debate that, even as I write these words, still rages in some places.

I have been writing this book for ten years. I have been thinking about it for thirty. In my last year of high school, at the tail end of the 1960s, one of my Hebrew school friends, chaplain of our synagogue youth group, announced: "I'm going to be the first woman rabbi." I remember my astonishment. What a bold idea, to presume, even as we all dreamed of futures bearing little "relation to the happy housewife image of the 1950s,"[2] to be that which no woman had yet dared to be. Several summers later, as we returned home from our various campuses, we all had read in the press the name of the one who would soon become the first woman rabbi. So I asked my friend, now that she knew she could become a rabbi, would she? No, she quipped, another had beaten her to the gate.

Even as I followed my own career path into academe, I found myself carefully watching the women, among them others of my classmates, acquire what they needed to know to lead them into the rabbinate. As I pursued graduate work in Jewish history, I regarded, with amazement, Conservative Judaism's highly public struggle with the issue. I followed the twists and turns as that rancorous debate dragged on into the 1980s, ending only, in 1985, with the ordination of the first woman to become a Conservative rabbi.

A decade ago, as I was finishing another book, my American University colleague, sociologist Rita Simon, invited me to combine our different scholarly perspectives in a study of the first women who had become rabbis.[3] Back then I assumed that the history of women's entrance to the rabbinate would comprise but a brief prologue of the very few who had dared to envisage this before 1972.

In the late 1980s, we interviewed several dozen of the first women rabbis in the history of Judaism. As I conducted my interviews, the women who had become rabbis repeated over and over: "I decided this when I was eight." "No, I didn't know women couldn't do this." "Back then, I didn't know women weren't rabbis." Their words, echoing those of my friend, sparked me to wonder had other Jewish women, those who had not come of age in the 1960s, asked the same question. As my research deepened and drew me further into the past than I had ever imagined it could, I turned from our plan to write about the women who had become rabbis to the women who would have, if they could have, become rabbis.

Others had already illuminated a handful of women who in earlier eras wanted to be rabbis. Rabbi Sally Priesand first disclosed that, a half century before her, on different continents, both Martha Neumark and Regina Jonas had also asked could not women be rabbis. Religion scholar Ellen Umansky added another name or two.[4] But gradually I not only found more women who had sought this office for themselves, but also many, many others who had engaged in the impassioned debates the question aroused. Not only had the proposal reached deeply into virtually every sector of American Jewish life, briefly resounding in Germany, but, to my great surprise, it extended back in time. For over a century, those championing the woman rabbi and those convinced that Judaism forbade her had argued publicly in the national and Jewish presses; privately in seminary offices, dormitories, and boardrooms; and eventually in the hotel ballrooms of rabbinical conclaves and in the synagogues where some American Jews assembled.

In "begin[ning] to notice what has been ignored,"[5] this century-long debate on the woman rabbi, I drew from different historical fields. From the historians who uncovered the institutional, social, and psychological barriers faced by women who had wanted to practice medicine and law and to preach, I heard echoes of the experiences of the women who had wanted to be rabbis. From those who unveiled women's historic struggles to learn and to use that learning in service to their communities, I drew parallels to the women who proposed to master Jewish learning, to preach it, and to teach it to others. Studies of American religion offered a comparative context. My own discipline, Jewish history, revealed that the growing desire of women to be rabbis was another of the changes made as Western Jews cast off the yoke of the ghetto and entered the modern world.

Toward the end of the eighteenth century as Jews, participating more fully in their broader societies, encountered modernity, many came to appraise life circumscribed by the yoke of Jewish law distasteful. Fearing that "Judaism is weakening in its hold upon its followers day by day," men and women in their Jewish communities and their rabbis decided they must, in order to preserve Judaism, hold up to scrutiny "the entire content of our religion." They believed that if they did not take charge of religious reform, Jews would lead their way out of Judaism.[6]

Subsequently, religious reformers began a process of modifying the customs and ceremonies, the rituals and laws of Jewish life. They revised the synagogue service. They addressed the "cleft between life and the traditional Sabbath observance." They adjusted aspects of the laws which historically set the patterns of Jewish life from birth to death and all that lay in between.[7]

Those who became the first generations of Reform rabbis hoped all modernizing Jews would welcome their revisioning of Judaism, embrace their responses to the challenges of their times. But not all Jews did. Others had different ideas about the proper balance between tradition and change. As these men articulated just what transformations of Judaism they could accept, they laid the foundations for "the more traditional movements of Jewish religious modernization."[8] Those who became Conservative Jews sought "to integrate tradition with modernity," to shape a movement reflecting "a modern mind and a Jewish heart, prophetic passion and western science."[9] Those who articulated modern Orthodoxy, while never immune to currents of change, ruled in favor of devotion to tradition.[10]

Even as the encounter with modernity reshaped Jews and Judaism, it revolutionized the rabbinate. Rabbi, literally "my master," described the sages devoted to study, to interpretation and to explication of Jewish law. In Europe, before the modern era, Jews appointed rabbis spiritual heads of their communities. They needed these men to interpret and to apply Jewish law, to serve as legal decision makers and to judge, tasks mandatory to the proper functioning of Jewish society. Barricaded behind their tomes of Talmud, these rabbis searched in the tradition of the past to judge the affairs of their day. Women compelled their daughters to run to the rabbi to ask if the chicken they hoped to cook for the Sabbath was kosher. Fiancés came to break their engagement contracts. The married came so the rabbi could arrange their writs of divorce. Businessmen asked the rabbi to arbitrate the "fractions" of their disputes. Others came to dictate their wills. Their heirs came to dispute the terms. Rabbis thus ruled on matters religious and affairs civil.[11]

But in the modern era rabbis lost most of their powers of jurisdiction. Modernizing Jews no longer turned to rabbis to ask if they could eat a chicken or to settle a business dispute. Jews now required rabbis less for their ability to interpret Jewish law, than to stand as exemplars of Judaism, men with a broad experience of Jewish life and culture and the ability to convey their knowledge. Nineteenth- and twentieth-century Jews came to expect that their rabbis would lead them in their congregations and preach at every service. They asked them to solemnize their weddings and to speak words of comfort at their funerals. They wanted men capable of inspiring their children and discussing great Jewish books with the sisterhood. They required rabbis to counsel the sick, the dying, the divorcing, and the disenchanted. In short, they expected their rabbis to minister, much like parsons, preachers, and pastors.

But no matter their prescriptions for modern Judaism, these rabbis, and all who identified as Reform, Conservative, or Orthodox Jews, found themselves compelled to reassess the position of women within Judaism. The encounter with modernity mandated certain shifts in women's presence, place, and roles in their Jewish communities. Eventually these changes would pave the way for some to raise the question of women rabbis. This debate thus figured as one more of the myriad and highly delicate negotiations Judaism faced at its new boundaries with the modern world.

As the story of the women who asked to become rabbis unfolds, this book echoes what so many others have already affirmed, that uncovering women's history remains a political enterprise. Women need to know that others preceding them have wrestled with the same questions and ideas. Without this knowledge, they remain disadvantaged, unable to build upon the creativity of those who came before. Explaining the grave consequences of the failure to recount women's history, the eminent historian Gerda Lerner wrote:

> Men created written history and benefited from the transmittal of knowledge from one generation to the other, so that each great thinker could stand "on the shoulders of giants," thereby advancing thought over that of previous generations with maximum efficiency. Women were denied knowledge of their history, and thus each woman had to argue as though no woman before her had ever thought or written. Women had to use their energy to reinvent the wheel, over and over again, generation after generation.[12]

This history of the debate on the woman rabbi follows Lerner's paradigm. It substantiates that for a century the women who wanted to be rabbis and their supporters invented over and over again the same arguments to prove that women were worthy, that they were capable, that they were serious, that they could learn, and that they should use their knowledge to become rabbis, teachers, and preachers. Given that Jewish men and women still debate the issue today, uncovering the history of the women who would be rabbis unequivocally brands this scholarship political. For those currently engaged in the question are about to discover that the arguments and strategies they believe they are constructing anew were visited by others a long century before.

Women Who Would Be Rabbis

Chapter 1

"Could not—our women—be—ministers?"

RAISING THE QUESTION OF WOMEN'S RABBINIC ORDINATION, 1889

In 1889, the journalist and Jewish communal activist Mary M. Cohen posed a provocative and unexpected question. On the front page of Philadelphia's *Jewish Exponent*, in the short story "A Problem for Purim," Cohen created a female protagonist who dared to ask "Could not—our *women*—be—ministers?"[1]

The story is set a few days before Purim. Lionel Martinez, a student preparing for the "ministry," a term then commonly used for the rabbinate, invites a few friends to gather to discuss Jewish affairs. Despite his concern that some of them might object, he decides—because "we require the help of the other sex"—to include three women. Meeting at his home on the night of the festival, Martinez asks his guests to govern themselves according to the rules then in fashion in societies and clubs, even though they have not met to form one. The circle elects him chairman. He then raises the evening's topic: "ministers and their work."

Initially, the discussion turns to sermons and the possibilities of exchanging pulpits in the hopes that this might offer, as one young man claims, "*some* vitalizing influence." In response, Dora Ulman, the superintendent of a local sewing circle, speaks up. Warning those assembled that her words "will shock you all considerably," she asks:

> "Could not—our *women*—be—ministers?" All but Lionel were struck dumb. Even Jack's boasted calmness had taken flight; he sate [*sic*] in open-eyed surprise. Martinez said quickly:
> "Will you explain your idea or plan, Miss Dora?" He was, however, secretly a little astonished; he had not expected anything from her until later on, and then, "views" on sewing-schools.

In the remainder of the story Cohen, through her female characters, sets forth in clear and forceful rhetoric just why Jewish women should become rabbis.

She begins by having Miss Dora argue "that there are trials in the lives of women that men do not and cannot understand," and that women can preach and teach about these better than men. As men now minister to both men and women, women surely can do the same. While she does not expect women to "supercede men in the pulpit," she brings forward the biblical models of Miriam, Deborah, Hannah, Huldah, and Esther to reveal Jewish precedent for female leadership. She then argues "women are created to the work of ministering just as they are to the painting of pictures, the writing of poems, or the moulding of statues." When one of the men remarks that even if congregations would accept women, he knows scarcely any women capable of rabbinical duties, she counters: "There are some among my friends . . . who have a strong inclination for the work and only need due preparation and a little encouragement to properly qualify them; their example would no doubt bring forward other candidates."

When one young man argues that people "would laugh openly to see a woman in the pulpit," Cohen's Isabel Harris, who has "large experience in various educational and charitable work," retorts: "Oh, every good cause is apt to meet with ridicule at first." Other innovations, Isabel points out, such as the English-language sermon, once considered "terrible," gradually won acceptance and are now considered essential. Surely, women ministers would similarly prevail as, despite the laughter, they proved themselves capable. After all, "Are not some of our present preachers ridiculed? It would be no worse for women than for men."

Yet the future Rabbi Martinez doubts "our people" are ready for this. "It would alarm them more than any previous novelty. They will probably imagine that our present preachers are becoming too weak to hold the reins of spiritual influence." Some would also voice "the usual objection to women going out of their proper sphere." After all, while the mothers and wives of rabbis do not take active roles in public worship, they have always participated in their sons' and husbands' charitable endeavors.

While Dora compliments such women's exemplary avocation, she believes his "fear of women out-doing men in ministerial work is just what would spur your sex on to better things, and thus give ours a higher ideal for which to strive. Competition is the safe-guard of the people." Responding to his circumscription of woman's proper sphere, she contends, "If women have a gift for the ministry, they are more in their place in the pulpit than if they were doing plain sewing, teaching music, or attempting any other work than the one to which their nature and their conscience call them."[2] Finally, she concludes by citing an anonymous Christian clergyman who wrote: "The pulpit will never reach its sublimest power until Woman takes her place in it as a free and equal interpreter of God."

Nevertheless, the advocates of women's ordination do not have the last word in Cohen's story. Wishing to match Miss Dora's quotation with one of his own, Harris, whose sister has already pointed out the promise of this innovation for American Judaism, counters with the words of the early woman's rights activist and journalist Margaret Fuller: "Man is not willingly ungenerous. He wants faith and love, because he is not yet himself an elevated being." And so, even though the group disperses, "some with new thoughts to mark the Festival of Queen Esther," Harris's words seem to signal society's inevitable resistance to change.

What remains striking about this story more than a century later is how Cohen uncannily anticipated much of the rhetoric and most, although not all, of the arguments that would, emerge[3]—as if *de novo*—every time the question of women's ordination would later surface in some sector of American Jewry. These same arguments favoring and opposing women rabbis would ring in decades to come in the Anglo-Jewish press; swirl through seminary offices, dormitories, and boardrooms; surface in the halls of rabbinical conclaves; and eventually eddy out both to the American press and to the synagogues. Without any sense that these points were not being made for the first time, in fact with the sense that these arguments were novel and immensely essential,[4] those opposed to and those in favor of women's rabbinic ordination would clash over and over again in the same terms.

Those opposed to female rabbis would often begin, like Lionel Martinez, from a position of surprise that women could see beyond their circumscribed horizons to broach the topic. They would claim that there were very few, if any, women suited for the task; that even if there were such women, they would meet ridicule if they attempted to become rabbis; and that no one would hire them anyway. They also would say that while Judaism had survived other radical innovations, they did not believe "our people" ready for this one; it constituted too severe a break with the past. Some would allude to the fact that women in the pulpit would feminize the profession, endangering the status and reputation of men who continued to choose this career.

So too, those in favor of women's ordination would voice the arguments Cohen's female characters raised. In this modern world, all professions, including the rabbinate, should be opened to women. Such female exclusion was not only patently unjust, it damaged the profession, for women, with their unique perspectives, could understand female issues and problems far better than the men who now had sole responsibility for the ministry. Ministering to others, rather than standing outside of woman's proper sphere, was integral to it. In fact, women, as a group, would bring to the rabbinate enormous strengths, especially the spirituality acknowledged as particular to their sex. Moreover, ordination for women did not mark a radical innovation, or a schism with the past, for Jewish tradition had produced both Miriam and Deborah. The entrance of women into the rabbinate would not feminize the profession and make it unattractive to men. Instead, it promised to raise the quality and status of all rabbis by raising the excellence of the entire field.

Who was Mary M. Cohen and how did she come, in 1889, to raise this question, presaging a century-long debate about the admission of women to the rabbinate? Like the female characters of "A Problem for Purim," she "had large experience in various educational and charitable work," was personally committed to Judaism and the Jewish community, and was determined to play an active role in negotiating and shaping their expression in America. Born in 1854 into an upper-middle-class Philadelphia Jewish family, Cohen joined an intergenerational coterie of privileged men and women committed to Judaism. Many, like herself, were single, worshipped together at Philadelphia's leading traditionalist synagogue, Mikveh Israel, and made "careers" out of their deep involvement in Jewish cultural, religious, and charitable institutions. Cohen was the third superintendent, after founder Rebecca Gratz and Louisa B. Hart, of Philadelphia's Hebrew Sunday School, the first institution to give women a public role in teaching Judaism. She also led Mikveh Israel's Religious School Committee and presided over the Mikveh Israel Association, a coeducational group interested in Jewish education and social life. She was the first corresponding secretary of the Jewish Publication Society and the only woman member of its first executive committee. Desiring the maintenance of traditional, but acculturated forms of Judaism in America, she railed against Reform, which she called "infidelity." She urged faithful Jews to do what in essence she did, to "rouse themselves from the indifference which religious liberty [can] promote" and to work to develop a viable American Jewish culture.[5]

Cohen envisioned educated Jewish women, like herself, playing a particular role in combating the religious indifference she derided. She championed universal secular education and Jewish girls' religious education. Surely, her own substantial and continuing Jewish education served as a fitting model. A graduate of Philadelphia's Hebrew Sunday School, she continued her studies, even toward the end of her life, learning Hebrew with a tutor in her last years. Not only did she teach in the Hebrew Sunday School, but she also taught English to the women who came to classes run by Philadelphia's Jewish

Young Women's Union. She championed Jewish women's religious education in the Jewish press, commending a New York innovation that saw women leading English-language High Holiday services for working girls. Her writings widely cited Jewish sources, including Isaac Leeser's Bible translation and works of Jewish history.[6]

Nevertheless, Cohen remained sensitive to the prevailing ethos of her class and day, the Victorian ideal of "true womanhood" which glorified the inherent piety of women. Thus, she celebrated Jewish women within that cultural context. The life of Louisa B. Hart, her predecessor at the Hebrew Sunday School, offers one such example. In editing Hart's *Memoirs*, Cohen praised her "intellectual spirituality" and "purity of soul" and her dedication to Judaism and Jews. In making a "career" out of her work in the Jewish community, Hart, a pious, single, Jewish woman, like Cohen, "gave up her life for her religion."[7]

As her familiarity with the larger culture's model of "true womanhood" suggests, Cohen's experience straddled the Jewish and gentile worlds. Beyond her involvement in a myriad of Jewish organizations, she participated in several literary—and largely gentile—clubs, including the Pennsylvania Women's Press Association, and reform organizations, such as the New York Social Economy Committee. Moreover, she took great interest in the 1876 National Centennial Exhibition held in Philadelphia. A member of its Women's Committee, she helped create the Women's Pavilion. In her articles in the popular press, just then beginning to appear under the pseudonym "Coralie," she publicized the committee's work.[8]

Other articles pasted in her scrapbooks reveal her interests in the expanding horizons of work opening to women. One clipping reports on a census of seventy-two jobs performed by American women, from actor to woolen mill worker—and including preacher. Another celebrates the successful careers of local women, among them a columnist, chemist, and physician. Meanwhile, her younger sister, Katherine M. Cohen, literally sculpted a career in "the moulding of statues." This evidence confirmed what Mary M. Cohen well knew from her own growing experience as a writer and a journalist, whose articles increasingly found a place in the general press and in Jewish newspapers, such as the *American Hebrew.* With the proper education, women could carve out for themselves new professional opportunities.[9]

These two overarching absorptions—that of the woman fully devoted to Judaism and its successful transplantation to America and that of a "career" woman, fully cognizant of the expanding professional opportunities opening to American women—converged in "A Problem for Purim." On the day of the Jewish year when Jewish boys and girls masque themselves and take on unfamiliar roles, on the day when Jewish men may dress as women, Cohen dared to envision a woman as rabbi. In so doing, she asked her story's readers to ponder the problem she posed for Purim: "whether a strong and constant belief that a thing will be, helps anything to the effecting of the thing." For Cohen, then and later, there was "no sex in spirituality. . . . The woman who is fitted by nature and experience to occupy the pulpit should do so."[10]

Cohen prophesied this "thing will be" because so many innovations had already taken place and, in fact, continued to take place, in American Jewish religious life. Indeed many of these changes far exceeded reforms, like the vernacular sermon, which she pointed to in "A Problem for Purim." Moreover, American Jews of very different bents, Reformers and traditionalists, had eagerly embraced many of these modernizations.

In his masterful history of Reform Judaism, Michael Meyer observes that, as the pace of synagogue building accelerated in America in the years after the Civil War, many ritual and liturgical innovations appeared. Congregations introduced organs, replaced cantors with gentile choirs, abolished the second day of festivals, abbreviated and in some places even eliminated the Torah reading, discarded Orthodox prayer books, exchanged the traditional Hebrew liturgy for an increasingly vernacular one, and dispensed with the prayer shawl and male head covering.[11] Collectively, these innovations, especially such radical ones as eliminating male ritual garb, came to be characteristic of synagogues affiliating with Reform Judaism.

Yet, most nineteenth-century American congregations experimented with reforms.[12] For example, from 1829 to 1850, Isaac Leeser, *hazzan* of the Cohen family's synagogue, Mikveh Israel, sanctioned changes "consistent with tradition," promoting enhanced synagogue decorum and English translations.[13]

Not surprisingly, women's presence, place, and roles in the nineteenth-century American synagogue underwent a similar transformation in adapting to modernity. The domestic sphere was the area of Jewish religious life traditionally presided over by Jewish women, but ironically it did not easily transfer to America, which located religiosity more in the public space of the church rather than in the private realm of the home. As a result, the identity and roles of women as Jews underwent a gradual reshaping in nineteenth-century American Judaism.[14]

The most visible shift from European, premodern forms of Judaism was the emergence of women as synagogue worshippers.[15] Paralleling a feminization of American Protestant churches that contemporary observers noted,[16] some middle-class, acculturating American Jewish women came to display their piety publicly by becoming synagogue-goers. This new pattern sharply contrasted with traditional Judaism's exemption for women from most occasions of public prayer and coincidentally was not copied by the German middle-class female cousins they left behind in the birthplace of Reform Judaism, Germany.[17] Including women in greater numbers in synagogue worship formed an explicit part of the early programs of American reformers. They argued: "[W]omen must not be excluded from the soul-satisfying experiences which come to us through a solemn worship service." And in nineteenth-century America, observer after observer commented on the growing presence of women in synagogue sanctuaries.[18] In some places they came to dominate as they replaced their husbands and sons who had fled to the secular worlds of work and clubs.

Moreover this shift affected congregations of all kinds.[19] Mikveh Israel's Isaac Leeser wrote, in 1844: "The females too belong to Israel, and they also must be taught, that they may understand and observe the law." And he welcomed the women who began to come to synagogue. He not only created—at their request—the revolution of the English-language sermon but also set about translating important sacred texts. With his translation of their Hebrew prayer books and his

English Bible, the first by an American Jew, his female congregants could better prepare themselves for their greatest task, rearing their children as Jews. Committed, knowledgeable Jewish women thus offered a potential solution to the problem of the waning interest so many American male Jews displayed with regard to Judaism. Leeser and other traditionalists like him, many the forerunners of what would later become Conservative Judaism, did not define new roles for women synagogue-goers. Yet, their sensitivity to enhancing women's understanding of Judaism revealed their acceptance of the transformation that had allowed for modernizing Jewish women to emerge as public worshippers.[20]

The emergence of nineteenth-century, middle-class, acculturated Jewish women as synagogue-goers represented but the first shift in women's presence, place, and roles in nineteenth-century American synagogues. Other experiments, especially the introduction by some congregations in the late 1840s of mixed choirs, expanded women's experience of their synagogues. Comprised of boys and girls from the religious school, or male and female congregants, or, in some places, gentiles, mixed choirs revealed the reformers' determination to create a more aesthetic synagogue service. Mixed choirs challenged, although many observers did not know this, Judaism's precept against women raising their voices in public prayer. Their introduction sparked the first specific discussions in the nascent Anglo-Jewish press of woman's place in the synagogue.[21]

By the middle of the 1850s new debate about woman's literal place in the American synagogue emerged. Traditionally, when they came to synagogue, Jewish women sat behind a screen in a balcony above the main floor.[22] In 1851, at Anshe Emeth in Albany, New York, Isaac Mayer Wise, the founding president of Hebrew Union College and the father of Reform Judaism in America, introduced—almost as an afterthought—the practice of seating men and women together. Anshe Emeth had recently purchased a church. Rather than spending money on renovating the church to accommodate a balcony for the women, the members made use of the existing pews for both men and women.[23] As modernizing synagogues battled over this break with the past, reforming rabbis would point to mixed seating as a marker of the successful emancipation of women in the synagogue.[24]

The introduction of confirmation for boys *and girls* revealed still other shifts not only in the creation of a public occasion for the affirmation of Judaism but also in new patterns of educating Jewish girls. Attention to the education of Jewish girls had periodically surfaced in various Jewish communities in the past, often as part of a general trend of reforming the local Jewish education system.[25] Early German leaders of Reform Judaism had, in particular, considered the religious education of Jewish girls in need of serious improvement. They worked to replace the traditional pattern of a girl learning in her mother's kitchen all she needed to know about Judaism with a new emphasis on formal religious instruction.[26]

In the United States, as nineteenth-century American Jews experimented with various systems of Jewish education, they accommodated to the growing American norm of coeducational instruction. From its inception in 1838, the Philadelphia Hebrew Sunday School taught boys and girls.[27]

Now not only did modernizing Jews plan to instruct their daughters alongside their sons, but they also introduced them to subjects Jewish girls traditionally had not studied. In the all-day schools established by Jewish immigrants in New York in the 1840s, both boys and girls in the grammar classes had an hour of Hebrew instruction. Nevertheless, during the hour the boys studied Torah and haftarah cantillation, the girls practiced needlework.[28] Emily Fechheimer Seasongood, who grew up in Cincinnati in the 1850s and 1860s, recalled in her memoir that, for a time, the curriculum in the schoolhouse annex of Bene Yeshurun included "Chumish," the five books of Moses, taught in Hebrew.[29]

More surprisingly, for the first time, many of those teaching these boys and girls were women. As the teaching profession in American public schools rapidly became feminized, Jewish women also emerged as teachers in the new Jewish schools. Historically, formal Jewish education had remained the exclusive domain of men. But over the course of the nineteenth century, American Jewish women pioneered new roles as teachers of Judaism in the Sunday schools and supplementary schools then emerging to educate the next generation of American Jews. The Philadelphia Hebrew Sunday School offered Jewish women their first public role as teachers. Later, only its female graduates could join the faculty. Meanwhile, Jewish women in Baltimore, Charleston, and Savannah solicited advice from Rebecca Gratz, the school's founder, on taking up the mantle of Jewish educator.[30]

The goal of such education, to raise Jews committed to their communities and synagogues who would, in turn and in time, come to rear their own Jewish offspring, was manifested in the new ceremony of confirmation. Obviously borrowed from Christianity, where it marked the end of the study necessary to assume adult responsibilities in the church, the idea of confirmation appeared as one of the early reforms envisioned by members of the first generation of German Jews engaging Reform. They critiqued the "theatrical act" of the bar mitzvah. This ceremony historically signified a thirteen-year-old boy's coming-of-age, that now he had to take on the obligation of fulfilling all of the commandments of Jewish law. But in the modern era, so the Reformers believed, a young boy no longer received the "moral religious training" necessary to "become a man who will stand up courageously against all storms of fate." Thus the bar mitzvah, which signaled the religious maturation conferred by age, had become a "meaningless ceremonial."[31] Moreover, girls, who reached religious maturity at age twelve, experienced no solemn occasion comparable to the bar mitzvah. For reforming rabbis, this omission revealed yet another case where "[o]nce again, the female sex is here treated as less capable, as in Oriental custom." Aware that no such rabbinic custom marked the "significant landmark in the life of both boys and girls which consists of the knowledge of religion they have achieved," reforming rabbis proposed confirmation.[32]

Apparently the first confirmation ceremony dates to the German city of Dessau in 1803, where it involved an examination of what the thirteen-year-old boys knew about the precepts and duties of Judaism. By the second decade of the nineteenth century in Germany, the examination, initially held in the school or home, had moved to the synagogue and the first female pupils were confirmed.[33]

In the decades that followed the practice of confirmation spread to the United States. An individual confirmation ceremony appeared in 1830 in the prayer book of the Reformed Society of Israelites, the first such group on American soil. By 1846 confirmations including girls as celebrants, had been introduced in New York City by Max Lilienthal. Isaac Mayer Wise soon followed Lilienthal by holding them in Albany, New York.[34] More traditional congregations quickly followed, without, however, seeing confirmation as a replacement for bar mitzvah. "[I]n the course of time, virtually everyone was won over to the constructive effect of this ceremony."[35]

Emily Fechheimer Seasongood, who was confirmed by Isaac Mayer Wise at Bene Yeshurun in Cincinnati in 1864, and Wise, himself, have both left descriptions of the confirmation as celebrated at mid-century. By this time the "modern confirmation" had acquired ceremonial elements beyond a public examination of what the children had learned in their twice-weekly instruction with the rabbi. Held on the first day of Shavuot, the holiday marking the giving of the Torah to the Israelites at Mount Sinai, acculturating American Jews gathered in their synagogues to affirm the entrance of "our sons and daughters into the same covenant." Marching up the aisle to the hymns sung by the choir, the thirteen-year-old Emily Fechheimer placed a bouquet on the pulpit. She and her thirty classmates then listened solemnly as Wise reviewed the doctrines of Judaism and examined the students. After each confirmand recited a poem, they declared their consent to live according to the precepts of Judaism. Then "the congregation [rose] to witness the act of confirmation; the minister [laid] his hands upon the heads of the pupils and blesse[d] them two by two." As the choir sang the priestly prayer, the pupils were then blessed by their parents. Afterwards, friends and relatives visited Emily's home to offer congratulations, enjoy refreshments, and view her gifts.[36]

The communal confirmation, coming at the end of the academic year (for Shavuot typically falls in May or June)—with its procession, music, flowers, display of the students' erudition, and gift-giving— echoes the graduation ceremony students, like Emily, celebrated upon completing private or public school. Through the confirmation ceremony, these acculturating American Jewish teens marked the end of their Jewish educations and their admission to the Jewish community of the synagogue.

Confirmation also promised, for a few, a glimpse of something more than the experience of the congregant. It provided a once-in-a-lifetime opportunity for Jewish teens to stand briefly and speak before the congregation, to demonstrate publicly their commitment to Judaism and their desire to play a role in maintaining their community. Boys who found themselves moved by this experience, could, if they sought, find other occasions to stand up and be counted as Jews. If they wished, they could even aspire to lead their communities, to make a career in the rabbinate.

This was not the case for girls. Even though the confirmation was utterly novel for girls within Judaism, it also marked the *only* occasion for them to ascend the *bimah* and speak before the congregation. That fact did not dissuade girls (or at least did not dissuade their parents) from participating in confirmation. Photos and lists of confirmands published in the Anglo-Jewish press present confirmands, by the early twentieth century, if not before—much like congregants in many synagogues—as largely female. At Congregation B'nai Jeshurun in New York City, at Isaiah Temple in Chicago, and at Temple Israel in Omaha, Nebraska, the majority, sometimes the preponderant majority, of those confirmed, were female.[37] After their confirmations, the young women returned to take their places in their family pews awaiting the day when they would move from the pew of their father to that of their husband.

As Mary M. Cohen well knew by 1889, even though her own synagogue prohibited many of these reforms, the presence, place, and roles of women in American synagogues had already changed significantly from the past. Yet, Jews engaged in the process of confronting modernity made still other adaptations affecting Jewish girls and women. As rabbis and scholars sought to reconcile the traditions of the past with the times they found themselves living in, they embraced yet other changes, sanctioning amendments to and even abrogations of certain of the Jewish laws regulating women's lives.

Early reformers had effected changes in the position of Jewish women by calling for their religious instruction, confirming them alongside their brothers, and welcoming them into the synagogue. But a broader concern with the overall status of women within Judaism emerged in a series of conferences held in Germany and in the United States. Here relatively small groups of reforming rabbis, responding to the changing political and cultural climates already impacting their modernized and increasingly fragmented Jewish communities, reexamined virtually every aspect of the tradition they had inherited.[38]

Probing Jewish tradition against "the idea that pure religious faith is essentially moral"[39] and influenced by the scientific rationalism of the day, modernizing rabbis tested the inviolability of the customs and praxis of the past. They scrutinized the body of Jewish law known as *halachah*, attempting to reconcile each of its precepts with their new-found sensibilities and roles as participants in larger societies. They reconsidered traditional patterns of Jewish dress and diet, the holidays and Sabbaths, religious services, their language, liturgy, and aesthetics, and central religious tenets, including the notion of the Jews as the chosen people, the belief in the coming of the messiah, and the promise of the return to Zion.

All these were burning topics at the rabbinical conferences, as individual rabbis vehemently argued over the parameters of the changes each could sanction. Some willingly abandoned tenets historically central to Judaism, such as the particularism of biblical laws governing diet and the hope for the return to Zion, as incompatible with the spirit of the age. Others eagerly embraced some modernizations, such as changes in dress and openness to secular education, but could not abide jettisoning Hebrew as the language of prayer. The results of their passionate debates evolved into not only Reform Judaism, but also into the "more traditional movements of Jewish religious modernization," Orthodoxy and Conservative Judaism.[40]

The religious emancipation of Jewish women and the rectification of the disadvantages they incurred under the yoke of Jewish law naturally fell within the sweep of the Reforming rabbis' attack on tradition. By 1837, when the first of these rabbinical conferences convened in Wiesbaden, various communities had already reformed the religious instruction they offered their daughters and introduced confirmation to include them. Now modernizing rabbis began scrutinizing the laws affecting the status of women within Judaism. At a subsequent conference in Breslau in 1846, Rabbi David Einhorn, then one of the more radical Reform rabbis in Germany, and later a rabbi in Baltimore, Philadelphia, and New York, summarized the theme of these discussions. He argued in favor of the "complete religious equality of the female sex" as a natural outcome of "our religious consciousness, which grants all humans an equal degree of natural holiness." As a result, he believed "[t]he halakhic position of women must undergo a change."[41]

Essentially, discussions of women's status within Judaism revolved around three central issues: ameliorating the position of women within the Jewish laws of marriage and divorce, equalizing their opportunities in Jewish ceremonials, and emancipating them in the synagogue. Initially much concern centered on the laws of marriage and divorce, many of which, by the middle decades of the nineteenth century, seemed particularly distasteful, if not disgraceful, to modernizing Jews, male and female.

Levirate marriage and the plight of the *agunah* engendered the greatest disapproval. Levirate marriage, as required by biblical law, demanded that a childless widow marry her brother-in-law or that they enact *halitzah*, a ceremony of renunciation. During *halitzah* the brother-in-law frees his widowed sister-in-law from the obligation to marry him and to rear their first child in the name of her deceased husband. But more Jewish women faced the fearsome possibility that a marital disaster could brand her, who had once been a wife, an *agunah*. Jewish women found the plight of the *agunah* potentially more disabling. A woman becomes an *agunah*, bound to her husband forever, unable to wed another, when he has refused to divorce her, disappeared, or his death remains unconfirmed.[42]

Once Reformers began amending and even revoking Jewish laws, they tackled these and other marital precepts they deemed inimical to their age. In 1837, Abraham Geiger—a key figure in the second generation of German Jewish reformers, who, for articulating and shaping its ideology, deserves more than anyone else the title "founding father of the Reform movement"[43]—called for the abolition of *halitzah* and *agunah*.[44] In 1871, at a synod held in Augsburg, Reform rabbis agreed that where the secular authorities had declared a missing person dead, the widow could remarry. And they adopted, almost unanimously, a resolution dispensing with *halitzah*.[45]

This Augsburg synod may well have been influenced by the decisions made by a group of liberal rabbis who had met in Mary M. Cohen's hometown of Philadelphia in November 1869.[46] Organized by Einhorn to promote his radical views of Reform Judaism in America and to deal with key practical issues, especially marriage laws, its thirteen participants decided *halitzah* "has lost all sense, significance, and binding force for us" and that the question of whether a husband or wife could be declared "presumed dead" "should be left to the laws of the country." They also decreed that "the bride shall no longer play a passive role." In the traditional Jewish wedding, she neither spoke nor gave her groom a ring. Yet, these American rabbis now endorsed both. Furthermore, viewing divorce as "a purely civil matter," they dispensed with the *get*, the document a divorcing husband gives to his wife.[47] (Without this document, which only the husband can give, she becomes an *agunah*, chained within an untenable marriage.)

Reformers recognized other aspects of Jewish tradition also required emendation. In the spirit of ceremonial equality which brought confirmation for girls and the double-ring wedding ceremony, Joseph Johlson, a teacher in the liberal Frankfurt Jewish community school, proposed that ceremonial equality begin at birth. In Judaism on the eighth day following the birth of a boy, Jews mark his entrance into the covenant with a ritual circumcision, *brit milah*, and name the baby before the community. Finding ritual bloodletting repugnant to the age and an unnecessary physical danger, Johlson created a new rite, "The Sanctification of the Eighth Day," in 1843. In so doing, he surprisingly—for no such parallel ritual existed for female infants—conceived the ceremony of naming and entrance into the covenant for both boys and girls. Unlike confirmation and the double-ring ceremony, "The Sanctification of the Eighth Day" did not find acceptance among nineteenth-century German Reform Jews. Despite the spirit of the age, the Reform rabbinical conferences of the mid-nineteenth century did not reject circumcision. But the experiment reflects the spirit for equality between the sexes already evident in Reform Judaism.[48]

Reforming marriage laws and equalizing girls and women within the ceremonies of Judaism were not the only areas of *halachic* change involving Jewish women. Indeed, transformations in one other venue of change, emancipating women in the synagogue, would eventually push forward the question, "Could not our women become rabbis?"

In 1837, in the same year Abraham Geiger convened the first conference of Reform-oriented rabbis, he wrote:

Let there be from now on no distinction between duties for men and women, unless flowing from the natural laws governing the sexes; no assumption of the spiritual minority of woman, as though she were incapable of grasping the deep things in religion; no institution of the public service, either in form or content, which shuts the doors of the temple in the face of women . . . our whole religious life will profit from the beneficial influence which feminine hearts will bestow upon it.[49]

Geiger—much like Mary M. Cohen's fictional rabbinical student—knew women could help in the effort to develop a revitalized Judaism. To attract them, he proposed ending the distinction Judaism traditionally made between the sexes vis-à-vis their religious responsibilities. Tradition obligated Jewish men to fulfill all of the laws of the Torah, the positive and the negative prescriptions, those bound by time and those outside of time (with the obvious exceptions of certain precepts particular to women, such as those governing women's sexuality). However, Jewish law generally exempted women, largely because of domestic responsibilities, from fulfilling the *mitzvot* that were positive commandments fixed in time. Because for Jewish women domestic needs took precedence over such *mitzvot* as the requirement to pray with a quorum of ten three times a day, women experienced a form of spiritual minority within traditional Judaism. Geiger envisioned opening the temple doors and requiring Jewish women to cross that threshold just as Judaism commanded their fathers and brothers, husbands and sons. Yet his call for emancipation included a caveat: female responsibilities within Judaism must remain circumscribed by the "natural laws governing the sexes."

Others shared Geiger's opinion. Several discussants at the conference of liberal rabbis held in Frankfurt-am-Main in 1845 raised the matter of women's religious minority. In calling for the abolition of *aliyot*, the honor of being called to the Torah, Abraham Adler contended it accentuated the distinction between the sexes, since men alone went up to the Torah. He asserted Judaism must insist upon the equality of men and women in religious functions. Samuel Adler and David Einhorn concurred. Samuel Adler then proposed a resolution proclaiming that

> she has the same obligation as man to participate from youth up in the instruction in Judaism and in the public services, and that the custom not to include women in the number of individuals necessary for the conducting of a public service is only a custom and has no religious basis.

Rather than voting then, the conference charged Geiger, Adler, and Einhorn with bringing to the next gathering specific proposals for women's religious equality. In Breslau a year later, Einhorn presented their report.[50]

It went beyond Geiger's sweeping call for women's emancipation within Judaism by listing the steps required to effect it. Opening with the demand that the *halachic* position of women must change, its authors argued that women "have received assurances of their capabilities for emancipation, without, however, being indeed permitted to become emancipated." After surveying why in the past this was so—in part because "it was believed that God Himself had pronounced the damning verdict over her"—they proclaimed: "[I]t is a sacred duty to express most emphatically the complete religious equality of the female sex." This meant "the female sex as religiously equal with the male, in its obligations and rights." Women must observe all the commandments—that is, those modernizing Jews still kept—even those pertaining to fixed times. To prepare them to do so, girls would, alongside their brothers, receive Jewish educations and reach religious maturity at age thirteen. After that point, girls would both participate in public worship and count in a *minyan*, the quorum of ten necessary for public prayer. And since a woman would now pray equally with her husband, the reformers would abolish the demeaning benediction in which men thanked God for not having made them female (*shelo asani ishah*).[51]

Although historian Michael Meyer indicates widespread support for these measures, the men at the 1846 conference in Breslau neither discussed nor voted upon them. They claimed their failure to consider them was for lack of time.[52] Thus, the legal emancipation of women within German Reform Judaism remained an ideological desideratum for some Reformers, never achieving the status within the German Reform synagogue of legal mandate.

Nevertheless, in future years many would hail Einhorn's 1846 report as a hallmark of women's emancipation within Reform Judaism.[53] Those who did apparently failed to recall that it was not confirmed and also that, like Geiger, its authors fixed limits to woman's emancipation, proclaiming: "It is thus our task to pronounce the equality of religious privileges and obligations of women *in so far as this is possible"* (emphasis added). Like Geiger's caveat that women would share in the duties of Judaism in consonance with "the natural laws governing the sexes," these rabbis expected women to achieve equality in the synagogue only "in so far as this is possible."

Although the Reformers did not delineate their restrictions, they had no need to. Not until the first decade of the twentieth century would Germany allow women to matriculate in its universities.[54] Einhorn and the other rabbis shared the assumptions of their time and place. As natural laws fixed the rising and setting of the sun, so too, they circumscribed woman's religious emancipation. Women could pray and count as spiritual equals. They should prepare themselves for these responsibilities through Jewish education and confirmation. But in the nineteenth century, in a humanity constrained by the "natural laws governing the sexes," man led and woman followed everywhere, including in the synagogue. The German Jewish Reformers of the 1830s and 1840s never imagined that others would find woman's emancipation in the synagogue incomplete so long as she could not become a rabbi.

On the other side of the Atlantic, the discussion of woman's emancipation in the synagogue had also risen among those seeking to modernize Judaism. Here, Isaac Mayer Wise, now rabbi of Cincinnati's congregation Bene Yeshurun, championed expanding the woman's role in the synagogue. In 1867 he had written in his German-language magazine, *Die Deborah*, an article outlining his proposals for the advancement of Jewish women. In 1876 he repeated his suggestions in forceful rhetoric in his English-language *American Israelite.*[55]

Like many of those who, in the future, would come to write on this theme, Wise opened his article by referring to Genesis and its first account of the creation of human beings. Elaborating upon "And God created man in His image, in the image of God created He him; male and female created He them" (Genesis 1:27), he concluded: "According to Moses, God made man, male and female, and both in his own image, without any difference in regard to duties, rights, claims and hopes." Thus woman's inequality in the synagogue stemmed not from within Judaism but rather from without. He blamed it on: "[t]he influence of oriental society and the Koran [which] gradually excluded woman from all public affairs of the synagogue and the congregation, so that we found her in a garret in the synagogue, isolated like an abomination, shunned like a dangerous demon, and declared unfit in all religious observances." To call a woman to the Torah or to grant her synagogue honors "would have appeared preposterous, and would to-day be considered a desecration of the Orthodox synagogue."

As he did on so many other occasions, Wise used his topic of the moment, in this case women, to attack Orthodox intransigence in the face of modernity.[56] "Those people are brutally pious and stupidly faithful to what they call ancient custom, whatever an abuse may be." Reform—and Wise—had taken the initiative to end the abuses in woman's position in the synagogue and he enumerated its stages. First women joined the choir. Then reformers expected girls to come to worship. Next they confirmed boys and girls together, where, by the time he wrote this, "girls read the Thorah publicly" in his synagogue. Then came family pews and an end to the laws of marriage and divorce that demeaned women. The result, self-evident to Wise, had brought, as Geiger had sought, "the beneficial influence which feminine hearts will bestow upon" Judaism: "Now the mothers and daughters in Israel are in the temple, and with them came again order, decorum, and devotion. A hundred abuses have fallen down to the ground dead in our houses of public worship, since woman occupies again her place in the temple, as she did in the temple of Jerusalem."

Many nineteenth-century American Reformers believed that these achievements sufficed to celebrate Reform's successful emancipation of the Jewish woman.[57] But for Wise, the promise of her emancipation remained unfulfilled. Echoing the nineteenth-century American woman's rights movement, which regarded political suffrage as the symbol of female emancipation within American society,[58] Wise argued:

[T]he reform is not complete yet. You must enfranchise woman in your congregations. The principle, the advancement of the cause, justice to woman, and the law of God inherent in every human being, require that woman be made a member of the congregation, of equal rights with any man. . . . All laws contrary to this principle, on any statute book of a congregation, should be wiped out as reminiscences of barbarism and degrading to the cause of religion.

Wise wanted to see women on synagogue boards, especially school boards and choir boards where their special talents—for he shared the reigning assumption of the differences between the sexes—would be influential. He saw women as both more understanding of music than their husbands and "not as lazy as their liege lords." While "their husbands are at the lunch houses, at the gambling tables, napping at the counting rooms, or talking nonsense at some place or another," women were in the synagogue. Therefore it was only just that the influence they exercised by virtue of their presence be secured by their right to vote "for the benefit of Israel's sacred cause."

The belief Wise expressed in his 1876 *American Israelite* article that suffrage was the last barrier to woman's emancipation in the synagogue reflected the ongoing American debate about woman's rights, and especially about suffrage. This debate, which had opened in the United States in 1848 at the first woman's rights convention in Seneca Falls, New York, was still decades away from conclusion with the passage in 1920 of the Nineteenth Amendment giving women the right to vote. Calling woman's suffrage "one of the three great reform efforts in American history," scholar Ellen Carol DuBois observed that "for three-quarters of a century . . . American women centered their aspirations for freedom and power on the demand for the vote." Suffrage, a white middle-class affair, failed in nineteenth-century American political culture, according to historian Carl Degler, because it could not be subsumed under the headings of woman's traditional role as mother, wife, and sustainer of the family. But it succeeded once its proponents shifted their focus away from the individual rights of women. When those in favor of woman's suffrage began to point instead to the special contribution enfranchised women could make to society, one that came precisely from their character as women, as wives, as mothers, and as homemakers, female suffrage became law.[59]

In advocating woman's suffrage in the synagogue, Wise allied himself with the new priorities of the social and economic class he and his congregants had so recently joined. And he showed himself willing to apply these priorities to women in the key arena of American Jewish life, their modernizing synagogues. Emphasizing the special character of women and their new role as sustainers of Judaism in the synagogue, he argued: "We need women in the congregational meetings to bring there [their] heart, soul, piety and mutual respect." Within a few years of the publication of Wise's article, a few modernizing congregations accomplished just what Wise—and the suffragists—called for: they enfranchised their women.[60]

For Wise, the right of women to vote and to count as full members of their congregations signified the finale of the process, the pinnacle of woman's emancipation in Jewish life, her winning of equal rights. In the synagogue, as in American political culture, suffrage then symbolized woman's full and complete equality. And it was a symbol adopted not only by those specifically shaping Reform Judaism, but also by all those engaged in the process of modernizing Judaism. For example, in 1894, Mary M. Cohen's congregation Mikveh Israel, a traditional synagogue which maintained separate seating, became the first in Philadelphia, and among the first in the nation, to enfranchise women.[61] Thus, at the time that she dared ask "Could not—our *women*—be—ministers?" Cohen perceived, even from within her own congregation, the many shifts in the status of women within the synagogue and the laws of Judaism.

Cohen saw that women, like herself, were synagogue-goers and, in many places, had become the majority of those who came to pray. She knew from her experiences as a student, teacher, and superintendent of the Philadelphia Hebrew Sunday School, that middle-class American Jewish girls had access to Jewish education. She appreciated that respect for woman's new-found place as congregant, and the status that position conferred, had won her the right to exercise her voice in congregational affairs and even beyond. In 1896, Mikveh Israel asked Cohen to represent the congregation at a convention of the Jewish Theological Seminary of America, the Conservative rabbinical school, which the congregation had helped found a decade before. Cohen celebrated that "the selection of a woman delegate will bear witness to the marked liberality of our congregation."[62] Even if many of the changes in Jewish law had not won acceptance at Mikveh Israel and elsewhere, Cohen found empowering the changes that had occurred. That and her leadership experience within her congregation, surely explain her willingness to challenge Judaism to look beyond suffrage as the end point of woman's emancipation. Given her times and achievements, it no longer seems such a stunning leap—even though it struck Miss Dora's listeners "dumb"—from the ongoing debates about women's new rights and responsibilities in Judaism to Cohen's suggestion that perhaps "our *women*" could become rabbis.

For as Mary M. Cohen penned "A Problem for Purim," her scrapbook clippings make clear that she knew the woman's rights movement was also calling for an end to the restrictions placed on women's economic opportunities and arguing for opening the professions to women. And Cohen was determined to bring this issue home to American Jewry. In 1879, in the essay "Hebrew Women," she wrote of the responsibilities of Jewish women. While Cohen agreed that they included keeping "their lineage pure" and awaiting the return to Jerusalem, she insisted that they also required "identifying (ourselves) ... with the social and political interests of the countries wherein (we) reside."[63] Cohen, absorbed by the woman's rights movement, wanted to see American women enter all professions, even the rabbinate.

It is perhaps not surprising from our vantage point on the cusp of the twenty-first century that the question of women as rabbis belongs to the history of women in the workforce. But it was far more rare to make this connection when Mary M. Cohen did in 1889. In the pioneering study *Out to Work*, Alice Kessler-Harris wrote of the changing patterns of wage-earning women in the United States. She observed that in 1840, about 10 percent of all American women took jobs outside their homes. But those who did found opportunities for gainful employment limited. Most female jobs offered women little but the barest sustenance. Those with some education found few avenues for their talents. Nevertheless, gradually over the course of the nineteenth century, women's labor force participation and categories of occupation expanded. Some educated women carved out for themselves new and fulfilling careers as teachers, missionaries, and writers, in addition to the typically female jobs of governess and companion.[64]

But others dreamt different dreams. Entree into all the professions became one of the goals of the woman's rights movement. The Declaration of Sentiments and Resolutions of the 1848 Seneca Falls Convention, "the single most important document of the nineteenth-century American woman's movement," railed against men for "monopolizing nearly all the profitable employments" and for excluding women from medicine, law, and theology.[65] In fact, some would deem women's advancement in the professions to be more significant than the vote.[66] Over the course of the nineteenth century, small numbers of American women gradually entered the male-dominated professions, first in medicine and the ministry, and then in law and the academy.

Histories of women's efforts to become physicians, lawyers, scholars, scientists, and ministers reveal a largely forgotten record of the struggles of individual women to enter the "brotherhoods" of the male-dominated professions.[67] They also uncover the institutional, social, and psychological barriers these pioneers faced in common, no matter their field. Moreover, these studies establish the tremendous resourcefulness of these women, who, largely as isolated individuals, devised independent—although, in retrospect, often common—strategies to cope with the roadblocks they encountered. The ordeals of the nineteenth-century women trying to become the first physicians and lawyers mirror what the first women seeking rabbinic ordination would brave.

In 1835, after a haphazard, but not atypical, medical education, which included a brief apprenticeship to a husband and wife medical team, Harriot Hunt of Boston became the first woman in America to practice medicine successfully. As professional education and licensure became formalized, she sought, at the age of forty-two, admission to Harvard Medical School, not "out of 'love of novelty, [or] bravery in an untried position,'" but out of "a simple and single desire for such medical knowledge as may be transmitted through those professors, who from year to year, stand as beacon lights to those who would be aided in a more full knowledge of the healing art." In rejecting her application, not once but twice, Harvard Medical School called it "inexpedient."[68]

Meanwhile, Elizabeth Blackwell, popularly considered the first female physician, was, in actuality, the first female American medical school graduate. Described as "a pretty little specimen of the feminine gender ... [who] comes to class with great composure ... [and] takes notes constantly," she would later suffer criticism for graduating from an irregular school, Geneva Medical College. Yet, in 1849, few of her male colleagues held medical degrees from any institution. By the time she had graduated, new venues for women seeking medical degrees had led to the creation, in Boston, of the New England Female Medical College, the first such school for the training of female physicians.[69]

In 1869, after having her request for admission to Columbia University Law School denied, Lemma Barkaloo, "a large heavy built, cheerful looking woman of twenty or thereabouts," won permission to study law at Washington University. She thus became the first American female law student. Rather than completing the course, she chose, after a year's study, to sit, successfully, for the bar examination. Hers was "the most creditable examination of a class of five," whose ranks included a lawyer with fifteen years' experience in the bar of another state. In becoming Missouri's first female lawyer, she, so a contemporary wrote, "depart[ed] from the usual employments of her sex ... to enter into an arena in which men, oft times rude and ungallant, are the gladiators."[70]

But while Lawyer Barkaloo succeeded, other women found themselves fighting a state-by-state battle for admission to local bar associations. In Illinois, Myra Colby Bradwell, wife of a Cook County judge, did not share Barkaloo's success. Having passed the Chicago bar exam in 1869, she was refused, on the basis of her sex and marital status, admission to the Illinois bar. As she continued to wage legal efforts to win admission to the bar, sixty prominent Chicago lawyers unsuccessfully petitioned the state to appoint her a notary public.[71]

Meanwhile, in Philadelphia, in 1870, Carrie Burnham Kilgore, who already held a medical degree, was refused admission to the University of Pennsylvania Law School. Eleven years later, determined to get a law school education, she had her husband purchase a ticket for her to attend its lectures. On her second day there, so she later recounted in *Women Lawyers Journal*, the Board of Trustees wrote "to inform me that if I attended the entire course and passed all the examinations, it was not at all sure that the University would graduate me or confer upon a woman its diploma." Tenacious Kilgore prevailed, graduated, and won admission to the Pennsylvania Supreme Court in 1886. In 1890, she advertised unsuccessfully for a woman law student to work with her. For at least a decade she remained the only woman lawyer in Philadelphia.[72]

These professional breakthroughs for women were held up as models by the woman's rights movement, but for someone like Mary M. Cohen, thinking that American Jewish women could and should become rabbis, the ministry surely epitomized the most analogous profession. And, as she well knew, Protestant women had already joined it.

Antoinette Brown Blackwell attended Oberlin College, the first institution of higher education open to women. Although she hoped to become a minister, the college denied her, as a female student, the training in rhetoric essential for the ministry. In defiance, she formed a secret women's debating society. Later, after she completed the undergraduate women's literary course, Oberlin permitted her to take its graduate theological courses but, in 1850, refused her a degree. In 1853, the members of a small New York Congregational church ordained her their pastor. She thus became the first American woman ordained a Protestant minister.[73]

As a young girl growing up in the 1870s, Anna Howard Shaw was so eager to preach that liberal-minded local ministers occasionally invited her to deliver Sunday sermons. Later the Reverend Dr. Anna Howard Shaw earned degrees from Boston University's seminary and medical school. In 1880, she applied for ordination to the Methodist Episcopal Church Conference. It refused to consider her application. Subsequently, the smaller Methodist Protestant Church ordained her.[74]

Meanwhile, the nineteenth-century press helped stir up interest in the issue of women in the ministry. An 1872 biography of Maggie Newton Van Cott, a woman preacher, reprinted twenty-three articles about her which appeared between 1869 and 1871 in papers across the United States, including Philadelphia.[75] Other pamphlets and articles promoting women in the ministry followed.[76]

One of these, *Woman in Pulpit*, sets Frances E. Willard in the forefront of the advocates. An educator and moral reform leader, not a minister, Willard was among the most influential figures of her day. A graduate of the North Western Female College, she rejected marriage in favor of a career. After a number of years in teaching, she became, in 1871, president of the Ladies College of Northwestern University in Evanston, Illinois. In 1874, she joined the woman's temperance movement and later that year became president of the Chicago Women's Christian Temperance Union. From 1879 until her death in 1898, she headed the national WCTU, which, with over 200,000 members, stood out as the largest and the most influential women's organization of its day. Under her "Do Everything" policy the WCTU exploded into a multi-interest reform society, advancing a broad agenda, including women's rights.[77]

In 1889 in *Woman in the Pulpit*, Willard, who in her other writings portrayed American women "in all walks of life," argued for women in the ministry. She estimated that some 500 women were evangelical preachers, another 350 were Quaker leaders, and that at least a score functioned as pastors in the six mainstream Protestant denominations then ordaining women—Methodist, Baptist, Free Baptist, Congregationalist, Universalist, and Unitarian. She argued that combining motherhood and the ministry promised significant advantages to a woman's children. After all, Queen Victoria confirmed that women could effectively care for their children and for others.[78]

Accounts of women's efforts to become doctors, lawyers, or ministers, and the arguments they made for the benefits of their efforts, uncover the commonalities of female pioneers in the professions. And their experiences resonate for the history of women who would, without ever knowing this, follow in the wake of Mary M. Cohen's call to open the rabbinate to women. Like Lemma Barkaloo at Columbia University Law School, the women who would have become rabbis met with rejection—often, like Harriot Hunt at Harvard Medical School, more than once—based on their sex when they applied for admission to rabbinical seminaries. And the rejections came even when they were, like the judge's wife Myra Bradwell, the wives or daughters of men influential in the profession. Some would find themselves permitted to sit in classes but warned, like Carrie Burnham Kilgore, that such attendance, and even completion of the entire curriculum, would not promise them the professional title they so desperately sought. Others would find that those who denied them access to the professions, but felt pressured to heed women's call for meaningful work, would recommend alternative careers, as happened to Myra Bradwell who became neither a lawyer nor a notary public. Or they would find themselves pushed to separatist institutions, as the women in the first female medical colleges.

As pioneers, these women found that because they had left behind accepted female roles to do battle in a man's world, men—fellow students, professors, and the press—evidenced great concern for their femininity whether they were young, single "pretty little specimen[s]" like Elizabeth Blackwell, forty-two-year-old spinsters like Harriot Hunt, or married women like Carrie Kilgore. These same men judged female pioneers' intellectual ability severely, demanding that they outperform their fellow students and colleagues—as was true of Lemma Barkaloo in her bar exam.

In order to cope with the rejections, harsh judgments, and the stresses of being among the first, these women crafted new strategies as they battled to gain access to the professions for themselves and to open the doors—as Lawyer Kilgore tried to do—for others. Where possible, where they were not alone—like the female physicians in Boston, "a hotbed of feminist medical activity"[79]—they sought out the company of other women. As Antoinette Brown did at Oberlin, they bonded together in formal and informal groups to gain access to the knowledge denied them and sororial solidarity. When necessary, some found themselves switching affiliations, as Anna Howard Shaw switched churches, when what they sought in one place they could find only in another. Others schemed to gain "back-door" entree, piecing together the education they needed and apprenticing to those willing to train them, as Harriot Hunt had done. But most would find themselves, like Carrie Kilgore, on their own and valiantly carrying on.

Surely, many not named here, because they did not succeed, just gave up the fight and went off to live the life Justice Joseph P. Bradley painted in denying Myra Bradwell's application to the Illinois bar: "The paramount destiny and mission of women are to fulfill the noble and benign offices of wife and mother. This is the law of the Creator."[80]

When Mary M. Cohen wrote "A Problem for Purim," in 1889, the experiences of the female pioneers in the American rabbinate lay in the future. The frustrations and difficulties of their struggles were fixed only in her imagination. Yet, in writing "Could not—our *women*— become ministers?" she had not made a radical break with the past. Rather she wrote from within the perspective of her late nineteenth-century communities. In her Jewish world, she had seen, often firsthand, the changes that had taken place in the lives of Jewish women. She well understood their new opportunities for enhanced Jewish educations, the efforts made to equalize their status within various spheres of Judaism, and especially their new places and opportunities in their synagogues. In the larger sphere of changes taking place in the lives of middle-class American women, she had perceived through her career as a writer and in the occupations of others, expanding opportunities for women to engage in meaningful work. In "A Problem for Purim," albeit under the guise of the Jewish holiday of masquerade, she took the next, and by no means illogical, step of proposing that Jewish women become rabbis. In so doing, she presciently anticipated the raising of the question of women's rabbinic ordination across a broader spectrum of American Jewry. Within a year, others in real life would take up the question she had disguised as fiction.

Chapter 2

"Make a highway for woman"

RISING EXPECTATIONS FOR WOMEN'S ORDINATION, THE 1890s

Contemporary observers proclaimed a "revival" underway in nineteenth-century American Judaism, a time historian Jonathan Sarna has persuasively termed the "great awakening." The chief architects of this renaissance, Sarna has also pointed out, came less from American Jewry's self-proclaimed elite, the rabbis and scholars, than from the "bottom up," from "[y]oung people and others alienated from the religious establishment," whose ranks included women.[1]

In 1892 Rabbi Adolph Moses paraphrased the prophet Isaiah to proclaim: "Make a highway for woman, remove every obstacle from her path, let every mountain of inequality and injustice be made level, let every valley of ignorance and prejudice be raised. . . . Let all her powers grow and expand, and be added to the working forces of civilization."[2] In fact, even as Rabbi Moses called for leveling mountains of inequality, many in the synagogue had already toppled. And even as he exhorted women to add their powers to the work of building civilization, American Jewish women were already shouldering new roles that helped shape American Judaism's "great awakening."

Building upon what had already emerged—a new woman's presence in the synagogue and even dominance in some settings; the breaking down of gender barriers through mixed seating, mixed choirs, and confirmation ceremonies for girls; the emergence of female Jewish education and educators; and, in Reform settings, the abrogation of many of women's legal disabilities—American Jewish women "became significant players in the campaign to revitalize Judaism to meet the needs of a new era." The cultural and religious renaissance they helped shape, one whose institutional by-products included the Jewish Theological Seminary of America, the Jewish Publication Society, and the National Council of Jewish Women, laid many of the parameters for Jewish cultural life in America well into the twentieth century.[3]

The changes which occurred in American Judaism during the "great awakening" afforded some Jewish women utterly new opportunities to function as scholars and preachers. Their new participation in debate on theological topics and their ability to stand before Christian America and before other Jews as exemplars of American Jewry—roles traditionally left to the province of the rabbinate —helped push forward the question of women's ordination. Consequently, the question Mary M. Cohen had first raised in 1889—could not our women become rabbis—eddied out to American Jewry. By the first years of the twentieth century, the proposal for women rabbis sat so squarely on the agenda of American Judaism that most of those sharing in the task of modernizing Judaism, not just the Reformers, had faced the question. For some, the matter seemed settled. The 1890s had created a climate of rising expectations which promised that in the very near future, "should women desire to enter the ministry, there will be no obstacles thrown in their way."[4]

Chicago matron Hannah Greenebaum Solomon stood among those convinced that soon women would be rabbis. Born in 1858, Hannah was the fourth of ten children of a German Jewish immigrant family. At the age of eighteen, she and her sister Henrietta became the first Jewish women invited to join the Chicago Woman's Club. Solomon well knew that to "join an organization of 'women'— not 'ladies'—and one which bore the title 'club,' rather than 'society,' was in itself a radical step." For the literary culture clubs emerging all across the nation in the 1870s and 1880s promoted women's self-education and advancement and thus constituted radical challenges to the established social order. Critics cried that while the members of women's clubs busied themselves researching, writing, and presenting papers, "[h]omes will be ruined, children neglected, woman is straying from her sphere."[5]

The Chicago Woman's Club, among the most influential in the country, kept its members very busy, setting them on a seven-year study program of key political, social, and philosophical currents. As they read, wrote papers on, and discussed Karl Marx and Friedrich Engel's *Das Kapital* and Sidney and Beatrice Webb's *The History of Trade Unionism*, "untrained women without business habits or parliamentary experience" schooled themselves for the leading roles they would assume in virtually every municipal reform effort in Chicago.[6]

As a member of the Chicago Woman's Club, Solomon extended the boundaries of her limited early education. As a child, she had attended the alternative to the public school run by Zion Temple, studied with private tutors, and had some high school instruction. Now at her club, she studied Plato's *Republic*, Moore's *Utopia*, and St. Augustine's *City of God*.[7] Here, too, she also advanced her study of Judaism. In 1891, Solomon, who by this time was married and the mother of three children, agreed to review Benedict de Spinoza's *Tractatus Theologico-Politicus* for the club's Philosophy and Science Department. In this rationalistic attack upon religion, the seventeenth-century philosopher Amsterdam rabbis expelled for his "evil opinions" on the supremacy of natural law, critiqued Judaism. With no English translation available, Solomon based her analysis on the German edition.[8] A year later, her paper, "Our Debt to Judaism"—the first time the club undertook the sensitive study of religion—was so well received that club members invited her to present it before other organizations to which they belonged, and *Unity*, the magazine of the Unitarian Church, published it. Here Solomon showed herself not only conversant with major periods and key intellectual figures of Jewish history but also with critical biblical scholarship and Reform Judaism's critique of rabbinic Judaism.[9] Thus, even before she began her pioneering work organizing the National Council of Jewish

Women, Hannah Solomon already stood, before the gentiles in her community, as an erudite spokeswoman for Judaism.

In the early 1890s Chicago's elites began planning for the 1893 World's Fair. Chicago Woman's Club members Bertha Honoré Palmer and Ellen M. Henrotin volunteered to orchestrate women's participation in the Fair. Palmer, head of the Fair's Board of Lady Managers, appointed Henrotin, later president of the General Federation of Women's Clubs, to arrange for women's participation in the more than two hundred auxiliary congresses Fair planners scheduled. These brought together experts to discuss recent developments in science and technology, culture and the arts, and religion. Thanks to the efforts of the Fair's Board of Lady Managers, one fourth of all congress speakers were female. Four hundred women from the Chicago Woman's Club took part in the various congresses.[10]

As Henrotin sought women from each major religious denomination capable of spearheading the various women's committees for the World's Parliament of Religions, she failed, according to National Council of Jewish Women historian Faith Rogow, "to find Jewish female clergy or nationally known Jewish suffragists."[11] Instead she asked club member Solomon to head the Jewish Women's Committee. As Solomon began searching for women to participate, she discovered that tracking down knowledgeable Jewish women to speak at the Congress of Jewish Women was a gargantuan task. In the end, after having personally written to the ninety women whom various rabbis had suggested, Solomon, along with social reformer and Chicago Woman's Club member Sadie American, and the other members of the organizing committee, determined to use the upcoming forum of the Congress of Jewish Women to create a permanent organization. The National Council of Jewish Women that they envisioned would "bring together thinking Jewish women, who have the advancement of Judaism and Jewish interests at heart."[12]

Plans for the Congress of Jewish Women proceeded. The committee ambitiously organized a program spanning four days. It invited no less than twenty-eight women to speak, chose another two outstanding figures to represent Jewish womanhood before the Parliament of Religions, and announced its intent to the conveners of the World's Parliament of Religions. Then, unexpectedly, in March 1893, with the World's Parliament less than half a year away, those organizing the Congress of Jewish Women encountered unanticipated opposition.

In the summer of 1892, a committee of five rabbis from Reform Judaism's rabbinical conclave, the Central Conference of American Rabbis, had begun designing their auxiliary congress, the Jewish Denominational Congress. By the end of that year, the committee had sketched out a program covering the archaeology, history, and ethics of the Jewish people. It called for assigning these topics "to well-known scholars who have made these branches their special study," and extended "a special invitation to representative men and women to take part." Incorporating "polemics and apologetics" into its program, those mapping out the Jewish Denominational Congress seized upon an opportunity to clarify Judaism's relationship to Christianity and in so doing to "silence slander in the name of humanity forever."[13]

Three months later, representatives from Reform Judaism's Union of American Hebrew Congregations, the Central Conference of American Rabbis, the local Chicago organizational committee, and the Congress of Jewish Women gathered to finalize their plans. With the World's Parliament of Religions but six months away and the program for the Congress of Jewish Women "far advanced," the committee chairman asked Hannah Solomon, "[W]ill you Jewish women cooperate with us in our sessions?" In her memoirs she recalled her answer:

"We will . . . be very glad to join with you if you will accord us active participation in your programs."

The program committee then retired to deliberate, and when they returned, lo and behold! not a single woman's name appeared in the recommendations!

"Mr. Chairman," I inquired, "just where on your program are the women to be placed?"

"Well," hemmed and hawed the chairman, "the program seems complete just as it stands."

"Very well," I replied, "under these circumstances we do not care to cooperate with you . . ."[14]

Subsequent publicity for the Congress of Jewish Women proclaimed its independence: "In most of the Religious Congresses the men's and women's committees have acted together and will hold one Congress. But the rabbis refuse to give the women adequate time, place or representation, so they were compelled to hold a separate Congress."[15]

Solomon's determination to prevent the rabbis and male lay leaders of American Judaism from co-opting her plans for a separate gathering of American Jewish women resulted in an unprecedented assembly of women displaying their knowledge of Judaism, their scholarship, their erudition, and their piety. Not surprisingly, then, significant scholarly inquiry has focused on the Congress of Jewish Women, chiefly for its permanent outcome, the founding of the National Council of Jewish Women (NCJW), the first Jewish counterpart of the American women's culture and civic club movement.[16]

Yet, even without this outcome, the Congress of Jewish Women remains in and of itself revolutionary. As Sadie American, later NCJW's executive secretary, observed in her 1893 address to the Congress of Jewish Women:

> Never before in the history of Judaism has a body of Jewish women come together for the purpose of presenting their views, nor for any purpose but that of charity and mutual aid; never before have Jewish women been called upon to take any place in the representation of Judaism.[17]

Never before had a body of Jewish women stood collectively to preach and to teach, representing themselves to others, American Christians and Jews, as well as to the press, as exemplars of American Jewry.

The Congress of Jewish Women thus stands as a landmark event in the emergence for American Jewish women of what the distinguished historian Gerda Lerner has named *The Creation of Feminist Consciousness*. In her pathbreaking book she argues that, as a result of women's systematic educational disadvantaging, their "major intellectual enterprise for more than a thousand years was to re-conceptualize religion in such a way as to allow for women's equal and central role in the Christian drama of the Fall and Redemption" and, for those not Christian, a central place within their religious communities. Over and over again, in different times and places, individual women isolated from one another and from the historical consciousness essential to build upon the reasoning of those who preceded them, reinterpreted religious, especially biblical, texts to argue for woman's right to education and to the religious influence such knowledge bestowed upon similarly educated men. Including in her analysis pious and scholarly Jewish women, such as the daughters of the medieval sage Rashi and the "Maid of Ludomir," Lerner demonstrates the spiraling path of women intellectuals gradually escalating toward the group consciousness essential to their quest for equality.[18]

For Jewish women's history, the 1893 Congress of Jewish Women sits squarely within Lerner's paradigm. It unveils a small group of American Jewish women engaged in the essential work of reconceptualizing Judaism in order to expand their place there. As they stood and spoke in the Congress hall, they scaled the first three stages of feminist consciousness posited by Lerner: "authorization to speak; inspired speech, and the right to learn and to teach." This time they did so not as isolated individual women, like Hannah Rachel Werbemacher (c. 1815–92), the "Maid of Ludomir," who had won a following among Hasidic men for her teaching. Rather, for the first time in Jewish history, they stood as a collective body of Jewish women.[19] Thanks to an Anglo-Jewish press eager to broadcast this event and to the Jewish Publication Society which subsequently issued papers read at the Congress,[20] their message eddied well beyond those seated in the crowded Congress hall.

For four days, from 4 to 7 September 1893, the participants and those in the audience at the Congress of Jewish Women learned about Judaism and especially about Jewish womanhood chiefly from Jewish women. They began with historical overviews. Louise Mannheimer presented "Jewish Women of Biblical and Medieval Times," followed by Helen Kahn Weil who surveyed "Jewish Women of Modern Days." Speakers on the next day considered specific aspects of Jewish women's historic and contemporary roles. Ray Frank discussed "Woman in the Synagogue"; Mary M. Cohen contemplated the "Influence of the Jewish Religion in the Home"; and Julia Richman examined "Women as Wage-Workers." On the third day Minnie D. Louis, Rebekah Kohut (her remarks read by another), and others reflected upon Jewish women as mission workers and philanthropists and as combatants of anti-Semitism. At the conclusion of the Congress, Sadie American issued her call for "Organization," which culminated in the founding of the National Council of Jewish Women. While the discussants included clergy, among them rabbis Kaufmann Kohler and Emil G. Hirsch and the Reverend Ida C. Hultin, all presenters of papers were Jewish women.[21]

First and foremost, the speakers celebrated Jewish women's traditional roles as mothers in Israel.[22] For Louise Mannheimer, educated at the University of Cincinnati, married to a rabbi, a composer, poet, club member, and translator of Nahida Remy's *The Jewish Woman*,[23] "no title of honor . . . through all the generations of the adherents of Mosaic Law was more revered." Such women, devoted to the duties of their homes, abided "a deep and tender love for their children."[24] In discussing Helen Kahn Weil's paper on modern Jewish women, Henrietta Frank, Hannah Solomon's sister, maintained: "Woman as homemaker, as purveyor of happiness . . . is needed as much as ever . . . "[25] Ray Frank concurred. Although then unmarried, she nevertheless professed: "Sisters, our work in and for the synagogue lies in bringing to the Temple the Samuels to fulfil the Law. As mothers in Israel I appeal to you. . . . Nothing can replace the duty of the mother in the home. *Nothing can replace the reverence of children, and the children are yours to do as ye will with them*" (original emphasis).[26]

Yet, even as they exalted the Mother in Israel professing nothing could replace her, these women's performances belied their rhetoric. For rather than remaining secluded in the sanctuaries of their homes, they had come to stand in the hallowed halls of the Parliament of Religions, daring to represent Judaism to the world. Thus, at the same time that they glorified Jewish women as wives and mothers, they mined Jewish tradition to affirm woman's right to go outside her proper sphere. These women deliberately reread biblical and rabbinic texts, much the way modernizing rabbis did, so that the weight of the past would sanction the rights they now claimed. Hannah Solomon explained: "In the pages of history, in the lives of the heroes and heroines, the destinies and possibilities of a people are written. In them, we have been trying to discover ideals for ourselves, our daughters and granddaughters."[27]

The speakers maintained that, even as Jewish tradition extolled the Mothers in Israel, it authorized Jewish woman's right to speak, to advance her Jewish education, to receive rabbinic training, to exercise religious authority, to claim equality, to stand in the center of her Jewish community. And they averred this from the opening moments of the Congress when Ray Frank prayed: "Almighty God, Creator and Ruler of the universe . . . believing that Thou ordainest all things well . . . we feel that Thou hast, in the course of events, caused this glorious congress to convene, that it may give expression to that which shall spread broadcast a knowledge of Thee and Thy deeds." In asking the Almighty to "[g]rant, then, Thy blessing upon those assembled, and upon the object of their meeting,"[28] Frank thus declared that the Ruler of the Universe condoned woman broadcasting Judaism to the world.

Similarly, Louise Mannheimer claimed Jewish women's right to equality rested on the archetypes of ancient and medieval Jewish women: "the Mothers in Israel, the Prophetesses in Israel, and the women who solved the problem of the proper sphere of woman's activity in Israel at this early historical time." From the latter "group of energetic women," she inferred: "So we find woman in the full enjoyment of equality of rights in Israel, even to the extent of the highest office in the land, the office of ruler."[29]

Mannheimer also reconceptualized Jewish tradition to establish women's right to study and to claim the religious influence conferred by her studies. "[I]n Talmudic times there flourished many a woman whose authority in the expounding of the Law was acknowledged even by the rabbis." She declared that when the officers of King Josiah sought the prophetess Huldah, they naturally found her

> *in the College*. . . . What an abundance of conclusions can be derived from this statement! . . . There were, then, no restrictive regulations at that time to exclude women from colleges among the Israelites . . . even married women. . . . There is, then, even in those remote times a precedent for the liberal views of the Hebrew Union College.[30] (original emphasis)

Surely, Mannheimer alluded here to the fact that, from its inception in 1875, Reform Judaism's rabbinical seminary welcomed female students. The first, seventh-grader Julia Ettlinger, lasted but two years in what was then, according to Michael A. Meyer, "little more than an intensive religious school." But, by 1900, two young women had earned Bachelor of Hebrew Letters degrees, and others had taken classes, among them Ray Frank.[31]

Unquestionably, Ray Frank's career as "the girl rabbi of the golden west," ranks among the most influential forces in advancing the perception, among some, that women's rabbinic ordination was imminent. In the 1890s, those, like Louise Mannheimer, answering the question "Do you expect some time to see a Jewish woman in the pulpit?" would point to Frank to boast Jews already "have a woman in the pulpit."[32]

Born in 1861 in San Francisco, the largest nineteenth-century Western Jewish community, Frank, the daughter of Polish immigrants, came from a traditional Jewish family that claimed descent from the great Lithuanian sage, the Vilna Gaon. After completing her education in California public high school, she became a teacher in the silver mining town of Ruby Hill, Nevada. When, in the mid-1880s, its mining industry declined, she returned to Oakland, studied philosophy at Berkeley, and began teaching Sabbath school. Soon she won a reputation among her students' parents for her charismatic lectures. After the congregation's rabbi resigned, she took over the running of the school.[33] And she began, at least incipiently, to ponder the topic of women rabbis.

In May 1890 she wrote a lengthy letter to the editor of the *Jewish Messenger* who had asked his readers to consider "What would you do if you were a rabbi?" Responding to her own question, "What I would not do if I were a rabbi," Frank seized the opportunity to decry the materialism of the rabbinate, the mixing of religion and politics, the selling of "religion in the form of pews and benches to the highest bidder," and unbridled animosity between "reform" and "orthodox" rabbis. She concluded: "Women are precluded from entering the Holy of Holies; but it is a great satisfaction to contemplate *what we would not do* were the high office not denied us" (original emphasis).[34] Four months after writing this letter, Ray Frank gained her first experience of what that "high office" could be like.

In 1890 she had begun working as a correspondent for several local newspapers. It was this work which brought her, on the eve of the Days of Awe, to Spokane, Washington. Learning that there were to be no High Holiday services in the city, she approached one of the influential Jews there. He agreed to arrange for services if she would agree to preach. She did—to a packed Spokane Falls Opera House, chastising those assembled on the eve of Yom Kippur for failing to build a synagogue. She exclaimed: "I am tonight the one Jewish woman in the world, may be the first since the time of the prophets to be called to speak."[35] From then until shortly before her marriage to economist Simon Litman in 1901, she carved out a career as "The Jewess in the Pulpit." Before too long, the press, which considered her "a latter-day Deborah," acclaimed her "the only female rabbi" in America.[36]

By the time the Congress of Jewish Women convened, Ray Frank had won celebrity preaching from synagogue pulpits, from the podiums of B'nai B'rith lodges, and even in a Unitarian Church, throughout California and elsewhere in the West.[37] She thus joined the nineteenth-century tradition of the female orator. She stood alongside nineteenth-century women suffragists, the first female lawyers, physicians, and ministers, among all those women speaking from public platforms and from church pulpits. She brought a distinctively Jewish religious voice to what in the 1830s, when Sarah and Angelina Grimké began their speaking tours of female antislavery societies, had been a radically new American female role.[38]

Frank's preaching and her reception in the West offer striking parallels to the experiences of female ministers of the Western Conference of the Unitarian Church, a liberal religion, which, much like Reform Judaism, affirmed an "overarching commitment to human freedom" and reason. The first of these Unitarian women, dubbed by historian Cynthia Grant Tucker a "prophetic sisterhood," was ordained in 1880. Over the next years she and those who followed encouraged other "girl[s] of promise" as "prospective minister[s]." By the end of the decade, eight female ministers could gather for the ordination of one, unveiling a sisterhood radiating out from their center in Iowa. Many of them, like Ray Frank, had earned their ordination through active work preaching beyond their own communities and not in the hallowed halls of the only seminary then allowing Unitarian women to study for a degree in divinity.[39]

As "The Jewess in the Pulpit," Frank and those joining her at the Congress of Jewish Women stood, quite literally, next to the women of the prophetic sisterhood. The Reverend Ida C. Hultin, ordained a

Unitarian minister in 1886 and then a pastor in Moline, Illinois, was among the Congress's discussants. Even as Frank was writing "What I would not do if I were a rabbi," Hultin had been championing "Woman in the Ministry." In fact, the parallels strike deeper, for in the early 1880s, Hultin had tried, at least twice, to get the advanced education she believed necessary for ordination.[40] A decade later, Frank was to do the same.

Early in January 1893 Frank arrived in Cincinnati to study at the Hebrew Union College. Already some thirty years old, she had no intention of matriculating in rabbinical school. Rather as she wrote:

> I entered the theological college in Cincinnati, in order to learn more of the philosophy of Judaism, and was the first woman to take that special work at the college . . . it never having been my intention to take the regular theological course, having long prior concluded that while theologies are many, religion is one; and that ordination is not essential to preachers, or, better yet, to teachers.[41]

While in Cincinnati, she studied history with Professor Gotthard Deutsch, came to know the Hebrew Union College faculty, and continued her work as a lecturer. She was not the only female student then at the college. The press reported that another, Lena Aronsohn of Little Rock, Arkansas, was actually seeking the title of rabbi. At least one journalist hoped "more of the sex will follow suit."[42] Hebrew Union College president Isaac Mayer Wise offered high praise for Frank and also welcomed her as an example to other women:

> We glory in her zeal and moral courage to break down the last remains of the barriers erected in the synagogue against woman. . . . In the laws governing the Hebrew Union College the question of sex or race or confession is not touched upon at all. . . . We can only encourage Miss Ray Frank or any other gifted lady who takes the theological course, to assist the cause of emancipating woman in the synagogue and the congregation.[43]

Thus by the time she arrived in Chicago in September 1893 for the Congress of Jewish Women, Ray Frank had not only firmly established a reputation as a charismatic lecturer and preacher, she had also achieved recognition from established Judaic institutions and scholars. At the Congress Frank not only presented a paper, she also acted as its rabbi. Her opening prayer convened the Congress and her final benediction closed it.[44]

In the paper she read there, "Woman in the Synagogue," she too began by glorifying Jewish women's traditional roles as Mothers in Israel, praising them as "[t]rue help-mates," endowed with "the softest maternal qualities."[45] Nevertheless, like Mannheimer and many of the other Congress speakers, she used the occasion to offer an alternative model of exemplary Jewish womanhood, one which also rested on historical precedent. Surely, she meant her survey of the learned Jewish women of the past to resonate favorably against the image she herself projected.

Frank especially celebrated "learned mothers and teachers," who "rose to eminence intellectually and socially." These female scholars—almost always the mothers, sisters, wives, or daughters of great rabbis—typically taught women their religious duties. But Frank also uncovered learned women of the past who dared venture beyond the well-accepted convention of women teaching women. Recollecting that in the Middle Ages, Jewish woman was "[f]orced by circumstances at times to become a leader," she praised the medieval woman who, modestly screened from view, "delivered in public biblical lectures to men." She named women so pious they "regularly attended synagogue, morning and evening" and those so learned they became scribes and disputed with the great scholars of their day. She applauded one who was principal of a rabbinical college and cited the German-Jewish historian Leopold Zunz who praised another as "well nigh a lady rabbi."

Ray Frank intended her long list of erudite women to inspire her audience. She exhorted:

Women of the nineteenth century! These are but a few names from among the many on the old grave stones, testifying to the splendid work done for the synagogue by women, at a time when obstacles made up their lives. . . . But enough has been given to disprove all doubts as to the Jewish woman's capability in religious matters . . .

Alone among the women of the Congress she insisted woman "may be ordained rabbi or be the president of a congregation—she is entirely able to fill both offices." But Frank did not ask for ordination, for herself or for others. Rather she carefully couched the radical notion of women as rabbis, of a woman stepping as far outside her sphere as Frank herself did, in a traditional posture: "What matter whether we women are ordained rabbis or not? We are capable of fulfilling the office, and the best way to prove it is to convert ourselves and our families into reverent beings." For the then unmarried Ray Frank, the role of the pious Mother in Israel remained preferable—even if for her personally it was then hypothetical—to a life as rabbi.

Yet, for the remainder of the decade, Frank's own experience was closer to that of rabbi than to that of Mother in Israel. For the next several years, until she sailed for Europe in June 1898, where she married Professor Simon Litman and settled into life as a faculty wife, she traveled and lectured, read services and wrote, and corresponded with influential writers, among them Ambrose Bierce, Charlotte Perkins Gilman, and Israel Zangwill. Occasionally she led services, declined offers to head congregations, and insisted that she did not wish to become a rabbi. All during this time, until she married, she continued to receive significant coverage in the Anglo-Jewish press as the first "lady rabbi."[46]

In their article "The Girl Rabbi of the Golden West," Reva Clar and William M. Kramer argue that Ray Frank achieved much of her fame by employing Samuel H. Friedlander, a Portland, Oregon, impresario, as her manager. Friedlander, they say, seized upon the young Frank, who was both a charismatic speaker and so well-schooled in Judaism, as a star attraction. He shepherded her career, booked lectures for her, and kept her name in the press and before the public— all of which, they say, proves that "the much-acclaimed Ray Frank was too good to be true."[47] Yet, in hiring a manager, Frank was by no means atypical of other orators of her day, among them the first female minister, Antoinette Brown Blackwell, and the woman's rights leader, Elizabeth Cady Stanton, who used such agents to arrange lecture circuits and secure their fees.[48] Moreover, Frank's sensation, whether orchestrated by another or not, neither diminishes her power as a preacher nor her critical importance for stoking the fires of debate around women's rabbinic ordination. For, as she continued to preach and to teach, often to function like a rabbi, the rhetoric around female ordination escalated.

Frank was apparently so well received at the Congress of Jewish Women that immediately afterwards she remained in Chicago where Christian and Jewish clergy welcomed her to their pulpits. In his invitation, Rabbi Joseph Stoltz asserted his conviction of the "need for Jewish women in the pulpit." A month later the *San Francisco Chronicle* reported that some wealthy Chicago Jews, similarly impressed, had asked her to help them form and then lead a congregation. Although the press indicated that Chicago rabbi Isaac S. Moses, who had commented on her paper at the Congress of Jewish Women, encouraged her to accept their offer, she declined the call.[49]

At the same time that Frank was receiving so much notice in Chicago, Rabbi Emil G. Hirsch came to ponder the question of women in the pulpit. Hirsch was one of the most influential figures then in Reform Judaism. Rabbi of Chicago Sinai Congregation from 1880 to his death in 1923 and professor of rabbinic literature and philosophy at the University of Chicago, which he helped found, Hirsch was also editor of the *Reform Advocate*. In November 1893, he wrote a front-page editorial, "Woman in the Pulpit." Decrying synagogues as either lecture associations or mourners' societies, he argued that our congregations should follow the example of Christian churches. These had greatly benefited from giving over many activities to women, who intuitively expressed "richer religious sentiments. . . . This being so, the question whether woman should be admitted into the Jewish pulpit admits of no negative solution. She is as much in place there as she is in any other profession."[50]

Hirsch specified the training necessary for this exalted calling. Perhaps thinking of Ray Frank, who despite some collegiate course work lacked formal credentials beyond a high school diploma, he argued that "[z]eal, good intentions, fervor, depths of religious convictions cannot make up for ignorance on all or most questions of Jewish theology or history and literature." Hirsch expected rabbis to have strong general educations in philosophy, classics, psychology, history, and religious thought. And obviously they also required "a comprehensive knowledge of the literature and history of Judaism," the lan-

guages to read them, and the tools critical to evaluate them. Refusing
to lower his image of rabbi as scholar—although, he admitted, many
congregations had done so—he concluded, begrudgingly true to the
liberal spirit of the day which expected women to enter all professions: "Let us, if we must, have women rabbis, but let them be not
only women but also rabbis."[51]

Hirsch also happened to be Hannah Solomon's rabbi. At the conclusion of the Congress of Jewish Women, the founders of the National Council of Jewish Women had elected Solomon president. As
president, she had accepted on NCJW's behalf, an invitation to join
the National Council of Women (NCW), a broad coalition of women's
organizations which had been founded in 1888 during the fortieth
anniversary celebration of the Seneca Falls Convention and which
had chosen Frances Willard as its founding president.[52]

At the NCW's 1895 convention Solomon shared a platform with
Willard. Perhaps Solomon knew of Willard's promotion of women in
the ministry, her 1889 polemic *Woman in the Pulpit*. Perhaps the
memory of her own rabbi's editorial encouraged her. In any event, she
proclaimed before the NCW: "We are receiving every possible encouragement from our rabbis, and should women desire to enter the
ministry, there will be no obstacles thrown in their way."[53]

Two years later, again in the *Reform Advocate*, Hirsch asked others, besides liberal rabbis and their progressive congregants, to consider the question. In February 1897 he inaugurated the symposium
"Woman in the Synagogue," stating: "The *Reform Advocate* gladly
yields the floor to woman.... In the synagogue, orientalism precluded her active participation. The bars are falling. Upon her is a
new consecration.[54] The impetus for the exchange came not only
from what Hirsch had witnessed as one of the discussants at the Congress of Jewish Women—about which he had initially expressed mis-
givings[55]—but also from the burst of activity then evident in the nascent Jewish women's organizations, especially the National Council
of Jewish Women.

The National Council of Jewish Women stood on the pillars of wom-
en's dedication to "Religion, Philanthropy, and Education." In its

early years it promoted members' study of Judaism; supported Sabbath schools and religious schools for immigrant children; combated Christian missionaries in Jewish neighborhoods; and championed social reform and philanthropy. Reform rabbi Kaufmann Kohler greeted those assembled at its first triennial convention with rhetoric celebrating the possibilities NCJW embodied for Jewish women: "We thank Thee, O God, that Thou hast endowed the woman of to-day with new vigor and courage, and called her out of her long reserve, that she may retain her heritage from Eden, and spell forth her holy message with a new and fiery tongue."[56]

The NCJW also found a ready champion in Rabbi Hirsch. He saluted the three hundred women who convened in his synagogue to establish local Chicago sections. In 1896, when NCJW numbered over fifty sections with four thousand members, almost half of whom were involved in Council study circles, he praised this "agency for fostering Judaism as a religion," claiming, "[i]n recent years, no movement within Judaism has asserted itself which is freighted with greater possibilities for good than this."[57]

Hirsch had good reason to believe in the promise of Jewish women's religious activism. The "sisterhoods of personal service" had an already established record of presenting Jewish women with new opportunities to extend their religious activities outside the synagogue. In 1887, New York Reform rabbi Gustav Gottheil told his congregants at Temple Emanu-El that authentic religious life required prayer and worship, acts of goodness and deeds of charity. He challenged women to fulfill the latter commandments by rendering direct personal aid to those in need, especially the sick, children, and working girls and women among poor, immigrant Jews. In response, they formed the first sisterhood of personal service. Eventually its activities included home visits; religious, industrial, and cooking schools; nurseries and kindergartens; employment bureaus; vocational and recreational programs for women and children; and even counsel for juvenile delinquency. By 1896, not only did a federation of uptown New York sisterhoods coordinate their efforts, but Jewish women in San Francisco had also created similar organizations.[58]

In the 1890s these newer and more expansive Jewish women's religious organizations joined earlier models of individual, local synagogue-based and community-based Jewish women's associations. These organizations, which proliferated especially in the years after the Civil War, as the Jewish community grew and spread throughout the United States, continued to appear in towns and cities all across America, even as the sections of the NCJW and the sisterhoods of personal service, were emerging. For example, in Detroit, between 1882 and 1891, the rabbis and Jewish women of Temple Beth El created the Hebrew Ladies' Auxiliary Relief Society (later the Hebrew Ladies' Sewing Society), the Self-Help Circle, and the Woman's Club of Temple Beth El (which did not become the Detroit Section of the NCJW until 1925). Elsewhere, in these same years, Jewish women joined the Daughters of Israel or the Ladies' Deborah Society. And at the same time, according to Rebekah Kohut, "the first national as well as the first fraternal Jewish woman's organization in the United States," the United Order of True Sisters, founded in 1846, continued its religious work.[59]

In this era, too, one Jewish woman, Rosa Sonneschein, created an utterly new outlet for the expression of Jewish woman's religious sensibilities. Born in 1847, Rosa Fassel was the youngest of nine children of a distinguished Moravian rabbi. In 1864 she married Rabbi Solomon Hirsch Sonneschein. The Sonnenscheins had three children before, and one child after, they moved to America, a step Rosa hoped would curb her husband's alchoholism. It did not, and, in America, they divorced.

Rosa Sonneschein settled in St. Louis. There, in 1879, she founded the Pioneers, the first Jewish woman's literary club in the United States. In 1893, inspired by what she saw at the World's Columbian Exposition, where she read a paper at the Press Congress, she conceived of the idea for an English-language, Jewish woman's magazine. The first issue of the *American Jewess* appeared in April 1895, a remarkable blend of two nineteenth-century journalistic traditions, that of the burgeoning woman's press with that of the flourishing Anglo-Jewish press. By the time it ceased publication in 1899, its readership had grown to twenty-nine thousand.[60]

Hailed "as a sign of the times, a manifestation of the spirit that led to the organization of the National Council of Jewish Women," its columns open to all "who actively participate in the questions pulsating and throbbing in our national, social and religious life," the *American Jewess* appealed to middle-class Jewish wives and mothers. Its regular columns featured domestic life and fashion, fiction, and reports on the happenings of the NCJW and other Jewish women's organizations.[61]

Many in its pages, including editor Sonneschein, championed woman's rights, especially the progressive changes then paving the way for the expansion of Jewish women's religious opportunities. Its very first issue printed Rabbi Adolph Moses' exhortation to "make a highway for woman."[62] In the next, Reform rabbi Henry Berkowitz extolled woman's new economic opportunities:

> As physicians, preachers, dentists, lawyers, journalists, compositors, type-writers, bookkeepers, sales-women, telephone and telegraph operators . . . women are proving themselves efficient. Every day a bolt is wrenched off, some bars are pulled down, and an entrance to some new occupation is being forced open for women.[63]

The *American Jewess* turned attention to how such progress specifically affected Jewish women. Sonneschein claimed, in 1895, to have read the 20,000 names on the membership rosters of 102 American synagogues. All began "Mr." Not one listed members "Mr. and Mrs." Decrying that synagogues refused married women membership, that even widows who paid for pews could not vote, and unaware that the year before Philadelphia's Mikveh Israel had granted women voting rights, she agitated as "befitting the spirit of our time," to extend membership to women, to allow them to attend congregational meetings, to vote, and to be elected to Sabbath-school boards. Later, after Rabbi Joseph Stoltz's Temple Isaiah had made women members, she boasted of her success.[64]

Sometimes obliquely and sometimes overtly, the *American Jewess* also presented readers with the issue of woman's rabbinic ordination. The *American Jewess* introduced its readers to women who had become ministers. In its pages, the Reverend Ella Bartlett, following the long-established literary tradition of women engaging in biblical criticism, drew inspiration for the prototype of the "new woman" from Miriam, Hannah, and the daughters of Zelophehad. Asking

"Does the new woman preach the word?" Bartlett recalled that, in the time of King David, "The Lord gave the word," and "a company of women" preached it. While Sonneschein did not directly address the question of women becoming rabbis, she did write: "We have shouldered the burden of journalism because we believe the time has again come when Jewish women will play an important part in the Synagogue; that they are fully as capable to fill the pulpit as the pew . . ."[65]

Not surprisingly, the *American Jewess* also shared the popular fascination with Ray Frank. In one issue of the journal, in the article "The Jewess in San Francisco," Rebecca J. Gradwohl called her "the woman rabbi." In a later issue, Louise Mannheimer modified the claim: "We have a woman in the pulpit, though she has not been ordained."[66]

Frank was perhaps the best known female "rabbi," but she was not the only woman spurred by the new directions of women's Jewish activism in the 1890s to claim a place in the pulpit alongside the rabbis. Having stood on platforms at the Congress of Jewish Women, founding NCJW leaders ascended the *bimah* to preach their message. As they did, they followed Christian women, ordained ministers, preachers, and social activists, who by the 1890s not only sermonized from church pulpits, but even, on occasion, in synagogues. Rabbi Hirsch had invited Hull House's Jane Addams to his pulpit long before he invited a Jewish woman to join him there. In 1891, in Rochester, New York, suffrage leader Susan B. Anthony shared a pulpit with Reform rabbi Max Landsberg. New Orleans Temple Sinai listed among the "distinguished women who spoke in our pulpit," Jane Addams, municipal reformer Florence Kelley, and social critic Charlotte Perkins Gilman, and boasted that Sadie American was the first Jewish woman to preach there.[67]

In February 1897 Hirsch invited Hannah Solomon to preach in his stead. Standing "in the place of our great leader," she began by referring to the novelty of her position: "When the invitation was extended to me to stand in this pulpit, to have the honor of addressing you, I dreaded a catastrophe. The event itself may be a catastrophe for you." Chicago papers hailed Solomon as "the first woman in the history of Judaism to act as rabbi." And she subsequently claimed incorrectly, given the experiences of Ray Frank, that she was the first Jewish woman to occupy a Jewish pulpit.[68] Not surprisingly, others would make similar claims for themselves or their synagogues that "[t]he first time . . . that a woman occupied the pulpit of a Jewish congregation was in this temple."[69]

The liberal rabbis who issued such invitations, like Joseph Stoltz who had welcomed Ray Frank, and Emil G. Hirsch, paved the way for Jewish women's new role. Perhaps New York rabbi Kaufmann Kohler spoke for them too, when, in 1896 at the first triennial meeting of the National Council of Jewish Women, he heralded women's ascension to the pulpit, claiming: "They will do more good than we ministers have so far done." But as historian Karla Goldman has shown, Kohler, much like the rabbis of the Jewish Denominational Congress at the Parliament of Religions, was highly ambivalent over the extension of Jewish women's sphere to areas customarily the province of the rabbinate. Woman as Jewish preacher on occasion was becoming a possibility. But Kohler—and many others—perceived that woman's natural essence set limits to the equality sought by those calling for women's emancipation. Thus at the same meeting that he welcomed women to the pulpit, he warned the women of NCJW, then debating the highly controversial matter of moving Sabbath observance to Sunday, to "leave such theological disputes to the Rabbis." While Jewish women could claim the relatively new rabbinic role of preacher, they dare not assume the traditional mantle of the rabbi, the decider of the law. He propounded: "The time has not come for woman to take issue with the rabbis or occupy their place."[70]

Nevertheless, despite Rabbi Kohler's warning, the combined force of the Congress of Jewish Women, Ray Frank's career, the National Council of Jewish Women, the sisterhoods of personal service, the plethora of local female Jewish organizations, the *American Jewess*, and Jewish woman's occasional role as synagogue preacher all suggested an army of Jewish women on the move. Marching to sustain Jewish life in America, they changed the parameters of their participation in the cultural and religious practices that defined Jewish life. Sometimes these new settings and roles even gave them occasion to ponder, however briefly, whether or not the nineteenth-century woman's rights vision of the admission of women to all the learned professions would come to include the rabbinate. Confronted with the shifting boundaries of Jewish women's participation in and on behalf of their Jewish communities, in February 1897, Rabbi Emil G. Hirsch convened the symposium, "Woman in the Synagogue." Opening the pages of the *Reform Advocate* to representative Jewish women, Reform and "orthodox," he asked them to consider specifically how this activity could benefit the synagogue.

He began: "The woman question can no longer be considered to have more than one side. The new woman is rapidly—aging," no longer an object of curiosity or a target for wit. He invited Jewish women to become "new allies" in the essential work of mending the critical condition of the synagogue. He then asked prominent Jewish women to contribute short essays responding to specific questions: "How can she best serve its interests? Should she take an active part in the administration of its affairs?" What could she offer its schools? How could the societies of Jewish women benefit the synagogue? And most critically for the topic at hand, "Should she occupy the pulpit?"[71]

Twenty-six women joined the symposium. They came from across the United States, from Savannah, Vicksburg, St. Louis, and Detroit, as well as New York, Baltimore, Chicago, and Oakland. They included NCJW leaders Hannah Solomon, Sadie American, and Louise Mannheimer, the educators Minnie D. Louis and Julia Richman, the writer Mary M. Cohen, the preacher Ray Frank, and American Jewish womanhood's most distinguished exemplar, Henrietta Szold, a writer, executive secretary of the Jewish Publication Society of America, and also one of the two women chosen by Hannah Solomon's organizing committee to speak at the World Parliament of Religions.

Many began, as did Chicago's Mrs. Emanuel Mandel, with the assertion: "By making of her home a temple a woman can best serve the interests of the synagogue." To that Mary M. Cohen added that she should attend services regularly. Ray Frank, reiterating what she had said at the Congress of Jewish Women, noted that this included bringing her children there. Not only were Jewish women to lead the young to services, they were also to get them to Sabbath-school. Miriam Landsberg, wife of the Rochester rabbi who had shared a pulpit with Susan B. Anthony, specified that this required getting up early enough on Sunday mornings to give children breakfast before Sabbath school and impressing upon them "that it is even a greater disgrace not to behave well in the Sabbath-school than in the daily school . . ."[72]

Yet while these respondents lauded what had become nineteenth-century Jewish women's customary religious role of regular worshipper, they also saw women taking on new roles in their synagogues. Overwhelmingly, the writers expected, as Minnie D. Louis argued, that women could and should be a "potent factor" in the administration of the synagogue. Several argued that she merited representation—some even claimed equal representation—with men on congregational and Sabbath-school boards. Still others saw Jewish women preparing themselves to be Sabbath-school teachers and superintendents.

As for the last question, "Should she occupy the pulpit?" nine of the twenty-six respondents felt compelled to "draw the line at the woman-rabbi." As Katherine De Sola of Montreal exclaimed: "No—by all that is sacred—a hundred times no! Let woman be as she has ever been, content to let *men* preach while *she* practices" (original emphasis). Those who could not envision women rabbis preferred woman "exalted in the school as a teacher." One argued that the rabbinate required knowledge and voice. While women could acquire knowledge, "nature" denied her the voice essential to this calling. Another worried "when that crowning jewel of woman, motherhood, comes to bless her," the woman rabbi would struggle to balance family with vocation. One naysayer, however, conceded that woman would be welcome in the pulpit "as an occasional guest," but not "as a proprietress."[73]

But two-thirds of the participants—although most, like social welfare worker Rose Sommerfeld, had never before given the subject much thought—contemplated the possibility. These women revealed that, no matter where they personally fell on the spectrum of Judaism, the admission of women to the rabbinate was a logical consequence of the nineteenth-century woman's rights movement. Echoing its rhetoric, Mary M. Cohen affirmed: "There is no sex in spirituality." NCJW leader Henrietta Frank concurred: "Sex does not determine fitness for any position requiring brains and culture. Women have become physicians, professors, poets, sculptors, writers, teachers. Why should they not be teachers of congregations ... " In fact, the expansion of Jewish woman's religious sphere had already paved the way. "As Jewish woman has so well succeeded on the platform, there seems to be no valid reason for excluding her from the pulpit," wrote Louise Mannheimer.[74]

However, the correspondents easily foresaw the barriers hindering any woman aspiring to the rabbinate. First she would require proper training. Therefore, as one respondent pointed out, the key to women's ordination belonged to the seminaries: "*If women are to be given that training*, there is no reason that they should not occupy the pulpit" (emphasis in original). Another understood that, while a woman might receive such training, her success ultimately rested on the reception of "the Jewish congregants of America." Expecting "the decision of this tribunal, for the nonce," she offered disappointed women the "one possible loop-hole of escape," to become Sabbath-school teachers. A third recognized that one essential element was still missing. Where were the female rabbinic candidates? Not a single writer, not even Ray Frank, laid claim to the calling. Therefore, she concluded: "the question does not confront us practically yet."[75]

Still, given the obstacles, were such a woman to present herself, the writers set extraordinarily high standards for a woman rabbi. Hannah Solomon decried any who would turn to the ministry just to earn a living. Only one "capable of fulfilling the highest good in that noble calling" would ever be worthy. And Henrietta Szold spoke for virtually all in demanding that such a woman be "extraordinary":

I believe that woman can best serve the interests of the synagogue by devoting herself to her home ... and by occupying the pulpit only when her knowledge of the law, history, and literature of Judaism is masterful, and her natural gift so extraordinary as to forbid hesitation, though even then it were the part of wisdom not to make a profession of public preaching and teaching, the old Jewish rule of not holding women responsible for religious duties performed at definite times having a deep-seated rational basis and wide applicability.... In other words, the Deborahs and Miriams need not hide their light under a bushel, but they and the world must be pretty sure that they are Deborahs and Miriams, not equally admirable Hannahs and Ruths.[76]

Here Szold, who was already at the time and would continue through the first half of the twentieth century to be a towering figure of American Jewish womanhood, voiced the ambivalence that virtually all discussants—whether these women of the symposium or Reform rabbis—expressed about Jewish women taking on the mantle of the rabbinate. The shifting boundaries of woman's place in the modern world required American Jewish men and women determined to keep pace with the times to welcome, at least rhetorically, the possibility. But most, reluctant to see this become an actuality, set standards impossibly high for any female aspirant. Thus when the question would become practical—as it may in fact have already been for a few of the women who studied at Hebrew Union College at the end of the nineteenth century—the issue would by no means be easily resolved.

Szold's hesitancy about women's ordination, apparently first expressed in this 1897 symposium, takes on added importance given that less than a decade later she was to find herself among the students at the Jewish Theological Seminary of America. By 1893, when the committee organizing the Congress of Jewish Women chose Szold, along with well-known writer Josephine Lazarus,[77] to stand before the World's Parliament of Religions as exemplars of Jewish womanhood, she had already emerged as a significant figure in American Jewry. By the time of her death in Jerusalem in 1945, she had become a giant in American Jewish life, the founder of Hadassah and Youth Aliyah, a distinguished journalist, speaker, organizer, Zionist, tireless Jewish communal worker, editor, and translator, the only Jewish woman future historians would rank among the greatest American Jewish leaders of all time.[78]

Born in Baltimore, Maryland, in 1860, Henrietta Szold was the eldest of eight children, all daughters, of Hungarian rabbi Benjamin and Sophia Schaar Szold. She received in Baltimore schools and from her father the intensive education customarily reserved for the eldest son. The only Jew at Western Female High School, Szold graduated at the top of her class, but, since Baltimore then had no female colleges, she could not continue her formal education. Instead she became her father's secretary, editor, ghost writer, and most important intellectual companion. She also taught, wrote essays for the Jewish press, and organized night classes for East European Jewish immigrants. In 1893 she moved to Philadelphia to become the executive secretary—in effect the underpaid editor and translator—of the Jewish Publication Society of America, a post she held until 1916.[79]

In the same year that Szold first took on this important job, she appeared at the World's Columbian Exposition, where she gave two presentations at the Parliament of Religions. In one, she spoke about the work of the Jewish Publication Society. In the other, at the invitation of the Committee of the Jewish Women's Congress, she delivered the paper, "What Judaism Has Done for Women" to the Religious Parliament. This address brought the question of women in Judaism to an audience other than that reached earlier by the Congress of Jewish Women.[80]

In "What Judaism Has Done for Women," Szold joined with those who had reconceptualized Jewish tradition at the Congress of Jewish Women to show that Judaism professed the equality of the sexes. Genesis proved "the ideals of equality between man and woman that have come down to us from the days of the Patriarchs." However, because surrounding nations did not share "Israel's ideals of womanhood . . . and Israel was not likely to remain untainted," Mosaic legislation had laid "down stringent regulations ordering the relation of the sexes," safeguarding woman's rights with respect to inheritance, marriage, and divorce.[81]

Cautioning that the laws of marriage and divorce are "so multifarious and exhaustive that only a very skilled Talmudist and an equally systematic mind" can comprehend them, she nevertheless presented "some instances and some laws in order to illustrate how the rabbis accept woman's exceptional position." Determined to read into the Jewish past confirmation of the equality of the sexes, she alleged "women, as well as men, could sue for divorce," willfully ignoring that under Jewish law only men have the power to grant a divorce. With regard to education, she claimed, "[a]ccording to the Mishnah, girls learn the Bible like boys," deliberately disregarding the favored classical maxim obstructing women's learning.

Like the speakers at the Congress of Jewish Women, Szold, too, paused toward the end of her address, to honor the Mother in Israel, who teaches her children, speeds her husband to synagogue, and makes for all a "godly and pure" Jewish home. But "What Judaism Has Done for Women" did not close here. Before the august Parliament of Religions, Szold weighed the implications of the "new woman" to fashion a modern vision of Jewish womanhood:

> Our pulses are quickened and throbbing with the new currents of an age of social dissatisfaction and breathless endeavor. The nineteenth century Jewess is wholly free to do as and what she wishes, nor need she abate a jot of her Judaism. Judaism does not, indeed, bid her become a lawyer, a physician, a bookkeeper, or a telegraph operator, nor does it forbid her becoming anything for which her talents and her opportunities fit her. It simply says nothing of her occupations. . . . Judaism permits her daughters to go forth into this new world of ours to assume new duties and responsibilities and rejoice in its vast opportunities.

Still, her reticence led her to warn Jewish women going forth into this new world—and Szold, a spinster and working-woman of thirty-three, appeared to be among them—to: "[b]eware of forfeiting your dignity." Yet the speech reveals her fully cognizant of the woman's rights question of her day and its implications for women in the professions. Her presence at the World's Parliament of Religions and her scholarly address in this unprecedented setting revealed the ways in which her words and her work, not unlike that of Ray Frank, provided a new model for modern Jewish womanhood.[82]

Six years after she had written in the *Reform Advocate* that "the Deborahs and Miriams" wishing to be rabbis "need not hide their light under a bushel," Henrietta Szold found herself in rabbinical school. In the summer of 1902 her father died. As her despondency over his death persisted, Sophie Szold reminded her daughter that, as the eldest, she had inherited his manuscripts. According to biographer Joan Dash, her mother suggested that she organize these papers and prepare them for publication. Henrietta, however, believed she lacked the training in rabbinics essential to the task. So her mother proposed that she ask Solomon Schechter, the new president of New York's Jewish Theological Seminary, to see if she could become a student in the rabbinical school founded, in 1886, "in sympathy with the spirit of Conservative Judaism." Could she, when classes resumed in the fall of 1903, study there, "not to be a rabbi, simply to train herself for work on the manuscripts."[83]

In a later era, those advancing woman's emancipation within Judaism, especially within Conservative Judaism, would recover the story of Szold's admission to the Jewish Theological Seminary.[84] Writing "she was accepted on the condition that she not ask to become a rabbi," some presupposed that Seminary moguls set the condition and Szold bowed to their request to win the education she sought.[85] One would even wish to claim her as "the first woman rabbi."[86] Yet Szold's prior ambivalence about women rabbis, her sense they needed to be outstanding "Deborahs and Miriams"—which her modesty precluded her from claiming for herself—and her own record of the meeting with Solomon Schechter suggest a different reading of the event.

In 1897, Szold had not only publicly expressed her ambivalence about women rabbis, she had also privately written, to her friend Elvira N. Solis, a much more negative assessment of "this question of woman in the Jewish pulpit." Not only was she "tired of Woman spelled with a capital W. ... ," but she was growing "afraid of Woman," who threatened to "force man out of every field of spiritual endeavor, and make every high aspiration fall under the odium of effeminacy."[87]

In February 1903, Henrietta Szold discussed her plans to attend the Seminary in a letter to Judge Mayer Sulzberger, chairman of the Publication Committee of the Jewish Publication Society: "While in New York this week, I had a talk with Dr. Schechter about my entering the Theological Seminary as a student. After he was assured that I was not an aspirant after Rabbinical honors, he agreed to put no obstacles in my way. It remains to be seen what the attitude of the Seminary authorities will be."[88]

A week later she received a letter from Cyrus Adler, then president of the board of the Seminary. He told her that Schechter could admit "special students *not candidates for degrees* who in his opinion are capable of profiting by the instruction given in the Seminary" (emphasis added).[89] It seems clear, given Szold's ambivalence about women rabbis, that she neither expected nor sought any other outcome from her studies at the Seminary. Most likely, of her own accord she had assured Schechter that she had no intention of using Seminary training to seek ordination.

Certainly, Szold personally transcended the customary roles of Jewish women, and not only in her career. For example, after her parents' deaths, she recited *kaddish*, the memorial prayer traditionally said only by men, contending "that the elimination of women from such duties was never intended by our law and custom. . . . It was never intended that, if they could perform them, their performance of them should not be considered as valuable and valid as when one of the male sex performed them."[90] Nevertheless, when it came to the question of women rabbis, which Szold, true to the rhetoric of her time and place, found she had to entertain, she envisioned the privilege as reserved for one whose "knowledge of the law, history, and literature of Judaism is masterful, and her natural gift so extraordinary as to forbid hesitation," a standard so impossibly high that she could never claim it for herself.

By 1903, when Szold was seeking admission to the Jewish Theological Seminary, representatives of a more traditional element of American Jewry than that of Hannah Solomon and Emil Hirsch showed themselves fully cognizant that debate about women's ordination had commenced. Even New York's leading Anglo-Jewish weekly, the *American Hebrew*, a paper "strong for traditional Judaism" but willing to recognize some accommodations to American conditions,[91] broadcast the topic. In an editorial discussing the *Reform Advocate*'s "Woman in the Synagogue," *American Hebrew* editors claimed they gave significant space "to the matter of women occupying the pulpit . . . simply because this question has not been so ventilated before."[92] Now as Szold, at the age of forty-three, entered the Seminary, she unwittingly played a role in keeping before her contemporaries the question of women rabbis. And she helped spread it to another sector of American Jewry, the East European immigrant readers of the Yiddish press. In 1904, she noted with glee the consternation her studies aroused as reporters of the Yiddish press claimed she planned to use her training to do what rabbis traditionally did, to rule on questions of Jewish law.[93]

In 1906, when Szold ceased her course work at the Jewish Theological Seminary, the more than decade-long conversation about women's rabbinic ordination came, for a time, to a close. For from then until the end of World War I, the debate that had swirled so widely, reaching almost every sector of American Jewish life, ceased.

Middle-class Jewish women bent upon service to Jews and Judaism apparently found other challenging outlets for their talents. They turned to new organizations of synagogue sisterhoods (formed in 1913 and 1918) and Henrietta Szold's Hadassah (1912), which now joined the National Council of Jewish Women in hosting national forums where such capable women could display their piety and erudition on a regular basis. There other and more pressing discussions—immigrant welfare, Zionism, and most urgently Jewish women's war work—interrupted the debate about woman rabbis.

Meanwhile Ray Frank had disappeared from the popular press. In 1898, she left for Europe. There in an interview in London she made very clear that while, "women whom circumstances do not permit to marry" could be independent and turn to the professions, she did "not believe in their being taken up by married women." When she returned to the United States, it was as Ray Frank Litman, to settle on the campus of the University of Illinois at Champaign-Urbana, where she became a model faculty wife, involved in sisterhood, Hadassah, and Hillel, and devoted to Jewish students.[94] No other woman emerged to take her place as a charismatic preacher and unofficial rabbi.

With women no longer pressing the question either rhetorically or as real-life examples, the press ceased to broadcast the debate about whether women could and should become rabbis. Not only did the *American Jewess* stop publication in 1899, but the Anglo-Jewish press and even the general press lost interest in the issue of women clergy.[95] Perhaps for Christian audiences, the novelty about women in the pulpit had, for the time being, worn off.[96] Rabbis, like Emil G. Hirsch and Kaufmann Kohler, who had taken up the question as the "new woman" loomed, no longer talked about woman in the pulpit as the logical extension of Reform's commitment to women's religious equality.

Instead, by 1912 the *American Hebrew* could editorialize with confidence: "It is now some years ago that we were threatened with a woman rabbi.... During the time Miss Frank was in the public eye other Jewish women believed they had a message to give from the pulpit ... but in recent years Jewish women have been content to leave the pulpit, as they are ready to leave their religion—to the rabbis."[97] Perhaps that was true then. But to the surprise of many, less than a decade later, a new group of female pioneers, utterly ignorant of the debates of the previous generation, would insist that they would be glad to leave their religion to the rabbis, just so long as they could join their exalted ranks.

Chapter 3

"[W]oman cannot justly be denied the privilege of ordination"

1922

The long struggle over woman's suffrage reached its resolution with the ratification of the Nineteenth Amendment in 1920, when once again the woman rabbi took her place on the agenda of modernizing Judaism. From then until the eve of World War II, the question of ordaining women regularly surfaced in Jewish life, chiefly in America, but also for a time in Germany. In these years, however, the debate took a new, more urgent turn. Progressive rabbis and their wives, club women, and female public speakers no longer debated the question "Should she occupy the pulpit?" as a mere abstraction. In the 1920s and 1930s the practical issue confronting Reform Jewry was what to do about the first serious female seminary students who were then presenting themselves as rabbinical candidates.

Beginning in the 1920s a small number of women tried to push the question of women's ordination from the "bottom up." Five women—Martha Neumark, Irma Levy Lindheim, Dora Askowith, Helen Hadassah Levinthal, and, in Germany, Regina Jonas—spent enough time in rabbinical schools to

force their faculties, fellow students, and other Jewish leaders to respond to their quests to become rabbis. Apparently unaware that only
thirty years earlier there had been much serious talk about ordaining
women, and the role of Ray Frank, Henrietta Szold, and others in this
debate largely forgotten, these new post–World War I pioneers and
their champions looked further back in history for affirmation. Together, just like their predecessors at the turn of the century, they reread Jewish tradition and searched in the history of Jewish women to
legitimize the woman rabbi. Arguments based on contemporary sociological and political realities—the revolution in women's status in
their own time—did not suffice; so once again they asserted that the
Jewish past authorized woman's right to learn, to teach, to exercise
religious authority, to demand equality, and to stand in the center of
her community as a rabbi. Across the divide, those opposing women's
ordination would search the same texts to conclude: "It is contrary
to all Jewish tradition and Jewish religious teaching to have women
perform the functions of Rabbis in Israel."[1] As the two sides squared
off, they unknowingly added their voices to the already open debate
about the woman rabbi.

Martha Neumark (1904–81) was the first of the early female rabbinic candidates. In 1921, her petition to the faculty of Hebrew Union
College for a high holiday assignment launched a lengthy debate
among the professors, their graduates in the Central Conference of
American Rabbis, and HUC's Board of Governors over whether Reform Judaism would break with tradition and permit women to become rabbis. Her challenge prodded the members of Reform's Central Conference of American Rabbis (CCAR) to proclaim: "Woman
cannot justly be denied the privilege of ordination."

Born in 1904, the second of three children of David and Dora
Turnheim Neumark, Neumark emigrated to America in 1907 from
Berlin, when her father accepted the position of professor of philosophy at Hebrew Union College.[2] In an autobiographical sketch, Martha Neumark described herself as a "deeply and sincerely religious"
child, one who misbehaved at public school, not at Sunday school. A
prize-winning pupil at Cincinnati's Rockdale Temple, she also studied privately with her father. As a teen, her confirmation deeply

moved her. "I was one of those who read from the Torah in Hebrew, and the recitation of those ancient words crystallized a vague restlessness of mine into the desire to serve my people."[3]

Her matriculation, in 1918, when she was fourteen and a student at Hughes High School, as a special student in Hebrew Union College's Preparatory Division generated no controversy, since other girls had preceded her in the precollegiate course. There she studied Bible, Hebrew, Aramaic, rabbinics, liturgy, and Jewish history. Two years later, another brief experience of religious leadership helped crystallize her decision to become a rabbi.[4]

The Neumarks regularly spent their summer vacations at a Michigan resort where Professor Neumark served as rabbi for the Jewish vacationers. One Friday night he turned over the conducting of the entire service, except for his sermon, to sixteen-year-old Martha. Later she remembered that the radical experiment led the congregants to buzz afterwards "both pro and con, but in the main they were kindly." Again the experience of religious leadership was inspiring: "It was as I incanted the Hebrew that the witchery and charm of the service surged through me."[5]

Her exemplary Jewish education and brief tastes of spiritual authority compelled her to do just what her male classmates were doing. Having completed three years of intensive study, she felt ready to sally forth to display her erudition and mastery before those Jews, isolated in the hinterlands of America, who annually turned to Hebrew Union College for proto-rabbis for the Days of Awe. As she later wrote, "The doubt never entered my mind as to whether I, a girl, would be ordained."[6]

But it surely entered the minds of others. Neumark's petition for a High Holiday pulpit and the implications of honoring that request prompted Kaufmann Kohler, president of HUC, to take the matter up with the HUC Board of Governors. He noted that her request really raised two questions: the first, whether or not women should be ordained after completing their studies, and the second, the particular case of Neumark "who has not given any special proof of her capacity to lead a congregation in prayer and to address one for such a position." As Kohler noted, logic would dictate that if she were sent out to preach, she should later be ordained rabbi.[7]

Unexpectedly, a two-year-long debate ensued.[8] It swirled beyond college faculty, alumni, and lay leaders to their wives and daughters, and even to leading American Jewish figures not then confronted with challengers to the male rabbinate on their turf.[9] Rabbis argued, scholars searched the tradition, women who wanted to become rabbis opened up to the press, and once rabbis, seminary leaders, and laity had fixed their positions, neither Neumark nor those who followed her over the next half century won seminary ordination.

When the faculty split, in the late spring of 1921, on whether or not to send Martha Neumark out to preach on the High Holidays, Kohler asked Rabbi David Philipson to chair a committee comprised of board members and faculty members Jacob Lauterbach, Julian Morgenstern, and Henry Englander to study the question of graduating women as rabbis. One month later they reported by a vote of four to two, that "practical considerations," which they saw no need to detail, precluded encouraging women to become rabbis. Nevertheless, "[s]ince Reform Judaism teaches the equality of women with men in the synagogue, your committee can see no logical reason why women should not be entitled to receive a rabbinical degree."[10]

Professor Lauterbach and board member Oscar Berman objected vehemently, arguing against women's ordination on historical and sociological grounds, against its implications for world Jewry, Reform Judaism, and Hebrew Union College. They believed it "contrary to all Jewish tradition," an "absurd and ridiculous" innovation which would "outrage the feelings of a large part of the Jewish people." As for Reform Judaism, women already made up "the majority" in its synagogues. Ordaining them as rabbis only increased "the danger of the Synagogue and Judaism becoming altogether an affair of the women ... " While Reform's other innovations, such as "taking off the hat ... were absolutely necessary for the preservation of Judaism," this was not. No one, except for "two or three girls" wants it.[11]

Hebrew Union College, it was argued, could not possibly accommodate female rabbinical students. To do so, it would need "[s]eparate rest rooms, wash rooms and locker rooms," a special section of the proposed dormitory, and women supervisors to look after their welfare. Moreover, their presence in the classroom would prove detrimental, since it would distract the other students from their serious work.

Lauterbach and Berman reminded all that Judaism assigns women "a certain sphere of duties." They expected women to marry, a "privilege" that sometimes makes it impossible for them "to appear in public and perform public functions." Moreover, when she complies with nature and marries, she must "make her choice between following her chosen profession or the calling of mother and homemaker."[12] Hence she will abandon her profession. "The college will have trained and supported her for eight years for nothing ... will have made a "very bad investment."

Yet, the professor and board member did concede American Judaism offered new opportunities to women, who, like Neumark, wanted to preserve Judaism by teaching and leading others. They concurred Reform Judaism should enable such women to acquire the knowledge "to do religious work and to become superintendents of religious schools, teachers, leaders in study circles and bible classes."

Presented with these conflicting opinions, HUC's Board of Governors decided to appeal to the past, to ask the faculty to rule on whether or not Jewish law permitted women to become rabbis.[13] The assignment fell to Jacob Lauterbach, a professor of rabbinic literature. Ordained at Berlin's Orthodox *Rabbinseminar* and holding a doctorate from the University of Göttingen, Talmudic scholar Lauterbach subsequently headed the CCAR's Responsa Committee (1923–33), charged with guiding Reform praxis. Here the professor, much more so than his predecessors in this post, linked Reform Judaism to the classical rabbinic legacy of textual interpretation. While personally committed to Reform, his opinions, on such topics as the Jewish view on birth control, invariably rested on talmudic and rabbinic texts.[14] Already on record as opposed to woman rabbis, he found, as he told his colleagues in December 1921, the body of Jewish law "unanimous in excluding woman from the office of Rabbi."[15]

But the faculty postponed its vote until another committee of one, this time Professor David Neumark, could weigh in. Obviously, Neumark represented the one faculty member with the greatest personal stake in the debate. His daughter believed him "an ardent champion of women's rights," her first and constant teacher, the one who eruditely pleaded her cause before all who would listen.[16]

David Neumark's reading of the sources challenged that of Lauterbach. He concluded: "The question of ordaining women as rabbis has never been raised in Jewish legal literature." Searching instead for analogous issues, he raised the problem of woman's inability to serve as witness and its ramifications for her right to assume the classic rabbinic functions of judge and "ritual decisor." Finding at least one authority ignoring the "generally accepted" prohibition on women as witnesses, he ruled: "in my opinion . . . there is no legal authority to debar women from any of the above functions." But even though he concluded *halachah* permitted women to act as legal decision-makers, ordaining women surely violated "orthodox Jewish custom." Yet the faculty did not contemplate ordaining "a woman as rabbi to serve within the orthodox scope of this office." Rather they debated whether or not Hebrew Union College would ordain women as well as men, certifying their "fitness and ability . . . to instruct and to teach religion." Convinced "[t]he orthodox will not object to the ordination of woman rabbis more than they do to our ordination of men," the father championed his daughter, the pioneer.[17]

Before the faculty voted, Moses Buttenweiser reminded his colleagues that surely Miriam, Deborah, and Hulda illustrated Judaism's historical attitude toward women's ordination. He wanted the men to view these prophetesses "not in the light of the far-fetched construction placed upon them by the Talmud, but in the light of the facts of the case as narrated in the Bible." There, so he recalled, the prophet Micah assigned to Miriam "an equal share" with Moses and Aaron in delivering Israel from Egypt and in "the birth of the nation."[18]

Subsequently, the faculty, even Lauterbach, agreed that given Reform's history of departure from tradition, HUC could not "logically and consistently refuse the ordination of women." While the majority determined nothing now stood in the way of women preparing for the rabbinate, the Talmud professor—later joined by his disciple, Reform's emerging *halachic* expert, Solomon Freehof—dissented fearing this radical departure would provoke "schism" in world Jewry.[19]

Having heard from the faculty, the HUC Board of Governors decided to canvass the alumni, scheduled to meet as the CCAR the following summer. Meanwhile, "no women students of the College" could plan to officiate on the High Holidays.[20]

Now Lauterbach prepared a full-length "Responsum on Question, 'Shall Women Be Ordained Rabbis?'" Understanding that the external issue of women's admission to other male professions drove the question, he held that Judaism, unlike law or medicine, demands its official representatives to be male. Admitting women to the rabbinate remained contrary to the very spirit of Judaism the rabbis had to uphold.[21]

He found his proof in the key passages of Jewish law those engaged in later debates about women rabbis would also scrutinize. Since Judaism exempts women from performing the commandments fixed in time,[22] rabbinic law excluded women from representing the congregation, as "one who is not personally obliged to perform a certain duty, cannot perform that duty on behalf of others." Consequently, women could not become religious leaders. The Talmud took this for granted; medieval sages upheld it; and this view remains "strictly adhered to by all Jewry all over the world throughout all generations even unto this day."

Lauterbach asked, "[S]hall we adhere to this tradition or shall we separate ourselves from Catholic Israel and introduce a radical innovation?" Arguing that Reform rabbis constitute "the latest link in that long chain of authoritative teachers," he asserted ordaining women would shatter this historic bond.

Going beyond rabbinic sources, Lauterbach brought forward sociological realities. Women could not possibly enter the rabbinate as they did any other profession, for it was unique in its arduous demands. No woman could marry and raise a family and give the rabbinate the whole-hearted devotion it required. On the contrary, a successful rabbi required a helpmate for a wife, one to make "his home a Jewish home, a model for the congregation to follow." No married woman rabbi could expect this from her husband. Even if she found a man to "take a subordinate position in the family" and assist her, her family model would not provide a "very wholesome" influence for the congregation.

Excluding women from the rabbinate in no way deprecated them. It merely affirmed the Torah's wisdom in assigning man and woman their respective "spheres." Woman's sphere remained the home where she reigned as wife and mother. In concluding he returned to the other new possibilities open to modern Jewish women, an array of avenues for religious and educational work. Thus, he saw "no injustice done to woman" in upholding the rabbinate as a male preserve.

When the CCAR met in July 1922 to consider Lauterbach's *responsum*, most of the fifteen rabbis on the record sharply disagreed with the professor. They decried his traditionalism as "reactionary," not in keeping with the "revolution in the status of woman" of their time. They criticized his thesis as "inadequate," since in all of Jewish tradition the professor could not find a single statement opposing ordaining women. Instead he had relied upon inference, upon the absence of women rabbis in the past.[23] As progressive men, they parroted the liberal rhetoric of their time, expecting woman's social and economic emancipation to follow quickly in the wake of her new right to vote. Surely, her emancipation should extend to the profession of rabbi.

As they argued, several of the rabbis looked over their collective shoulder at Christian America. One sought out the favorable opinion of members of a nearby Unitarian church. Another, Toronto rabbi Barnett Brickner, pointed to a recent close vote against ordaining women in the Methodist Church in Canada. Rabbi Levinger, likely Lee Levinger of Ohio State University's Hillel organization, observed, "[I]f in the next thirty or forty years we produce but one Anna Howard Shaw, we want her in the rabbinate."[24]

These men easily could have appealed to other recent evidence of Christian America's absorption with women in the ministry. In 1918 the Baptist General Conference became the nineteenth denomination to ordain women. A year later, female ministers bonded together across denominations to establish the American Association of Women Ministers. It planned to "promote equal ecclesiastical rights for women and to encourage young women to take up the work of the ministry." Even as the men of the CCAR debated the woman rabbi, Anglicans, Presbyterians, and members of the Methodist Church struggled with woman's right to the ministry. Although these denominations then rejected ordaining women, others, including the Cumberland Presbyterian Church and the General Association of General Baptists, opened their pulpits to women in these years.[25]

But most joining in the rabbis' debate that summer had no need to look outside of Judaism to women and their new roles in American life nor to search for parallel examples of women in other Christian ministries. Instead they referred to women's changing position in their own world of American Judaism. One observed that already in his congregation women conducted summer services, an innovation newly championed by the women of Reform Judaism united as the National Federation of Temple Sisterhoods.[26] Another reported on a different experiment in expanding woman's proper Jewish sphere. "In the city of New York a professor in the Seminary, the rabbi of an orthodox congregation had a Bar Mitzva of girls."[27] Unquestionably, he referred to the bat mitzvah Jewish Theological Seminary professor Mordecai M. Kaplan had arranged for his daughter Judith but a few months before.

The men also responded to Lauterbach's concern that women rabbis would create a schism in Israel. These rabbis well knew that their predecessors had taken many stances with "no regard for mere keeping of the peace" and that "there are many actions that we would not have taken had we feared this."[28] They had little need to catalog for each other such Reform departures as the abolition of the *get*, the dismissal of the *agunah*, the suspension of the dietary laws of *Kashruth*, or their opposition to Zionism.

Moreover, the woman rabbi would enter a transformed, modern rabbinate, not the old profession Lauterbach would "carr[y] over into America . . . whose function is that of a lawyer, one who renders decisions in an ecclesiastical court." Reform rabbis had jettisoned that role and "broke[n] with tradition long ago when we declared that a rabbi need not be an authority on questions of *Kashruth*." Instead they had assumed other functions, preaching and teaching, appealing to the young and the old in the congregation, and presenting Judaism to a wider world. Surely women with the requisite academic training could take on these responsibilities.[29]

Finally, the rabbis turned to the problem of combining motherhood and the rabbinate. Although at one time women indeed sacrificed marriage for a career, they presumed this no longer the case. They argued against the assertion that the rabbinate "involves the totality of life to the preclusion of even the function and offices of motherhood." They believed this "no more applicable to the Jewish woman as rabbi than it is to the Jewish woman as lawyer, doctor, dentist, newspaper writer, musician, business woman or teacher." David Neumark even assumed that after a woman bore a child, "she will be a better rabbi for the experience."[30]

In joining the rabbis at Cape May that July, Neumark brought along his daughter.[31] He came to refute Lauterbach's interpretation of the sources prohibiting rabbinical roles to women. Where Lauterbach argued women's exemption from certain "religious duties" precluded her from "acting as the religious leader or representative of the congregation," Neumark retorted: "[T]he traditional functions of the rabbi have nothing to do with representation of the congregation." Where Lauterbach quoted Talmud to prove women did not sit in the "academies and colleges where the rabbis assembled and where the students prepared themselves to be rabbis," Neumark read the text to claim "a woman is not *often* to be found in the Beth-ha-Midrash," the house of study. Where Lauterbach saw tradition denying women the privilege of reading Torah before the congregation, Neumark observed Reform Jews had parted with this tradition.[32]

Next the rabbis took the unusual step of opening the floor to their wives and daughters. Three women, Mrs. Frisch, Miss Baron, and Mrs. (Henry?) Berkowitz spoke for the record. All welcomed the woman rabbi. One, in fact, found her initial opposition changed by the men's debate.[33]

But these three women and Miss Neumark were not the only Reform women confronting the female rabbi. Reform's leading spokeswoman, Carrie Simon, had also noticed her. The founding president (1913–19) of the National Federation of Temple Sisterhoods and wife of Washington [D.C.] Hebrew Congregation's Rabbi Abram Simon, Carrie Simon led NFTS to pioneer the expansion of woman's roles in the Reform synagogue. In the 1910s and 1920s, she traveled around the country organizing new sisterhood affiliates and broadcasting "What Can the Women Do for Judaism?" By now, her preaching from synagogue pulpits no longer signaled the remarkable departure from custom it had been when, some twenty years earlier, another president of a Jewish women's club, Hannah Solomon, stood before Temple Sinai. Even before the CCAR rabbis gathered, Simon, without ever referring to the teenager whose request to become a rabbi had caused all this furor, urged the women of Reform Judaism to contribute not only their husbands and sons, but also their daughters, to the Jewish ministry.[34]

In the end the liberal spirit prevailed and the CCAR voted fifty-six to eleven that "woman cannot justly be denied the privilege of ordination." When Martha Neumark advanced to HUC's collegiate department in the fall of 1922—by then she was also in her third year at the University of Cincinnati—she had every reason to expect that despite the "persistent discouragement and laughter"[35] she met in rabbinical school, soon she would become the first woman rabbi in the history of Judaism.

But ultimate responsibility for HUC's policy rested neither with the faculty nor the alumni but rather with the HUC Board of Governors. In February 1923 its members voted, so Martha Neumark recalled, six laymen to two rabbis, that "no change should be made in the present practice of limiting to males the right to matriculate for the purpose of entering the rabbinate."[36]

Their decision, however, did not end Martha Neumark's studies. Despite the fact that she was no longer, as the press had proclaimed, "destined to be the only and first woman in the rabbinate,"[37] she continued to be "the only female in a class of 99 boys."[38]

And she continued to argue for the woman rabbi. Understanding the question as "merely another phase of the woman question," of the struggle which "ensues each time that a woman threatens to break up man's monopoly" in any field, she contended the "usual feminist recapitulation of the achievements of women . . . too threadbare for use." Instead she proffered: "We need but look at the noteworthy contributions which our own American Jewesses have made to their people and the country. Henrietta Szold stands out as the most zealous worker in the cause of the restoration of the Jewish homeland."[39] For Neumark, Szold was the "[i]ndefatigable and ceaselessly energetic" Zionist, and not her model predecessor in rabbinical school.

In 1925, in the wake of Neumark's marriage to fellow University of Cincinnati student Henry Montor and the death of her father, her champion, she withdrew from Hebrew Union College. By then she had completed more than seven and a half years of the nine-year rabbinical course.[40] For her efforts, HUC officials granted her the first certificate for Sunday-school superintendentship awarded by the new and short-lived Hebrew Union College New York Teachers School.[41]

That spring, the Montors moved to New York City. Although Martha Neumark Montor claimed Rabbi Stephen Wise offered to help arrange private ordination if she completed the curriculum, she never tested his gesture. Many, many years later, she would ruefully recollect her failure "then to follow through."[42]

By the time Wise met Martha Neumark Montor, the noted orator had already had his own experience with the question of woman's ordination. Indefatigable Zionist and passionate social reformer, Stephen Wise towered among the preeminent Jews of his era. Born in Budapest, Hungary, and raised in New York City, Wise decided against matriculating at Hebrew Union College. Instead he received private ordination, in which, outside the walls of the modern rabbinical seminary, a rabbi examines the applicant. After finding him capable of answering questions of *halachah*, he ordains him rabbi in Israel.

After several years as a rabbi in Portland, Oregon, Wise returned to New York City. When his negotiations with New York's premier Reform synagogue, Temple Emanu-El, broke down over its lay leaders' efforts to muzzle his freedom of speech in the pulpit, he started the Free Synagogue. Increasingly dissatisfied with the quality of Hebrew Union College and especially with its anti-Zionist stance, Wise determined to act on a dream he had long held to launch his own school. With the aid of the Free Synagogue, he founded, in 1922 in New York City, the Jewish Institute of Religion (JIR), a nondenominational, but nevertheless liberal, rabbinical school. The nontraditional nature of the seminary and its dedication to the free expression of all forms of Judaism marked the school as liberal while avoiding the label Reform.[43] Just as it registered its first class, a chance meeting with Wise brought Irma Levy Lindheim to its doors.[44]

Born in New York City in 1886, Irma Levy was the daughter of well-to-do German Jewish immigrants. In 1907 she defied her father's wishes to arrange a suitable marriage. Instead she wed Norvin Lindheim, socially her peer, but whose career as a fledgling attorney her father deemed unsuitable. Together the Lindheims raised five children and made their New York City home a center "for a mixture of important people from the worlds of business, diplomacy, finance, and the arts," many of them Germans her husband met in his growing international law practice.[45]

Yet raising a family and the life of hostess could not fully absorb Irma Lindheim. Her fourth child was but five weeks old when, in the spring of 1917, she enlisted for active service in the Motor Corps of America, established when the United States went to war with Germany to recruit female volunteers to drive and do odd jobs for the military. Quickly she rose to first lieutenant, the only Jewish woman to become one of its high officers. In the midst of her service, Lindheim became increasingly aware of "the disgrace of [her] basic ignorance as a Jew." While on weekend leave from the Motor Corps, she visited Baltimore, spending an evening at the home of the ardent Zionist Harry Friedenwald. Returning on the train to New York, she had what she later described as a "conversion," the moment when her life mystically changed, and she determined to use her vast energies on behalf of Zionism.

Lindheim met Henrietta Szold and began to work for Hadassah. After she became chairman of the Seventh District of the Zionist Organization of America, she used the money she inherited from her father to purchase a building for its educational and cultural center. At its housewarming, Bernard Flexner hailed her "the Zionist rabbi" for her work. With Professor Mordecai M. Kaplan as her guide, Lindheim planned the center's programs. They included a children's Jewish story hour, Sunday forums for women, and for older children instruction with Hunter College professor Dora Askowith.[46]

Throwing herself into Zionist work helped distract her from what came to be a family tragedy. In 1919, the federal government charged her husband with conspiring to conceal that during World War I German monies had been used to buy the *New York Evening Mail*. In 1920, he was wrongfully convicted of making a false report concerning the registration of enemy property in wartime America.[47]

Meanwhile Lindheim's Zionist work made her increasingly aware of her woefully inadequate knowledge of Jewish history, tradition, and culture. As a child, she had attended religious services with her grandmother. Her "confirmation was the tremendous event of my youth." Later she claimed that afterwards: "For a while I felt an acute regret that I was not a man, and therefore could not become a rabbi." Nevertheless, she considered her childhood family "completely assimilated."[48] Not only did the Lindheims not celebrate Jewish holidays, but told that she had to serve her dinner guest, the Zionist Herbert Bentwich, kosher food, she prepared smelts stuffed with lobster.

As the Jewish Institute of Religion prepared to open, Lindheim, by now acutely aware of how little she knew of Judaism and all things Jewish, asked Wise if he would accept her as a special student. Wise's enthusiastic response led her to pause in her work for Zionism. In October 1922, Lindheim joined the opening class. What began as a corrective to her basic Judaic ignorance escalated into a three-and-a-half-year period of intensive study.

As with her earlier work for the Motor Corps and Zionism, Lindheim wholeheartedly threw herself into her studies. She sent her children out of the city to the family's twenty-two-room mansion on Long Island and set up a small studio apartment a block from the Institute. She then devoted herself to ten-hour days of classes and study, pausing only to cook dinner in the evenings for her husband and to spend weekends with her family.

Lindheim succeeded in school as she had elsewhere. Applying to study in a special graduate course with the influential Columbia University educator John Dewey, she was asked "Have you a bachelor's degree?" Her reply—"No. But I have five children"—won her a place. Later, she claimed, both the JIR faculty and students voted her best in scholarship two years in a row.[49]

In February 1923, just as the HUC Board of Governors was deciding against female rabbis, Lindheim petitioned JIR faculty to change her status to that of a regular student in the rabbinical program. She recognized that "[e]ven for a Stephen Wise that was to be confronted with a monumental issue. A true feminist at heart, who had battled valiantly to help women achieve the vote, he was—though in practice a Reform Jew—a traditionalist at heart. To take such a step as I proposed was to fly in the face of all precedent."[50]

A lengthy discussion among the faculty ensued. While "[i]t was clearly understood by all those present that it was not against the principles of the Institute to admit women students," the professors reiterated objections voiced in the earlier debates at HUC. This innovation would add to the burden of establishing the new school; it had no dormitories for women; and it would be easier to encourage the students to "seriousness" if no women were present. At first, the faculty voted to admit women only as auditors to Extension courses, basically adult education classes. But they allowed the three women already enrolled in the JIR, including Irma Lindheim, to remain.[51]

However, Lindheim refused to take no for an answer. Instead she waged her campaign "with seriousness and satire." Again, in March, the faculty debated. Finally, after a third airing of the subject, in May 1923, the men changed their minds and unanimously recommended the admission of women to the JIR on the same basis as men. While the JIR's original catalogue described it as a school training men for the Jewish ministry, its 1923 charter stated it did "train, in liberal spirit, men *and women* [emphasis added], for the Jewish ministry, research and community service."[52] Subsequently, Wise responded to colleagues, like Rabbi Lee Levinger, who had discovered "girls" wanting to be rabbis: "Yes, we do admit women on the same terms as men."[53]

Meanwhile, Irma Lindheim continued her studies. But in March 1924, the personal crisis that had tested her family since her husband's trial and conviction in 1920 came to a climax. Norvin Lindheim, whose conspiracy conviction would subsequently be overturned—but posthumously, was called to serve his jail term. The month in jail, a "terrible experience," and the long haul of the legal battle took its toll on the Lindheims. The seemingly unflappable Irma Lindheim sagged under the burden. In 1925, on the verge of collapse, she was ordered by her doctor to rest. The change of scenery he prescribed led her to make her first trip to Palestine, a journey recorded in the letters published as *The Immortal Adventure*.[54] Already from Palestine, she wrote Wise that upon her return to America, she did not plan to resume her studies.[55] True to her word, when she landed in New York, she decided that she could no longer indulge herself in the luxury of student life, that she had to act upon what she had seen and learned in Zion. Later she wrote that Wise was disappointed that she did not complete her final year at the JIR and become a rabbi, but that as a devoted Zionist, he understood it more important for her to work for Palestine than to win ordination.[56] Anyway, as Lindheim later recollected: "It was not that I had any plan to function as a rabbi. I simply believed, in a time of women's gradual emergence as individuals in their own right, that if I prepared myself in accordance with the requirements of being a rabbi, the door would be opened for other women, should they wish and have the gift to minister to congregations."[57]

But just as Irma Levy Lindheim was abandoning, of her own accord, her quest to be a rabbi, another woman was moving toward testing JIR's promise to prepare men—and women—for the Jewish ministry.

Among the three women enrolled as special students in JIR's opening class was Dr. Dora Askowith. Shortly after her birth, in 1884, in Kovno, Russia, her family journeyed to America. At Boston's Girls' High School she displayed a talent for history. In 1903, she won the Old South Historical Prize for her essay and first publication, "The Purchase of Louisiana." After earning a B.A. with honors at Barnard College in 1908, she began graduate work in history at Columbia University. She earned an A.M. there in 1909. Her thesis, "The Reforms of Joseph II, Emperor of Germany," examined the Holy Roman emperor (1765–90) who, in 1782, promulgated the first edict limiting the social and economic isolation of the Jews. In 1915, Columbia University awarded her a Ph.D. in history. The subject of her dissertation, *The Toleration of the Jews Under Julius Caesar and Augustus*, which drew widely upon sources in German and French as well as Latin, proclaimed that Jewish history remained her abiding scholarly passion.[58]

While pursuing graduate studies, Askowith taught history in New York City public high schools, and in 1912 became a temporary instructor at Hunter College. From then until shortly before her death in 1958, she taught a variety of courses at Hunter, first in the regular daytime sessions, and then after 1916 in the Evening and Extension Programs. Some, such as a graduate course in ancient history and classes in comparative religion, permitted her to teach aspects of Jewish studies, long before this subject entered university curricula.

She organized the school's Menorah Society[59] and acted as a Jewish spokeswoman, reminding the college, well known for its high percentage of Jewish students, that opening classes on the High Holidays would adversely affect these women.[60]

Surely, Askowith's intense interests in Jewish communal life, especially Zionism, had introduced her to Stephen Wise long before she enrolled at JIR. She came from an ardent Zionist family and credited her father with displaying the first model for the Zionist flag.[61] In Hadassah's early years she sat on its Central Committee.[62] In 1917, she became national director of the Women's Organization for an American Jewish Congress. Its treasurer was the former Louise Waterman, Mrs. Stephen S. Wise.[63]

Rabbi Wise established the democratically elected and pro-Zionist American Jewish Congress to champion Jewish civil and political rights in the postwar world. In 1917, in "a stunningly unique event," over 335,000 American Jews, men and women, elected delegates to its opening convention. In the pamphlet "A Call to the Jewish Women of America," Women's Organization national director Askowith proclaimed: "[N]ot until now, with one accord, were all the Jewish women of America of voting age, numbering over a million, given the ballot." Askowith broadcast to all Jewish women the promise and possibility of the upcoming elections, which the "Women's Suffrage Party ... [deems] an important step in the ultimate attainment of suffrage for all the women of America."[64]

"A Call to the Jewish Women of America" also included her overview of "the part played by the Jewish woman in Jewish history."[65] Here the historian paraded before a new audience the exalted position held by Jewish women in the past to justify expanding their sphere in the present. She lauded brave and pious Jewish women, the biblical heroines Miriam and Deborah and "the Jewish queens who held the reins of government"; and medieval martyrs and learned scholars, like Ima Shalom, "who founded schools and was noted for her knowledge of Jewish law." She explained Judaism's historic preference to preserve woman's "perfect equality of right" despite the practice of surrounding nations. Turning to the modern era, she praised recent developments of modern Jewish womanhood, including the work of the National Council of Jewish Women, sisterhoods, and Hadassah. And she observed: "There is hardly a profession which does not count Jewish women among its followers. . . . In the journalistic world, from the pulpit, from the platform and in the court room, the voice of the Jewish woman is heard."

Although Dr. Askowith sat alongside Lindheim in the first classes held at the JIR, she had not yet fixed her ambition on the rabbinate. Rather her sense of women's expanding professional opportunities led her to hope for a promising academic career. A Barnard College alumnae fellowship permitted her to travel in 1924–25 to Europe and Palestine. There she studied at the American Academy in Rome and the American School for Oriental Research in Jerusalem. Although publication followed, Askowith failed to receive the regular faculty appointment she hoped for.[66]

Meanwhile, she continued to write about Jewish women. In 1928, in another article, she asserted "The Jewish Woman Claims Her Place." As she had done in "A Call to the Jewish Women of America," she first paraded the great Jewish women of the past, like the judge Deborah and the sage Beruriah, to prove "woman was the vital factor in the development of Jewish civilization." This was especially true for "modern times," now that Jewish women had won the "[r]ights and privileges that had been sought and fought for in vain, for centuries." And she surveyed just what Jewish women had done with their new-found rights and privileges. In America, they had organized various Jewish women's groups: Hadassah, Women's League for Palestine, and Pioneer Women awakened women's Jewish sensibilities. They encouraged their members' philanthropy and inspired them to Jewish study. At home and in the colleges, women, like those of her own Hunter College Menorah Society, learned Hebrew, Bible, and Jewish history. Some prepared themselves to teach. Others would enter new fields of professional activity. Similarly, "the Jewish women's voice is heard in all matters affecting the welfare of Jewry in the Holy Land." There in Palestine, organizations like the Hebrew Women's Union for Equal Rights "assure[d] the legal status of women."[67]

Given Askowith's celebration of women enhancing their Jewish educations, her sense of the professional possibilities opening to women, and her faith in the attainment of women's equality, it was but a short leap from writing "The Jewish Woman Claims Her Place" to her claiming her own place in the rabbinical program at the Jewish Institute of Religion. From 1928, when she returned to the JIR, until 1937, she pursued her studies, hoping "to open the road for women who might be desirous of becoming ordained and willing to devote their efforts to furthering the interests of Jewry.[68]

As early as 1930, the faculty conceded that she had done sufficient work in all departments to be in the fourth year of the rabbinical curriculum. Yet, they found her unable to meet the requirements set for her in Hebrew. Despite her repeated requests for admission to the rabbinical program, she was denied regular status pending passing the second-year Hebrew examinations. Askowith, however, never took those exams.[69]

Still she argued for the woman rabbi, preaching a trial sermon, "The Woman in the Rabbinate," before President Wise and the student body.[70] Here naturally she "turned to the literature of the tradition." She "pointed out that nowhere in the vast body of material examined does one find clear-cut opposition to women serving in the rabbinate." Biblical women were "worshipper[s] and official[s]." Rabbinic literature granted "equality of the sexes in religious functions." Several women "were actually accepted by their contemporaries as '*rabbinim.*'" She named not only Rashi's daughters and the "Maid of Ludomir," but also one Frume Rifka Cherniavski, in whose honor, in 1879, a Williamsburg synagogue was named Ezrath Nashim, after the women's court in the ancient Jerusalem temples. Askowith could not "ascertain whether she actually received *Semikah*," rabbinic ordination.

In 1937, Askowith left JIR. Perhaps her failure to master Hebrew was decisive, although surely other students struggled with this requirement.[71] Perhaps her professors' discouragement persuaded her to abandon her plan. At least one of them ranked the historian and scholar "a poor student."[72] Perhaps she had already fulfilled her plan to deepen her knowledge of Jewish studies, for Askowith too denied that she ever planned to function as a rabbi. Instead, she wrote: "I took the work at the Institute because of my deep interest in Judaica and Hebraica rather than because I sought to enter the ministry though I hoped to open the road for women who might be desirous of being ordained."[73] Before she left JIR, Askowith stopped to encourage another young woman, Helen Levinthal, to stay the course.

The daughter of Rabbi Israel and May Bogdanoff Levinthal, Helen Hadassah Levinthal (1910–89) came of age in Brooklyn's Crown Heights in the shadow of her father's synagogue, the Brooklyn Jewish Center. Like her peers, the American-born children of the East European immigrants, she attended public schools. But as the daughter of a leading Conservative rabbi, Helen Levinthal had a much more intensive Jewish education than many other Jewish youth, especially girls. The daughter of a rabbi deeply "concerned with the education of Jewish girls and with strengthening their loyalty to Judaism," she graduated in the first class of the Brooklyn Jewish Center Hebrew School at a time when approximately three-fourths of American Jewish elementary school children received no Jewish education whatsoever. Apparently no confirmation, certainly no bat mitzvah, accompanied her studies. Not until she was in her twenties did her father inaugurate a consecration service to initiate girls into Jewish religious life.[74]

At a time when the New York Jewish women who indeed attended college commuted to Hunter and other New York City schools, Helen Levinthal went away, to the University of Pennsylvania, where she earned a B.S. in education in 1931. Returning to New York, she simultaneously registered as an auditor at the Jewish Institute of Religion and began studying for an M.A. at Columbia University (1932). Meanwhile, other involvements in Junior Hadassah, Junior Federation of Jewish Charities, and the Young Folks League of the Brooklyn Jewish Center absorbed her, as did her engagement to Leon Sukloff, which her parents announced late in 1932.[75] In the early 1930s, Levinthal thus appeared yet another in a small, but continuing, group of women at JIR, well connected to Jewish life and learning and inspired by these involvements to Jewish study.[76]

But Helen Levinthal trod a different path. In 1939 she became the first woman in American Jewry to complete the rabbinical curriculum. She did not leave for the record an explanation of what led her, in 1935, to change her status from that of auditor to that of a regular student, the only woman among some fifty men in the rabbinic program. Although the class register of 1937–38 listed her as Helen Sukloff, by 1938–39, her brief marriage had ended and she had reclaimed her place as Helen Levinthal.[77]

Later Levinthal would explain that she had begun her studies at JIR, inspired by the classical Hebrew epigram, "study the law for its own sake." But she came to "love Hebrew research," sensing that for her, the descendant of twelve generations of rabbis, it was "the call of the blood."[78]

This distinguished rabbinic line would end with her generation. Her grandfather, Philadelphia rabbi Bernard Levinthal, founded the Union of Orthodox Rabbis, the *Agudat ha-Rabbanim*. Her father was among the most highly regarded Conservative rabbis of his day, an outstanding preacher, and a national leader in Zionist affairs. Israel Levinthal also held a law degree from New York University, but he had found practicing law spiritually unfulfilling. While his son took up what had been for the father but a brief diversion, the law,[79] his daughter tried to extend the Levinthal rabbinic line unto the thirteenth generation.

Since other women before her had come and gone at JIR without ever reaching the point of ordination, the problem of whether or not to ordain Helen Levinthal only became real as she approached her senior year.[80] In December 1937 the faculty debated her verbal application to be a candidate for ordination. With the exception of Hebraist Shalom Spiegel, the men declined her petition, reporting: "It was the consensus of opinion that Miss Levinthal was an average student with no special qualifications, that the question of principle is too tremendous to settle in a casual way."[81]

Yet the father continued to champion the daughter. From Boaz Cohen, the unofficial head of Conservative Judaism's court of Jewish law, Rabbi Levinthal learned that the only responsum on the question was the one Jacob Lauterbach had written back in 1922.[82] Unconvinced that this held the last word, Levinthal continued to raise the matter privately with Stephen Wise.

The two rabbis used to run into each other frequently in those days. Wise once quipped: "If your father . . . will give his approval to our ordaining Helen, we will do so." (Obviously, for Bernard Levinthal, a woman in the pulpit was anathema.) Meanwhile, Helen Levinthal also lobbied privately, and the faculty continued to debate off the record. Later Wise told Rabbi Levinthal the men felt: "while Helen did excellent work, the time was not ripe for the J.I.R. to ordain a woman."[83]

Instead Helen Levinthal graduated with a Master of Hebrew Literature degree. The educator Samson Benderly, who proposed this JIR track in 1931, observed that after the first year, the curriculum was "similar for both groups of students." Certainly, Levinthal's classmates saw no difference between their program of study and hers. Levinthal would not be the first JIR student to receive only this degree. But she would be the first and only woman ever to do so. Meanwhile, her fellow male students graduated as rabbis and masters of Hebrew literature.[84]

In the fall of 1938, Helen Levinthal entered her senior year and began researching her thesis, "Woman Suffrage from the Halachic Aspect." In fact, she had already demonstrated elsewhere her abiding interest in the place of women in Jewish tradition. When, in 1936, Israel Levinthal created a consecration ceremony to mark girls' assumption of their Jewish responsibilities, he numbered his daughter among their teachers. Not only did she stand as a role model for her students, but she also taught them much about the history of Jewish women. Of the eleven talks the teens delivered at that first service, eight recounted women in Jewish history.[85]

Now in seeking out a topic for her thesis, the equivalent of the rabbinic theses her fellow students were then writing, Helen Levinthal found the contemporary issue of woman's rights in Palestine compelling. Could she search the literature of the Jewish past and find that it affirmed woman's right to vote, woman's right to equality? Could she justify the aims of the Women's Equal Rights League, established in Palestine in 1919, to demand female suffrage in all local and national elections?

Once she faced the topic of woman's rights within Judaism, she did what her predecessors only two decades ago had done, and apparently unaware that they had already done much of the work for her. Levinthal once again exhaustively searched the body of Jewish literature for commentary on the question of woman suffrage, turning to the distant past, to the history of Jewish women, for precedent that established women's right to equality within Judaism.

In more than one hundred pages in English and Hebrew, Levinthal explored women in Jewish law, claiming from the beginning women stood with the men in receiving the Revelation at Sinai. She critically examined women's exemption from fulfilling the commandments fixed in time, observing that historically they held a place in public worship. She found that *halachah* included "no *isur*," no prohibition on teaching women Jewish law. And she summoned the female leaders of the Jewish past to testify. Knowing that the rabbis claimed woman cannot judge over the people, she countered: "It is my humble opinion that all the opposing responsa fail to reconcile successfully the unalterable and glaring Biblical example of Deborah."[86]

The questions of woman suffrage and woman's right to hold elected office afforded her indirect parallels to the specific challenge she posed, woman's right to become a rabbi. Considering recent responsa on woman suffrage, especially that of her thesis advisor, JIR Talmud professor Chaim Tchernowitz, she wrote:

> While it is true that never in the past did women vote within the Jewish community, this in itself does not constitute a valid legal argument (as some authors would have us believe) against the extension of the franchise to women. For it is not strictly accurate to claim that in the past women were *denied* the right to vote or even to claim that legal disabilities as such were imposed upon them. It would be more accurate to suggest that historical phenomena and the concomitant habits and customs of the community, whether of society generally, or the Jewish People in particular, were responsible for the *non-voting* of women[87] (emphasis in original).

Undoubtedly she intended a deliberate parallel to her own situation. Just as only in recent years had *halachah* come to grapple with the question of woman suffrage, so too, only recently had Jews specifically entertained the question of the woman rabbi. Even as it was "not strictly accurate to claim that in the past women were *denied* the right to vote," surely she intimated neither was it strictly accurate to claim that Jewish law denied woman the right to become a rabbi.

In March 1939, Tchernowitz, a graduate of Kovno's Isaac Elchanan Yeshiva and the former chief rabbi of Odessa,[88] gave Levinthal an honor grade for her work.[89] That month too, for the first time, her father invited her to preach in his synagogue. A consummate master of the classical Jewish sermon, Israel Levinthal stood out as one of the great preachers of the twentieth century. Because he subsequently published many of his sermons, he not only saved his preparatory notes, he also had the habit of grading himself on each one. After Helen gave "The Jewish Woman Faces a New World" from his *bimah*, the proud father recorded: "most excellent 100 + +."[90]

But no matter how successful the student, no matter how gifted her preaching, as the faculty, and as Helen Levinthal herself later conceded, the time was not yet ripe for a woman rabbi.

Nevertheless, the impending graduation of a woman, even as a Master of Hebrew Literature, distressed her classmates. A full year before she would complete her studies, the junior class petitioned Wise and the faculty "occasioned by the fact that one member of the class is a woman and may be graduated in 1939 either as a Rabbi or Master of Hebrew Literature or both." The ten young men, including future rabbi Earl Stone, unanimously agreed that "the presence of a woman in the group will detract from the dignity and force of our ordination into the ministry as rabbis in Israel.... While we do not necessarily believe that the opportunity for study and acquisition of the M.H.L. degree should be denied to a member of the female sex ...," they wanted her diploma conferred in a separate ceremony.[91] Wise and the faculty demurred, refusing to prevent any candidate who fulfilled degree requirements from appearing at commencement.[92]

Subsequently, in June 1939, Helen Levinthal graduated from the Jewish Institute of Religion. Both her father and her grandfather attended the ceremony at which Wise conferred upon the men of the senior class "the degree of Master of Hebrew Literature and Rabbi."[93]

To Helen Levinthal he granted two diplomas, one in English verifying her as Master of Hebrew Literature and a special certificate in Hebrew, proposed by Israel Levinthal but most likely crafted by Professor Tchernowitz. Wise had once told Levinthal that Tchernowitz conceded a new title "could be conferred upon a woman" since the Hebrew title *rav* was masculine. The Hebrew diploma bestowed upon Chavah Hadassah, the daughter of the Rabbi Israel Chaim Levinthal, the title of *musmakah*, certified in the literature of Israel (*lasifrut yisrael*), thus echoing in the feminine the Hebrew term *musmakh* of rabbinic ordination.[94]

Helen Levinthal's peers were right. Widespread press coverage of her exploit came before reports on their "ordination into the ministry as rabbis in Israel." *Time* magazine proclaimed her "as near to being a rabbi as a female might be." The *Brooklyn Jewish Center Review* exaggerated she became "the first woman rabbi (even if unordained)." And Jewish papers in Warsaw and Jerusalem joined the Yiddish and Anglo-Jewish presses in observing "on account of her sex ordination was not conferred." Although she averred, "I haven't made up my mind yet whether I'd like to be a rabbi," she held out hope for the future. Certainly the press saw her as a symbol of change. The *New York World-Telegram* claimed that "[o]nly tradition prevented her ordination as a rabbi." And Levinthal herself agreed, telling the *New York World-Telegram*, "it is all a process of evolution. . . . Some day there will be women rabbis."[95]

Neither Levinthal, nor the press, were aware that already one woman had indeed become a rabbi.[96]

In 1930, in Germany, the birthplace of Reform Judaism, twenty-eight-year-old Regina Jonas wrote of the rabbinate: "I personally love this profession and want very much to pursue it when that will be possible."[97] Five years later, Rabbi Max Dienemann granted her a rabbinic diploma.

Born in 1902, Regina Jonas completed her secondary education and, in 1924, received a license to teach in girls' schools. Shortly afterwards, she began studying at the Hochschule für die Wissenschaft des Judentums (College of Jewish Studies). Founded in Berlin, in 1870, the Hochschule became the rabbinical seminary and institute of advanced Jewish studies German Reformers had long hoped to build. Training rabbis and certifying Judaica teachers, it quickly became the heart of Reform Jewish intellectual life.[98] But when Jonas crossed its portals, she sought more than the diploma certifying "Academic Teacher of Religion" which the Hochschule granted women; she wanted to become a rabbi.

Of Jonas's career at the Hochschule as a student, little is known. Religion professor Katharina von Kellenbach has discovered that Jonas completed her thesis, "Can a Woman Hold Rabbinical Office?" in 1930. In it, she turned to the past, to the weight of tradition and to Jewish women's history, to prove the woman rabbi "merely the elongation of a line which is sketched already by our scriptures."

Jonas examined the modern rabbi as scholar, teacher, preacher, and Jewish role model. It was clear, Jonas argued, that modern women could assume these roles if properly trained, so the question became whether Jewish tradition prohibited women from acquiring the training. She concluded that not only was there no prohibition on woman's learning, but that the radical changes in woman's status wrought by contemporary life rendered earlier prohibitions against women's teaching and preaching null and void for the modern world. Indeed Jewish women in the past had taught. For prooftexts, she paraded the clever and learned Jewish women of the past, Deborah and Hulda, Beruriah and Rashi's daughters. The latter not only taught, they had also given rabbinic opinions.

She argued that when Israel stood at Mt. Sinai, its sons and its daughters had received the yoke of the Torah together. Thus, she concluded, women could, if they desired, take upon themselves the religious obligations traditionally expected of Jewish men. In fact, remarkable Jewish women in the past had done so, and she pointed to a woman in Mainz who wore *tefillin*, the phylacteries men wear in morning prayers. Where she could not surmount *halachic* objections, such as the classical position forbidding women from bearing witness, she, in good rabbinic fashion, held to the letter of the law but circumvented its intention. Thus, she found nothing in Jewish law precluding the woman who would become a rabbi from assembling men eligible to serve as witnesses.

Jonas too searched outside Jewish tradition, turning to the women who had become doctors and teachers, attorneys and judges. Just as they had joined these professions, so too could women enter the rabbinate. And since "the world consists of two genders due to G'd," the contemporary synagogue would benefit from hearing the "essentially different" voice of a woman rabbi. In the end she decided "other than prejudice and unfamiliarity, almost nothing opposes a woman holding the rabbinical office *halakhically*."[99]

In 1930, Professor Eduard Baneth, the distinguished scholar of talmudic and rabbinic literature, accepted Jonas's thesis.[100] But before he could give her the oral exam in Jewish law required of rabbinical candidates, he died. At the Hochschule only a Talmud professor could ordain. Whether or not Baneth would have acted upon the conclusion of the thesis he approved remains unknown. Talmud *Dozent*, Professor Hanokh Albeck, believing Jewish law forbade it, refused to ordain Jonas, and other faculty concurred.[101] Subsequently, along with a teaching diploma, the Hochschule awarded Jonas a special transcript indicating that she "participated in the homiletic exercises" and that she was becoming "a thoughtful and skilled preacher."

Shortly after her graduation, Jonas began to draw upon her training, finding some places willing to let her preach. Already in June 1931, the *Israelitisches Familienblatt* reported that "overnight we received the first Jewish female preacher in Germany."[102]

Four years later, in December 1935, Jonas appeared in Offenbach to take her long-postponed oral exam in Jewish law before Rabbi Max Dienemann, one of the leaders of German Reform Judaism.[103] After testing her, he awarded her a rabbinic diploma (*Hatarat Hora'a*).[104] There he wrote:

> Since I have recognised that her heart is with God and Israel and that she gives her soul to the purpose which she intends for herself, and that she is God-fearing; and since she passed the exam which I gave her in *halakhic* matters, I attest that she is capable of answering questions of *Halakhah* and *that she deserves to be appointed to the rabbinical office*. And may God support her and stand by her and accompany her on all her ways.[105]

Although Dienemann cautioned her against using the title "rabbi" until she consulted with other authorities, from then until her death, some knew her as *Rabbiner Doktor Regina Jonas*, "Miss Rabbi Jonas."

The point at which each pioneer found her hopes for seminary ordination crushed uncovers obstacles the pioneers confronted in common. Each trying on her own to do what none before had ever done,
the women who wanted to become rabbis, isolated as individuals, encountered similar forces of resistance. The gatekeepers to the rabbinate in the 1920s and 1930s reiterated the same arguments. If they did
not proclaim that Jewish law forbade this, the men believed the time
not ripe; that Judaism afforded woman other opportunities for creative work; and that, anyway, the particular candidates who presented themselves were "average," not sufficiently worthy to compel
such a drastic break with the past.

But the pioneers' experiences in rabbinical school raise questions
beyond that of what prevented them from achieving their goal. The
timing of their quests and the responses their challenges evoked im-
part a great deal not only about the history of women's ordination but
also about expectations for proper Jewish womanhood in America in
these years. Why was this question constantly before liberal Judaism
in the 1920s and 1930s? And why, with a small, but committed, cohort
of women challenging its leaders, did the men not then resolve it in
favor of the woman rabbi?

When Martha Neumark first petitioned Hebrew Union College
for a High Holiday pulpit, the men of Reform Judaism took her application very seriously. Similarly, faculty at JIR found that Lindheim,
Askowith, and Levinthal's challenges required reflection. Unquestionably, the "times" explain, in part, not only why these women
themselves believed they could fulfill their dreams but also the consideration extended them then by the men in power.

The early 1920s heralded an era of great hopes concerning the
emancipation of women in the United States. As the old debate about
woman suffrage came to its favorable conclusion, many affirmed the
realization of woman's emancipation. Certainly this held true for
leaders of American Jewry, who evidenced a widening sense of expanding opportunities for women in all sectors of Jewish life. As one
rabbi had observed in the CCAR debate around Neumark, a rabbi at
Conservatism's Jewish Theological Seminary had just devised a "Bar
Mitzvah" for a girl. In Reform Judaism women leaders of the National Federation of Temple Sisterhoods not only called for women

rabbis, they also developed their own roles and responsibilities in the Reform synagogue, conducting, as Martha Neumark had, summer services and devising the first Sisterhood Sabbaths, where women led services and preached.[106] At the same time George Zepin, secretary of Reform's Union of American Hebrew Congregations, found himself welcoming as delegate to the customarily male UAHC conclave, Sara Lewinson, an "intense believer in the possibilities of useful service for women in . . . fields of activity ordinarily occupied by men."[107] Even Jacob Lauterbach and Oscar Berman, who opposed women rabbis, conceded women could and should acquire the knowledge necessary to do religious work and to teach. Elsewhere, in Conservative Judaism and among Orthodox Jews, women also extended the boundaries of their religious activities beyond the home into their synagogues and communities.[108] By 1927, the *American Hebrew* editorialized:

> During the short period, as time goes, of the emancipation of woman-hood, women's interests have so widened that they parallel those of men in practically every walk of life. . . . The Jewish women of America are abreast of their sisters in this feminine participation in domains the mas-culine contingent of the species had previously appropriated to itself.[109]

And if Jewish women indeed stood "abreast of their sisters" in en-tering domains formerly claimed by men, then the widening sphere of possibilities for women's Jewish activity could, and some thought should, extend to the learned Jewish profession, the rabbinate.

Since the 1848 Seneca Falls convention, women's progress in the professions had served as a major index of their emancipation. Be-tween 1890 and World War I, as the historian Alice Kessler-Harris has shown, the number of women seeking professional training mushroomed. The manpower shortage of World War I not only opened new professional areas to women, it "finally destroyed resid-ual myths that women lacked the physical stamina or intellectual prowess for the most demanding jobs." Moreover, the war promoted the "sense that enormous possibilities were there for the taking. . . . Women, like men, demanded their share of the world's rewards. Am-bition crept into their vocabulary. To aspire, to achieve, not merely to do a job, became at least a possibility for daughters as well as sons." As a result of such heightened expectations, the 1920s saw the number of women in the professions rise by 50 percent. Although the preponderant majority of them remained in the feminine fields of teaching, librarianship, social work, and nursing, increasing numbers entered law and science. Others found new places as journalists, editors, professors, civil servants, and in business.[110]

Their ranks came from the expanding numbers of women graduating college. In 1900, 85,000 women attended college. By 1930, the number had mushroomed to 481,000.[111]

Not only did women enter college in greater numbers than ever before but they evidenced rising hopes for the kind of work they would do upon graduation. The vast majority of female college graduates of the 1920s and 1930s anticipated either taking a job after commencement or continuing to study for professional work. Moreover, by 1922, only one-third of them, compared to some three-quarters a generation earlier, planned to enter the female bastion of teaching. The remainder fixed their career sights on business, social services, and the professions.[112]

The women who came to college in the years just before and after World War I believed: "We came late enough ... to take education and training for granted. We came early enough to take equally for granted professional positions in which we could make full use of our training. This was our double glory."[113]

These women rested their double glory on their personal merits, on their indisputable worthiness. As Penina Migdal Glazer and Miriam Slater argue in their history of women's entrance into the professions, aspiring professional women believed firmly "in the ideology of merit that was so closely associated with all professional work."

> Women banked so heavily on merit—the belief that if only they were good enough, trained enough, committed enough, their achievement of superior performance would be regarded—because it seemed so incontestable. Merit and achievement were, presumably, a matter of personal control and volition, and therefore, protected from political manipulation by others.[114]

These co-eds expected that, properly trained, their superior performances would win them a place in the professions. Moreover, they presumed they would be the first ones to do it all, to combine marriage and career, not to have to choose one over the other. In the late nineteenth century nearly half of all college-educated women never married. Prospects for marriage remained even gloomier for women with advanced educations. In 1910, only 12 percent of all professional women married. Seventy-five percent of the women who earned Ph.D.'s between 1875 and 1924 never wed. Until the 1910s college women anguished, compelled to choose between marriage and career.[115]

But those who followed them presumed otherwise, neither to shun marriage for career nor to give up careers when they married. In the 1910s women college students began to talk of combining marriage and career. Ruth Sapinsky's "bird's-eye view" of "The Jewish Girl at College" in 1916 addressed the truism that college women do not marry. But the Jewish collegiates she surveyed planned to enter the workforce and to wed.[116]

In fact, not only did such college women expect to marry, they did marry. A survey of alumnae who graduated between 1919 and 1923 from five women's colleges, including Barnard, showed marriage rates as high as 90 percent. In the 1920s women graduate students too began to marry in increasing numbers. By 1930, the number of married professional women had more than doubled over the 12 percent of 1910, and one-third of women doctors and lawyers had married by the 1930s.[117] Historian Barbara Miller Solomon argues the significance of this transformation:

> Just as the issue of woman suffrage before 1920 had seemed to portend a redefinition of women's roles in American society, so the idea of women's multiple identities in combining marriage, motherhood, and career seemed radical. Affirmation of this choice by a majority of graduates, whether married or unmarried, represented a giant step in the thinking of educated women.[118]

The American women who tried to blaze the path to the rabbinate stood amidst these educated, career-bound women. Martha Neumark graduated from the University of Cincinnati in 1924; Dora Askowith earned her B.A. in 1908 and Ph.D. in 1915; Helen Levinthal graduated from the University of Pennsylvania in 1931. Of this group, only Irma Lindheim never attended college. In the 1920s these women had either just come of age or had witnessed the promises blazoned forth for women in the professions.[119] Surely, so they expected, the profession they set their sights on, the rabbinate, must give way before meritorious women, like themselves.

Undoubtedly, the new thinking that professional life no longer precluded marriage and motherhood influenced the women who wanted to become rabbis. The learned Jewish profession had long required its men to set an example, to take a wife to make for them, as Jacob Lauterbach asserted, "a Jewish home, a model for the congregation to follow." Although Askowith remained single, as did 75 percent of the women who earned doctorates when she did, both Lindheim and Levinthal were married during rabbinical school. Although Levinthal divorced, one month after her 1939 graduation, she wed lawyer Lester Lyons.[120] Apparently Martha Neumark too assumed she could combine marriage and career. Her daughter Rae Montor remembered her mother recalling the frustration of her student years, of wanting "to be taken seriously as an intellect and at the same time to be taken seriously as a woman."[121]

Not only did these female rabbinical students not expect to remain single, they and those engaging the woman rabbi voiced the expectation that the women who would become rabbis need not reject their traditional role as "Mothers in Israel."[122] The energetic Irma Lindheim stood out as a paradigm. When she entered rabbinical school, she had already given birth to her "ideal family of five children." Stephen Wise praised her "glorious children," claiming: "Anyone who can breed such children should have been the Mother of a thousand!"[123] So too David Neumark observed: "The practical difficulties cannot be denied. But they will work out the same way as in other professions." And he pointed to scientist Lydia Rabbinowitz who had raised "a family of three children and kept up a full measure of family life while being a professor of bacteriology." As for the woman rabbi, he believed: "If she marries and chooses to remain a rabbi, and God blesses her, she will retire for a few months. . . . When she comes back, she will be a better rabbi for the experience." Not long after Martha Neumark found her hopes to become the first woman rabbi quashed, the daughter quoted the remarks of her father to confirm women could combine family life with the rabbinate.[124]

Convinced they need not forfeit marriage and family for career, the pioneers set out. As they looked about them, they sensed their ambitions reflected the times, that indeed they constituted but a small part of a much larger stream of ambitious women striving to break new ground in the professions.

Certainly, the ministry seemed to confirm this. In the 1920s, new challengers stormed leading Protestant denominations which had not yet come to count women among their clergy. The Anglicans and Presbyterians struggled with woman's right to the ministry. In the Methodist church, Georgia Harkness, who later became the first woman to teach in a major seminary outside the feminine bastion of Christian education, proclaimed ordaining women would bring on "the advancement of the Kingdom."[125] In the 1920s and 1930s seven Christian denominations joined the nineteen already admitting women to their clergy.[126] Concomitantly, the press broadcast "Woman's Progress Toward the Pulpit," highlighting new "firsts"— the first women to preach in the Methodist Episcopal Church, the United Lutheran Church, and the Evangelical Church.[127] The press's perception of change was justified. In 1910 there were 685 female clergy; by 1930, there were 3,276.[128]

With the national press fueling the perception of women's headway in the professions, the Anglo-Jewish press chimed in, featuring successful Jewish career women, symbols of American Jews' engagement with the "times." In the 1920s the *American Hebrew* regularly profiled "Jewish Women Headliners," lauding those who had carved out careers in law, medicine, business, politics, and the arts. Commending Mrs. Clarice Baright on her appointment as magistrate, the *American Hebrew* described her the only woman in her law school class of one hundred, in the "days when a woman lawyer was not only a rarity, but a freak." Still "it never occurred to her that there was an obstacle in the fact that she happened to belong to the feminine sex."[129]

The pioneers assumed that if they persisted, if they demonstrated their merit, they could pave the way, and other women would follow. Indeed they were right, for other young women too contemplated becoming rabbis. Martha Neumark presumed that because of the publicity she had received, other women applied to HUC. But they all received the same reply; they could study "and take all the work, but under no conditions would they be granted the regular scholarships nor the privilege of being ordained." Such was the message HUC officials sent to aspiring rabbinical student Dora Landau in 1921. Later, at JIR, in New York, Adeline Seltzer left behind a record of her efforts to win admission to rabbinical school.[130]

Earlier, another teen recorded her thoughts on the subject. In 1919, fifteen-year-old Lucile Helene Uhry wrote in *The Guardian*, the religious school newspaper of Stephen Wise's Free Synagogue:

> Jewish women today are in every walk of life, except the Rabbinate. Everywhere women are gaining their rights to study by the side of men, to work by the side of men, to serve by the side of men. . . . The war has proven that women are equal to tasks that heretofore no one ever dreamed they could accomplish. Surely, they are equal to the tasks of the rabbi.

Miss Uhry had done her homework. She rested her argument in part on the past. "Throughout the ages," the Jew had championed woman's education and the "advancement of his Womankind." Somehow she had even learned that Ray Frank "actually acted as rabbi," but "could not be ordained." With Jewish women already "teachers, preachers, and social reformers," rabbis in all but name, she asked: "Today, when the World has come to realize that women can, and will hold great positions in every phase of life, will the Jew, the progressive, democratic, liberal-minded Jew fall behind, and prevent his women from entering that most noble of professions, the Rabbinate?"[131]

So years before Irma Lindheim walked through the doors of Stephen S. Wise's JIR, the "progressive, democratic, liberal-minded" rabbi had encouraged Miss Uhry. "I am beginning to feel that if you are really in earnest and wish to study for the ministry, there is no reason why you should not. The fact that no woman has served as rabbi is no reason why no woman should so serve. If you were my child, as in a sense you are, and felt you wished to enter the ministry,

I should urge you to go on and prepare yourself."[132] Later Uhry declined to study at the JIR. Instead she married Rabbi Louis I. Newman and became "First Lady of Rodeph Sholom" in New York City.[133]

But the heightened expectations for educated women's full participation in American and American Jewish life do not alone explain the regard given the pioneers. Surely, their positions as insiders in their seminary communities, to the extent that women could be, ranked as significant to the consideration they received. Neumark was the daughter of Hebrew Union College Professor David Neumark. The Lindheims and Wises shared a long friendship. Stephen Wise had officiated at Norvin Lindheim's confirmation. The Lindheims named their fifth child after their rabbi. Convinced that the lawyer's conspiracy conviction revealed a grave miscarriage of justice, Wise used his not inconsiderable political connections to win presidential clemency (and later to overturn the judgment) even as Irma Lindheim poured her energies into her JIR studies.[134] Moreover, Norvin Lindheim, a trustee of JIR, supported the school financially.[135] Later, Helen Levinthal, the daughter and granddaughter of distinguished rabbis, colleagues of Wise, could presume the same kind of deliberate consideration of her request for ordination. It was one thing to dismiss Dora Askowith, who could not boast these powerful family connections, as unsuitable for the rabbinate. It was quite another to refuse admission to the daughter of a professor, or that of a rabbi, or the wife of a trustee—even when she lacked, as did Irma Lindheim, the formal academic credentials requisite for admission.[136]

Nevertheless, these women presumed that, if they were good enough, their excellence, not the *yichus* (prestige) of their family connections,[137] would carry them towards their goal. But as they found out, no matter how commendable their performance, individual merit played little role then in woman's quest for ordination. Askowith's Ph.D. and publications demonstrated intellectual credentials worthy of the rabbi as scholar. Levinthal stayed the entire course hoping a thesis in the most important seminary field, *halachah*, would proclaim her worthiness to join this exalted profession.

But, as these women came to discover, the gatekeepers to the rabbinate "felt that the first women . . . ought to be outstanding."[138] And this test, reflecting both the judge and his object, proved so exceptional that none of the aspirants, could pass. For what one judge deems exceptional, another may well mark just "average." None of the women, no matter how gifted their scholarship, preaching, or teaching, could surmount the hurdle decreeing the first woman rabbi must be "outstanding."

In fixing this unreachable ideal, the gatekeepers to the rabbinate proved themselves men of their "times." In claiming only an "outstanding" woman could compel such a radical departure from the past, the faculty, administrators, and lay leaders of the seminaries revealed themselves. Levinthal could receive an honor grade for her thesis, but elsewhere the faculty would judge her just "average." Askowith had already published scholarship worthy of a doctorate, but one professor found her "a poor student." These men thus affirmed that despite great hopes voiced for women's equality, despite all the flattering portraits of career women in the press, and despite how they fueled the perception of women's greater role in the professions, women did not progress smoothly in all the learned professions in the 1920s.

In fact, as historian William Chafe has shown: "[S]tatistical gains inflated the degree of progress actually achieved. . . . Instead of breaking down barriers to positions from which they had previously been excluded, career women in the 1920s clustered in occupations traditionally marked out as women's preserve." Not only did professional women remain in the feminine professions of teaching, librarianship, and nursing, but the history of women's achievement in the male-dominated professions does not constitute an unbroken record of numerical and statistical gain. As historian Nancy Cott has demonstrated, while women's participation in the labor force steadily increased from the nineteenth into the early twentieth century, women's advance in the professions depended upon the profession. In medicine, for example, women as a percentage of American physicians declined from 6 percent in 1910 to 4 percent in 1930. In other professions, press attention masked the reality of but token access. In 1910, women constituted 1 percent of all lawyers; twenty years later they comprised only 2.1 percent.[139]

Similarly, the record of women's advance in the ministry remained mixed. Although Congregationalists boasted that with the ordination of Antoinette Brown Blackwell in 1853, they became the first Protestant denomination with female clergy, as of 1919, only sixty-seven women were Congregational ministers.[140] Although the number of female clergy climbed in the 1920s, the 1930 figure of 3,276 broached, but failed to exceed, the 3,405 female clergy of the peak year of 1900. Between 1900 and 1910, the number of employed female clergy had plummeted some 80 percent. Not until after 1940, did female clergy exceed the numbers of their peak year of 1900.[141]

Data culled from the profession of Jewish education provides additional evidence for the constraints binding women who aspired to this Jewish profession. In 1930, educator Israel Chipkin presented what he had learned about "The Jewish Teacher in New York City and the Remuneration for His Services." Two-thirds of the 1,801 teachers in the 417 schools he surveyed were male. Although the number of women in Jewish education had increased since 1916, only in the least intensive educational setting, the one-day-a-week schools, did women outnumber men. In the supplementary Hebrew schools, the Talmud Torahs, male teachers outnumbered female teachers, two to one.[142]

And the higher one went in the field of Jewish education, the greater the bias for male educators. Of the forty-two members of the professional association, the National Council for Jewish Education, in 1930, only one was a woman. A 1933 survey of principals in Jewish schools found but a single woman.[143]

Helen Levinthal's father, Rabbi Israel Levinthal, evidenced the prevailing sentiment empowering those in Jewish education to prefer one sex over the other. In 1940 he responded to Annie Linick's application to teach in the Brooklyn Jewish Center's Hebrew school. Mostly boys attended this supplementary school five days a week. There they learned all they would need to know to take on, at their Bar Mitzvahs, the responsibilities of Jewish manhood. At the same time the center offered a one-day-a-week Sunday school and the Brooklyn Jewish Center Academy, an elementary day school. To Miss Linick, Rabbi Levinthal wrote: "[I]t is the unanimous opinion of our committee that for this vacancy a man should be secured and not a woman. Not that our committee has any definite viewpoint on woman teachers, but they feel that in a small school like ours where we have one woman teacher, the rest should be men. In the Academy it is the reverse, all of the teachers are women."[144] Although Levinthal claimed his committee did not have "any definite viewpoint on woman teachers," its members did. They believed educating elementary school children belonged to the realm of women's work. Educating boys to their responsibilities as Jewish men must remain a predominantly male domain.

That the Nineteenth Amendment had, in fact, done relatively little to transform women's economic profile reflected, as Chafe affirms, "[d]iscrimination against women remained deeply rooted in the structure of society—in the roles women and men played and how those roles were valued."[145] Surely, the present and future leaders of American Judaism, no matter their rhetoric, shared these basic assumptions of gender roles. Professor David Neumark, Martha's father, had one son, the "brilliant" Immanuel Kant (Mannie) Neumark, and two daughters. And Martha Neumark's male classmates never doubted that sons, not daughters, inherited their father's mantle, when they crooned to the tune of "Mammy":

> Doc-tor Neumark!
> Your son shines east, your son shines west.
> Your daughter shines too, but your son shines best.
> Man-nie Neu-mark . . .
> He'll be a great professor, his father's successor.
> Man-nie.[146]

The rigidity of these gender roles had real ramifications for career women trying to combine marriage and all that went with it and their profession. Despite their own expectations that they would work after college, the majority of female college graduates did not work for long after marriage. Even though an increasing number of women attempted to combine marriage and career, "the real question confronting potential career women" remained marriage or career.[147] This held true for women in Jewish education, most of whom "stop teaching when they have children."[148] That the small numbers who did mix career and family merited, like Magistrate Baright, so much attention reveals, according to historian Nancy Cott, just how iconoclastic the combination really was. By looking at women's participation in all white-collar fields, including the professions, she showed that less than 4 percent of married women in the 1920s experimented with combining marriage and career.[149]

Moreover, by the time Dora Askowith and Helen Levinthal raised their challenges in the 1930s, prospects for all professional women had worsened. "[A]s the Depression swept the country, it became less likely that women would enter male-dominated careers."[150] In the 1930s women were more likely to be excluded from, than admitted to, the professions. In these years professionally employed women constituted a declining proportion of all employed women, as well as a declining proportion of all professional workers.[151]

During the Depression, the American rabbinate too was under siege. In the 1920s, a real shortage of rabbis for American Israel may have fueled optimism for women's entrance into the rabbinate.[152] If Judaism needed more rabbis, worthy women could help fill their ranks. But, by the 1930s, the situation had reversed. Not only did American Judaism not have enough jobs for qualified men trained in the United States, but rabbis and their families fleeing German atrocities desperately sought havens in America.[153] And Helen Levinthal knew this. In 1939, after her graduation, she explained she felt it presumptuous to seek a congregation, as "she would not want to take the place of a young rabbinical graduate, or perhaps a refugee, anxiously awaiting a call."[154]

Consequently, despite support for woman rabbis voiced by many of the men then leading American Judaism, and despite their willingness to envision to some extent the reshaping of woman's roles and responsibilities there, they evidenced no real intention of acting upon their liberal rhetoric. In fact, the wording of many of the statements on women's ordination belies these leaders' aversion to fulfill their promises, to realize Reform's mandate to do what was right and fair, what was moral,[155] in affirming "the complete religious equality of woman with man." Over and over again, those who held the power to confer rabbinic ordination found themselves forced to concede the virtue of a woman's desire to be a rabbi. But paradoxically their proclamations acquiesced to the woman rabbi chiefly in the negative. In voting on Neumark's application, Hebrew Union College faculty felt they "*cannot* logically and consistently withhold ordination" from a woman.[156] The men of the Central Conference of American Rabbis

decreed "woman *cannot* justly be denied the privilege of ordination."
In reviewing Lindheim's application, the JIR scholars assured that all
present clearly understood "it was *not* against the principles of the Institute to admit women students" (emphases added). These collective
pronouncements thus stand as striking barometers of these leaders'
extreme reluctance to make a radical break with the historic past.

Rabbi Stephen S. Wise, the one figure faced with the most important challengers, exposed the tensions the men faced when summoned to act on their liberal promises. As Irma Lindheim knew, Wise
was both "a true feminist at heart" and "a traditionalist at heart."
Wise's biographer, Melvin Urofsky, confirms her judgment:

> [T]here are internal contradictions in Wise's own life and views regard-
> ing women which were never resolved in his own mind nor in his public
> statements.... He called for equality for women, yet declared that
> women inherently were more moral than men, and therefore had to pro-
> tect the moral standards of the nation. He was one of the first to speak
> out for allowing women to enter the rabbinate, yet never did anything to
> implement this idea.[157]

Wise's own family divulges the polar models then set before American Jewish women. The rabbi held a romantic view of his wife, the
former Louise Waterman, and he encouraged her art and voluntarism. Yet, much of the latter, like her founding of the Women's Division of the American Jewish Congress and the Child Adoption Committee of the Free Synagogue, reflected the rabbi's wife sharing in
and sustaining her husband's commitments.[158] But the same man encouraged his daughter, later Judge Justine Wise Polier, to continue
her education at Yale Law School. She earned her LL.B. there in 1928,
the same year Dora Askowith returned to JIR. The first woman to
graduate from Yale Law had earned her degree but five years
before.[159]

If *Who's Who in American Jewry, 1928* offers a fair measure of
American Jewish women's activities in this era, it reveals that more
women earned merit following the path of Mrs. Wise than in following that of her daughter. While women comprise less than 6 percent
of those listed here, more than a third of those who won a place did so
for volunteer, social, welfare, or civic work. Less than 15 percent of the

235 women named won a space because they were doctors (6), lawyers (8), professors (7), or other professionals.[160]

Jewish Theological Seminary Professor Mordecai Kaplan, father of the Bat Mitzvah girls, divulged just which archetype American Jewish religious leaders preferred. In 1932 he explained this to the model Jewish women of Hadassah's eighteenth annual convention, women who were married, mothers, and volunteer workers among American Israel. He claimed that earlier as "men—both leaders and laity" strove to make Judaism viable for the modern world, few women joined them because of "the limitation which the man has always imposed upon [woman's] creative energies." But now, thanks to Hadassah and to similar associations, "Jewish womanhood is being reclaimed for the Jewish people." The prototypical Hadassah woman not only cared for the sick in Palestine, but she also undertook "Judaizing her home" and Jewishly educating her children. Now he hoped Hadassah could go further and "launch a great popular movement for Jewish adult education." Nonetheless, he paused to remind the ladies that "higher Jewish learning of the specialized type will *naturally* remain the province of the man" (emphasis added).[161] And, since nature decreed it thus, obviously the prize awarded those who acquired higher Jewish learning, the honorific rabbi, would also remain, in these years in American Judaism, the exclusive province of the man.

Thus, even as the "times" fueled the perception that women could crash the Jewish professions, even as the tenor of the "times" kept this question before liberal Judaism in America in these years, the reality of the "times" belied those who held rising expectations for women's rabbinic ordination. In the 1920s and 1930s, gender roles remained rigidly constrained in American life and American Jewish life. The women who wanted to become rabbis, who dared to presume they could overcome the barriers of sex, ultimately confronted insurmountable hurdles. As the men who held the keys to the rabbinate affirmed, indeed the time for ordaining a woman rabbi had not yet come.

After their journeys to ordination ended, the American trailblazers—Martha Neumark, Irma Lindheim, Dora Askowith, and Helen Levinthal—led long lives which reflected upon their Jewish educations and desire to lead and to teach their people. Across the ocean Miss Rabbi Regina Jonas lived a life cut violently short. Yet before it ended, she too served her people. In all cases, these women came to draw upon their higher Jewish educations, finding, as Stephen Wise wrote, in 1925, to Irma Lindheim, during her first visit to Palestine: "It is good to read your word that the three years at the Institute prepared you for the work that is now to come."[162] Rather than becoming embittered by their failure to become rabbis, these women used, as befitted the "times" and their sex, their Jewish educations to serve their people. Furthermore, before they died, all returned to the question of the woman rabbi. As each did, she turned yet again to the past, this time to claim her own place in the history of women's ordination.

For Martha Neumark, the work "now to come" was not that of Sunday school principal, the career mapped out for her on the certificate she earned for her seven-and-a-half years at HUC. Instead of entering educational administration, she joined her husband, Henry Montor, in his Zionist and Jewish communal work. Not long after the Montors moved to New York City, Henry Montor carved out a career with the United Palestine Appeal. As its executive vice-president (1939–50), in what one historian termed the Montor-Morgenthau era (for Henry Morgenthau, Jr., who became national chairman in 1947), he reshaped the focus of American Jewish philanthropic life, so much so that David Ben Gurion hailed him for his pivotal role in creating the State of Israel.[163]

In the early years of that work, Martha Neumark Montor, with her superlative Jewish education and demonstrable qualities of leadership and intellect, contributed materially to his endeavors. As the Montors' son, Karel, born in 1925, recalled, from the time he was five or six, he stayed with a housekeeper and his mother went to the office with his father. There the ambitious Montors ran, together with Harry Montor's sister and brother-in-law, Seven Arts Publishing and two newswire agencies, Palcor News and Palestine Independent Press.[164]

Later Martha Neumark Montor's interests shifted. Following the birth of her daughter Rae, seventeen years after that of her son, she settled into suburban domesticity in Bayside, New York. There she pursued another of her passions, music. As a rabbinical student, Martha Neumark had played piano in a silent movie theater. Now she earned a masters in musicology from Columbia Teachers College, taught music, composed, and wrote about music.[165]

Later, in the 1950s, unanticipated change shook the Montor household. In 1956 the Montors divorced, and Martha Neumark Montor found the boundaries of wife and mother, teacher and musicologist permeable. In her long life, she explored many careers. In her own words she worked as a "research specialist, publicist, psychologist, teacher, lecturer, psychological social worker, literary secretary, and administrator." A writer of, she claimed, thousands of articles, including sermons, she even copy edited the *Central Conference of American Rabbis Yearbook*. When she retired in 1975, she was earning her living working as a counselor for New York City's Department of Corrections.[166] In 1981, Rabbi Bonnie Steinberg, whom Martha Neumark Montor never knew, conducted her funeral.[167]

Throughout her life, her Jewish commitments, those she had once planned to fulfill as rabbi, remained central. She taught her daughter to appreciate her "connection to my own past, and my people's past."[168] She continued to write about Zionism and to stand for Israel, protesting the anti-Israel mural displayed in the Jordan Pavilion at the 1964 New York World's Fair. A half century after she left Cincinnati, she reflected on the legacy of her rabbinical education. Her classmates, like Maurice Eisendrath who became president of the Union of American Hebrew Congregations, had gone on to become rabbis in American Israel. While she had never become a rabbi, she had remained "closely identified with my former fellow students and also with the whole field of Jewish journalism."[169]

As she met the challenges of living on her own, Martha Neumark Montor became part of an increasing number of American women and American Jewish women, entering the paid labor force. Eventually, as historian Alice Kessler-Harris has shown, the cumulative effect of the incremental changes that had occurred in female participation in the American labor force over the course of the twentieth century had radical consequences, including the renewal of the challenge for the opening of all professions to women.[170]

The former rabbinical student came to sense this. Again she raised the question of women rabbis, this time not for herself, but for others. Turning to Hebrew Union College administrators and faculty, she asked would they join her, in 1964, in "some sort of reactivation of the idea of women in the rabbinate." Back in 1925, she had recognized this as merely another aspect of the woman's question.[171] By the mid-1960s, this aspect of the woman's question seemed poised to emerge yet again.

By this time Hebrew Union College and the Jewish Institute of Religion had merged, maintaining, as HUC-JIR, campuses in Cincinnati and New York. Nearly half a century after her initial challenge, Martha Neumark Montor wrote that in these new times "only individual inertia now stands in the way of a woman's successfully completing the rabbinical course and being ordained as a rabbi." In 1964, she shared with the Cincinnati HUC historian Jacob Marcus that she had approached New York's Dean Paul Steinberg about reopening the question of women in the rabbinate.

> I have a feeling that the time is ripe for active recruitment of women students—or at least open welcome for them. . . . I remember that in that long ago I was promised the necessary blessing by a group of indignant rabbis, including Stephen S. Wise. But I guess I was just too young and too foolish then to follow through. Now I'd like to complete the circle by helping some more mature young woman to set the precedent.[172]

For Irma Levy Lindheim the work "now to come" was Zionism. During her trip to Palestine, she had met the Chief Rabbi of Stockholm, who found her rabbinic education so impressive that he asked her to become his assistant chief rabbi.[173] Nevertheless, when she returned to New York in 1925, Lindheim did not return to JIR to complete her education. Instead, in 1926, one pioneer in rabbinical school succeeded another, when she followed Henrietta Szold as National President of Hadassah. As Mordecai Kaplan taught, so Lindheim knew, gifted women of her day, Judaically knowledgeable and skilled as leaders, could, as volunteers, guide their people, especially the women of American Israel. That was their calling. If they reached high office, that was their ordination. Lindheim understood this. In writing to Henrietta Szold of her nomination, of the call to lead Hadassah's 30,000 women, she claimed: "If, at the Convention, the decision of the National Board is confirmed, I shall feel that I have been ordained, more truly so, even, than had I been confirmed as a rabbi." Later she remembered: "As Elisha had prayed that a double portion of the spirit of Elijah might fall upon him, so I prayed that the spirit of Henrietta Szold would fall upon me." And that spirit was not that of Szold, the lone female rabbinical student, but rather that of Szold, the consummate worker among the community of Israel. Szold wished her well, noting that Lindheim's special "preparation, personality, and convictions" were just what Hadassah needed.[174]

Throwing herself into eighteen-hour work days, Lindheim left home and family to travel around the country appealing for Hadassah. Angered over what she and others, including Wise, deemed to be the disastrous leadership of the Zionist Organization of America under Louis Lipsky—who wanted "nothing short of [the] absorption of Hadassah and its full cessation as an autonomous body"—she became embroiled in a public controversy to reorganize the ZOA. Preaching from synagogue pulpits, Conservative as well as Reform (including that of Lucile Uhry's husband, Rabbi Louis I. Newman), she pleaded Hadassah's cause before rabbis and lay leaders of American Jewry. In the midst of this campaign in the spring of 1928, her husband died at the age of forty-seven.[175]

Distraught, Lindheim refused reelection as Hadassah president. Once again she turned to Palestine to settle her and her family's spirit. This visit, the first with the children, and then the collapse of the family fortune in the stockmarket crash of 1929 convinced her to make a radical break with the past. Later she would preface her autobiography with Robert Frost:

> Two roads diverged in a wood, and I—
> I took the one less traveled by,
> And that has made all the difference.

The road less traveled took the Lindheims to Palestine. There in 1933, at the age of forty-seven, Irma Levy Lindheim joined the Labor Zionist kibbutz Mishmar Ha-emek.

From her new home Lindheim retained her passionate interests in

American Jewish life and continued to return frequently to America. In 1935, the woman who had never had any plan to function as a rabbi, preached yet again in American synagogues, including Stephen Wise's Free Synagogue Carnegie Hall pulpit,[176] appealing this time not for Hadassah but for the Jewish National Fund.

While the socialism of her Labor Zionism distanced her somewhat from Hadassah, she nevertheless continued to turn to its leaders from time to time, trying to persuade them to promote her schemes for educating American Jewish youth to their responsibilities. She called upon Hadassah to develop a Jewish youth farm experience, to sell her autobiography *Parallel Quest* (1962), and to try out "Gramsie's Hour," an educational program she created to train Jewish grandmothers to imbue their children with a sense of Jewish identity.[177]

Six years before her death, the first woman in American Judaism became a rabbi. If Irma Lindheim knew that one had done what she had failed to do, the records have not preserved her comment. Yet much, much earlier, she mistakenly thought another had reached the end of the road she had paved. In July 1939, from Palestine, she wrote her old friend Stephen Wise: "I was very much moved when I saw that Miss Leventhal [*sic*] has actually been graduated as a Rabbi. It gave me a little pang of regret that it was not I. But on the other hand, if I had not made the fight, she might not have gotten the degree."[178] In 1978, the pioneer of women in the rabbinate, Irma Levy Lindheim, died and was buried on her beloved kibbutz.

The work "now to come" for Dora Askowith remained "the very rugged road"[179] of adjunct professor of history in the evening and extension division of Hunter College. There Askowith continued to teach undergraduates and graduates ancient, Roman, medieval, and Renaissance history. When she could, as in courses on comparative religion and "The Near and Middle East," she introduced her passion, Jewish history. Her students reported that she held them "spellbound."[180] Her many activities outside the classroom revealed her utter devotion to her work and her students' welfare.[181]

Askowith's continuing Jewish commitments made her a valuable role model for students interested in their Jewish history and culture.

Not only did she intervene with the Hunter College administration when opening classes were set for the High Holidays, but she also continued her work with Hunter's branch of the national collegiate Menorah Society. When she had founded the society in 1912, Askowith had brought Henrietta Szold to open its initial program of a year-long survey of Jewish history. Later, she persuaded Menorah students to study Hebrew, to send books to Palestine, and to exhibit books on Jewish culture for the inaugural National Jewish Book Week. She even managed to persuade some faculty to assign research papers linked to the anniversaries of the deaths of Jewish historical figures Sa'adia Gaon, Heinrich Graetz, and Leon Pinsker. And she continued to use this setting to teach her students about women in Jewish history. In 1933, they joined other college women in presenting in New York the "Pageant Dedicated to the Women of Israel Throughout the Ages," a series of "tableaux" tracing "the contributions of women to the historic development of Israel's ideals."[182] Askowith's decades-long work with Hunter Menorah students demonstrated the teacher's passion for transmitting to the young women the richness of Jewish heritage and especially women's contributions to it.

Meanwhile, while living in the straitened circumstances set by an adjunct professor's hourly wage,[183] she continued to write. Her subjects remained Jewish women, Jewish history, and contemporary Jewish affairs. In 1941, she published *Three Outstanding Women: Mary Fels, Rebekah Kohut, Annie Nathan Meyer.*[184]

And she continued to return again and again to women in the rabbinate. In 1947, she countered, in a letter to the editor of the *New York Times*, Rev. Dr. John H. McComb's contention that ordaining women was "absolutely contrary to the Bible and to common sense." Opening with her own experience of studying at the Jewish Institute of Religion, she explained she had entered rabbinical school, "not with the intent of entering the rabbinate" but in order to enhance her "chosen field of work as a college instructor of history." Nevertheless research for her student sermon "The Woman in the Rabbinate" had revealed that nothing in Judaism, nor for that matter in Christianity, barred women from religious leadership. Not only did ancient Israelite customs assure the equality of women in religious practice, but "Jesus imposed no restrictions on woman, domestic, social or religious." The injunctions in later rabbinic and patristic literature against women's learning and leadership represented "isolated, disparaging statements," divorced from the "prevailing attitude ... of granting equality to the sexes." Furthermore, female religious leaders of the past and present, including medieval Jewish women "were actually accepted by their contemporaries as rabbinem." If men remained reluctant to admit women as rabbis and ministers, "I can only say that it is due, primarily, to a different outlook upon the world in which we live and that time will, undoubtedly, bring a change in attitude."[185]

A year later, having learned that Hebrew Union College and the Jewish Institute of Religion planned to merge, she asked Stephen Wise and HUC President Nelson Glueck to see if in the revisioned seminary, women, as well as men, could be ordained. Less than a decade later, she again raised the matter, informing the readers of *Judaism*, not only of how Jewish literature failed to present "clear-cut opposition to women serving in the rabbinate," but also of her own precedent. She, "the writer ... sought ordination, not with the intent of entering the rabbinate, but ... to open the field for other women desirous of seeking ordination."[186]

Two years later, in October 1958, Askowith died at the Hebrew Hospital and Home in the Bronx. At the time of her death she was reportedly at work on her autobiography, *Within My Reach*.[187]

For Helen Levinthal the work "now to come" briefly found her donning rabbinical robes.[188]

Israel Levinthal's first pulpit had been Brooklyn's Congregation B'nai Sholom. In 1939, its members, finding themselves without a leader for the High Holidays, asked their rabbi's daughter to be their rabbi. Helen Levinthal, now Mrs. Lester Lyons, agreed to preach but demanded that the synagogue engage another, an ordained rabbi, to lead services.[189] As she had explained earlier, nothing in Jewish law and life precluded her from preaching in a liberal congregation. In fact, she had done so already from her father's pulpit. But without ordination, she believed it presumptuous to lead a congregation.[190]

In the next year Helen Levinthal Lyons continued to teach and to preach. She taught Jewish history and religion at Brooklyn Jewish Center's Adult Institute for Jewish Studies. She preached from her father's pulpit, this time on "What of the Future of the Jew?"[191] Shortly thereafter, she carved out a brief career as one of only three women— the others were Judith Kaplan Eisenstein and Avis Shulman—sent by the Jewish Center Lecture Bureau to speak throughout the country on Jewish subjects. Levinthal Lyons lectured before sisterhoods in Richmond and Brookline, before Zionist and synagogue groups in New York and Philadelphia, and even at the Women's Institute of Jewish Studies, the Jewish Theological Seminary's women's adult education forum. Her topics included "The Jewish Woman Faces a New World" and "Jewish History in the Making." In lecture series, like "The Jew and the World Scene," she stood alongside such highly respected figures as professors Salo W. Baron and Jacob Marcus and rabbis Stephen S. Wise and Ira Eisenstein.[192]

Her success led the Yiddish paper *Der Tog* to exclaim:

[T]he young Hadassah Levinthal began to forge a path in Yiddish life, which will certainly not shame her honored grandfather, the Rabbi Dov Ber Levinthal from Philadelphia, and her oft-heard-from father, Rabbi Israel Levinthal from Brooklyn. Her voice is already heard from pulpits, religious as well as cultural.... She is in great demand from all corners of the land.... Who knows, perhaps her service to her people will be so worthy and her influence so spiritual to her young generation in America, that the rabbinate will recognize the need to make certain changes in the laws which prevent women from becoming rabbis.

But, in adding her voice to the rhetoric speculating on the woman rabbi, *Der Tog*'s columnist also commented: "I didn't ask her if from her future children a rabbi would emerge, who will continue the name Levinthal. I am sure that it will be so."[193]

As expected, within a short time, marriage and motherhood saw Helen Levinthal Lyons settle comfortably into domestic life. In addition to the roles of wife and mother, she drew upon her training and superlative Jewish education to work as a communal volunteer, especially among the women of American Israel. President of her local Hadassah chapter and of the Parent-Teacher Association of the West-

chester (Jewish) Day School, she was honored, in 1984, as a "Woman
of Valor," one who "set an example in Jewish living" by her service to
her suburban Conservative synagogue. Her volunteer interests dove-
tailed with those of her husband, a board member of the Westchester
Day School and a trustee of their synagogue.[194] Thus in the decades
after her graduation from the Jewish Institute of Religion, Helen
Levinthal Lyons found that, like other committed and educated Jewish women of her day, she could serve her people as teacher and as volunteer.

But, despite her satisfaction with these accomplishments, Helen
Levinthal Lyons never abandoned her dream to win the ordination
denied "on account of her sex" so long ago. Unlike Martha Neumark
who wanted to "complete the circle" by helping someone else do what
she had never done, Helen Levinthal sought for herself that which
she had earned. In 1971, as the press began to swell with news of the
impending ordination of Sally Priesand, Levinthal's former classmate, Rabbi Earl Stone, one of those who long before had shared in
the junior class's objection to having a woman join its graduation, revealed that with the changing times came a change of heart.

In May 1971, Stone wrote, of his own accord, to HUC-JIR President
Alfred Gottschalk. HUC's press release about the impending ordination of the first woman rabbi claimed that the only woman previously
enrolled had failed to complete the course. Stone pointed out the er-
ror. Not only did he want the world to know that more than a quarter
of a century before one had already done what another was about to
do; but he also hoped "something could be done, even at this late date,
to correct the situation." Levinthal Lyons, "surprised and delighted"
by Stone's unexpected interest, confessed that she felt "cheated" that
the publicity ignored her own pioneering role and that another was
about to receive that which she had been denied. She thanked him,
saying "I shall be deeply grateful for your kind assistance in convincing the administration to acknowledge *officially* my status and to
make appropriate rectification" (emphasis in original).[195]

In May 1972, HUC-JIR President Alfred Gottschalk responded to
Israel Levinthal, who shared his daughter's enthusiasm for Stone's
campaign: "All of us who attended the JIR knew that your daughter
had graduated with the full rabbinic curriculum, but, for reasons per-

taining then, had to forego the honor of Ordination." But Gottschalk felt that to ordain Levinthal Lyons today, after so many years, "would be but a gesture." Instead he promised to recognize her accomplishments in the publicity surrounding the impending ordination of the first woman rabbi.[196]

But this time Helen Levinthal Lyons refused to abandon her dream. Over the next decade, she continued to correspond occasionally with Earl Stone, determined to "keep picking away until . . . this inequity will be rectified," for she "should have been the first woman ordained."[197] In 1985, after learning that the Jewish Theological Seminary was about to ordain its first female rabbi, Levinthal Lyons, now ailing, again called upon her classmate for help.[198] This time Stone convinced former classmates to join him in bringing the matter again to Gottschalk. Meanwhile Helen and Lester Lyons persuaded a friend to raise it with Rabbi Alexander Schindler, president of the Union of American Hebrew Congregations.[199]

The combination of forces pushed Gottschalk to investigate the matter. HUC-JIR administrators searched JIR records. They found that not only had the faculty denied Levinthal's verbal application to be a candidate for ordination, but that no "regular academic transcript" for her existed. The latter was decisive. Gottschalk wrote Stone: "In view of the fact that we do not have in our possession an academic record of courses taken and successfully completed, I regret to note that I cannot see how she can be granted ordination."[200] Although in June 1939, none of those associated with the Jewish Institute of Religion had ever refuted the national and international press's claim that Helen Levinthal had completed the entire rabbinic curriculum, and although Gottschalk himself had earlier affirmed "[a]ll of us who attended the JIR knew that your daughter had graduated with the full rabbinic curriculum," the missing transcript became the grounds for denying Helen Levinthal Lyons ordination. Still Gottschalk held out hope for further consideration of the matter, and Stone optimistically expected that "at next year's ordination" something would be done for her.[201]

But nothing was. Rather, three years later, a full half century after she had asked JIR for ordination, HUC-JIR formally acknowledged Helen Levinthal Lyon's pioneering role. On 11 November 1988, New

York Dean of Faculty Paul Steinberg conferred, in a private ceremony in her home, a special award upon the then desperately ill trailblazer. It lauded her:

> Pioneer in setting new directions in higher Jewish learning and scholarship for women.
>
> Descendant of rabbis and daughter of an esteemed rabbi and scholar, you truly studied the law for its own sake, your love of learning was manifest in all your life.
>
> Ever zealous for learning, you added a special dimension for women in transmitting the Jewish tradition and cultural heritage.
>
> You are blessed, that in your lifetime, you are able to see others travel the path that you had cleared.
>
> Wisely has it been written: "Many daughters have done valiantly, but thou excellest them all." Indeed, your works praise you in the gates.[202]

Thus Helen Hadassah Levinthal Lyons claimed her place in the history of women's ordination. Less than a year later, on 13 August 1989, the pioneer who never became a rabbi died.

The American women who would have become rabbis in the 1920s and 1930s, Martha Neumark, Irma Levy Lindheim, Dora Askowith, and Helen Levinthal, found their paths blocked. Some found that lives connected to men with power who shared their interests helped them satisfy some of their aspirations. As Adrienne Rich has said, "To have some link with male power has been the closest most of us could come to sharing in power directly."[203] Others found that as long as they restricted their sphere to education and to Jewish women, the times afforded them opportunities to lead and to teach, even to preach, to fulfill some of the roles they would have realized as rabbis. Eventually each would return to the subject of the woman rabbi and to the dream she had held not only for herself but for paving the way for others. As each did, she claimed her place in the history of ordaining women rabbis. Yet, none of these women apparently ever knew that in the crucible of Nazi Germany one had won the title they had failed to receive and had attempted the difficult work of trying to be the first woman rabbi.

By the time Dora Askowith again raised before an American public the question of women's ordination in 1947, Miss Rabbi Regina Jonas had perished, a tiny figure lost among six million others, in the Holocaust. To what extent, in the 1930s, Jonas stood within a movement among German Jewry for women's ordination, remains obscured by the tragic history of German Jewry and the terrible loss there. Certainly, the scholarship on German Reform Judaism and German Jewish feminism does not point to an atmosphere of rising expectations for women's ordination comparable to that evident in the United States from the 1890s onward. This was true despite the early pronouncements by German liberal rabbis claiming, "the halakhic position of women must undergo a change," and "it is a sacred duty to express most emphatically the complete religious equality of the female sex." As historian Marion Kaplan succinctly conveys, among German Jewry "in the years before World War I there was no whisper of religious equality from any quarter . . . "[204]

Furthermore, preconditions which in the United States created high hopes for women's ordination were absent, or emerged much later, in Germany. In the United States, with American women already doctors, lawyers, and ministers, American Jews who were confronting, in the 1890s, the proto-rabbi Ray Frank, as well as Hannah Solomon on the pulpit, and the learned leadership of Henrietta Szold, found the question of the woman rabbi close behind.

But in Imperial Germany, women won admission to the learned professions decades after American women won, at the very least, token access to medicine, law, and the clergy. In fact, German women ranked among the last European women to win admission to the learned professions. Not until 1899 were German women allowed to practice medicine. Only in 1922 were they permitted to function as full-fledged lawyers.[205] Similarly, the Protestant ministry offered no comparable role models. In 1927 German Protestant women won the right to become vicars, an "inferior theological office" created especially for women by the Evangelical Church. Only small numbers of German women entered these professions. For example, in 1915 Germany had 233 female and 33,000 male doctors. And they had to defy, as did the German Jewish women who in disproportionate numbers aspired to the professions, the prevailing middle-class German ethos.

"Comfortable middle-class families of all religions considered public employment unladylike and improper for their daughters."[206]

As for the lone German Jewish feminist organization, the Jüdischer Frauenbund, founded in 1904, it concentrated largely on political, not on religious reforms. Religious equality never became part of its program. Rather the Frauenbund tried to enlarge middle-class woman's sphere, seeking new opportunities for women to broaden their outlook beyond their bourgeois roles as housewives.[207]

Holding that women who brought their children to synagogue had a "duty, not a right" to a say in religious matters, the Frauenbund remained, according to Marion Kaplan, "relatively moderate in its demands that women be allowed to perform certain religious rituals." It did, nevertheless, encourage its members to analyze Jewish texts from a woman's perspective. And its members strove to alleviate the misery wrought by the intractable Jewish law of *agunot*, which, especially after the upheavals of World War I, left thousands of widows, whose husbands' bodies had disappeared, unable ever to marry again.[208]

Given this moderation, no discussion of woman's right to the pulpit surfaces among German Jewry until its final decade. Not until 1928 did a woman—Lily Montagu, the British religious organizer, leader, and preacher of Liberal Judaism[209]—preach in a German synagogue. But, unlike Ray Frank or Hannah Solomon, she came not from within the community but from without. Only in the early 1930s— perhaps not coincidentally just as the *Israelitsches Familienblatt* reported that with Regina Jonas "overnight we received the first Jewish female preacher in Germany"—did the topic surface. As Frauenbund circles debated "Can Jewish Women Become Rabbis?" they pointed out that "in the United States women could preach in some synagogues."[210]

Whether any of Regina Jonas's other female classmates joined her in aspiring to the rabbinate is unknown. Hebrew Union College Professor Israel Lehman, who had known Jonas, thought her the only woman at the Hochschule studying for the rabbinate. And he wondered, had the faculty known she sought ordination, whether they would have admitted her.[211] Certainly Jewish women in Nazi Germany, especially those, unlike Jonas, with husbands and children, faced other devastating concerns. Even as "[b]rigades of German feminists had silently accommodated Nazism . . . Jewish feminists focused every spark on welfare for the Jews."[212] Thus, for now, it must be assumed that Jonas trod her path to rabbinic ordination alone. Not only did none of the other women students there[213] accompany her, but she apparently never knew that across the ocean others sought what she obtained from Rabbi Dienemann. Of all the pioneers in the 1920s and 1930s, only Jonas won ordination.

Yet, her ordination remains qualified. Although none would question the legitimacy of private ordination—after all Stephen Wise held the same, Rabbi Dienemann warned her not to use the title "rabbi" until she consulted on an appropriate title with Rabbi Leo Baeck. Furthermore, private ordination—and Dienemann insisted that he signed neither on behalf of the *Vereinigung der Liberalen Rabbiner* (Association of Liberal Rabbis) nor the Hochschule—"did not give Jonas official recognition as a rabbi." The question remained, to what extent she would "be allowed to see the last bulwark of prejudice fall and to speak to the people from the pulpit as a rabbi."[214]

As Katharina von Kellenbach shows, Jonas was never officially installed as a congregational rabbi. In 1937, the *Jüdische Gemeinde zu Berlin* hired her to be an "academically trained teacher of religion," the calling conferred upon her and others by her Hochschule diploma. But in addition to teaching in its schools, the *Gemeinde* charged her with carrying out "rabbinic-spiritual care" elsewhere in the Berlin Jewish community, among the elderly and the ill. Hochschule Professor Alexander Guttmann has suggested that it assigned her to work in "homes for the aged, as it did not want to create a problem by assigning her to preach in the major synagogues." There, as one survivor of Berlin's Jewish community recalled, when Jonas tried to sit in the rabbi's seat among the men, one of them would tell her that for praying she should go upstairs and sit with the women. Jonas herself acknowledged the difficulty of butting up against the disbelief and hostility she met.[215]

But von Kellenbach asserts, "as Nazi antisemitism unfolded her actual duties as a rabbi expanded." With the breakdown of institutional order, when arrests, deportations, and emigration left many congregations without rabbis, German Jews' need for spiritual sustenance unexpectedly opened to Jonas avenues for service that prejudice in less turbulent times would otherwise have blocked. Now, in addition to lectures, sometimes in synagogues, often on Jewish women of the past, she occasionally replaced absent rabbis. In 1942, she was deported to the "model" concentration camp, Theresienstadt. There she volunteered to meet new arrivals at the train station, to use her preaching to soften their horror and to sustain her co-religionists with her lectures and sermons. And from there, on 12 October 1944, Miss Rabbi Regina Jonas took her last journey, to Auschwitz.[216]

For a long time, her legacy as the first woman rabbi was obscured. Much later those who would survive, who had met her then, would remember "Rabbiner Doctor Regina Jonas ... the first woman rabbi"[217] and claim on her behalf her place in the history of ordaining women. But in the 1950s and 1960s none of those continuing the discourse about the woman rabbi seemed to know of her. Only in 1972, would another young woman asking for herself the very same question, "Can a Woman Become a Rabbi?" search the Jewish past and recover Regina Jonas's place in the history of women rabbis.[218]

During World War II, as is common in such crises, the affairs of women were pushed to the background. American Jews, male and female, had other far more pressing wartime preoccupations. While women saw new job opportunities opening to them in a nation facing a man- and woman-power shortage, none, in these taxing years, stopped to raise the question of the woman rabbi for herself.

But at the war's end, some women began, yet again, to dream the dream of becoming rabbi. In 1947 Henry Slonimsky, dean of the Jewish Institute of Religion, returned Mrs. Nettie Stolper's application. Explaining that it been sent to her "through an oversight," he wrote, contrary to JIR's history: "Our school is so small and so exclusively geared to male students that we find it impossible, much to our regret, to admit any women students."[219]

Nevertheless, Slonimsky understood that contemporary woman's roles indeed had changed. Elsewhere he conceded, woman "should be accorded at least an equal position with man. . . . it is insulting to believe that looking after a modern small family under present conditions is a lifework for a woman of average strength and intelligence."[220] In espousing the rhetoric of woman's equality but refusing to extend the principle to the rabbinate, the professor epitomized the equivocal stance taken in the 1920s and 1930s by those with the power to confer ordination in liberal Judaism.

Yet the tide of rhetoric about woman's rights continued to flow. The next quarter century would see it swell and see an increasing number of women "all over America and indeed the world . . . beginning to feel this same way, beginning to feel the great blessing and the horrible curse of enormous possibility."[221] Some plunging into that current, clamoring for the realization of enormous possibilities, would set their course toward the rabbinate. As they did, they unknowingly followed the road already paved by Martha Neumark, Irma Lindheim, Dora Askowith, Helen Levinthal, and Regina Jonas, the women who would have been rabbis.

Chapter 4

"An idea whose time has come"

1972

In 1947, when Jewish Institute of Religion Dean Henry Slonimsky wrote to Mrs. Nettie Stolper that, "much to our regret," his seminary did not admit female students, his rejection of her application seemed to close the door on woman rabbis. Yet, within the decade, young women bent on becoming rabbis would indeed find places in rabbinical school classrooms. In the 1950s and early 1960s, these aspiring rabbinic students joined female proto-rabbis, ordained rabbis, *rebbetzins*, and lay leaders in sustaining the more than half-century-old debate about the woman rabbi. By the end of this era, the question debaters in the 1950s deemed "purely academic"[1] reached its resolution. Exactly a quarter of a century after Slonimsky's comment, one young woman, spirited, remarkably tenacious, and propitiously aspiring to the rabbinate at a time of "enormous possibility" for American women, succeeded in crashing the gender barrier to the Jewish profession. In so doing, she proved the woman rabbi indeed "an idea whose time has come."

At the time when Dean Slonimsky quashed Nettie Stolper's plan to become a rabbi, popular images of feminine conformity and domestic contentment were emerging as the defining paradigms for Cold War America. While veterans found upward mobility in going to college on the GI bill, women, veering away from fifteen years of privation and war, sought their futures in marriage and motherhood. Although the numbers of college women actually increased from 601,000 in 1940 to 806,000 in 1950, their proportion of all enrolled students declined from 40.2 percent to 30.2 in these years. Moreover, as women's average age at marriage fell to twenty, many of these young women dropped out of college. Never embarking upon careers, these youthful wives began their postwar work of giving birth to the demographic bulge of the baby boom. With growing families in tow, they and their husbands, the fathers who knew best, fled to the newly burgeoning suburbs. There, so popular culture recalls, the young mothers spent their days driving to Little League, Sunday school, and PTA meetings.[2]

Yet, despite these popular images, historians have uncovered an opposing reality for many American women in these years. Between 1940 and 1960, the proportion of women who worked rose from 25 to 35 percent, and, strikingly, the percentage of married women who worked doubled to 30 percent. While the 1955 White House Conference on Effective Uses of Woman-power lauded women's primary role as homemaker, it also anticipated the charge, broadcast in *Womanpower*, a report issued by the National Manpower Council, in 1957, that the nation had dramatically failed to utilize women's talents fully, especially in the strategic areas of math and science, essential to win the Cold War.[3]

In the decade immediately after World War II, those women who aspired to the professions found that they competed unsuccessfully with returning veterans who sought the training necessary to become doctors, lawyers, ministers, and professors. Although in most professions the absolute numbers of women increased, their relative proportions decreased. In 1930 women held 18 percent of the doctorates awarded by American universities; by 1950 and again in 1960 the percentage of doctorates claimed by women had dropped to 10 percent.[4]

But the dearth of women's professional training lasted only for the decade from 1946 to 1956. As the veterans completed their educations and embarked upon careers, some spaces for aspiring women opened in the professional schools. Moreover, despite the media attacking or ignoring the women's rights movement in these years, its graying heirs marched. Even young suburban matrons may not have been utterly isolated from these undercurrents. As Eugenia Kaledin has suggested: "[I]n the broadest sense the 1950s may finally be seen as the most active period of consciousness raising for modern American women; women pushing baby carriages still may have time to think."[5]

Not unexpectedly, American Jews joined in constructing their versions of the middle-class ideal in the 1950s and early 1960s. As they congregated together in suburban subdivisions and built elaborate new synagogues on the main thoroughfares of their new communities, they announced their claim in the American dream.[6] Yet, the same undercurrent that in American life permitted *Womanpower* to encourage girls to become high school science teachers, so that men might be freed for research,[7] also enabled the debate about women in the Jewish profession to flourish. In fact, the 1950s opened with American Jews confronting a striking example of the woman as rabbi, Paula Herskovitz Ackerman of Meridian, Mississippi.

Born in 1893, the daughter of immigrants, Paula Herskovitz grew up in Pensacola, Florida. There, as her family journeyed from Orthodoxy to Reform, she received her early Jewish education and was confirmed at Temple Beth El. The valedictorian of her high school, Herskovitz wanted to become a doctor. But her father refused. When she won a scholarship to Sophie Newcomb College (now Tulane University), he told her if she went to college, she must become a teacher. In the end, Paula Herskovitz never left for college. Instead she began teaching in the local high school and giving private music lessons.[8]

In 1919, at the age of twenty-six, she married Rabbi William Ackerman. Ordained at the Jewish Theological Seminary, Ackerman had become rabbi of Pensacola's Temple Beth El. A year later, the Ackermans set out for a new congregation in Natchez, Mississippi. Their son was born there. In 1924 they moved again, when Temple Beth Israel in Meridian, Mississippi, the second largest congregation in the state, invited William Ackerman to become its rabbi.

At Beth Israel, like many *rebbetzins* who were "an intrinsic part of their husbands' success," Paula Ackerman joined as an active partner in her husband's rabbinate and stood as a leader in her own right.[9] During the thirty-one years of her marriage, she embodied for her community the exemplary Jewish wife, mother, and communal volunteer. In the synagogue she taught in the Sabbath school. While her husband taught confirmation youth, she taught the pre-confirmation class. "[A]dvisor in every capacity" to the sisterhood, its secretary and program chairman, she refused its presidency, only because she felt a congregant should hold that office. Helping the sisterhood raise funds to build the "House of Living Judaism," a home for Reform Judaism in New York City, she and its members devised "ingenious methods," even giving mah jongg lessons, to raise money.[10]

But the rabbi's wife did more for Temple Beth Israel. She also frequently substituted in the pulpit for her husband in his absence or when he fell ill.

Outside the confines of the temple, Paula Ackerman found herself—like Carrie Simon, another *rebbetzin*, who had sought a wider venue for her religious service—a leader among the women of Reform Judaism.[11] A member of the board of the National Federation of Temple Sisterhoods (NFTS) and chairman of its National Committee on Religious Schools (1944–45), Ackerman beseeched qualified Sisterhood members "to rally to the noblest responsibility our Jewish inheritance requires today," to prepare to teach Jewish youth.[12]

On 30 November 1950, Rabbi William Ackerman, her husband of thirty-one years, died. A week later Beth Israel's president, unanimously supported by his board, asked the fifty-seven-year-old widow "to carry on the ministry until they could get a Rabbi."

Ackerman fully understood the implications of the invitation. Earlier she had observed how Sisterhood's campaign for the House of Living Judaism "graciously reciprocates our debt to the UAHC [Union of American Hebrew Congregations] for emancipating the Jewish woman—for taking her out of relegated galleries and placing her on Temple Boards and Union Commissions."[13] Now the possibility that she might carry on her husband's work signified an even greater expansion of woman's role within Reform Judaism, the woman as rabbi. As she contemplated the possibility, she wrote: "I also know how revolutionary the idea is—therefore it seems to be a challenge that I pray I can meet. If I can just plant a seed for the Jewish woman's larger participation—if perhaps it will open a way for women students to train for congregational leadership—then my life would have some meaning."[14]

As Paula Ackerman weighed the offer, she began consulting with Reform leaders to gauge their support and reactions. Among those she turned to was the rabbi who had confirmed her in her youth, Jacob D. Schwarz, now the national director of the UAHC's Commission on Synagogue Activities. In fact, it was her "dear friend['s]" prior invitation to join that commission which had demonstrated to her that Reform indeed accepted women "on Temple Boards and Union Commissions." Now as she contemplated whether or not "to blaze a new trail," he advised her by reviewing what he knew of the history of the question of the woman rabbi.[15]

Rabbi Schwarz offered a new approach to the question. Instead of searching the distant past for guidance, like others who had sought precedent for the woman rabbi, he offered Paula Ackerman what he knew about the very recent history of women who wanted to become rabbis. He wrote to her that "in 1922 to be exact . . . a prospective candidate for matriculation and ordination as rabbi at the Hebrew Union College" had propelled a thorough discussion of the question. He told Ackerman that he believed that the "faculty of the College [had been] opposed to the granting of ordination to a woman" and that their "decision at the time was influenced by the fact that the person who wanted the ordination was not particularly a persona grata." He summarized for Ackerman the negative responsum on the subject of woman's ordination that Professor Jacob Lauterbach had written when Martha Neumark had attempted to break the gender barrier in the rabbinate, and suggested that she read it for herself. Her friend also urged Ackerman to consider the demands of the job, of undertaking "a new career somewhat late in life."[16]

Nevertheless, Paula Ackerman decided, for the sake of the congregation, to become Temple Beth Israel's interim "spiritual leader." Having no intention of "serving as 'Rabbi' except [in] Meridian," she heeded the call because she feared that the small Southern congregation would need quite some time to find a man capable of the job and willing to accept its limitations. Responding to Schwarz's caution about the demands of the rabbinate, she reminded him that the one-hundred member synagogue had but sixteen children in its school and that, after all, she had been teaching since he had confirmed her. As for her qualifications to give sermons, she knew the congregation did not expect her "to preach philosophy or higher criticism of the Bible." Rather she would "give them some of the faith I have in my own heart—the Jewish way of life that I've lived every day of my life."[17]

Decision made, Ackerman's election signified to others the promises of woman in the pulpit. Apparently utterly unaware that the press had showered similar attention upon Helen Levinthal a mere decade before, Ackerman reported that the press widely broadcast she was "the first woman in the U.S. to execute a rabbi's functions." Her friends sent dozens of Uniongrams, the fund-raising cards of NFTS, some congratulating her as the first woman rabbi. Writing that the time had come for women to be spiritual leaders in Reform Judaism, NFTS Executive Director Jane Evans informed Ackerman that she was not really the first, that England's Lily Montagu had preceded her as a preacher and that Evans herself had already officiated at High Holiday services. Responding to the accolades that her appointment served as a milestone for Reform Judaism, Paula Ackerman no longer demurred that she was merely Temple Beth Israel's "interim spiritual leader" but claimed instead: "I am glad to pioneer in this movement, which we hope may lead to the ordination of women."[18]

But Reform leaders preferred not to see her in this light. It is easy to understand why Beth Israel's president, Sidney Kay, believed that UAHC President Maurice Eisendrath would sanction Ackerman's appointment. Even *Time* magazine quoted Eisendrath as saying: "Women should not be denied the privilege of ordination.... There is nothing in the practice and principles of Liberal Judaism which precludes the possibility of a woman serving as a rabbi." But Eisendrath was simply adding his voice to Reform's long rhetorical tradition of favoring women rabbis. When it got down to the specific case of Paula Ackerman—just as had been true for Martha Neumark, Irma Lindheim, Dora Askowith, and Helen Levinthal—Reform Judaism found questions about the candidate which precluded her from becoming a rabbi. In Ackerman's case, objections to her temporary rabbinate rested on the fact that she was neither formally trained nor ordained.[19]

Rabbi Samuel H. Goldenson, past president of the Central Conference of American Rabbis, raised a different objection. At first, he had seemed so enthusiastic that Paula Ackerman hoped he would attend her installation. Now, after reflection, he cautioned that "the step that your congregation is taking might lead to more problems raised than solved." He feared her appointment might set a precedent for the "exceedingly able wives" of other rabbis, not all of whom shared her "personal and mental qualities." Beth Israel's naming Ackerman her husband's successor might thus provoke "considerable embarrassment in other communities."[20]

Despite the discouragement and her dismay over Eisendrath's denial that the UAHC had sanctioned her appointment, Paula Ackerman forged ahead. Hoping "[i]f I can carry on here for a few months it would be so wonderful for me,"[21] she steered Beth Israel for the next three years. Ackerman led weekly and holiday services; officiated at confirmations, marriages (as permitted in Mississippi), baby namings, funerals, and unveilings; addressed congregational meetings; preached; and handled the tasks essential to sustain the congregation and its congregants. She even participated in Mississippi rabbis' meetings.[22]

Like the pioneers who had gone before, she drew inspiration for her work from the heroines of the Jewish past. In her last report to the congregation, in the fall of 1953, after Beth Israel had found an ordained rabbi to take charge, she spoke of how she drew strength from the sage Beruriah and the judge Deborah, "the first Jewish woman spiritual leader." In daring to accept the congregation's call, she had found wisdom in Mordecai's challenge to Esther: "Who knoweth whether thou art not come to royal estate for just such a time as this?" (Esther 4:14). And now that she was about to leave behind the pulpit, she looked to Naomi "quietly and simply living her Judaism." Finally, in a subtle comment on what her three years as spiritual leader might mean for others, she quoted the rabbinic sage of *Pirkei Avot* (2:21): "It is not incumbent upon us to complete the work but neither are we free to desist from it altogether."[23]

For the most part, Paula Ackerman did, like Naomi, live quietly in the years after her "rabbinate." Yet, in the spring of 1962, when the rabbi of Pensacola's Temple Beth El, her childhood congregation, suddenly quit, its leaders, proud of their "rabbinic" alumna, pleaded with her to "hold them together" for the remainder of the year. And so once again, for a brief time, Paula Ackerman found herself "spiritual leader," a real live example of the woman as rabbi. When she died on January 12, 1989, having lived long enough to see women ordained as rabbis, Rabbi Constance A. Golden conducted her funeral.[24]

It was true, as NFTS Executive Director Jane Evans had informed Paula Ackerman, that she was not, even in 1951, the first woman to serve as rabbi in Reform Judaism. Moreover, although Paula Ackerman surely did not know this, she was not the only female proto-rabbi of these years. In the 1890s Ray Frank had stood out in sharp relief as an isolated individual testing the question of the woman rabbi by serving as one. By the 1950s, however, a small number of women could be found, who for a time did just what Paula Ackerman did, stand before their congregations as rabbis.

In congratulating Paula Ackerman on her appointment as Beth Israel's interim rabbi, Jane Evans pointed to one of these women, England's Lily Montagu (1873–1963). Like others who supported the claim that the time had come for women to stand as spiritual leaders in Reform synagogues, Evans sought precedent in Jewish history to buttress her claim.[25] But when she pointed to Lily Montagu, Evans, like Ackerman's friend Rabbi Schwarz, affirmed that recent events provided adequate guidance on the subject.

Religion scholar Ellen Umansky has illuminated Lily Montagu's career as an author and religious thinker who led services, preached widely in England and abroad, and deserves credit for founding England's equivalent of Reform Judaism, its Liberal Jewish movement. Yet, as Umansky has observed, "even when Lily Montagu did assume a position of religious leadership, her functions were not those of 'rabbi.'" Rather her model of religious leadership, her responsibilities as teacher, preacher, and administrator paralleled the work undertaken by her peers, British Christian women. Moreover, except for a brief tour, which brought her to the United States in 1931, where she did speak at the Jewish Institute of Religion and received an honorary doctorate from Hebrew Union College,[26] Montagu was geographically far removed from the locus of the largely American discussion of the question of women rabbis. While Montagu's religious leadership suggested precedent to Jane Evans, others engaged in the debate about the woman rabbi, before and after 1951, rarely referred to her.[27]

Aside from Lily Montagu, however, examples of women proto-rabbis in the 1950s could have been found, if anyone had cared to look, far closer to home. In that decade, three other women in American Reform settings stood as the functional equivalents of rabbis. In fact, even before Paula Ackerman set what Samuel Goldenson feared to be the dangerous precedent of the *rebbetzin* succeeding the rabbi, Tehilla Hirschenson Lichtenstein had done just that. In 1922, her husband, Rabbi Morris Lichtenstein, had founded, in New York, the Society of Jewish Science, one of a number of Reform efforts to stem the tide of Jewish defections to Christian Science. Unlike Christian Science, Jewish Science affirmed modern medicine, but it also taught that God alone restored health. With its Sabbath and holiday services, it stood on the periphery of Reform Judaism, without formal affiliation.[28]

Tehilla Lichtenstein joined her husband in his work. In the early years of the society, she ran its religious school and edited its monthly periodical. When, in 1938, her husband died, she became its spiritual director. From then until shortly before her death in 1973, she gave weekly sermons, taught classes in Jewish Science and Bible, trained practitioners in religious healing, counseled, broadcast its message over the radio, and edited its magazine, *Jewish Interpreter.*[29]

The second instance comes not from that of a rabbi's wife succeeding the rabbi, but that of the president's wife following in his footsteps. In 1883 the Jewish merchants in the mining town of Trinidad, Colorado, had founded Temple Aaron. When the mines flourished, the congregation thrived. But after they closed, the Jewish community dwindled, too small to support a regular rabbi. For many years, lawyer Gilbert Sanders, a member of the UAHC Board of Directors and Temple Aaron's president, had led its weekly services. After his death in 1952, his wife, Beatrice Sanders, took over. For more than three decades, she conducted Temple Aaron's weekly and High Holiday services. In 1981, after Hebrew Union College awarded her an honorary doctorate, the local press ordained her Temple Aaron's "rabbi."[30]

Finally, a third example comes not from the wife stepping up, but from that of the exemplary Jewish educator expanding her sphere.[31] Libbie Levin Braverman (1900–1990), the daughter of a rabbi, had received—as was customary for rabbis' children—an intensive Jewish education. While preparing for the "dignified career" of public school teacher, she began teaching, in Cleveland, at Euclid (later Fairmount) Avenue Temple. Quickly, Braverman, married to synagogue architect Sigmund Braverman, won a nationwide reputation as an outstanding Hebrew and Judaics educator. She left public school teaching behind and eventually became education director (1946–1952) of Euclid Avenue Temple. There Rabbi Barnett Brickner and his wife, Rebecca Aaronson Brickner, shared her enthusiasm for pioneering innovative Jewish educational approaches. But in 1952, when the temple hired an assistant rabbi with educational training, Braverman found herself displaced. Refusing to work under him, she resigned.[32]

As she was contemplating her future, she received "an emergency call" from Akron's Temple Israel. The board had just fired the rabbi. Would she "come to help them out"? For the next five months, until Temple Israel hired a replacement, Braverman untangled the disorder left by a disastrous rabbi-congregational relationship. Doing "everything except, what I called in my lighter moments, Hitch and Ditch (marry and bury)," she ran the school, wrote the bulletin, prepared bar mitzvah boys, taught the confirmation class, and on Sisterhood Sabbath conducted the service and gave the sermon.[33]

That both Beatrice Sanders and Libbie Braverman took on their rabbinic roles a year after the press proclaimed Paula Ackerman "the first woman in the U.S. to execute a rabbi's functions" suggests other than happenstance. In addition to the obvious evidence of coincidental timing, it is likely that press reports about women rabbis—joined to news reports about the first women to become Reform temple presidents and to a growing discourse in mainstream Protestant denominations about women ministers—paved the way for the female proto-rabbis. Likely, these reports helped plant the seeds that would permit synagogue-goers—especially those in tiny communities on the periphery of Jewish life, like Meridian and Trinidad and in small communities with limited Jewish resources, like Akron, as well as those in "the fringe phenomenon" of Jewish Science—to grow accustomed to the notion of the woman rabbi.[34]

Certainly, the "commotion created by Mrs. William Ackerman's appointment as spiritual leader" had excited many American Jews, including those outside Reform circles. Readers of Trude Weiss-

Rosmarin's *Jewish Spectator* "literally swamped" her with queries as to whether she thought it "proper for a woman to serve as rabbi."[35]

Author, scholar, editor, and lecturer, the German-born Weiss-Rosmarin stood among the " 'other' New York Jewish intellectuals," the group whom scholar Carole Kessner defines as intellectual Jews rather than as "intellectuals who happened to be Jewish."[36] After earning a Ph.D. in Semitics, archaeology, and philosophy from the University of Würzburg in 1931, she and her husband, Aaron Rosmarin, set out for New York. In search of an academic job, but unable during the Great Depression to find one, she created her own opportunities. In 1933 in New York, she opened the School of the Jewish Woman, a forum offering Jewish women, ages eighteen to seventy-one, the chance to acquire the Jewish educations they had never received. By 1936, its newsletter had evolved into the *Jewish Spectator.* Although at first Aaron Rosmarin was its editor and his wife his associate, from the time of their divorce in 1943 until her death in June 1989, Trude Weiss-Rosmarin single-handedly edited this independent monthly.[37]

Weiss-Rosmarin stands out as one of the few Jewish women of her era to choose, as her vehicle for contributing to Jewish life, "the path of professionalism," rather than that of voluntarism. A popular lecturer, she wrote and spoke widely about issues central to contemporary Jewry—Zionism, the future of American Jews, and the destruction of their European families.[38] And very much in common with the women who would have been rabbis, she shared a deep commitment to and passionate interest in the affairs of Jewish women, past and present. Like Dora Askowith, a member of the board of the School of the Jewish Woman,[39] Weiss-Rosmarin wrote about women in Jewish history. In the pages of the early *Jewish Spectator,* then a magazine read chiefly by women, she surveyed the women of valor of the Jewish past, the queens, martyrs, and heroines, from the biblical era forward.[40] But the affairs of Jewish women of the present also absorbed her. Although a "religious traditionalist," Weiss-Rosmarin sharply critiqued those areas of Jewish law, especially the rules of divorce, which continued to encumber women in all streams of modern Judaism other than Reform.[41]

Not surprisingly, then, when confronted with an example of the woman rabbi, she weighed in with her opinion. Her readers, who by now included close to a thousand rabbis,[42] wondered how she could possibly object. After all, Weiss-Rosmarin, who had been called "the most Jewishly learned woman in the world,"[43] herself preached at "Orthodox" services. Surely, the woman rabbi followed as the next logical step. And she concurred: "In point of fact, I am not at all 'opposed' to 'women rabbis.' . . . '[E]xceptional' women—exceptional in their professional aspirations and interest—should enjoy all the rights and privileges which are considered the birthright of men."[44]

Indeed, even as she wrote, a small number of "exceptional" women found their congregations according them a right and privilege previously considered the "birthright of men," as they became synagogue presidents. In Frederick, Maryland, Jeanette Weinberg served as president of Temple Beth Shalom (1943–1959). In Philadelphia, Natalie Lansing Hodes became founding president of Main Line Reform Temple-Beth Elohim in 1952. And in Baltimore, Helen Dalsheimer moved from the presidency of the National Federation of Temple Sisterhoods to that of Baltimore Hebrew Congregation. In so doing, she took over the helm of one of the oldest and, with 1,450 families, largest congregations in the country. Weiss-Rosmarin understood that the attention focused on female presidents climbing up the *bimah* "shows how far we are still from according women real and genuine equality." But perhaps, she hoped, they heralded "an auspicious turning point in the attitude of the Jewish community to its female constituency . . . a new and salutary trend toward giving women their due share in Synagogue leadership."[45]

Meanwhile, public discourse about women ministers heated up yet again. In 1947, the Presbyterian Church, one of the largest and most important of the mainline Protestant denominations, began a new round of deliberations about ordaining female clergy, a question it had first broached in 1929. That same year the *New York Times Magazine* aired for its readers the pros and cons of the debate.[46] By the late spring of 1955, the question had wended its way to the Church's General Assembly. Its vote to ordain women smoothed the path for the Reverend Margaret E. Towner to become, in October 1956, the first female minister in the Presbyterian Church (northern).[47]

Acquiescing to women's ordination a century after Antoinette

Brown Blackwell had raised her challenge, the Presbyterians marked an important milestone in the history of women in the clergy. Permitting women's ordination signified, as scholar Mark Chaves has shown, the Church's embrace of the principle of gender equality, that as its General Assembly proclaimed, "it is proper to speak of equality of status for men and women in the Church and in its ministry."[48]

Mid-century observers of woman's progress in the ministry could easily point to evidence of other gains. Press reports suggested female ministers rising in their profession and an increasing number of Christian women heeding the call to preach. In the same year that the Presbyterians agreed to ordain women, a woman minister was elected to the "top job in British Congregationalism"; the Methodists "voted to sweep away all barriers that have kept women ministers from enjoying privileges equal to those granted their male colleagues"; and Harvard Divinity School began admitting women on terms equal with men. But five years before, the United States Census of 1950 had reported the all-time high figure of 6,777 female clergy, more than double the number in 1940. Although women comprised but 4.1 percent of the total,[49] the developments of the mid-1950s suggested the promise that more and more women would soon join this learned profession as full equals. Indeed, over the next fifteen years, a dozen other churches, for example the African Methodist Episcopal Church, and those in leading denominations, Lutherans and Southern Baptists among them, began ordaining women.[50]

News of the growing acceptance of women ministers propelled Reform rabbis to take up, yet again, the question of women rabbis. In June 1955, Barnett Brickner, rabbi of Euclid Avenue Temple and president of the Central Conference of American Rabbis, Reform's rabbinical conclave, challenged his colleagues to act. More than the example of Paula Ackerman and even more than the case of his own former educational director, Libbie Braverman, Brickner was struck by how much things had changed for women since he and his colleagues had first discussed the woman rabbi back in 1922. At that time he had signed the statement, "we declare that woman cannot justly be denied the privilege of ordination," but he had questioned its "practicability."[51] Now, pointing specifically to the Presbyterian Church and Harvard Divinity School, he observed: "Many Christian

Protestant denominations have also changed their minds and now ordain women." Omitting the recent examples of Paula Ackerman and the other women, who, to all practical purposes, functioned as rabbis, Brickner referred instead to Reform's "pioneer[ing] in granting equality to women." Without naming Helen Dalsheimer, he indicated that "soon one of the oldest Reform congregations will elect a woman as its president." These were for him markers of Reform's "liberalism." But despite Reform's "liberalism," it still fixed its vision for women of talent and limited their sphere to education. He wondered: "Why should we grant women degrees only in Religious Education, qualifying them to be educational directors yet denying them the prerogative to be preachers as well as teachers?" Arguing both that women "have a special spiritual and emotional fitness to be rabbis" and that "there is a shortage of rabbis," he called for his colleagues to re-evaluate the subject and to report back at the next convention.[52]

Brickner's query once again sent the question of women rabbis eddying out to American Jews. This time, perhaps since the rabbis collectively—not an isolated, lone figure like Paula Ackerman—propelled the question, Trude Weiss-Rosmarin reflected on the matter in greater depth. For her, "[t]he issue [was] not whether women can be proficient Jewish scholars, eloquent preachers, sagacious community leaders and wise spiritual counsellors. They assuredly can." She knew Jewish history substantiated her claim. She pointed to Miriam, Deborah, and Hulda; to learned women in the talmudic and medieval eras; and to one who had filled "rabbinic functions," Hannah Rachel Werbemacher, the Maid of Ludomir who "acted as a full-fledged Hasidic Rabbi . . . had her own Synagogue . . . even donned Talith and Tefillin like a man." Even as modern American women—doctors, scientists, and lawyers—excelled "in the so-called 'masculine professions,' surely, American Jewish women could "fill the intellectual requirements and the skills associated with the Reform rabbinate."[53]

But for Weiss-Rosmarin, this time, the question hinged not on whether women could handle the job, but on whether they should aspire to it. She cautioned that she feared what women might lose in their charge to storm the rabbinate. She argued that women should "seek emancipation—as women, and not by attempting to prove that they can do as featly as men in what are considered 'masculine professions.' " If her readers would "emancipate Jewish women as *women* —recognize that their contribution as women is as unique, as important and as valuable as the contribution of men in their male roles," they would give the *rebbetzin* her due. For, in modern America, "the Rabbinate means team-work of the Rabbi *and* the Rabbi's wife." Public recognition of this work, rather than having women become rabbis, would begin the process of "emancipat[ing] Jewish women as *women*."

A month after publishing this editorial, Weiss-Rosmarin appeared alongside "the first lady of Reform Judaism," Jane Evans,[54] on a platform at Brooklyn's Union Temple to debate "Should Women Be Ordained as Rabbis?" Advance publicity indicated the editor would speak against the question. Certainly Evans expected her to oppose the innovation. Yet, true to what she had already affirmed with the pen, albeit with qualifications, the "religious traditionalist" surprised the "full house" by acknowledging that women could become rabbis.[55]

Weiss-Rosmarin and her fellow disputant, Jane Evans, both kept the question of women's ordination open for consideration. Weiss-Rosmarin's *Jewish Spectator* presented the issue to a wide swathe of American Jewry, while Evans played a pivotal role in keeping Reform Judaism focused on the woman rabbi question. She was the guiding spirit behind the National Federation of Temple Sisterhoods from 1933 to 1976, when she retired as executive director, and as such stood at the heart of the organized women of Reform Judaism. In the midst of a Jewish world rocked by the turbulence of the Great Depression, the horrors of World War II, and the emergence of the state of Israel, she led this organization, initially limited to philanthropy, Jewish education, Jewish families, and the synagogue, to broaden its political and social vision.[56] And along the way, she inherited from NFTS founding president Carrie Simon the charge of pushing forward the question of the woman rabbi.[57]

A lone voice, from the time of Paula Ackerman forward, if not earlier, Evans sustained debate on the subject, at first within Sisterhood circles and later beyond them. As executive director of NFTS, Evans was required to travel across the country bringing Sisterhood's message to Reform Jews. She later reminisced that, when the moment permitted, she would introduce the possibility of women rabbis in the speeches she gave.[58] Thus by 1955, when she was called to debate Trude Weiss-Rosmarin, Evans stood, as she had earlier affirmed to Paula Ackerman, as a staunch and well-practiced advocate of women's ordination.[59]

Two years after her debate with Weiss-Rosmarin in Brooklyn's Union Temple, Evans sensed the time had come to take the question to a wider audience. As Brickner's proposal remained before the CCAR rabbis, Evans determined to win allies for the woman rabbi by bringing the matter to Reform's lay leaders. That year the National Federation of Temple Sisterhoods and the Union of American Hebrew Congregations held joint biennial meetings in Toronto. Before their one thousand delegates Evans asserted: "[W]omen are uniquely suited by temperament, intuition and spiritual sensitivity to be rabbis." Her declaration made headlines. The *New York Times* reported "Women as Rabbis Urged at Parley."[60]

By the time Evans raised the woman rabbi issue in Toronto in 1957, however, the CCAR had effectively quashed discussion of the matter—for the moment—and, paradoxically, they had done so asserting the matter was already settled in the affirmative. The previous year the men had heard a committee "Report on the Ordination of Women." The report claimed that the CCAR had "resolved" this issue long ago and affirmed, one more time, the rabbis' conviction of the justice of admitting women to their ranks. Again the committee report relied upon history, in this case Reform Judaism's own history, to prove that their predecessors had long proclaimed men and women to "have equal status in Reform Jewish affairs," to affirm that Reformers had "already settled [the] subject of the religious equality of the sexes in Reform Judaism."[61]

In addition, committee members, led by Chairman Rabbi Joseph I. Fink, looked beyond history to the world in which they lived. The rabbis knew, from their observations of American religion, that "the religious equality of women with men can be assumed as universally confessed in all liberal denominations." Their perspective on American society led them to profess: "[T]he emancipation of woman applies to life within the synagogue as well as to life outside the synagogue." As Americans wrestled with the implications of *Brown v. the Board of Education* (1954), which posited that segregation of black school children automatically generated a sense of inferiority, the rabbis presciently extended this argument to relations between the sexes. By ordaining women rabbis, they would "remove from woman the degradation of segregation."[62] In a conclusion, remarkable in Reform rhetorical history for its positive formulation, the men wrote:

> In view of woman's parity with man, we believe that the unwarranted and outmoded tradition of reducing woman to an inferior status with regard to ordination for the rabbinate be abandoned. Specifically, we believe that she should be given the right to study for the rabbinate, that she should be ordained if and when she has properly completed the course of study, and that she should then be admitted into the CCAR upon application for membership.

But the signators of this 1956 CCAR report, among them Maurice N. Eisendrath, UAHC president, and Nelson Glueck, HUC-JIR president, also assumed: "The question before us is purely academic at this time. We have no particular case in point."

Despite proclaiming the matter resolved, the rabbis did not then vote in favor of women's ordination. Instead they tabled the topic until such time as "those who have an opposite point of view may have an opportunity to present a report."[63] But not only did that report not materialize, the CCAR never revisited the "purely academic" question.

Frustrated by the stalling of the issue, Evans decided to push it forward in the one arena where she had unparalleled influence, among the women of the National Federation of Temple Sisterhoods. In November 1961, she met with NFTS's Board of Directors as the women prepared for their first biennial meeting in Washington, D.C., since 1935. Since then much had happened vis-à-vis women in American life. As one board member claimed: "we are a kind of different woman than our mothers and our grandmothers were."[64]

Not only had Sisterhood women changed, but just at this time American women began to stir anew. In Washington, a young, new president, John F. Kennedy, had already established a Presidential

Commission on the Status of Women. Scholars Leila Rupp and Verta Taylor argue that convening the commission "implicitly recognized the existence of gender-based discrimination in American society." Moreover, it revealed that the postwar women's rights movement—a movement chiefly sustained by women who had forged their feminism early in the century in battles over suffrage and the equal rights amendment—had had an impact.[65]

Much like those activists, Jane Evans had honed her feminism in her lifelong career in Jewish communal service. But, unlike the 1950s women's rights activists, Evans's arena was not the politics of gender relations in American life writ large but rather the gender inequities of her world of Reform Judaism. There the chief sign of gender-based discrimination remained the exclusion of women from the rabbinate. Evans, who had attended her first NFTS biennial convention in Washington in 1935, decided that with Sisterhood's impending return to Washington, its members should launch their own study. Rather than turning their attention to the status of women in American life, they would focus on the leading inequity that remained within their venue, the exclusion of women from the rabbinate.[66]

In November 1961, the executive director met with her board to give them advance warning of the recommendations she intended to make at the upcoming convention. She began by joking that, this way, "I can know in advance if you are going to fire me as soon as the report is read." Then she got down to business by informing the board that despite a growing number of denominations "admitting women as organized ministers, despite sympathetic presentation of the subject of women as rabbis by the late Dr. Barnett R. Brickner . . . , no woman had yet been ordained a rabbi in Israel." Therefore, "the time has now come . . . for sisterhood women to take a definitive stand on the question" of opening the rabbinate to women. As NFTS headed toward 1963 and the golden anniversary of its founding, Evans asked its members to prepare to resolve once and for all in favor of women rabbis.

In discussing Evans's proposal, board members revealed that recent history had an impact. "Is it true that the widow of the rabbi took over the position of the husband?" they asked about Paula Ackerman. Yes, replied Evans, as she told them, moreover, others had stood alongside Paula Ackerman. "The Honorable Miss Lillie H. Montague [*sic*] of London, England has for fifty years been the rabbi ... of her own congregation." Even Evans herself had led services, especially "during the war years when there was a great shortage of rabbis."

Board member Rebecca Aaronson Brickner, widow of CCAR President Barnett Brickner (who had died three years before), also joined in the discussion. Rebecca Brickner constituted a formidable Jewish presence in her own right. A protégé of Henrietta Szold, the fluent-Hebrew speaker had studied at Columbia University's Teachers College and at the Jewish Theological Seminary's Teachers' Institute in the group known as the "Benderly boys," the first generation of American-trained Hebrew educators taught by Samson Benderly.[67] In 1919, after teaching, working with Benderly at New York's Bureau of Jewish Education, and joining Hadassah's first national board, the educator wed fellow "Benderly boy" Barnett Brickner. In Cincinnati during their first year of marriage, she continued her studies at Hebrew Union College.[68]

Thereafter, Rebecca Brickner became an exemplary *rebbetzin*, working among Jewish women through Sisterhood and Hadassah, first at Toronto's Holy Blossom Temple and then at Cleveland's Euclid Avenue Temple. And there, too, the educator continued to teach. In Toronto, she was expected, or so she later claimed, to run the school. In Cleveland she prepared the confirmation class. In her husband's absence, she filled in. This made Brickner, as her publicity materials boasted, "the first woman in the country to conduct religious services in a Temple ... read from the Torah and preach a sermon." Of her experiences, she told the NFTS Board, "It is not as difficult as you think it is, it's a joy, it's a pleasure."[69] In fact, according to her husband's biographer, "the paramount reason for [Barnett] Brickner's belief that women were able to function as rabbis is that he was married to just such a woman." His wife's "learning, eloquence, insight, and administrative ability"[70] compared well to, if not surpassed, that of many of his colleagues.

Now Rebecca Brickner shed some light for the NFTS Board on what she thought had happened to her husband's proposal to welcome women rabbis. She claimed the CCAR planned to discuss it again in 1957, but that other matters took up most of the evening. Only after midnight did the men turn to the matter. By then, "too late to have a discussion on these very important questions," the rabbis postponed their debate for another year. Unfortunately, before that meeting, her husband died. Without him to bring up the woman rabbi, she failed to reappear.

In his stead his widow took up the charge, carrying her late husband's message forward to NFTS. Reiterating the arguments Barnett Brickner had made six years before, Rebecca Brickner told the women, the Protestants do this and do so in increasing numbers. Reform Judaism has a great shortage of rabbis. And since "women were specially minded and especially adapted to teach and to inspire ... [they] would make marvelous rabbis."

Then she added her own arguments, relying not upon ancient precedent but upon evidence of "the times." "[A] woman is really capable of doing most anything." If women judges, surgeons, ships' captains, and university presidents could do their jobs, women rabbis could do theirs. Not only did her own experiences of conducting services prove this, but so did the example of an unnamed Jerusalem woman who had recently led Rosh Hashanah services. Trying to anticipate and forestall objections, such as the problems raised by a pregnant rabbi, she pointed to an expectant Queen Elizabeth II touring her Canadian dominions. After all, she reminded the women, "[t]hese things are very temporary things." In concluding, she turned for inspiration to another Jewish dream, one once also deemed preposterous, Zionism. Paraphrasing its motto, she closed: "If you are only willing, it is not legend, it is not a myth, it can become a reality."[71]

Roused by Jane Evans and Rebecca Brickner, the board decided to send the question of women rabbis out to the convention floor. As the women of Reform Judaism gathered in Carrie Simon's hometown, pausing to memorialize their founding president who had died earlier that year, they, at long last, converged behind her dream.[72] They resolved that over the next two years all Sisterhoods would study the possibility of women rabbis. Those deliberations would prepare the women to vote at NFTS's golden anniversary to "request the Hebrew Union College-Jewish Institute of Religion and other liberal seminaries to ordain women as Rabbis..."[73]

At that meeting, in New York City in November 1963, NFTS's one thousand delegates reviewed Reform's history on the question of the woman rabbi. They learned of how the CCAR had debated the matter in 1922 and again in 1955. They heard "the fact that some women have completed at least part of the required course of study at the Hebrew Union College-Jewish Institute of Religion." In the end, en masse, they demanded the convening of a conference of all Reform institutions—the CCAR, the UAHC, HUC-JIR, and NFTS—to resolve the matter of the woman rabbi once and for all.[74]

Not surprisingly, that conference, an event unprecedented in Reform history, never took place. Instead the abstract debate about women's ordination in the centers of Reform institutional life seemed to quiet for a time. Possibly because the rabbis knew of no women rabbinical students then, they felt no urgency to heed NFTS's call. But these men had little idea that indeed among the women who continued to find their way to HUC-JIR, as women had done since its founding, were some who aspired to the rabbinate. In the late 1950s and 1960s, a small group of such aspiring women crossed the portals of HUC-JIR's Cincinnati campus. There they expected that, if they persisted, if they proved themselves worthy, in the end they would emerge with what they sought, Rabbi before their names. Although they entered as isolated individuals, they coalesced to constitute what another of the early pioneers deemed crucial to women winning ordination, the nucleus of "a group—even a small group—of women at the Seminary."[75]

That early pioneer was Avis Clamitz Shulman.[76] Born in Chicago in 1908, Avis Clamitz had grown up in Emil G. Hirsch's Sinai Congregation. Fascinated by the towering rabbi, Avis Clamitz later recalled that, as a child, she would "creep up in the front to listen, to devour," his words. His "formative influence" propelled her to plan a career in Jewish education.[77]

That quest led Clamitz, at the age of sixteen, to Hebrew Union College. The year was 1925. The semester before, another female student, Martha Neumark Montor, had left Cincinnati for New York City. Avis Clamitz thus found herself the only woman at HUC. Wanting "to become an expert in religious education . . . not think[ing] at all about becoming a lady rabbi," she matriculated in the preparatory department. Yet, even with this goal before her, she met, so she later recalled, discouragement from many. She claimed HUC President Julian Morgenstern told her that "although he could not prevent me from attending classes, for I had influential recommendations, I could never be . . . a candidate for a degree. I was further informed that there were no facilities there to deal with females and that from now on I was on my own." But gradually, perhaps due to her fine academic performance, she began to win support from some. After a successful first year, she returned, a regular student, a candidate for the Bachelor of Hebrew Letters. As she neared the end of her four years, she discovered the "more radical faculty members wished to make me a new test case" for women's ordination.[78] But Clamitz, shunning the sensationalism of the challenge, did not seek ordination. Later she claimed: "I really felt that as a Jewish educator in a Synagogue, I could do as much as I could as a rabbi. And I didn't want the notoriety and the publicity that would make what I was doing meaningless because of the fight."[79]

Subsequently, like so many other women who sought lives of Jewish service, she fulfilled her aspirations, not only in teaching, but in marrying a rabbi.[80] In 1929, Hebrew Union College awarded her a Bachelor of Hebrew Letters, marking her, along with Martha Neumark, one of the few American women then holding its degree. Shortly before her graduation, Avis Clamitz married Rabbi Charles E. Shulman.

Ordained at Hebrew Union College in 1927, Charles Shulman led congregations in Wheeling, West Virginia; Glencoe, Illinois; and, after 1947, Riverdale, New York. Inside and outside these synagogues, he and his wife worked together as partners and as individuals for a wide range of Jewish and Zionist causes. Early in their marriage, Avis Clamitz Shulman—her full name appeared in all her press clippings—worked as the paid field secretary for the West Virginia Federated Sisterhoods, a region of NFTS. Finding that, as she was "one of the very few women in the world who has studied for the rabbinacy [*sic*]," Jewish and Christian women's groups, synagogues, churches, and civic groups welcomed her to speak.[81] Sometimes, because very few rabbis lived in West Virginia, the former seminary student found herself "serv[ing] as a sort of unofficial rabbi in such cities as Parkersburg, Wheeling, and Fairmount, West Virginia."[82]

Thus like the other women who had learned in rabbinical school in the 1920s and 1930s, Clamitz Shulman, for a time, carved out a career as "one of the most able speakers from the feminine ranks."[83] She spoke about Hebrew literature, Jewish history, and the problems of modern Jewish life. She stood in interreligious forums as a representative for Judaism—on one occasion sharing the platform with the famous lawyer Clarence Darrow.[84] Inevitably her audiences saw her as a spokeswoman for contemporary Jewish women. In one such forum, she and Jane Evans appeared together to examine "The Jewish Woman in the World of Today." In another, she commented upon "The Future of the Woman in Palestine."[85]

Most of the time, the press would correctly report that she was "one of the few women who have received a degree from the Hebrew Union College."[86] But sometimes reporters exaggerated her credentials. Presumably, they, like many in her audiences, would not have understood that Hebrew Union College awarded a degree other than rabbi. Thus newspapers and synagogue bulletins proclaimed "Avis Clamitz Shulman . . . is herself an ordained rabbi," "one of the few graduate women rabbis," "a Rabbi in her own right." One broadcast: "Although she dare not use the title of rabbi, she has all the rights of a rabbi with the exception of not being able to perform marriages."[87] Years later, some in West Virginia and Ohio would remember that long before the 1970s and 1980s, a woman rabbi had visited their congregations.[88]

From her unique vantage point of having spent four years at HUC in the 1920s, Avis Shulman watched, with interest, as the issue of women rabbis heated up again in the 1950s. In "Ordaining Women as Ministers," she used "the historic ruling of the Presbyterian church" to comment upon "women's stubborn and tedious fight for equality." She highlighted the long history of the question in American Christianity, and she mined the recent Jewish past, using her own "experience to illumine in some small degree the subject of Jewish women in the ministry." She credited her success in overcoming resistance at HUC, not to "any exceptional capacities," but rather because "of a tedious and remarkably unglamorous process during which the Seminary became accustomed to having a woman around who quietly and tenaciously carried out her desire to learn." And she knew that her "path had become a little easier" because of the few women, including Martha Neumark, who had preceded her.[89]

Believing that her personal history typified "surely that of all women who pioneer on however small a scale in any field," she understood what neither Jane Evans nor Rebecca Brickner could, what it would take for women in the future to overcome the gender barrier to the rabbinate. As she looked back on her years at HUC, she felt most keenly "the absence of the group, the feeling of being a single feminine voice that I found disturbing."

> It is obvious to me that if there are to be women rabbis, the women themselves will have to demonstrate their sense of dedication and earnestness by undertaking the course of training even before promises of full equality are made. The greatest step toward ordination of women in the reform [*sic*] rabbinate will be found in the strength of those who dare to go forward even though there may be some initial liabilities. *When there is a group—even a small group—of women students at the Seminary enrolled in a rabbinical course, the now theoretical question will become a vital issue*[90] (emphasis added).

The former rabbinical school student sensed that no woman could do this on her own. She would need the support of others, especially of other women. When a core of such women would emerge, when those who championed her cause from a distance and those who backed her from inside the seminary would coalesce around the question, the woman who would be a rabbi would no longer stand as a lonely "single feminine voice."[91]

Gradually over the course of the 1960s, the crucial group of supporters took shape. Among them, outside HUC, stood the women of the National Federation of Temple Sisterhoods. They voiced enthusiasm for women rabbis just as in numerous places in American life, many different voices began clamoring anew for the equality of women in all the professions.[92]

Simultaneously, around and inside HUC, a small group of young women, like the group Avis Clamitz Shulman envisioned as pivotal to women's ordination, began to emerge. By the late 1960s, their existence, coupled with the changes wrought by feminism in American life, signaled the imminence of women's ordination. For by then, the men with the power to confer ordination realized that if one particular candidate did not make it, others, with their supporters behind them, already stood in the wings primed to raise the same challenge, to become the first female rabbis.

Reform's responses to dramatic changes in American Jewish life unexpectedly paved the way for an emerging nucleus of female students in Cincinnati. In the 1950s, the Reform movement—in fact, all denominations of American Judaism—exploded. As hundreds of new synagogues mushroomed, all seminaries rushed to train more rabbis. Endeavoring to meet the demand, HUC officials found that as they recruited college seniors, some did not know enough Hebrew to pass the entrance exam. Others were put off by six years of postgraduate study. In an era when unprecedented numbers of young American, including Jewish, teens were attending college,[93] the faculty decided to recruit men directly from high school. If a prospective rabbi would attend the neighboring University of Cincinnati, he could simultaneously begin his work at Hebrew Union College in its new undergraduate program. The young men who would complete this program would gain much. Not only would they have enough time to master Hebrew, but they would finish the first year of rabbinical school while earning their B.A.[94]

To uncover these future rabbis, HUC administrators naturally turned to Reform's youth movement, the National Federation of Temple Youth, popularly known as NFTY. Founded in 1939, NFTY, originally for Reform "youth" in their twenties, shifted its focus to high school students after World War II. Its camps, conclaves, leadership training institutes, study and social service programs offered high schoolers a Jewish version of the then regnant youth culture.[95] In these new settings, especially in its camps, committed Reform youth lived "their vision of what we wanted our world to be like." That world was epitomized by the slogan of its first camp, Union Institute in Oconomowoc, Wisconsin (1951): "Study and pray, work and play." Future leaders of Reform Judaism would come from NFTY's ranks. And NFTY would spur some of them, especially those who had summered at its camps, to want to continue to live Reform Judaism by spending their college years in Cincinnati.[96]

In 1957, HUC admitted its first class of twenty-four University of Cincinnati undergraduates.[97] Joining the fresh*men* in their Hebrew classes were three UC women.[98] One, Roberta Sholin, "never had any intentions of becoming a rabbi." Instead, she expected study to lead to a career in religious education. But another, Toby Fink, did have her heart set on becoming a rabbi.[99]

Toby Fink grew up in a rabbinic household, in a highly observant Reform home in Buffalo, New York. Her older brother, Arnold, followed the family tradition by becoming a rabbi. While in high school his sister too turned her sights in that direction. Given her background and interests, this NFTY regional vice-president and Oconomowoc camper saw her choice as "no great revelation." In fact, since her girlfriend, NFTY's regional president, also wanted to be a rabbi, Fink did not find herself alone in planning her future career. Her family's reaction to her decision, despite their awareness of women's historical exclusion from this profession, was "why not?" Surely, so they had raised their daughter to believe, in their time, women could achieve their ambitions. Their support did not surprise her, for Toby Fink was the daughter of Rabbi Joseph Fink, former president of the Central Conference of American Rabbis and chairman of the CCAR committee which produced the "Report on the Ordination of Women" while his daughter was still in high school.[100]

As an undergraduate bound for the University of Cincinnati, Fink planned on getting a jump start on some of the graduate credits she needed for rabbinical school. Later she recalled her correspondence with HUC undergraduate program officials.[101] She wrote she wanted to be a rabbi, and they wrote back that she could become a religious educator. Eventually, HUC officials sent her a letter which "grudgingly acknowledged" that once she had earned her B.A., they would consider her for the rabbinical program.

But Fink left HUC long before testing that promise.[102] Excluded from the camaraderie of the men who lived in the dorm, she sensed that, in the late 1950s, no one outside her family backed the idea. Finding the "world not ready for it," her fellow students "not welcoming," and that her future husband "was not going to be Mr. Rabbi," she abandoned her plan. Later she reflected: "Men don't recognize how much energy it takes to do something outside the mainstream."

Years later she commented, with the hindsight of one who had watched the feminist movement unfold, that she had lacked a "support group" to help her stand up to the "social pressure." Instead, although she had never considered any career other than the rabbinate, she had bowed to pressure to conform to feminine roles and female careers and became a social worker.

But some of the women who followed her path into the undergraduate program knew that she had tried to become a rabbi. Like Fink, Norma Kirschner explicitly chose the University of Cincinnati because of its proximity to HUC. In 1959, in her senior year of high school, Kirschner made an NFTY "pilgrimage" to HUC. By then she had become the first, or so she believed, female president of her Temple Youth Group, NFTY's synagogue base. She had also spent summers at NFTY camps and taught religious school. Wanting to continue Jewish studies in college at a time when few universities offered such an opportunity, Kirschner decided to combine study at the University of Cincinnati and HUC. During her interview for the undergraduate department she was told, just to make sure she and HUC "were on the same wavelength," that women could not be considered for ordination. Nevertheless, for a time, she hoped the men would change their minds, especially since she wanted rabbinical education to lead to a career in academe, not to the pulpit. She figured, if HUC-JIR were to change its position, it would do so first in Cincinnati, where it admitted undergraduate women. For she knew a bit about Reform's recent experience with women who wanted to become rabbis. She knew Toby Fink had preceded her.[103]

For three years Kirschner studied at HUC. In June 1963, the University of Cincinnati awarded her a B.A., and, that same month, she married. Her new husband, Stanley Skolnik, was a rabbinical student at HUC-JIR in New York. When his bride contemplated continuing her studies there, she found all women pushed to the education program. Since she did not want that course, she shifted direction, abandoning plans for a rabbinical education in favor of another of the well-established and socially acceptable female careers, that of librarian.[104]

The experiences of Fink and Kirschner, two of the women who, as undergraduates, turned to HUC in the late 1950s and early 1960s, re-

ABOVE.
Martha Neumark,
ca. 1920.
Courtesy her son,
Karel Montor.

RIGHT.
Irma Levy Lindheim.
Courtesy Hadassah
Archives.

Hebrew Union College faculty, staff, and students, 1925–1926. Avis Clamitz is in the second row, fifth from the left. Seated second from the right is Jacob Z. Lauterbach; seated third from the right is Julian Morgenstern. Charles Shulman, Avis Clamitz's husband-to-be, stands immediately behind and to the left of the three women who are two rows behind Avis Clamitz. Courtesy Deborah Shulman Sherman.

Helen Levinthal with her father,
Dr. Israel Levinthal. From
"Girl Completes Rabbinic Study;
9 Men Ordained," New York Herald-
Tribune, *29 May 1939. Courtesy*
Library of Congress.

*Paula Ackerman. Courtesy American
Jewish Archives, Cincinnati, Ohio.*

ABOVE.

Sara Kahn Troster and Rachel Kahn-Troster, January 1980. Their t-shirts read "Rabbinical School, Jewish Theological Seminary, Class 2001?" Courtesy Elaine Kahn and Rabbi Lawrence Troster.

LEFT.

Rabbi Sally Priesand, on the twenty-fifth anniversary of her ordination, 1997. Courtesy Ente Studio, Maspeth, New York.

veal that while these young women held rising expectations for their futures, HUC officials still assumed they would follow the paths well-trodden by the women who had preceded them. The co-eds could, if they wished, use their rabbinical school educations to become Jewish educators. Otherwise, such training fitted them to marry—especially to marry rabbis—to take their places as the next generation of exemplary Jewish wives, capable of raising the next generation of committed American Jews, and apt to devote their leisure time to worthwhile Jewish communal pursuits. For these young women, becoming rabbis themselves, expecting their husbands to be "Mr. Rabbi" remained, as it had been since the 1890s, simply out of the question.

In presuming Jewish women would mirror popular culture's gendered middle-class ideal, the men of HUC revealed themselves men of their times. A survey of the prominent American Jewish women included in *Who's Who in World Jewry 1955* affirms the propriety of their expectations. By far the largest category of American Jewish women who won a space in that volume—over 40 percent—did so for their work, preponderantly unpaid work, in the Jewish community. They volunteered for Jewish communal and welfare organizations and headed Jewish women's organizations. Of those whose paid labor propelled them into the ranks of illustrious Jewish women, the vast majority pursued careers long open to women. A quarter of the American Jewish women listed were artists, writers, including journalists and editors, or performers. Another 10 percent had turned to the feminized professions of teaching and librarianship. No matter their "career," the vast majority of the women had both married and borne children.[105] This evidence validates HUC officials' assumptions for proper Jewish womanhood at mid-century. The young women passing through their classrooms were, in the rabbis' and scholars' eyes, chiefly on their way to futures as wives, mothers, volunteer workers, and maybe as teachers among American Jewry.

Nevertheless, the data in the 1955 survey disclosed some women already taking another path. By the mid-1950s, a small, but increasing, number of American Jewish women—20 percent of all those listed—were recognized for careers atypical of middle-class women. A comparison of the data on the American women featured in *Who's Who in American Jewry 1928* with that of those listed in *Who's Who in World Jewry 1955* uncovers the changes wrought by three decades. By 1955 the number of female Jewish physicians listed had quadrupled, and the number of lawyers and jurists had doubled over the 1928 index. Moreover, the range of occupations American Jewish women pursued had expanded, suggesting that educated Jewish women, like their Christian contemporaries, were pushing beyond the boundaries of the women's professions. Although often only one or two American Jewish women had won prominence in the male-dominated professions, their presence suggested the changes underway. By 1955, some American Jewish women were already celebrated anthropologists, archaeologists, art critics, business executives, chemists, economists, government officials, historians, hospital administrators, insurance brokers, producers, publishers, radio commentators, statisticians, and zoologists. One, Tehilla Lichtenstein, was a "religious leader."[106] The wide diversity of careers and the increasing numbers of American Jewish women so employed, suggests that already some American Jewish women—those listed and those behind them whose names did not appear[107]—were expanding their horizons and advancing, at mid-century, an alternative model for proper Jewish womanhood.

Surely, this harbinger of tiny, but incremental change, helps to explain why in the mid-1960s, the old question of women's admission to the rabbinate burst out anew, as more and more young women, in Reform circles and elsewhere in American Judaism, now raised this question for themselves.

For women aspiring to the rabbinate in Reform Judaism, NFTY helped shape their rising expectations for themselves and their futures. In the late 1950s and early 1960s the co-eds NFTY spurred to Cincinnati had already had powerful experiences of Jewish leadership. Toby Fink was vice-president of her NFTY region. Norma Kirschner was president of her Temple Youth Group as were Georgia Sperber (Davis) and Judith Pilzer (Rudolph), who followed them into the undergraduate department in 1964. Some declared they became the first teenage girls in their temples to become youth group president. Furthermore, so Judy Pilzer Rudolph recalled, NFTY, especially its camps, gave girls, as well as boys, unusual opportunities for religious leadership. For the first time, girls, or so she remembered, as

well as boys, planned services, engaged in Torah study and philosophical discussions, and were encouraged to speak about what they had
learned, to give "sermonettes."[108] If, as teens, they could lead their
peers, why could they not, plan, as adults, to become rabbis and lead
their fellow Jews? The result was that these young women remained,
as Toby Fink was, surprisingly blinded to the gendered role divisions
outside Reform's youth culture—or, at the least, they believed them
surmountable.

Moreover, as another of the undergraduate department women,
Ann Blitzstein Folb recalled, the early 1960s, the Kennedy years, had
begun to give all people, even women, a sense that "they could be
more than anybody thought they could be." "People began to question all the previously held assumptions about what women had
been."[109] Between the establishment of Kennedy's Commission on
the Status of Women in 1961 and the birth of the National Organization for Women in 1966—the latter seen as the landmark launching
the contemporary women's movement—manifold signs of the resur-
gence of American feminism appeared. In 1963, Betty Friedan published *The Feminine Mystique* chronicling the discontent of her generation of female college graduates. That same year Congress passed
the Equal Pay Act. And, most important of all, despite early reluctance to enforce it, Title VII of the 1964 Civil Rights Act banned discrimination in employment on the basis of sex as well as race.[110]
When in New York, in November of 1963, NFTS's one thousand delegates called for a resolution of the woman rabbi question, they mir-
rored the changing times.

The fall after Norma Kirschner left HUC, another young woman
wanting to be a rabbi turned up. Once again, in admitting Ann
Blitzstein, HUC officials remained "very cautious." As they had
warned Toby Fink and Norma Kirschner, so they repeated to her,
completing the undergraduate program did not automatically guarantee her entrance to the rabbinic department.[111]

That first year, 1963–64, Blitzstein found herself the only woman.
But, by the spring of 1964, she knew more were on the way. One,
Georgia Sperber, she had already met. But Sperber saw HUC as a
place to explore Jewish Studies. She had no intention of becoming a
rabbi.[112] However, Blitzstein was especially eager to meet another. Al-

ready she had seen a newspaper clipping titled "Girl Sets Her Goal to Be 1st Woman Rabbi." That girl was Sally Jane Priesand.[113]

The second child in Rose Elizabeth and Irving Theodore Priesand's family of two boys and two girls, Sally Jane was born in Cleveland on June 27, 1946. Her parents' involvements in their Jewish community included their synagogues and the fraternal society B'nai B'rith. As a child, Priesand attended classes at the Conservative Community Temple. But when as a teenager she looked back at those early years, she wrote that then she neither enjoyed Sunday school nor felt particularly religious.[114]

However, when she was in junior high school, the Priesands moved from the east side of Cleveland to the west side. There they joined a Reform synagogue, Beth Israel—The West Temple. At first Priesand "was rather shocked" by her experience of its services. "Naturally, it was not necessary for a man to wear a yarmulke or a tallith. Furthermore, a girl was called upon to chant the blessings before and after the Torah reading. This is what probably surprised me the most, for at Community Temple the women had done very little in connection with the services." Sunday school, too, in the new synagogue seemed very different. In its small class all could participate. For the first time Priesand found herself really interested in Judaism. She joined the Temple Youth Group, gave the sermon at its annual youth service, and, in the summer of 1961, accepted a scholarship from Beth Israel's Sisterhood to attend Reform's Union of American Hebrew Congregation Camp Institute at Zionsville, Indiana. Shortly thereafter, the teenager came to set her sights on the rabbinate.[115]

Notes from the friends she made during that and in subsequent summers reveal that they knew she hoped to become "Rabbi Sally." Her fellow campers wished her good luck and expected to meet her again, this time "at the College." One friend complimented Priesand's sermons and roles in the camp services, demonstrating that the Jewish camp institutes truly offered teenage girls rare and moving opportunities for religious leadership, just as Judith Pilzer Rudolph would assert decades later. Only one friend glimpsed that difficulties might lie ahead: "I know that if the College will allow it, it won't be Miss Sally Priesand, but *Rabbi* Sally Priesand." Her friends' remarks revealed that already high schooler Sally Priesand had claimed her place in the annals of those who had planned to become "one of the first women Rabbis in the history of the world."[116]

Surely, her peers' enthusiasm for her plans was not uncharacteristic of the "middle-class children who came of age in those years." In his book, *The Sixties*, Todd Gitlin describes the youth who grew up in the fifties and came of age in the sixties as following "an approved track for running faster and stretching farther," pursuing college and university training in order to obtain credentials, their "tickets" to the future.[117] And, like other Jewish teens of these years, the NFTY teens, even the girls, joined the credentials' race. Several of the women who passed through HUC's undergraduate program followed a track straight from their B.A.'s to graduate school, earning—once they had given up on the rabbinate—master's degrees in social work, education, and library science.[118] Surely, in seeking an advanced degree, albeit one as unusual as a rabbinical diploma, Priesand did not appear so very different from her NFTY peers and from the increasing numbers of young American women who, within the space of that decade, would double the numbers of the nation's female doctors, lawyers, and dentists.[119]

In her last years of high school Priesand continued to prepare for her future at the HUC. She celebrated her confirmation, graduated from Hebrew high school, and organized Sunday school services. She became chairman of her youth group's ritual committee, compiled a notebook of prayers for its meetings, planned its annual youth services, gave sermons, and even wrote for the congregational newsletter. She returned again to the Union Camp at Zionsville and made an NFTY "pilgrimage" to HUC. Toward the end of her junior year, she wrote to find out what she would need to do to win admission.[120]

As Priesand corresponded with college officials, she wrote of how she wanted to be a rabbi and they responded she should become a teacher. In June 1963, Joseph Karasick, assistant to the provost, graciously welcomed Priesand's interest in HUC. But since her letter indicated she wanted the rabbinate, he cautioned: "[W]e would have to inform you candidly that we do not know what opportunities are available for women in the active rabbinate, since we have, as yet, not ordained any women. Most women prefer to enter the field of Jewish religious education."[121]

In forwarding her application materials, HUC-JIR secretary Miriam O. Weiss indicated that the question of women in the rabbinate was not yet decided. Apparently unaware of Helen Levinthal's work at JIR, she reported: "While we have had women students, none, so far, has taken the full course of study which would lead to graduation and ordination as a rabbi." Perhaps Weiss remembered that less than a decade before, the rabbis in the Central Conference of American Rabbis had delayed voting on the issue, for she warned: "The question of a woman as a rabbi is a question for the rabbis rather than the School. There is no attempt on our part to discourage you but to direct your thinking."[122]

In February 1964, Sally Priesand secured a place in the undergraduate department of Hebrew Union College-Jewish Institute of Religion as a "Special Student," "enrolled for credit but not enrolled as a Pre-Rabbinic student." In response to her query about what this meant, Karasick wrote that the words "Special Student" had "no adverse connotation." Rather since the college required unmarried undergraduates to live on campus and since it did not have housing for women, the term "Special Student" meant Priesand had permission to live off-campus.[123]

Shortly thereafter, a friend showed Ann Blitzstein a picture and the *Cleveland Plain Dealer* article on Sally Priesand and her plan to become the first woman rabbi.[124] Eagerly, Blitzstein wrote the high school senior to welcome her and to tell her that with her arrival in the fall of 1964, there would be at least "three girls in the Undergraduate Program." Although Blitzstein knew Georgia Sperber had no interest in the rabbinate, she was excited that Priesand shared her own dream. And she wanted to give her some idea of what she would soon face.

Blitzstein wrote that when she first came to Cincinnati, the "boys ... were quite cynical about my reason for coming to H.U.C."; they assumed "I wanted a husband more than an education." But as she had succeeded as a student there, they had come to take her "academic ambitions seriously." Nevertheless,

[o]pinion is divided on the idea of a female Rabbi, and most people are still of the opinion that marriage will eventually remove me from the

competition. I have developed a line of replies for all comers about why women can be Rabbis which serves me in good stead with those who wish to argue the subject.

The hard thing to fight is those who don't want to talk about it. Most of their thoughts are based on emotion & not reason, & emotion is a tricky thing to deal with.[125]

Although Ann Blitzstein could not have sensed this then, in welcoming Priesand to HUC she signaled the beginnings of the network of support Avis Clamitz Shulman deemed essential to women's ordination. Priesand, like the pioneers of the earlier generation, prepared to take the course of training even before she knew the men would ordain her. But utterly on her own, so Clamitz Shulman believed, she would fail. Only with others sharing in and championing her ambition, the very "support group" Toby Fink so sorely missed, could she succeed.

When Sally Priesand arrived at HUC in the fall of 1964, the year the first cohort of baby boomers swelled the nation's freshman classes,[126] she not only found Blitzstein and Sperber formally enrolled in the undergraduate department, but she also met other University of Cincinnati co-eds who centered their lives around HUC. Together these students helped sustain both the future rabbi and the question of women's ordination. Priesand roomed with Sperber. She attended the college services required of undergraduate department students with Karen Hirsch (Harari), who entered HUC in 1965, and another UC friend, Sherry Levy (Reiner). So much attention focused on the "novel" notion of women wanting to be rabbis, that Sperber Davis later recalled being teased because she did not want to be one. Levy-Reiner remembered that she too was told she should become a rabbi.[127]

Although by the time Priesand passed, in 1968, from the undergraduate department into the rabbinical track, she stood alone at HUC as the only female rabbinical student, she no longer stood alone in her ambition. By then her goal to become a rabbi was joined to the resurgent feminist movement. By then too, other women, convinced that they could do what none had yet done, were matriculating elsewhere, at HUC-JIR's New York campus and at the new Reconstructionist Rabbinical College. Some of them had, much like Sally Priesand, been drawn to the idea of becoming a rabbi as children and teens. Sandy Eisenberg Sasso, who, in 1974, became the first woman ordained by the Reconstructionist Rabbinical College, recalled that after her confirmation in 1963, she sat on the edge of her bed thinking she wanted to become a rabbi. Back then she had no idea women did not do this. Others made their decisions propelled by the news reports that soon Sally Priesand would become the first woman rabbi in the history of the world.[128]

As the 1960s waned, these women already inside the rabbinical seminaries found an ever widening circle of acclaim for their aspirations outside seminary walls. The press continued to play a pivotal role in raising the question of women's rabbinic ordination, sustaining it before a wide audience. Stories broadcasting Priesand's dream in both Jewish and national presses reflected the media's fascination with the transformations underway in the lives of American women impacted by a new wave of feminism.[129] While in the annals of American Judaism Priesand then appeared unique, in the annals of the new wave of feminism her story appeared but part of a larger one of the metamorphosis of women's roles in American life, including religious life. Newspapers reported that the National Organization for Women had created an ecumenical task force on women and religion and that major Protestant denominations had at long last changed their stances and would admit women to the ministry. Headlines blazoned "Women's 'Lib' on the March in the Churches," "male bias against women ministers," and "Black Nun Power."[130] Together they presented a picture of feminism storming the bastion of American religion.

Media interest in the women trying to become the first rabbis thus represented but a small part of its pursuit of women's shifting religious roles. When, in June 1969, the *New York Times* covered a symposium critiquing rabbinic training, it reported that Reform rabbi Daniel Jeremy Silver proposed the radical innovation of ordaining women.[131] Less than a year later both *Newsweek* and *Time* wrote about "Rabbi Sally" and her plans to become the first woman ordained in American Judaism.[132] Those articles sent the news of Priesand's ambition far afield. Major national papers, synagogue bulletins, and Jewish papers as far away as Israel and South Africa picked up the story.[133] Priesand saved these articles in her scrapbook along with accounts of NFTS's call for women rabbis and reports speculating whether women rabbis would appear first in England or America.[134] The attention of the press helped not only to sustain her desire and to plant the seeds of such ideas in others, but also to convince many to champion her cause. As one friend, who well understood both the power of the press and the reality that women's ordination rested ultimately in the hands of the leaders of American Judaism, quipped: "You certainly are famous! And now you *better* be ordained."[135]

Priesand came to enjoy the fruits of the media attention, recognizing it as one of the responsibilities of "being the first." For her, its real advantage lay in the fact that by the time she was ordained, people would know she existed, and it might be easier to find a congregation to serve.[136]

As her name and dream became known, Priesand increasingly found herself, while still a student, in demand as a speaker. Even as an undergraduate, she had received invitations to speak in churches and synagogues as "the one who may become the first woman rabbi."[137] As the press broadcast her plans, she found herself in demand. With sermons and speeches titled "A Woman Rabbi ... Her Prerogatives, Principles, and Problems" and "The Dream of Yesterday and the Vision of Tomorrow," she brought home to congregants, sometimes on Sisterhood Sabbath, and to Jewish women's groups, like B'nai B'rith Women, the message that Judaism too, with the times, was "a-changing."[138]

Such addresses presented her audiences, who had no memory of a Hannah Solomon or a Paula Ackerman, with the "novelty" of a woman on the *bimah*. As her listeners heard of the difficulties that beset the path of the one they assumed to be the first woman ever to attempt to become a rabbi, they participated on a microcosmic scale in the heated debate about women's inalienable right to do all that men do in American life and culture. Sociologist Norman Mirsky, who, as a member of the HUC faculty, had the chance to observe Priesand's rabbinical school career up close, commented that the rabbinical student became "a genuine heroine to nearly every non-

Orthodox Jewish women's organization." The professor well understood the ambivalence many in these voluntary organizations felt about the challenges the emerging feminism posed to their way of life. In the early years of the second wave of feminism, their formal programs paid little attention to the movement. But when Priesand stood before them, she became "the perfect instrumentality for acting out in a non-threatening way whatever sympathies these women might feel for Women's Liberation."[139] Priesand herself called her appearances lessons in "consciousness-raising." As Dr. Sherry Levy-Reiner, her roommate for part of rabbinical school, would later affirm, "for a lot of women" in those tumultuous years Sally Priesand was "carrying their dreams."[140] And as the student rabbi carried the dreams of some of her public, she also found herself sustained by their enthusiasm for hers.[141]

As Sally Priesand presented her challenge to assume an historic male role, she found many in her audiences ready to accept her and her ambition.[142] While the changing profile of professional women in these years prepared the ground, Priesand's feminine persona also eased her way. Just as the press had commented about the appearance and demeanor of the first women to enter the professions in the nineteenth century, so too would reporters in the 1970s describe Miss Priesand as "petite" and run photos of the student rabbi perched on a desk in a modest miniskirt and heels. At a time when some American youth sported love beads, scruffy jeans, and flowing gauze dresses, Miss Priesand, even in a miniskirt, appeared the model of propriety.[143]

But, more importantly, her prudent words on feminism disclosed how she shaped her quest to become a rabbi in moderate, in fact, in traditional, terms. In 1968, after feminists demonstrating against the Miss America pageant were dubbed—inaccurately—"bra-burners," the new Women's Liberation appeared, thanks especially to the media, to be dominated by revolutionary radicals determined to overthrow patriarchy. When Priesand, in these same years, spoke to audiences and reporters about Women's Liberation, she carefully distanced herself from those who wanted to cast her challenge in a militant mold. She claimed:

I am not an active supporter of the movement and didn't go into the rabbinate to break down any barriers . . . I do, however, think that the feminist movement is a very important movement, that it is one that has suffered greatly from adverse publicity that it has received unfairly. Much of what we read, hear, and see about feminism generally isn't about its basic message. And I think that message is that it is about time for us to overcome our own psychological hangups and to regard every human being as a real person with talents and skills and with the option of fulfilling his potential as a creative individual in any way he or she feels. And I think that this is the message of the feminist movement and I certainly agree with this, although I don't need to be an active supporter out in the front of the movement.[144]

In speeches, Priesand followed her cautious expression of feminism, uttered in liberalism's language of the individual's inalienable right to fulfill his or her potential, with her credo, her affirmation of Judaism. Having spoken her piece on Women's Liberation, Priesand turned to God, Torah, and the Jewish people. She told her audiences of the power of seeing a rabbi raise the Torah and of how she prayed to God to let her be worthy of Judaism's great heritage. "I believe that a rabbi is a scholar, a teacher, a preacher, a leader, a counselor, a comforter, a preserver of Judaism, and a human being."[145] And within a short time, she hoped to join these exalted ranks. Juxtaposing her muted feminism with her religious credo enabled Priesand to persuade her Jewish audiences to empathize with her deep desire to preserve Jewish tradition—not to overturn it—by serving her people as rabbi.[146]

In her appearances Priesand simply told her story, of how since the tenth grade she had wanted to be a rabbi, of what her summers at Zionsville had meant, and of how when she first arrived at HUC as an undergraduate, the faculty "pretty much ignored me." She related that they expected she would choose marriage over career. In fact, as she then recounted, one professor asked a student she dated to do the school a favor—if he would marry her, they would get rid of her.[147]

But as Priesand grappled with whether or not she had the "guts" to persevere, she became convinced that if she abandoned her dream, she would come to regret it. And so she shared with her listeners not only her triumphs, but also the difficulties of her journey. Although the men who completed the undergraduate program with her gained automatic admission to the second year of rabbinical school, she was required to formally apply, to update her autobiography, and to pass the psychiatric exam required of new applicants. Already, a small core of her fellow students joined Priesand's growing group of supporters, evidence of a new circle of her champions. Angered by the inequity of her treatment, they urged her to protest. But patiently she told them to wait and see. If she were admitted, she would not allege that once again HUC had marked her out as a "special student."[148]

Formal admission to the rabbinical program, however, proved but her first hurdle. Priesand found her next test raised by her very first High Holiday placement. In the summer of 1968, as HUC prepared to assign holiday placements to her second-year class, but five congregations seeking apprentice rabbis remained for the twenty eligible students. When her classmates held a lottery to see who would get their first pulpits, the only woman in the class drew number one. After college officials assigned her to Beth Jacob Congregation in Murphysboro, Illinois, its president objected that he had expected an ordained rabbi, not a student. Although his correspondence did not divulge that he challenged Priesand on the grounds that she was not a he, the message had been conveyed. As Kenneth Roseman, who handled the High Holiday placements, wrote to her: "I suppose this is merely a first taste of the problems that you will be facing and that we all recognized in advance." Thus concern about acceptance at the college was quickly supplanted by concern about what she would face out in the field.[149]

Yet despite this first rejection, Priesand not only met congregations willing to brave her student-rabbinate, but she also found the work all she had hoped it would be. Now congregants' enthusiasm for her ambition, her rabbinate, and herself helped sustain her quest. Although congregations still proved reluctant to take her—Congregation B'nai Israel in Hattiesburg, Mississippi, voted 10 to 9 in favor of hiring her—once she arrived, most people warmed to the person, her talent, and her dream. From Sinai Temple in Champaign-Urbana, HUC officials learned that with her very first service, "Rabbi Sally," as she was quickly becoming known, dispelled any doubts "about a girl rabbinical student."[150] In Hattiesburg, some congregants shared her excitement over the growing publicity and her hopes that "[o]nce I have broken through the barriers . . . I believe that more women will follow the dictates of their hearts and become spiritual leaders."[151] Although Priesand still met with rejection from some venues, by her last year in rabbinical school, she could say confidently: "It is hard for me to realize that after all these years I will finally be ordained. I imagine there might be some difficulty in finding a congregation. Not everyone will take me. But I don't expect there to be too many difficulties, and I am optimistic."[152]

By then Priesand's assurance that she would indeed be ordained was based on more than the outpouring of support of her friends and fellow students, the press, her fans and her congregants. By then her certainty that in less than a year she would stand at ordination, alongside her thirty-five classmates, rested on her belief that Reform leaders were ready to translate rhetoric into deed, prepared to break with the gendered yoke of the Jewish past.

In June 1972, HUC-JIR President Alfred Gottschalk told his board of governors that "Sally Priesand was the first woman admitted to the program leading to ordination with the assurance that it would be granted her upon the successful completion of her studies."[153] That claim, made from the vantage of days before her historic ordination, belied the reality of her first years at HUC, both in the undergraduate program and in her early years of rabbinical school. Then it was still possible, before all the publicity and acclaim and especially before the first of the national news stories in 1970, that something untoward would derail her, just another of the women who wanted to be a rabbi. But dramatic upheavals in American life during the years Priesand persevered at HUC unexpectedly cast a new light on her challenge to stand in American Israel as rabbi, teacher, and preacher.

Sociologist Todd Gitlin has called "[t]he years 1967, 1968, 1969, and 1970 . . . a cyclone in a wind tunnel." Opposition to the war in Vietnam and campus unrest, which in the spring of 1969 alone saw sizable demonstrations at colleges and universities holding one-third of the nation's students, created enormous anxiety about American youth and the future of the nation. Liberal causes, like the civil rights and women's movements, took radical turns to Black Power and

Women's Liberation. Meanwhile, other crusaders, like homosexuals, long obscured from the nation's collective consciousness, burst out in riots. These "days of rage" saw the assassinations of Martin Luther King, Jr., and Robert Kennedy, the bulldozing of People's Park, and the killing of students at Kent State and Jackson State universities.[154] Few Americans were utterly removed from the turmoil carried into their homes by the evening news and the morning papers.

The unrest sweeping the nation's campuses reverberated at HUC. Until the late 1960s, all new rabbis, upon ordination, had to serve the armed forces as chaplains. Now, in the wake of student resistance to the Vietnam War, the Central Conference of American Rabbis abandoned this policy. When in the spring of 1970, during college demonstrations against the bombing of Cambodia, the Ohio National Guard shot fifteen students, killing four, at Kent State, outraged rabbinical students, like millions of youth across the nation, gathered, first to mourn and then to protest. At HUC, officials narrowly averted a student strike by permitting those, including rabbinical student Priesand, heading to Washington to protest the war to defer their exams.[155]

Reform leaders' readiness by the early 1970s to sanction the woman rabbi as an "idea whose time has come" must be set against these "days of rage" when future rabbis protested the Vietnam War "by marching around the Federal Building in Cincinnati while blowing the shofar."[156] Given this backdrop, proclaiming a woman rabbi scarcely appeared the revolutionary act it once portended. Instead Reform's rendezvous with the woman rabbi now marked its engagement with the times, a symbolic embrace of the justice of women's renewed demands for equal rights.[157] By acquiescing to women's ordination and extending their rhetoric to deed, Reform leaders acted to continue their historic project of adapting Judaism to respond to modernity. In fact, even before they directly confronted the particular case of rabbinical student Priesand, a number of these leaders, rabbis and the men and women of their congregations, were already championing her cause. In the late 1960s, as they abstractly posed the question of women's ordination, they lengthened the conversation first opened in 1889 on the woman rabbi.

In 1966, while Sally Priesand was still a student in HUC's undergraduate program, UAHC President Rabbi Maurice Eisendrath told his board of trustees: "We must face the realities of life: Women are here to stay."[158] By then Eisendrath had personally experienced several phases of the recurrent cycling of the women's ordination question. He was Martha Neumark's high school and college classmate. When Paula Ackerman assumed her "rabbinate," he voiced approval of the principle of women rabbis while criticizing the *rebbetzin*'s assumption of her husband's mantle. Five years later, he signed the CCAR report endorsing women's right to the rabbinate.

Now against the backdrop of a resurgent feminism, he raised more broadly the problem of women's inequality within Reform Judaism. He decried the fact that only five of Reform's 700 congregations had women presidents and that only two women sat among the 180 members of the UAHC National Board, and that one of them, the president of the National Federation of Temple Sisterhoods, was ex-officio. And he argued:

> It is not always easy for us men to cop out on this perfectly apparent fact of life with snide jokes about Women's Lib and the like. But such jokes are no longer funny, and no longer becoming to a movement whose self-image is one of liberal thought, just action, equality, and moral motivation. . . . . We must stop dragging our feet on this subject and stop mouthing the same old tired bromides and act now to get women out of what many of them call "slave labor, kitchen squad" activities and into the mainstream of our work.[159]

Prodded by Eisendrath and earlier by the NFTS's 1963 call to Reform leaders to resolve the question of the woman rabbi, and inspired by the new climate for women's rights that Reform lay leaders sensed all around them, the Union of American Hebrew Congregations joined the women of Reform Judaism by endorsing, in 1968, women's admission to the rabbinate.[160]

Therefore, by the time Cleveland rabbi Daniel Jeremy Silver raised the subject of women's ordination—alluded to in the 1969 *New York Times* clipping Priesand had saved for her own record—the issue was already, once again, even for those who did not know of Miss Priesand, manifestly on the agenda of Reform Judaism. When, in May 1969, the editors of *Judaism* invited seminary presidents and professors, rabbis and rabbinical students to discuss "The Future of Rabbinic Training in America,"[161] they heard Rabbi Silver ask: "Why alone among the faiths must Judaism remain tied to the imbecility of a womanless ministry? Why alone among the professions is the rabbinate in violation of the Fair Employment Practices Act? Can we afford any longer to keep half of our human talent in the rabbinic deep-freeze?"[162] Although, at least in the published proceedings, none of the respondents reacted to Silver's summons to open the rabbinate to women, his pointed framing of the issue conveys the climate propelling Reform leaders to act, at long last, upon "the idea whose time has come."

As Silver's questions reveal, the wide-ranging impact of the new wave of feminism demanded that a movement committed to upholding, to borrow Eisendrath's words, "liberal thought, just action, equality, and moral motivation" champion the ideal of gender equality in American life. Silver well understood the role the federal government played in disseminating this ideal as it enacted new legislation and executive orders designed to promote gender equality for women in the work force and in the institutions of higher education preparing them for careers.[163]

Although originally prompted by the Civil Rights movement and intended to give African-Americans new economic opportunities, such legislation dramatically expanded women's economic and educational opportunities. Title VII of the 1964 Civil Rights Act not only prohibited discrimination in employment on the basis of race but also on the basis of sex.[164] Two years later President Lyndon Johnson signed an executive order requiring all companies wishing to do business with the federal government not only to provide equal opportunity for all but also to take "affirmative action" to bring their hiring into line with available labor pools. A year later the government extended this affirmative action to women. In 1970 the Women's Equity Action League decided to test its limits, to see if colleges and universities doing "business," holding government contracts, would also have to hire women and minorities. By the end of that year, women had challenged more than 160 institutions of higher education in court.[165] Two years later Title IX of the 1972 Educational Act prevented discrimination on the basis of sex in federally funded educational programs.[166]

As a religious seminary not doing "business" with the federal government nor housing federally funded education programs, HUC-JIR was not compelled to comply with such enactments. Nevertheless, such legislation demonstrated a national mandate for higher education to play a leading role in equalizing women's educational and economic opportunities. To limit women's access to rabbinical school and to champion an exclusively male rabbinate would brand the college and Reform Judaism intransigent, opposed to the ideal of women's educational and professional equality. On the other hand, ordaining the first female rabbi would symbolize Reform leaders' determination to do their part to foster women's equality in their particular niche of American life.

Moreover, the leaders of Reform Judaism knew they were not alone in American religion in grappling with "the imbecility of a womanless ministry." Although various Protestant denominations had long broken through the barrier to women's ordination, the American Association of Women Ministers, on its golden anniversary in 1969, counted but some three hundred members. Women then represented less than 5 percent of the American clergy. In fact, before 1970, even in the denominations ordaining females, relatively few women studied for the ministry. But by the early 1970s, as liberal feminism, the same feminism Miss Priesand espoused, with its goal of completely integrating women into American life, won greater support, it propelled more and more women to study for the clergy, even in denominations which did not—yet—grant them ordination.[167]

This time as churches which still did not have female clergy confronted the old question, the press, in articles, like "Bishop Betty? Rabbi Sally?" conflated the challengers. In 1970, while Priesand persevered in rabbinical school, the Lutheran Church in America and the American Lutheran Church voted to ordain women. As the number of women seminarians sharply increased, a new issue surfaced— how to integrate female clergy into the life of the church and to end continuing bias against women of the cloth. Now task forces on women and the church emerged in the United Methodist, United

Presbyterian, United Church of Christ, and the Lutheran Church in America. By 1976, when the Episcopal Church voted to ordain women, it became the last of the mainline Protestant denominations to do so.[168]

At the *Judaism* symposium Silver had stood alone among his rabbinical school colleagues in calling for an end to keeping "half of our human talent in the rabbinic deep-freeze." But as the news of Miss Priesand's ambition filtered out via the popular press, others echoed his support for the idea and, in particular, for her. Rabbinic student Priesand came to enjoy the backing of yet another circle of defenders—the very rabbis whose ranks she soon hoped to join. These men, along with her friends and fellow students, the press, and many in her congregations and audiences, sustained her on her way to ordination.

Among them was Alfred Gottschalk, dean of the Los Angeles campus of HUC-JIR, one of Reform's responses to the post-1945 migration of American Jews to this golden city.[169] Gottschalk complimented Priesand on her conduct of services, writing: "May you achieve all that you desire for your people and yourself." Rabbi Malcolm Stern, director of the Rabbinical Placement Commission of Reform Judaism, said that he looked forward to getting to know her in her senior year and to guiding her rabbinic placements. Others, sending their good wishes for her journey along the hazardous route of the pioneer, looked forward to the day when they would welcome her as colleague.[170] But chief—in Priesand's estimation paramount—among those encouraging in those years, head of all the circles of support sustaining her, was HUC-JIR President Nelson Glueck.

The man *Time* magazine described as "[a]n archaeologist-rabbi as lean and leathery as Joshua," Glueck had a distinguished career prior to assuming the presidency of Hebrew Union College. Born in Cincinnati and ordained at HUC in 1923, he earned a Ph.D. at the University of Jena (1926). Two years later Glueck joined the HUC faculty. But the archaeologist preferred the dust of the Negev to that of the chalkboards in Cincinnati. Over the next two decades, he spent as much time as possible in Palestine. There, during tours as director of Jerusalem's American School of Oriental Research, he supervised the excavation of ancient ruins. During World War II, his archaeological work concealed the surveillance operations he ran for the Allies. In

1947, HUC turned to Glueck to succeed Julian Morgenstern as president. Three years later Reform Judaism's Cincinnati and New York seminaries merged into Hebrew Union College-Jewish Institute of Religion. President Glueck headed HUC-JIR, overseeing its expansion not only to Los Angeles but also to Jerusalem, until illness forced him, in 1971, to step down.[171]

Priesand was convinced that Glueck played "a major role" in smoothing her path to ordination. She came to believe that he took care of "lots of little things in the background," that he personally arranged her first speaking engagement, and that at some point he had decided that she was going to be the first woman rabbi.[172]

Years later Helen Iglauer Glueck, who married Nelson Glueck in 1931, confirmed Priesand's impressions of her late husband's interest and support. At what point Glueck became convinced of the merits of women's ordination is unclear. A rabbinical student in 1921, he was presumably present at the HUC when his junior classmate Martha Neumark raised the matter. When Paula Ackerman first contemplated succeeding her husband, she turned to Glueck for approval. Although his letters to Ackerman failed to endorse women rabbis, he did tell her, "We need more people like you who are devoted to Judaism." A few years later he joined in signing the CCAR report which proclaimed "woman's parity with man," conceded her "the right to study for the rabbinate," and promised her ordination "if and when she has properly completed the course of study." At least one former NFTYite recalled hearing Glueck declaim in those years that he looked forward to the day when he would ordain a woman. As Helen Glueck put it, her husband's attitude was "quite simple." She believed Nelson Glueck to be "a man way ahead of his time" in his attitude toward women, that he was extremely interested in seeing women ordained, and that part of his fervor was due to her.[173]

Helen Glueck's boast that some of her husband's enthusiasm for women rabbis was due to her rested on the fact that the Gluecks did not fit the mid-century idealized portrait of the rabbinic couple. In this paradigm, the *rebbetzin* devoted herself fully to furthering the work of her rabbi-scholar husband in the synagogue and among the larger Jewish community. Such a pattern characterized the marriages of other participants in the debate around women's ordination. For

example, Barnett Brickner's biographer asserted that Rebecca Brickner's Jewish learning and communal leadership convinced her husband that women could function as rabbis. And Paula Ackerman had
prepared for her "rabbinate" by stepping up in her husband's absence
and by leading Sisterhood. Helen Glueck too supported her husband's
work. She tried, so she recalled, to invite every college class over once
a year. Yet, even before they married, Professor Glueck knew his wife
had powerful interests competing for her energies and time.[174]

When Helen Iglauer met Professor Glueck, she was a medical student at the University of Cincinnati's College of Medicine. Although
Mrs. Glueck took a year off from medical school to honeymoon in
Palestine, she returned to Cincinnati to earn her M.D. (1934). Dr.
Glueck then went on to complete her internship and residency. Afterwards, during a longer stint in Palestine, their son was born. When
the Gluecks returned to Cincinnati, the hematologist joined the faculty of her alma mater, was eventually promoted to full professorship,
and, as director of the university's coagulation lab, wrote some ninety
papers in her long career.

Helen Glueck's medical career gave her husband a first-hand
glimpse of the opposition and obstacles put in the path of professional
women. Dr. Samuel Iglauer, a professor of medicine at the University
of Cincinnati, disapproved of "women doctors" and initially tried to
discourage his daughter from entering medical school. Subsequently,
his daughter found herself among but a handful of women studying
at the UC Medical College in the early 1930s. Later, she was again
one of few—she thought but six—women to hold a full professorship
among several hundred faculty.[175] Surely his wife's scientific career
raised for her husband an example of women's professional aspirations and their ability to combine them with marriage and motherhood.

President Glueck, so his wife claimed, began to wonder "why
should we deny women the privilege of doing what they really want."
He would return from the annual CCAR meetings saying that the
rabbis argue and argue whether they should ordain women or not,
and "I don't say anything but, when I am ready, I am going to ordain
them."[176]

When Priesand completed the undergraduate program and won

admission to rabbinical school, she presented Glueck with the prospect of acting upon what he had told his board of governors four years
before: "The Hebrew Union College-Jewish Institute of Religion has
always been prepared to accept properly qualified Jews, male or female, to study for the rabbinate. If a female student should complete
the entire course, I, as the representative of the College-Institute,
would not hesitate to ordain her as a rabbi or as a rebitzen in
Israel . . . "[177] Helen Glueck recalled her husband wondering in "Sally's" first year what would happen to her. As the rabbinical student
stuck to her course, he took a real interest in her progress. His wife
claimed that he would come home saying he had checked her record
to make certain it was "okay." Responding to acclaim for one of her
speeches, he praised Priesand as an "outstanding student and a wonderful personality," adding "[w]e are very proud of her."[178]

In fact, so Helen Glueck averred, the college president ultimately
became "a father figure" to the lone female rabbinic student, stepping in for Irving Priesand who had died during his daughter's last
term at the University of Cincinnati. Priesand's rabbinic thesis, dedicated to the memories of her father and Nelson Glueck, affirms the
allusion. As he faced death, Nelson Glueck told his wife there were
three things he hoped yet to do—attend his grandson's bar mitzvah,
live in their apartment in Jerusalem, and ordain Sally.[179] But the
rabbi-archaeologist's death on 12 February 1971, of a form of leukemia
no hematologist could cure, prevented him from fulfilling his dying
wishes.

As Priesand entered her last year of rabbinical school, one major
hurdle remained—researching and writing her rabbinic thesis.
Originally she planned a critical study of the Yom Kippur Afternoon
Service. Early in 1971, Professor Jacob Petuchowski and the Committee on Academic Procedures approved her proposal to research its liturgy and current Reform practice and to compose her own service.
But, by the end of that year, Priesand had changed direction.[180]
Rather than studying the Yom Kippur Afternoon Service, she would
seek out evidence of women in the Jewish past and signs of Reform's
experience with the changing roles of Jewish women. As her research
deepened, she also found herself turning over a few pages in the history of the women who would have been rabbis.

Her rabbinic thesis, "Toward a Course of Study for Reform High School Youth Dealing with the Historic and Changing Role of the Jewish Woman," presented a curriculum for eleventh and twelfth graders surveying Jewish women from the biblical era to the present. In this wide-ranging work, she appraised the experiences of Jewish women throughout the ages, highlighting the changing role of women in Jewish history. She described women's legal position in the Bible and rabbinic literature and noted the advances Reform Judaism had made in emancipating women. She introduced future students to women's position in modern Israel, to great Jewish women like Israel's prime minister, Golda Meir, and to the contributions of women's organizations, such as the National Federation of Temple Sisterhoods. In another chapter, she examined the pejorative stereotypes of the Jewish mother and the Jewish American Princess.[181]

In the midst of her broad survey, she revealed that she had uncovered some of nearly a half-century's evidence of the debate on ordaining women rabbis. Even before her last year in rabbinical school, Priesand had become aware of a basic outline of the history of the question. Her scrapbook contained a copy of the National Federation of Temple Sisterhood's 1963 resolution on the "Ordination of Women As Rabbis," which briefly traced Reform's engagement with the question since 1922.[182] Now Priesand researched the subject further. She quoted from the CCAR report declaring "that woman cannot justly be denied the privilege of ordination." She found Martha Neumark's account of her motivations and the opposition she had faced. She uncovered Professor Lauterbach's responsum opposing women rabbis and Professor Neumark's rejoinder. And she discovered a predecessor none before her seemed to know, Regina Jonas, who, in her thesis, "Can a Woman Become a Rabbi?," had "[o]f course . . . set out to prove the affirmative."[183] In bringing to light the names of a few of the women who wanted to be rabbis, she unearthed for herself yet another tiny circle of supporters for what she hoped to achieve.

As Priesand prepared to close, at last, the history of women's quest for rabbinic ordination in Reform Judaism, she anticipated the raising of new questions and new challenges to Judaism. She called for "needed religious improvements in the Jewish woman's position," and she planned to teach her students that Reform Judaism had yet to realize, in fact, the spirit of women's equality it proclaimed, in principle. She criticized the masculine imagery dominating the liturgy, that baby boys were welcomed with far greater celebration than baby girls, that women played limited roles in Shabbat ceremonials and on Simchat Torah, and that religious school texts largely ignored Jewish women. Even as he evaluated and accepted her thesis, Professor Sylvan Schwartzman feared that "the author, in great zeal for her cause" overstated the case and that "the extensively critical tone of the work might tend to 'turn off' Reform young people from attachment to their faith." Rather than a feminist critique of Judaism, although he did not employ this term, he preferred "[m]ore of a positive approach," one that paraded "the achievement of noted Jewesses" which "would be more convincing of the enormous debt of Judaism to its women and of the justice of Reform's commitment to their total equality."[184]

That again and again the women seeking ordination appealed to the past and wrote about women and Judaism suggests far more than random coincidence. Even as Priesand dealt "with the Historic and Changing Role of the Jewish Woman," Regina Jonas had asked "Can a Woman Become a Rabbi?"; Dora Askowith had proposed that Jewish women claim their places; and Helen Levinthal had argued for woman "Suffrage from the *Halachic* Aspect." Why did these and the other debaters of the woman rabbi from the 1890s to the 1970s mine the past to illuminate the position and places of women in Judaism? Why did they constantly invoke tradition even as the women who wanted to become rabbis seemingly planned to overturn it?

Some of the answer lies in the isolation these pioneers experienced. As historian Sara Evans has observed of the young women preparing for professional careers in the 1960s, they found themselves "[t]rapped in the mystifying complexities of a popular culture" which offered them plenty of role models of women subordinating their careers to those of their husbands and few of women realizing their own ambitions. Such isolation could leave the career-bound woman, according to Evans, "paralyzed, unable to work because she had no models, no image of herself as a worker."[185]

Like the aspiring professional women Evans described for the 1960s, the women who wanted to become rabbis then and before had no models, no images of women leading in Judaism as they hoped to do. Unable to find contemporary models for their aspirations, they turned to Jewish history and tradition seeking archetypes in the female leaders of the Jewish past and asking if the weight of Jewish tradition would affirm, or at the very least not prohibit, what they hoped to do. Like Jonas, Askowith, and Levinthal and like so many of the other women all the way back to Ray Frank and Henrietta Szold engaged in the ordination debates of the past, Sally Priesand too did just this. Although the concentric circles of support—her friends and fellow students, her congregants and her audiences, the press and the men who would one day be her colleagues—helped sustain her as she persevered toward ordination, the single female rabbinic student ultimately trod a lonely path.

Thus when her turn came to explore Jewish tradition, she abandoned her plans to study liturgy for a topic far more relevant to the dream she was about to realize. And so she too invoked women in the Jewish past and the weight of its historic tradition, finding "[t]here is nothing in Jewish law that specifically prohibits the ordination of women as rabbis." Moreover, she unexpectedly revealed that indeed she "was not truly the first woman rabbi." In uncovering the example of Regina Jonas, Priesand disclosed that, in fact, the past had already set the precedent all thought was hers to claim. As she explained: "I was actually the second woman rabbi, then, although I was the first to be ordained by a theological seminary."[186] Collectively her invocation of Jewish tradition and the weight of its ancient and more recent pasts validated her ambition. Furthermore, they helped her confirm, that as a rabbi, albeit a woman rabbi, she would continue to appeal to that past, upholding the charge of her office, to maintain and affirm Judaism, never overturn it.

On 3 June 1972, the high school junior of a decade before who had written, "Although I am a girl, I would like very much to study for a rabbinical degree," was ordained rabbi, teacher, and preacher in American Israel. When HUC President Alfred Gottschalk, who had succeeded Nelson Glueck, placed his hands upon her head to confer ordination, Priesand's classmates rose to honor the first woman rabbi.

Female ordination symbolized the fulfillment of women's emancipation within Reform Judaism, the culmination of the proclamation made more than a century before that Reform held it a "sacred duty to express most emphatically the complete religious equality of the female sex."[187] The year 1972 thus came to stand then and forevermore as a benchmark for those crusading for gender equality in Judaism. But even as the new rabbi wept tears of joy and gratitude at the end of her historic journey to ordination day, Rabbi Sally Priesand was about to discover that she was beginning a journey which would soon reveal "the unbelievable and almost unbearable pressures of being the first woman Rabbi."[188]

Chapter 5

"[Q]ualifying her to teach... is one thing. Ordaining her as a rabbi is quite another"

THE DEBATE IN CONSERVATIVE JUDAISM

In March of 1972, three months before Sally Priesand stood at her ordination in Cincinnati, a group of women in New York, galvanized by the feminist movement and deeply committed to Conservative Judaism, appeared at the annual meeting of its Rabbinical Assembly. Excluded from the official program, these women, known as Ezrat Nashim,[1] organized a counter-session. There they conveyed to a sympathetic audience largely made up of rabbis' wives that "[t]he Jewish tradition regarding women, once far ahead of other cultures, has now fallen disgracefully behind . . . life-patterns open to women, appropriate or even progressive for the rabbinic and medieval periods, are entirely unacceptable to us today." Decrying the prescription "that Judaism views women as separate but equal," the young women contended it "now universally accepted that women are equal to men in intellectual capacity, leadership ability and spiritual depth." As girls, they had received the same educations as their brothers in Conservative schools and camps. As women, they saw themselves denied the "opportunity to act from this knowledge." As feminists, they deemed this "an affront to their intelligence, talents and integrity." Fed up with "apologetics" and with parades of the great Jewish women of the past, Beruriah, Deborah, and Esther, they cataloged how to bring "an end to the second-class status of women in Jewish life." In particular, they insisted "[i]t is time that: ... women be allowed full participation in religious observances" and "be permitted and encouraged to attend Rabbinical and Cantorial schools, and to perform Rabbinical and Cantorial functions in synagogues."[2]

In helping launch Conservatism's highly public wrestling with women's ordination, these women had scant knowledge of precedents, little inkling that they were not the first in Conservative Judaism to confront the question.[3] As they added yet another voice to the long debate, they, and the men and women who soon joined them, echoed those who had preceded them in constructing their explorations of the woman rabbi. Now new voices in the 1970s and 1980s appealed to the authority of the Jewish past, contending that while the tradition had never envisioned the woman rabbi, nothing in it prohibited her. And once again, those utterly convinced that Judaism forbade this, that this indeed proved one adaptation to modernity their concept of Jewish tradition could never embrace, banned her.

Conservative Judaism stands in the center of the "movements of Jewish religious modernization."[4] Struggling to stem the tide against Reform's radicalism while repudiating Orthodoxy's insularity, its leaders styled the movement as "the authentic bearer of the mainstream of the Jewish tradition."[5] As described by its premier historian, Abraham J. Karp, Conservatism evolved out of a coalition rooted in "the ideological ferment of nineteenth-century Jewish life and the sociological realities of twentieth-century America." As that ideological ferment, which challenged the inviolability of Jewish law and tradition, confronted contemporary realities, Conservative leaders sought to guide American Jews to strike the correct balance between "tradition and change," between their "insistence upon the validity of the *Halakhah* [Jewish law] and the need for taking the needs of modern American Jewish life into consideration."[6] Conservative rabbis believed themselves bound, like the sages of the Jewish past, to adjust that body of Jewish law, using time-honored legal mechanisms of interpretation. Whereas Reform jettisoned laws inimical to the spirit of the age and Orthodoxy refused, in the eyes of the Conservative rabbinate, to allow sufficient adaptations for modernity, Conservative leaders asserted their right, as a collective, to make Judaism viable for the modern world by interpreting its laws.[7]

By the early twentieth century these Conservative rabbis and scholars had developed the institutional settings of their visions. Its professors trained the men who would become rabbis at New York's Jewish Theological Seminary of America (JTS), founded in 1886. These JTS graduates found fellowship and the camaraderie of others, who shared their vision but whose rabbinical credentials came from elsewhere, in the Rabbinical Assembly, established in 1901. Its various law committees articulated just how far Conservative rabbis could adjust Judaism to speak to contemporary Jews. The congregations these men guided met for common purposes in the United Synagogue of America, created in 1913. Finally, in 1918, so that women could have their part in enriching Jewish life, the Women's League of the United Synagogue of America emerged.[8]

In these settings, the rabbis and professors worked out their vision of how to "conserve" Judaism while remaining sensitive to the realities of their day. As modernizing Jews confronted those realities, Conservative leaders struggled to preserve Judaism by sanctioning adaptations of Jewish laws. In the past, their responses to the sociological climate included permitting the use of unfermented wine for ritual purposes in Prohibition America. Contending with postwar suburban sprawl, they allowed for a change in the laws of Sabbath observance, to permit Conservative Jews to drive to synagogue on the Sabbath.

Modern Jewish life also compelled Conservative leaders to examine specific issues of women's status. In law, they had explored the permissibility of women studying Torah, and they struggled with the terrible condition of the *agunah*, which, as previously discussed, could keep a woman chained to an untenable marriage, often because her husband refused to grant her a Jewish divorce, a matter nineteenth-century Reform rabbis also had addressed. In the sanctuary, the men confronted the realities of men and women sitting together and the proliferation of bat mitzvah. In their prayerbooks, Conservative leaders emended the historic liturgy to reject as contrary to contemporary sensibilities the daily prayer in which men prayed "Blessed by He who did not make me a woman."[9] But before Ezrat Nashim decried that "[f]or three thousand years, one-half of the Jewish people have been excluded from full participation in Jewish communal life," before they demanded "women be considered as bound to fulfill all *mitzvot* [commandments] equally with men,"[10] the woman rabbi had scarcely entered the consciousness of those shaping Conservative Judaism.

Yet, the historical record does reveal that, on rare occasions, the question had butted its way briefly into Conservatism. In 1902, Henrietta Szold's application to study at the Seminary disclosed that both she and its president, Solomon Schechter, understood that others considered the woman rabbi a possibility.[11] In the early 1920s, with American Jews confronting other implications of women's newly won political emancipation and with Martha Neumark raising the question in Reform circles, both Cyrus Adler, then president of the Jewish Theological Seminary of America, and Rabbi David Aronson, a recent graduate, found themselves contemplating the woman rabbi.

Adler, a leading architect of many of the new communal institutions American Jews created in the decades around the turn of the twentieth century, was a religious traditionalist, a member, as Mary M. Cohen had been, of Philadelphia's Mikveh Israel. Holding a doctorate in Semitics, not rabbinic ordination, he succeeded Solomon Schechter as JTS president in 1916 and held that office until 1940. Nevertheless, Adler avoided ideological development of Conservative Judaism. In his autobiography he never used the term. Rather he insisted his vision of modernizing Judaism remained "orthodox."[12] In the early decades of the twentieth century, many others, like Adler, used "Orthodox" to refer to synagogues led by the men who had graduated from the Seminary, and much in the services in those synagogues then remained indistinguishable from Orthodoxy.[13]

To a reporter inquiring about the possibility of the woman rabbi, as Martha Neumark raised her challenge, the Seminary president responded unequivocally: "I am absolutely opposed to it." Given that "certain positive laws were not obligatory upon Jewish women," laws which prevented women from "presiding over the public worship," he found contemplating the prospect "utterly out of place and impossible." He averred: "I personally believe that so far as the Jewish Theological Seminary is concerned, it would not entertain the idea for a moment."[14]

Yet Adler recognized recent changes in woman's position within Judaism. He applauded efforts to educate Jewish girls and women, to create something which the Jewish people "never did have—a body of Jewishly educated Jewish women."[15] He asserted that even in matters of women's religious authority, "Jewish tradition is not so invariable on this point as people think." He uncovered that "a woman was at one time called to the Torah," that "a woman acted as 'Chazan' (Cantor) in special womens [sic] congregations," and that rabbis' wives, familiar with the Jewish dietary laws, often rendered decisions. Returning to the matter of the woman rabbi, he conceded, "I cannot say that the Jewish law expressly prohibits women from functioning as rabbis." But, so he believed, not only were no women in America qualified to become rabbis, but he could not envision "an orthodox Jewish woman desir[ing] to enter the rabbinate." Surely, any woman faithful to Jewish tradition and law, as he understood it, could not possibly contemplate stepping so far out of her assigned role. For Adler, the question of the "woman rabbi does not exist." Yet, he grasped that perhaps in the distant future, such a question would become viable. If it did, it would require an "overwhelming consensus of opinion" to violate "the tradition that the work of the rabbi, is to be done by men." Otherwise, he feared "separatist action resulting in schisms in Israel" would occur.[16]

Similarly, in 1922, a recently ordained JTS rabbi, David Aronson, revealed: "Woman is once more on the program. This time she comes chaperoned by the Central Conference of American Rabbis, and is on her way,—no, not to a Sisterhood Whist Party or to a Sabbath school entertainment,—but to assume her place in the pulpit." Aronson used this moment to bring forward "essential facts" crucial to understanding the historic position of women in Israel. He called the daughters of the biblical Zelophehad, who had demanded their share in the land of Israel, "pioneer suffragettes." He recognized that, although "a woman could not officiate in the Temple," she did join in its celebrations and that women "participated equally with the men" in rededicating the second Jewish commonwealth effected by Ezra and Nehemiah. He lauded learned Jewish women of the past, like Hulda, who "had supreme religious authority in her day." Of the rabbinic rule exempting women from the commandments observed at specific times, he noted that "even the Talmud had to admit that the rule was more honored in the breach than in the observance," that Jewish women tended "to observe, in part at least, all the possible ceremonies that the men did." However, Jewish women had not adopted the commandments of wearing prayer shawls and phylacteries, which some rabbis had ruled "obligatory upon women as upon men," nor had they historically enjoyed equal educations with their brothers.[17]

Aronson, like Adler, recognized that "coming nearer to our times," women's roles in Judaism had changed. In fact, possibly as "a result of the release of woman's energies pent up for ages," "the American Jewess takes a greater interest than her brother" in the synagogue and its attendant activities. Unlike Adler, Aronson thought that, "should any of our theological schools extend the right of ordination to women ... there will be no lack of candidates." Given that Reform congregations, so he believed, permitted women to participate equally with men, he assumed Reform Jews could offer "no logical objection to a woman-rabbi." Yet, he doubted that women would fill many pulpits, for, he surmised, the "woman who wants to live a normal life will find too many physical difficulties to prevent her from assuming such an office." As for "Orthodox congregations," there "the prejudice against woman's equality in religious matters is so great, that the very thought of the possibility of a woman-rabbi seems ridiculous."

For Aronson, as for Adler, other considerations of woman's status in Judaism loomed larger. He critiqued those synagogues which still confined women to the gallery. He recognized the need for women to advance their Jewish educations. Finally, he found inequities in Jewish divorce laws far "[m]ore important than the problem of the ordination of women." In concluding, he foresaw that the Jewish woman's "voluntary assumption of such Jewish responsibilities, and not the decision of any conference, [would] eventually determine her future position in Israel."

Adler and Aronson's early statements about women's ordination remain significant. They substantiate, as had the conversation of Szold and Schechter two decades before, that each time the possibility of the woman rabbi erupted elsewhere in American Judaism, it spilled over to Conservatism. As challengers pushed forward the question outside Conservative Judaism, those inside Conservatism discovered that the question swirling in American religious life compelled a response from their ranks too.

Moreover, their statements pointedly illustrate a key distinction between Reform and Conservative Judaism. Whereas, since the mid-nineteenth century, Reform had embraced, at least rhetorically, the liberal ideal of woman's equality, Conservative leaders in these years just as firmly upheld a Judaism which allowed for no such ideal. Thus when the struggle for women's ordination did ensue in Conservative Judaism, its champions could not advance the woman rabbi as the logical outcome of a long-standing affirmation of the parity of women with men. Instead they would have to establish that, while Conservative Judaism had never proclaimed women's equality, its interpretation of Judaism did not, in fact, preclude women from becoming rabbis.

Nevertheless, both Adler and Aronson already evidenced, as did others—rabbis, Seminary scholars, and sisterhood women—recognition and acceptance of evolution in Jewish women's places, roles, and responsibilities in America. Yet, the areas of such evolution in Conservatism remained, until the 1970s, carefully circumscribed. For example, in announcing the founding of the Women's League of the United Synagogue of America, Louis Ginzberg, Seminary professor of Talmud, who, as Conservatism's reigning *halachic* expert, was its "keeper of the law," remarked:

The changes brought about in the social-economical situation of the woman of our day demand readjustment of her position in the religious life of the Jew. Yet we feel no temptation at all to break in pieces the great legacy committed to us by the past. We must uphold the old Jewish ideal expressed in the words: "The glories of the king's daughter are within her home." . . . To make Jewish life in America function regularly, methodical work must be done by man and woman, each in his or her sphere.[18]

The women of Conservative synagogue sisterhoods found "methodical work" in their sphere in "activities . . . directed toward making our homes more truly Jewish," and they revisioned Judaism to champion educating themselves to succeed in this endeavor. For their daughters, they embraced the growing custom of confirmation, because in requiring "study of the essentials of the Jewish faith," it taught girls what they needed to know to become observant Jewish women. For both mothers and daughters, they encouraged attendance at services. There the revisioning of woman's place in Conservative synagogues permitted mixed seating. Furthermore, they sanctioned woman's right, as *The Three Pillars*, the Women's League 1927 manual, affirmed, to say *kaddish*, the memorial prayer for the dead, for their parents when there were no sons.[19]

For the Jewish Theological Seminary such revisioning of woman's place meant creating spaces for educating Jewish womanhood. In 1938, Louis Finkelstein, who soon thereafter succeeded Cyrus Adler as Seminary president, boasted: "the contribution of the Seminary to the higher education of Jewish women is in the tradition of the great rabbinic academies." He thought JTS's Teachers Institute, founded in 1909, "probably one of the first Jewish institutions of Higher Learning in this country to admit women as regular students." He credited it with bringing "into the field of Jewish education a devoted group of young women who . . . have made of our schools effective institutions for the transmission of the Jewish heritage." At the same time, he praised another JTS initiative, the Women's Institute of Jewish Studies, an adult education forum created in the early 1930s to prepare participants "for leadership in women's work."[20]

But, whenever readjusting woman's "position in the religious life of the Jew" raised the specter of women stepping outside their homes, pews, and classrooms onto the *bimah*, Seminary leaders flinched. Although the Jewish Theological Seminary "would not entertain the idea for a moment," in fact, both Adler and Aronson in the early 1920s did entertain the issue, even if only to reject it. Moreover, their responses remain striking because they presaged the points of what, a half-century later, became a vociferous debate. Adler could not say that Jewish law "expressly prohibits women from functioning as rabbis." Both understood women's *halachic* exemption from the positive time-bound commandments, including the right to lead prayer, central to the argument against their entrance into the rabbinate. Yet, both knew of exemplary women in the past observing these commandments and assuming unaccustomed roles. Furthermore, they sensed that the real underlying barriers to woman's ordination remained prejudice and tradition. Aronson fathomed the depth of "the prejudice against woman's equality in religious matters." Adler feared "schisms in Israel," because "[t]he entire fabric of Jewish law is opposed to women entering the rabbinate."[21] Half a century later these same arguments constructed in an era when the subject stood outside the boundaries of Conservatism would be reconstructed by those engaged in impassioned pleas for and against the ordination of women as Conservative rabbis.

But, in the 1920s, so Adler assumed, no woman committed to this interpretation of Judaism would possibly desire such a thing, to dare to step so far outside her sphere, to overturn tradition. In the years between Henrietta Szold's days at the Seminary and the mid-1950s, he may have been right. Apparently, no women tried to do at the Seminary what rabbis' and scholars' daughters attempted in the seminaries of liberal Judaism. The available records reveal no one pushing forward woman's ordination, or other issues of women's rights, broadly in the centers of Conservatism.[22] No Women's League leaders advanced the idea of ordination for others. No Carrie Simon or Jane Evans sprang from its ranks. No rabbis, seemingly favorably disposed, crafted abstract resolutions on the woman rabbi as had the men of the CCAR. No Seminary figure promisingly entertained the idea as had Stephen Wise. And, most critically, since without women pushing the question, the question was never practical, no women sought this for themselves at the Seminary. At HUC the professor's daughter, Martha Neumark, could raise the matter. At JTS, Helen Levinthal the daughter of the president of the Rabbinical Assembly, dare not. Even though she, like her father, remained deeply identified with Conservative Judaism throughout her life, her choice of JIR suggests that she discerned that the Seminary then denied women the training she sought.

That neither Sisterhood women, Seminary professors, nor Conservative rabbis embraced the woman rabbi in these years is not surprising. The pages of *Women's League Outlook* reflected the convictions of its writers, chiefly the wives of Seminary professors and the rabbis they trained. There one writer, typical of the Sisterhood magazine's tone in the 1930s, proclaimed: "At the risk of being declared reactionary, a menace to woman's freedom, I maintain that the greatest part the Jewish woman can play in the future of a healthy American Judaism is through the conduct of her own household."[23] Similarly, in 1936, another, Mrs. David Aronson, the by-line of Bertha Friedman Aronson, wife of the rabbi who reflected on ordaining women, cast educating Jewish women "to perpetuate the ideals of Judaism" at the heart of "Today's Challenge to the Jewish Woman."[24]

Meanwhile, in the halls of the Seminary, the scholars interpreted Conservatism's motto, "tradition and change," to favor the former over the latter. In the sacred space of the Seminary's synagogue, tradition mandated that the professors and their wives, the students and their fiancés, sit separately. Long after mixed seating symbolized Conservatism's concession to women's equality and long after it came to signify its "denominational boundary" from Orthodoxy, separation remained JTS's practice.[25]

In the years between World War I and World War II, young women sought Reform ordination on their own, spending enough time in rabbinical school to raise the issue. However, no such women appeared at the Seminary during these years. This difference not only reflects Conservatism's upholding of separate spheres for men and women's activity. It also reveals that the Seminary offered women a different place, one where they could gain the intensive Jewish education Conservative leaders embraced for them. In these years when women wished to study at the Jewish Theological Seminary, they turned or were directed to its Teachers Institute.

Founded in 1909, the successor to the Teachers Course which the Seminary announced in 1903, the Teachers Institute grew to comprise several departments. Its professional courses trained teachers for week-day Hebrew schools. Its academic department, later the Seminary College of Jewish Studies, attracted those seeking "a college for advanced Jewish studies." Its admission requirements revealed the advanced nature of these courses. Applicants had to prove that they could read biblical Hebrew, converse in the modern language, and display a broad understanding of all of Jewish history. Having won admission, students studied, in the advanced classes conducted entirely in Hebrew, a wide range of subjects, including the Bible and rabbinic literature, Hebrew language and modern Hebrew literature.[26] Here, women seeking to continue their Jewish educations beyond the Hebrew high schools of New York won access to the learning they sought.

When Henrietta Szold entered the Seminary in 1903, JTS did not yet offer the advanced courses of the Teachers Institute. The Teachers Course, whose first class convened in January 1904, "was conceived on a limited scale ... an adjunct of the rabbinical department," where first-year students began learning elementary Hebrew. In 1939, Teachers Institute Dean Mordecai M. Kaplan remarked on the striking difference between the Teachers Course and the Teachers Institute, noting "a graduate of the classes in its early years would scarcely be admitted as a student today."[27] Unquestionably, any woman, as Jewishly erudite as Szold, seeking to advance her Jewish education would not then have found it in the Teachers Course.

In fact, Szold did not stand as the only woman in these early years seeking the kind of education the rabbinical department offered. "Miss Fried[enrich?]" also appears on the roster Talmud instructor Joshua Joffe kept for the years 1905 to 1906. Perhaps she withdrew from that class, for her name was crossed out. Twenty-three years old when she entered the Seminary in 1905, with an M.A. from the University of California, Myra Mildred Friedenrich appeared again among the names of the 1906 to 1907 rabbinical course.[28] Who she was, what other background she possessed to win a place in the rabbinical course, and what she hoped to achieve from it are obscured by the dimness of the past. Only her name remains and the conviction that she must have possessed the learning essential to win a space in the classes training rabbis for American Judaism.

When, in 1909, the Teachers Institute opened, women desiring intensive, advanced Jewish educations had found their forum. They thus had little reason, as had Henrietta Szold and Myra Friedenrich, to turn to the rabbinical department.[29] Just as women constituted a majority—seven out of eleven of the graduates—of the Teachers Course, so too, they formed a majority of the students in the Teachers Institute. Its first class included twenty-two women and twelve men. By June 1935, the Teachers Institute and Seminary College of Jewish Studies had graduated 289 women and 202 men.[30] The Seminary's training of so many female teachers represented, in fact, another of its accommodations to America, a departure from the past; for historically Judaism excluded women, other than in their kitchens, from the sacred task of transmitting its legacy to the next generation.

Most of these graduates would teach "in religious schools at one time or other." Surely, many of the young women thus found themselves employed. Apparently, none of them tried to go further, to join their twenty-five male classmates, who had used this education as a springboard to the rabbinate. Instead, the women entered the classroom, staying perhaps until, perhaps even after, they began their real work, one for which their professional education had superbly prepared them, raising the next generation of Jews committed to this vision of American Judaism.[31]

Yet, in these years, on rare occasions, women did seek to go beyond the Teachers Institute. In 1923, Cyrus Adler reported that "two young ladies," graduates of the Teachers Institute, received permission to attend classes in Talmud at the Seminary.[32] Nearly two decades later, another woman made a similar request, asking if she could join the rabbinical students as they learned Talmud and Midrash. In 1941, the Seminary faculty approved Miss Zionah Maximon's request with the understanding that she would receive no credit of any sort and that she "is not to be listed as even a special student." Subsequently, Professor Louis Ginzberg examined her and assigned her a class placement.[33] Thereafter, Zionah Maximon, too, disappeared from the historical record. Who she was and what she hoped to achieve by this course of study remain unknown.[34]

Yet the particulars of the faculty's response compel reflection. The Seminary's stipulation that Zionah Maximon could neither receive credit for her work nor even claim a place as a special student provokes the historian to wonder if the men recalled the recent episode of Helen Levinthal, the daughter of one of their own rabbis. After all, only a year and a half before, *Time* magazine had ordained Helen Levinthal "as near to being a rabbi as a female might be."[35] In admitting Zionah Maximon, the professors exercised caution, granting her access to the knowledge she sought, but making certain she could never assert that having acquired this, she would claim the authority such knowledge conferred upon men.

In the interwar years, only one figure inside Conservatism, Mordecai M. Kaplan, envisioned a greater expansion of roles and opportunities for Jewish women. Kaplan, one of the most long-lived and most critical figures of twentieth-century American Jewry, was ordained at JTS in 1902. He went on to serve Orthodox congregations; to found a synagogue, the Society for the Advancement of Judaism (SAJ), to be a laboratory for his innovative ideas; and to add to his title of dean of the Seminary's Teachers Institute that of professor of homiletics. Subsequently, generations of Conservative rabbis fell under his spell. Among his greatest achievements were his comprehensive call for reconstruction of Judaism, as set forth in his classic *Judaism as a Civilization* (1934), and his ultimate creation of Reconstructionist Judaism, the fourth denomination of American Jewry.[36]

Kaplan's biographer, Mel Scult, describes him "as the father of the women's liberation movement in the Jewish community." For as Kaplan worked through his articulation of reconstructing Judaism to remain viable in the modern world, fashioning the bridge that would connect the Jewish past and the American present, he advanced, both rhetorically and, at times, in deed, the equality of women in Jewish law and in Jewish life.[37]

In *Judaism as a Civilization*, Kaplan recognized that talented Jewish women would "lose interest in Jewish life," unless Jewish leaders "find in Judaism a place for their powers." In *The Future of the American Jew* (1948), he developed this idea more fully:

Few aspects of Jewish thought and life illustrate so strikingly the need of reconstructing Jewish law as the traditional status of the Jewish woman. In Jewish tradition, her status is unquestionably that of inferiority to the man.... [T]his status must be changed. She must attain in Jewish law and practice a position of religious, civic, and juridical equality with the man, and this attainment must come about through her own efforts and initiative. Whatever liberal-minded men may do in her behalf is bound to remain but a futile and meaningless gesture. The Jewish woman must demand the equality due her as a right to which she is fully entitled.[38]

When Kaplan called for reconstructing Jewish tradition to grant women equality, he proved himself, as he did in other matters, prescient, for he understood, that only when Jewish women would take charge of the project, could their emancipation go forward. Until that would occur, all the actions of "liberal-minded men" were but gestures.

Kaplan's creation of the first bat mitzvah—in 1922, at the SAJ, for his daughter Judith—a landmark in the annals of women's emancipation in Judaism,[39] denoted one of these gestures. In its first years, the bat mitzvah did not mean, even at the SAJ, full equality for women. Then, although held on Shabbat morning, bat mitzvah girls ascended the *bimah* after the reading of the *haftarah* to read or chant not, as bar mitzvah boys do, from a Torah scroll, but rather "an interesting section from the Hebrew Bible." More importantly, while many girls had bat mitzvahs at SAJ, twenty years passed before the congregation called grown women to the Torah.[40] This suggests that, in the first half of the twentieth century, the roles assumed by the bat mitzvah girl marked a once-in-a-lifetime event, a concession to Jewish girls coming-of-age, not a vehicle for overturning traditional gender roles in the synagogue.

Moreover, Kaplan's rhetoric, in these years, disclosed that, even in his imagination, the paradigm of separate religious spheres, which Conservative Jews, and most American Jews, so staunchly honored, persisted. In 1932, while addressing Hadassah's annual convention, he pleaded with the women "to launch a great popular movement for Jewish adult education," as their contribution to American Jewish life. Here the professor pronounced that "higher Jewish learning of the specialized type will naturally remain the province of the man."[41] Thus, even Kaplan, the most liberal of the Seminary professors, could not then imagine that "higher Jewish learning," and the role it conferred, as other than the natural prerogative of men. Surely, in these years, the female rabbi did not yet represent for Conservative men and women the logical extension of reconstructing woman's roles in Judaism. She would wait in the wings until Jewish women themselves would take the "initiative." Then Kaplan and those who joined him would understand her to be the obvious outcome of "the equality due her as a right."

In the first postwar decade, while Reform leaders pondered the example of Paula Ackerman and studied anew the question of ordaining women rabbis, Conservative rabbis found themselves responding to the critique that "[w]e are still operating upon the Orthodox assumption that the basic inequality of the woman must be preserved in the law." Having "observed, in our own country, and in others, the struggle to emancipate the woman from the domination of the man in political and social life,"[42] the men of the Rabbinical Assembly resolved to seek "equalization of the status of women in Jewish law as a true expression of a Torah of justice."[43] They would find that equality not in the far-fetched notion of ordaining women but rather in granting another symbolic concession, the right of going up to bless the Torah, to have an *aliyah.* In 1955, two rabbis, Aaron Blumenthal and Sanders Tofield, presented to their colleagues responsa which sanctioned a change from the historic past, granting women the right, "whether in the blanket permissive form ... Or ... on special occasions," to have *aliyot.*[44]

But not everyone agreed. Rabbi Gershon Winer asked: "Is there a crying need of privileges being denied? Are our women folk asking for these particular privileges?"[45] Not only did Conservative women then not clamor for this right,[46] but, he believed, changing woman's role in the synagogue portended "dangerous implications for our movement."[47]

Another saw this danger too, but from a different perspective. In 1955, sociologist Marshall Sklare, in what became his classic work, *Conservative Judaism*, perceived the anomalous position of woman "[p]erhaps the single most disruptive force, or 'strain,' to American Jewish Orthodoxy." Noting that "the inferior position of women" transgressed Western norms, Sklare understood: "Even though change will entail a serious violation of the religious code and the overcoming of much resistance, a *status quo* position would mean organizational suicide." Yet, so far "there has been no widespread agitation for perfect equality. Conservative women have generally been satisfied with their limited status—a great advance over the age-old segregation."[48]

Certainly, in the 1950s, the only issue related to their emancipation pursued by those in Women's League was to request their rabbis to "take more definite and positive steps towards . . . [a] complete solution of the problem of equality in divorce and marriage," to resolve the *agunah* question.[49] Nevertheless, already some young women, who, in these years, thought they would like to become Conservative rabbis, left behind traces that once this was their dream.

In 1957, less than a month after the *New York Times* reported "Women as Rabbis Urged at Parley"[50] and but a few months before the first co-ed of the Undergraduate Program would find her way to Hebrew Union College, a young woman wrote Seminary president Louis Finkelstein. She claimed "Eversince [*sic*] I was a child it has been my ambition to become a conservative rabbi." The young woman had graduated from the Shulamith School for Girls, the first Jewish day school for girls in the United States,[51] and from the Yeshivah of Flatbush High School. Now she studied at Brooklyn College during the day and attended the Midrasha (Hebrew or teachers college) at the Yeshiva of Flatbush in the evening. "As you can readily see," she wrote to Finkelstein, "I have had an extensive Hebrew education. However, I am now interested in entering the Seminary as a rabbinical student. I feel that I am capable of overcoming any barriers that may stand in the way of achieving my goal; to be a religious and cultural leader of my people."[52]

A young man with these credentials would certainly have been welcome in the seminary's rabbinical school.[53] But Gladys Citrin received a different response. Louis Finkelstein told her:

There is no reason at all why you, or any other Jewish girl who so desires, should not devote her time to intensive studies of Judaism. However, in the Jewish tradition, the place of women in religion is to be high priestesses in the sanctuary of their home and we want them to become good wives and good mothers in Israel. It is not our thought that they should make a life calling out of the rabbinate. That would be contrary to the whole tradition for while the Jewish tradition knows of women who were prophetesses, like Deborah, but who were presumably also running a household at the same time, and while Judaism knows of many learned Jewish women, there is no precedent for a woman serving as rabbi in a congregation in the manner in which men serve. I would therefore encourage you in every way to continue your studies. Perhaps you would come to our Teachers Institute and become a teacher. It is not possible for a woman to be ordained as rabbi in our tradition.[54]

Like his predecessor, Cyrus Adler, Finkelstein believed "our tradition" had no place for the woman rabbi. Like all engaged in the debate, he comprehended the challenge to his position posed by women who had indeed in the past stood as religious and cultural leaders of the Jewish people. Thus he declared that surely Deborah ran her home at the same time that she prophesied. Registering the shifts he did endorse for Jewish women in his time and place, he welcomed Jewish girls devoting themselves to "intensive studies of Judaism." Thus he directed Miss Citrin to the Teachers Institute. Surely, this would help prepare her to become a good wife and mother in Israel, "a high priestess in the sanctuary of her home." Becoming a rabbi in the sanctuary of a synagogue was impossible. At the very same time that Finkelstein's Reform counterpart, Nelson Glueck, rhetorically embraced women's ordination, Finkelstein recorded unequivocal opposition.

Gladys Citrin, however, was not the only young woman, in the 1950s, to refute Cyrus Adler's contention that women in his sector of Judaism could not possibly desire such a thing. Perhaps because of the spillover of the debate from Reform circles, perhaps because of the attention then given to women in the ministry in the press, women committed to Conservatism years later recalled thinking back then they wanted to be rabbis. For example, Elaine Mann eventually did become a leader of her people through her career in Jewish communal work. Back in the 1950s, as a college and Hebrew college student, she thought, off and on, about the rabbinate.[55] In the late 1970s, other women reported that they had been waiting more than twenty years for the Seminary to consider ordaining women. As one explained, she never wanted to go to the Teachers Institute, never wanted to become a teacher; she wanted to become a rabbi.[56]

However, in the 1950s, except for the single record of Gladys Citrin's request, Conservative leaders had little reason to suspect that the growing debate about women's ordination in Christianity and in Reform Judaism could spill over to the Seminary. They did not foresee that, over the course of the 1960s, more girls would arrive at the same place that Sally Priesand, and those who had gone before her, had reached. Some, like Sandy Eisenberg, who began thinking about becoming a rabbi in 1963, came from Reform settings. But others sprang from Conservatism. Eileen G. Leiderman later wrote that she would have, if she could have, studied for the rabbinate at JTS in 1966. Jan Kaufman reached her decision to study there as a seventh-grader in 1967.[57] Some of these women, coming of age as the 1960s gave way to the 1970s, rode the crest of the new wave of American feminism. As they did, they discovered not only one woman persevering toward ordination at HUC but a new Seminary welcoming the women who wanted to become rabbis, the Reconstructionist Rabbinical College (RRC).

Frustrated by Conservatism's refusal to reconstruct Judaism to meet the modern world, as they believed it must, the Reconstructionists had at last broken ranks to found the fourth denomination of American Judaism. Although Kaplan had long preferred that Reconstructionism remain an influential "school of thought," in 1968, five years after he retired as Seminary professor, the RRC opened in Philadelphia.[58] Under its founding president, Ira Eisenstein, the RRC trumpeted that no longer would the Reconstructionists expect the Seminary to train rabbis disseminating their vision of modern Judaism. Now they would train their own. Moreover, the RRC would respond to Kaplan's call, of a half century before, to revision the position of woman in Judaism. In an earlier era according woman "religious, civic, and juridical equality with the man" still meant that "higher Jewish learning of the specialized type will naturally remain the province of the man." But by 1968, as women all over America "demand[ed] the equality due [them] as a right," the "higher Jewish learning" of the Reconstructionist Rabbinical College, and the degree it conferred, would be offered to men—and to women.

According to Eisenstein, the question of training women for the rabbinate had not come up earlier among the Reconstructionists.[59] As he explained, in resisting the denominational split indicative of the founding of a seminary, Kaplan was not thinking about ordaining rabbis of any kind. Not until 1967, when the Federation of Reconstructionist Congregations and Havurot committed to raise the money for the school, did plans go forward. When posters announcing a new school for the training of rabbis invited applicants, Eisenstein assumed they would include qualified women. It "never occurred to us even to debate the matter." He believed accepting women as candidates for the rabbinate the "obvious thing to do,"[60] the logical extension, in the midst of the burgeoning Women's Liberation movement, of the commitment to reconstruct woman's place in Judaism.

No women found their way into RRC's first class of thirteen. But a year later, in 1969, Sandy Eisenberg crossed its portals. Born in Philadelphia in 1947, Eisenberg became deeply attached to her Reform temple, Keneseth Israel, in her teens.[61] Vice-president of her temple youth group, she led services and gave sermons. Her entry in her temple's essay contest won her a trip to Israel. Keneseth Israel's rabbis, including Arnold Fink, brother of Toby Fink who had wanted to be a rabbi, became her role models. Inspired by the moment of her confirmation, she began thinking she would follow in their footsteps.

When Eisenberg first thought about becoming a rabbi, she did not, so she later claimed, know that women did not do this. Later she recalled reading something in religious school which observed that no woman had been ordained—yet. By and large she kept her dream secret. Although she wrote a short story about a girl who wants a career no woman has, she refused to divulge to her classmates what that career was. Finally, she told Rabbi Bertram Korn, senior rabbi of Keneseth Israel, who encouraged her.

In college at Philadelphia's Temple University, Eisenberg majored in religion. Thinking to do graduate work in this field, she wavered about the rabbinate. Aware of her indecision, Rabbi Korn invited her, in her last year of college, to write and lead a service for the congregation.[62] When it was over, the congregants were moved, and she had resolved: "Judaism is so important to me that I decided I wanted to devote my life to it, to being a leader in the Jewish community."[63]

By now, she knew of Sally Priesand at HUC. Yet, Eisenberg was drawn to the Reconstructionist Rabbinical College. As an undergraduate, she had discovered that much of what she had learned about Judaism derived from Kaplan's thought. Furthermore, the RRC expected all students to complete the rabbinical course and a Ph.D. at Temple University, and she had already received her acceptance from Temple's grad school. Uncertain about what kind of reception she would find out in the field, thinking the Ph.D. assured her the option of a career in academe, she enrolled in RRC in the fall of 1969.

In her first year of rabbinical school, she came to know fellow student Dennis Sasso. In June 1970, they wed. As they stood under the *huppah*, Bertram Korn called their wedding historic: "For the first time in the story of Judaism, two students for the rabbinate are being wed."[64] In reality this represented the first time that such a wedding did not mean that one of those students would find her title, not rabbi, but *rebbetzin*.

Meanwhile, the press began to circle around Eisenberg Sasso as it had circled around Priesand. It reported on the "rabbi in mini-skirts" and highlighted that she would not be the first woman rabbi, but that she would follow Sally Priesand. Some news accounts even added that "the only known female rabbi was Regina Jonas."[65]

As soon as the Jewish community discovered that Eisenberg Sasso, in a short while, would become a rabbi, she found herself parrying remarks like, "you look like a normal American girl" and "what would prompt a Jewish girl to have the *hutzpah*" to do this. She discovered that some thought she should teach in her husband's religious school, not lead as a rabbi on her own.[66]

To fashion responses to her critics, she turned, as so many others before her had, to the position of women in Jewish tradition. Not wanting, however, to be identified solely with this subject, she planned to write her dissertation on liturgy.[67] Nevertheless, as she sought in the Jewish past affirmation for what she hoped to do, she found herself speaking and writing widely about women in Jewish tradition.

In 1973, she published a birth ritual for girls in the same special issue of *Response* magazine which reported on Henrietta Szold's days at the Seminary and which Ezrat Nashim member, Liz Koltun, edited. There Eisenberg Sasso asserted that even as God made the covenant with Abraham, he also promised to make Sarah a mother of nations. For her, this affirmed that "it is through the whole community, males and females, that Jewish life is perpetuated."[68]

A year earlier, she presented to the annual meeting of the American Jewish Committee in New York City, "Women and the Bible: Lessons for Today." Using the book of Ruth as her springboard, she understood that the narrative of the great-grandmother of King David revealed that "[w]oman attains her highest station in Biblical life when she becomes the mother of sons." This and evidence of the biblical laws of marriage and divorce forced her to conclude that the Bible assigned women an "inferior status." Yet, she argued for "a positive side to the picture," bringing forward evidence of "women's social and religious standing in the community," by pointing to Deborah and Miriam, to women's right to take "part in religious gatherings," and to the tradition which required children to honor mother and father "equally." Turning to later eras in Judaism, she found that the rabbis extended "[m]any protections" to women, especially in the laws of marriage. But as times changed, Judaism changed. Now Reform and Reconstructionist Judaism have "granted women equal standing with men." Nevertheless, even here barriers of sentiment linger: "For with the same breath that liberal Jews praise woman rabbinical students, they ask the women to serve the coffee and cake." And so she asked Judaism to push forward, to create "full opportunity for women in all areas of Jewish life," to embrace the kinds of changes she, as a rabbinical student, had begun to develop in her "B'rit B'not Israel—A Covenantal Birth Ceremony for the Jewish Daughter." Yet, even as she urged a broader vision of the emancipation of women within Judaism, she paused to explode the charge that in seeking to change tradition, she was bent on its destruction. She affirmed: "This creation must necessarily be founded on a knowledge and commitment to Jewish life. . . . I do not propose to annul 2000 years of tradition."[69]

In 1974, newly ordained Rabbi Sandy Eisenberg Sasso became rabbi of Manhattan Reconstructionist Congregation. Three years later, in the fall of 1977, she and her husband found jobs at Indianapolis's Beth El Zedeck, a congregation affiliated with both the Conservative and Reconstructionist movements. She thus became the first woman rabbi in a Conservative congregation.[70] But by then the furor over women's ordination was well under way in Conservative Judaism.

In the early 1970s, even as the new wave of American feminism continued to surge, and with the first women rabbis finding their places in Reform and Reconstructionist Judaism, a new force, an emerging Jewish feminism, helped propel the debate into Conservatism. Jewish feminism began, as Anne Lapidus Lerner, an instructor in modern Hebrew literature at the Jewish Theological Seminary, described in 1976, "as a series of isolated questionings in the shadow of the women's movement."[71] These isolated questions emerged amidst the euphoria sweeping American Jewry in the wake of Israel's victory in the 1967 Six-Day War and out of the "counterculture" alternatives young Jewish activists, like those in the Havurah movement, created to the establishments in which they had been raised. The Jewish feminist movement included college and graduate students who found themselves "torn in two." Their feminism promised them intellectual and spiritual equality with their male peers, but their Judaism relegated them to second-class status in the synagogue and within Jewish law.[72]

Signs of this emerging Jewish feminism, and of its impact upon Conservative Judaism, surfaced even before Ezrat Nashim issued its public call to the Rabbinical Assembly in 1972. For example, in 1970, the National Women's League invited both Trude Weiss-Rosmarin and Judith Hauptman to speak. Hauptman, then a student in Talmud at the Seminary, presented a feminist critique of prayer, arguing that, in the past, Jewish women had been obligated to pray and that they should take it upon themselves to do so now. Already in 1970, Rabbi Philip Sigal, a member of the Rabbinical Assembly's Committee on Jewish Law and Standards, considered the question of the inclusion of women in the *minyan*, the quorum of ten necessary for public prayer. And in these early years, too, Rabbi Fishel Pearlmutter, who later led the crusade for Conservative women rabbis from within the Rabbinical Assembly, began calling from the convention floor for the admission of female rabbis to the RA.[73]

In the early 1970s, Conservative leaders, especially those in the Rabbinical Assembly's Committee on Jewish Law and Standards, launched a multipronged examination of the status of women, even before, even as the women of Ezrat Nashim clamored for this. Bound to abide by *halachah*, unable to utter the sweeping verdict of the Reformers who had deemed "it is a sacred duty to express most emphatically the complete religious equality of the female sex,"[74] Conservative leaders found themselves considering what adjustments they could accept to equalize women within Judaism. In 1973, by a vote of nine to four—after, as the press reported, "women students at New York's Jewish Theological Seminary argued vigorously for recognition of their rights as 'complete persons' "—the committee ruled that women could count in the quorum of ten necessary for a *minyan*.[75] In 1974, Rabbi Aaron Blumenthal, who, two decades before, had argued for the "gesture" of *aliyot* for women, surveyed a range of issues governing their status. He addressed, among others, emending the masculine language of the Hebrew liturgy to include women in prayer, having women recite reciprocal vows in the wedding ceremony, and requiring them to study Torah. He asked whether or not they could serve as witnesses and could fulfil *mitzvot* which they were not required to perform. Paramount among the questions he raised was the emblem of women's Jewish emancipation, the symbolic marker of her religious equality, ordaining women rabbis.[76]

Now for the first time those within Conservatism—articulate and feminist women, some of whom wanted to be rabbis; rabbis and Seminary scholars, including some of the first women to teach there—debated the woman rabbi in the open. As forces from without—"now two rabbinical schools do ordain women"[77]—collided with forces from within—including the first women to request admission to JTS rabbinical school since Gladys Citrin, they launched a protracted and agonizing debate with Conservative Judaism. As the first young women sought admission to the Seminary's rabbinical school, Conservative elites found themselves entertaining, for far longer than a moment, the idea of ordaining women as rabbis.

In a broad overview of the organizational diffusion of women's ordination, sociologist Mark Chaves asserted later conflicts over women's ordination proved "much more wrenching than early, truly innovative, adoption." Such later struggles "look more like 'bottom-up' social movements. . . . Post-1970 conflicts over women's ordination are much more contentious, much more divisive, and much more painful for denominations . . ." Pointing specifically to female ordination in the Episcopal Church and to the protracted struggle in Roman Catholicism, he argued that in these later conflicts "organizational elites still are key players," but they are joined by "key actors . . . female seminarians" who push the question from the bottom-up, as they "form organizations, mobilize constituencies, and conduct 'illegitimate' actions." Moreover, after 1970, those favoring women's ordination "face[d] organized countermovements."[78] Certainly, Chaves's observations provide a comparative context for understanding the difficult, if nevertheless, relatively short course of the question of women as Conservative rabbis.[79]

Over a bit more than a decade, from 1972 to 1983, Conservative leaders found themselves inextricably engaged in an intricate political dance of shifting alliances, studies undertaken, commissions formed, hearings held, motions tabled, and votes counted. Each twist and turn of the question in these years, as the ball was thrown from one arena of Conservative Judaism to another, and as the national and Jewish presses followed it, reflected just how "divisive" and "painful" the prospect of women's ordination was for those enmeshed in the debate.

The historian seeking to reconstruct the trajectory of the question could trace its course, at times, on a month-by-month basis.[80] In March 1972, at the Rabbinical Assembly convention, Ezrat Nashim clamored for women to become rabbis and cantors. In February 1973, the faculty of the Seminary refused to admit women to the rabbinical school. In November 1973, the United Synagogue of America resolved in favor of the admission of qualified women to JTS rabbinical school. In May 1974, Rabbinical Assembly President Judah Nadich urged his colleagues to admit ordained women to their ranks in the hopes of influencing the Seminary's policies on this matter. In June 1974, the Rabbinical Assembly's Committee on Jewish Law and Standards voted nine to three that women could not be rabbis and cantors. In April 1975 and March 1976, the Rabbinical Assembly tabled motions in favor of admitting rabbis regardless of sex and encouraging

JTS to admit men and women to its rabbinical school. In May 1977, the Rabbinical Assembly tabled this motion again, only after hammering out with the Seminary an agreement to create a commission to study the question.[81]

The Commission for the Study of the Ordination of Women as Rabbis convened in December 1977. It held public hearings and conducted surveys to ascertain Conservative Jews' opinions. Its members considered papers, examining aspects of the question, including whether or not *halachah* permitted ordination of women. At the end of its deliberations in December 1978, eleven commission members agreed *"[t]here is no direct halakhic objection to the acts of training and ordaining a woman to be a rabbi, preacher, and teacher in Israel."* Therefore, they recommended "that qualified women be ordained as rabbis in the Conservative Movement" and encouraged their admission in the class entering in September 1979. Three commission members dissented, opposing the ordination of women for, among other reasons "the possible disruption of the unity of the Movement," asking, instead, "that appropriate roles be created for Jewish women short of ordination so that their commitment and talents may be a source of blessing and not of unnecessary controversy."[82]

In January 1979, JTS Chancellor Gerson Cohen presented the findings to the Rabbinical Assembly. A vote by the Seminary faculty on the question was postponed—from May to the following academic year. By December 1979, the increasingly organized opposition, led by the Seminary's senior Talmud faculty, had mobilized. Sixteen faculty threatened to boycott a vote on the question, arguing in a well-publicized Conference on Halakhic Process that "Jewish law forbids the participation of women as rabbis." The result was that, in December 1979, the Seminary Senate tabled, by a vote of twenty-five to nineteen, the motion on admitting women to rabbinical school "until such time as a balanced committee of Talmudic scholars . . . has completed a systematic study of the status of women in Jewish law." In the meantime the Seminary tried to start a program of religious ministry for women seeking an alternative to the rabbinate. In May 1980, the Rabbinical Assembly responded by going "on record as favoring the ordination of women."[83]

As of 1980, the question appeared to be shelved—for a long or short run, no one knew. But in 1983 the RA tried to force the question out in the open again by considering admitting to its ranks a woman ordained at HUC-JIR. Her membership failed, only four votes short of the 75 percent majority required. That sparked Chancellor Cohen to announce in the late spring of 1983 that he would bring the issue forward again the following fall. In October 1983, the Seminary faculty voted to admit women to the rabbinical school. In the fall of 1984 twenty-three women entered the Seminary as rabbinical students. A year later, in May 1985, Chancellor Cohen presided over the ordination of Amy Eilberg as rabbi, teacher, and preacher in American Israel.[84]

The many accounts of Conservatism's political struggle over women's ordination highlighted the personal motivations, partisan strategies, and intellectual, ethical, and *halachic* rationalizations of Conservatism's elites—Seminary faculty and scholars, Rabbinical Assembly rabbis and their officers—embroiled in the debate. As the press broadcast to a wide public the twists and turns of the contest,[85] these elites, in some thirty-five responsa and *halachic* studies evaluated the question.[86] As they did, they turned both to Jewish tradition and to what they knew of the history of ordaining women rabbis, to see if, as they understood it, Judaism could embrace this response to modernity.

In these studies, like those written for the Commission for the Study of the Ordination of Women as Rabbis, these elites mined the Jewish past. They started from the premise, as Seminary vice-chancellor Simon Greenberg explained, that the Conservative movement mandates that "in studying, interpreting, and applying a traditional text one should take into account not only the literal meaning of its content, but also its history." Thus the scholars considered the "historic aspects of the questions before us." Given Conservatism's commitment to *halachah*, they surveyed the specific legal obstacles Jewish law placed in the path of the women who wanted to be rabbis.[87] These experts found, in the legal barriers to woman's assumption of certain roles in Jewish life, proof of "woman's generally subservient position in society." Nevertheless, they also brought forward evidence to the contrary to show women in the Jewish past who had led their people and who had asserted their rights. They recounted the examples of Miriam, who led "the Israelite women in dance and song"; of the daughters of Zelophehad, "the first women known to history who dare to speak up for their rights"; and, of course, of Deborah.[88]

Moreover, these scholars emphasized that the rabbinate they proposed opening to women was, as Seminary professor Robert Gordis explained, "virtually a new calling." Although the title was ancient, the functions of the modern rabbi, in which the rabbi had become chiefly preacher and teacher, counselor and guide, represented "a *novum* in Jewish experience."[89]

Some related what they knew of the particular history of this specific question. Seminary professor Anne Lapidus Lerner found in the experience of Henrietta Szold at the Seminary that "the idea of rabbinic ordination of women was not a complete impossibility in the first decade of the century" and that "the issue of ordaining women was probably first directly raised in this country in 1922" by Reform rabbis. She examined Conservatism's own encounter with other questions of women's status, such as the *agunah*. Others praised especially Conservative Judaism's ringing endorsement of teaching women Torah.[90]

Many referred to the way in which "the times" reflected changes, changes which, as Robert Gordis explained, proved that "expression of the inferior status of women . . . hardly comports with the realities of present-day life." To buttress their arguments, they reported that the times had not only affected Conservative women, but that Orthodox women too had expanded their sphere. Simon Greenberg specifically pointed to the charismatic Orthodox teacher, *rebbetzin* Esther Jungreis, who, before a "mixed audience," had "delivered a rousing Torah-filled address urging her listeners to return to the ways of the Torah."[91]

Even as such examinations retraced the paths taken by those who had encountered this question before, whether for themselves or for others, these later contestants in the battle over women's ordination by and large ignored the crucial key players, the women who wanted to be rabbis. While those with the power to ordain or to admit women rabbis to their ranks held the keys to the successful resolution of the question, without the women who wanted to be Conservative rabbis, there never was any question. For the prospect of women's ordination was never viable—not when women considered it in the *Reform Advocate* in 1897, not when Reform rabbis conceded it in their 1956 "Report on the Ordination of Women," and not at the Seminary in 1957 or 1972 or 1983—unless women wanted this for themselves.

Understanding these key players, who they were and how they came to raise the question, what paths they pursued as the political debates followed their torturous course, who encouraged them and discouraged them, and where they found themselves when the Seminary decided to allow them to become that which they wished to be, is imperative to this history. These women, the first to ask the Seminary to reconsider its stance on the admission of women to the rabbinical school, lived at the hub of the swirling controversy in Conservative Judaism. As individuals, they raised the issue; defeated, some went away, but others sought out new strategies to claim that which they so passionately sought. Moreover, in the end, they, and their growing collective body of supporters, affirmed that no matter how long Conservative elites denied women the opportunity to serve their people as rabbis, the question would remain open. As one commission member recognized, their presence assured that a negative decision on the question would be "merely a temporary one, one which will be appealed repeatedly until, in our lifetime or thereafter, it is overturned."[92]

In the early 1970s, the first women committed to Conservative Judaism and sensitive to the emerging Jewish feminism began to seek admission to JTS's rabbinical school. With their very first request they signaled that they constituted a nascent collective, that in Conservative Judaism women would not seek to become rabbis as isolated individuals. Within days of Sally Priesand's ordination, in June 1972, not one, but two Brandeis students wrote to Gerson Cohen. They told Cohen, the new Seminary chancellor, Louis Finkelstein's successor: "Learning, teaching and leadership are essential for the well-being of the community." Quoting the rabbinic text, *Ethics of the Fathers*, Beverly Weintraub and Nancy Forse asserted that it "implies that these must be pursued by all who take upon themselves responsibility as Jews. The paradox is that we feel this responsibility, yet we are denied the chance to fulfill our aspirations to become rabbis." They claimed to have reached this conclusion on their own, and that "[u]ntil recently we did not even know of any other group pressing for women's rights in Judaism." At Brandeis, they had organized a "women's *minyan*," played leading roles in Hillel, the Jewish student association, and taken courses in Jewish studies. Describing themselves as observant in practice, wishing to study only at JTS, and believing the rabbinate compatible "with a rich family life," they concluded: "We would not choose to be accepted as token women any more than we'd want to be rejected on the basis of sex. In light of this we request that you take steps to reconsider the Seminary's policy on admission of women to the rabbinical program. In a world full of perplexed Jews, please help us to be numbered among the guides."[93]

Already, they did not stand alone in their plea to be numbered among Conservatism's guides. Susannah Heschel, the daughter of JTS luminary theologian Abraham Joshua Heschel, hoped to follow in her father's footsteps. As a "big girl" of seven or eight, "Susie" had despaired when she found herself banished from her father's side in synagogue, required to take her place among the women. Later when she had pleaded to have her bat mitzvah at the Seminary, Louis Finkelstein had offered her, instead, a party. But now, with Cohen at the helm, she and, so she claimed, her father thought things might change. Even before Priesand's ordination, Susannah Heschel went to ask Professor Cohen if the Seminary would teach her to become a rabbi.[94]

Meanwhile, another young woman simultaneously turned to Cohen. In *Women's League Outlook*, in the winter of 1973, he shared part of her letter. Its author wrote, that given that Conservative institutions had "educate[d] girls on the same basis as boys,"

> the groundwork is laid to produce someone like myself who finds a great deal of fulfillment in studying Judaica and in working with people from a Jewishly oriented standpoint.
>
> Then what happens? If one is a Conservative Jew, one naturally looks to the Seminary to continue one's training in rabbinical studies—and ultimately to receive ordination as a Rabbi.[95]

Who were these young women and how, over the course of the mid-1970s, had they come to ask for admission to the Seminary?[96] Like the Reform women who sought a rabbinical education, they represented the shining products of their movement. As Sandy Levine, who first applied to JTS in the fall of 1973,[97] explained, they were reared in Conservative synagogues and educated in its Hebrew schools. If they had had a bat mitzvah, although only one girl in Beverly Weintraub's Hebrew class had, it had likely been on a Friday night, like that of Joan Friedman, not on a Saturday morning, like those of her male Hebrew school classmates. As teens, they had joined Conservative youth movements, traveling as Amy Eilberg did across the United States with United Synagogue Youth (USY). They had enjoyed powerful experiences of Jewish leadership in these groups, as for example, Sandy Levine, who became president of her USY region, and Debra Cantor, who served as vice-president of hers.[98] Summers had brought them to Ramah, the network of Conservative camps founded in the wake of World War II. Years later, many, like Carol Glass, recalled how Ramah inspired them; how, as Judith Hauptman recalled, Ramah allowed girls to lead certain prayers, which, in other Conservative settings then, girls and women could not do.[99]

Many of these young women had decided their course as children or in their teens, long before *Newsweek* discovered Sally Priesand. They had wanted to be rabbis ever since they were "rabbi" in their junior congregations where girls, like Sandy Levine, did all that boys did, leading services, reading Torah, and wearing a yarmulke. Some, like Beverly Weintraub, confided their youthful dream only to their diaries. Others remembered, as Joan Friedman did, that friends knew about their ambitions and teased them in high school—calling them "rabbi" or singling them out as the future "first lady rabbi."

Almost all fell under the influence, at least indirectly, of resurgent feminism's promise that women can and ought to be able to do anything men did. Leslie Alexander remembered that, when she was growing up in the 1960s and early 1970s, her parents told her, "I could do anything that I wanted to do." Feminism affirmed these young women's, and their parents', expectations that, of course, they would go on to college and then to graduate school and a career.

Most found themselves encouraged by their rabbis. Many mentioned Brandeis Hillel Rabbi Al Axelrod. Almost all recalled their own growing awareness of the emerging Jewish feminism. They had participated in the very first "isolated questionings in the shadow of the women's movement"—the women's *minyan* of Hillel's 1971 summer leadership conference, a *Simchat Torah* celebration at the University of Pennsylvania that gave co-eds their first chance to dance with the Torah, or their first glimpse of women praying with *tallit* and *tefillin* at the February 1973 Jewish Feminist Conference. They began to learn, as Nina Cardin had, if they did not already know, "how to read Torah, to *daven*, to put on *tallit* and *tefillin*, and to lead Services."[100] Already, some carried their new ideas about what they had learned home to Conservative institutions, this time not as campers, but as staff at Ramah.

To the very first of their petitions for admission—that of the Brandeis students in the summer of 1972, Chancellor Cohen responded by encouraging them to "write formally and individually to Rabbi Joseph Brodie, Registrar of the Rabbinical School, and request an application for admission to the Rabbinical School." He assured them that "to the degree that I can exercise my authority as Chancellor, your applications will be considered, and as objectively as possible." But, he cautioned: "even if the Seminary should admit women to the Rabbinical School, there is no guarantee that the Rabbinical Assembly will admit them as members." Well aware of the public interest in the question, he pleaded with them not to share his letter with the press, not to make of their "application a cause celebre. Indeed in avoiding sensationalism, it seems to me, you and your advocates have the best chance of expecting the kind of change to which you aspire."[101]

The chancellor's caution about the press's tendency to sensationalize the woman rabbi was well-founded. Even as he received Weintraub and Forse's letter, an enterprising *New York Times* reporter, tracking the challenge of Ezrat Nashim, concluded from his remarks that "the Conservative Jewish Theological Seminary would not summarily reject the idea today." Already Cohen had carefully, but publicly, put forth that this "would have to be a decision of a multiple nature. . . . I, for one, would urge serious consideration if a woman applied who was qualified academically, characterologically, and religiously, and I would urge the faculty and my colleagues in the Rabbinical Assembly to consider it."[102]

With the first of the women applying to the Seminary's rabbinical school, Cohen kept to his word, bringing forward to the faculty, early in the winter of 1973, the question: "Do we re-affirm the present policy of admitting female students to courses but not to a program leading to ordination, or do we change our policy?"[103] As the faculty "beg[a]n the conversation toward the eventual reaching of a consensus," Senior Talmud Professor Saul Lieberman summarily rejected the prospect. When the men asked if there were "any Halachic objections," he "replied that it was forbidden." But others disagreed, understanding that Jewish law in no way prohibited women from fulfilling most of the modern rabbi's roles. Another thought the solution lay in finding "another title for a woman reflecting on her academic preparedness to lead with religious expertise." The men understood that they had to consider the internal politics of the Conservative movement. What would the Rabbinical Assembly do if the Seminary ordained women? Finally, they briefly contemplated these women who sought "to be responsible agents of the Jewish community," who asserted they would take "on equal responsibility with men." Failing to reach consensus, the faculty tabled the matter for the time being.[104]

Thus, even as women who wanted to be Conservative rabbis continued to write to the Seminary, they received letters advising them "[f]or the present . . . every single course in the entire Seminary catalogue is available to every qualified student regardless of sex," but that "the present policy of the Rabbinical School is to admit only male candidates." The women who wanted to be rabbis were told, as was Beverly Weintraub, to turn to the Teachers Institute—"You should become a teacher, don't try to be a rabbi." Susannah Heschel and Jan Kaufman were advised to consider JTS's other graduate programs.[105] As Gerson Cohen explained, in these ways the women would honor the commitment of Conservative Judaism to its "deeply rooted patterns of law, custom and social posture," to its upholding "of the centrality of the special roles assigned to men and to women in our tradition." Rather than being "swayed by the private ambitions of some, or, what is more likely the case, by current feminist fads,"[106] these women should go on to do that which Conservative Judaism permitted women to do in its particular mix of tradition and change in American Jewish life. They could acquire the educations necessary to carve out fulfilling careers in service to the Jewish community, as teachers and camp directors, Jewish communal and social workers, even as scholars, but never as rabbis.

Nevertheless, some, like Sandy Levine, who first met with rejection, kept applying.[107] Then new faces followed. By 1979, according to one source, approximately forty women had applied to JTS's rabbinical school.[108] As Chancellor Cohen admitted to Sandy Levine in 1975, her letter was but "one of many that my colleagues and I receive from week to week expressing the anguish of talented and committed young Jewish women who feel that they have been deprived of the right to fulfill themselves fully as Jews because of the Seminary's current policy against the ordination of women."[109]

Some of these women even received preliminary applications because they had dared to mask themselves—a kind of " 'illegitimate' action"—as they made their requests. They signed their letters of inquiry using only their first initials, as had Joan Friedman; or they did not have to, having the luck of androgynous given names, like Jan Kaufman. Afterwards, when those reading their applications discovered that the candidate was a she and not a he, the men called the women and welcomed them to study at the Seminary, not in the rabbinical school, but in another graduate program.

Others never even asked to apply to the rabbinical school. Instead, they pursued a different stratagem, heeding the advice of Talmud instructor Judith Hauptman to enter the Seminary masked as graduate students.[110] That way they could complete on their own the curriculum they would need for ordination. Then a woman could "step forward with her transcript in 10 to 15 years when a majority of the faculty agrees to ordain women. She just can't have a pulpit now." Probably none of them knew that even as they contemplated this course, Helen Levinthal Lyons was asking HUC-JIR to recognize just such an accomplishment of forty years before.[111]

Many, in fact, looked to Hauptman herself as a pioneer—for her role in Ezrat Nashim, for her studies of Talmud, and as the one who might possibly become the first woman ordained in Conservative Judaism.[112] A graduate of the Yeshivah of Flatbush, she had studied Talmud at the Seminary College of Jewish Studies. Male students who took that course did so for the headstart it gave them in rabbinical school. But that was not possible for her. Instead, she entered the Seminary's graduate program in Talmud. Because the graduate courses she needed were then offered only in the rabbinical school, Judith Hauptman found herself, in the late 1960s, asking, as Zionah Maximon had done, in the early 1940s, permission to study there.[113]

In retrospect, so she would later recall, "I might have tried to be a rabbi if the option had been available to me." Instead she channeled her passion for Talmud into scholarship. As she pursued her Ph.D., she began to teach Talmud, first in the Seminary's high school department, later in the rabbinical school. As the first female member of the faculty in the field that lay at the heart of the rabbinical curriculum, she stood, to others, as an exemplar of the woman as rabbinical scholar.[114]

When, in 1984, the Seminary admitted the first class of women to rabbinical school, Professor Hauptman announced: "I plan in the near future to be ordained and have already been admitted into the Rabbinical School."[115] Yet, ultimately she chose not to return as a student to the classrooms where she was a professor. The honor of becoming the first woman Conservative rabbi would fall to another.

By the mid-1970s, some of the women who wanted to be Conservative rabbis had heard "the word on the grapevine" that they might convince the faculty, prove themselves "serious students," especially by studying Talmud. So, the women who wanted to be rabbis got themselves to the Seminary. There they took some, or as much as possible, of the rabbinical curriculum, earning one kind of credential— an M.A. in Jewish education, history, or Talmud—as they awaited the chance to earn the one they really sought.[116]

But others took a different tack. Even as they pursued the formal academic courses which could lead them one day to the rabbinate, they also began working as "rabbis." This way they would prove that women could do all that rabbis did, if only given the chance. As the press conveyed to a wide audience their experiences, they would thus mobilize supporters by showing how serious, how deeply committed, how utterly worthy they were of becoming Conservative rabbis.

A few women found congregations willing to permit them to do this kind of work, to do all—or almost all—that they would do if they were rabbis. In a small congregation, like the one Lynn Gottlieb led, she became its "rabbi." In a large congregation, like Minneapolis's Adath Jeshurun, Carol Glass filled in for the junior rabbi but took another title. No matter the formal label, these young women found themselves doing much of what Conservative rabbis did: leading services garbed in *tallit* and *tefillin*, conducting life-cycle events, counseling the distressed, teaching Judaism, and preaching its message.[117]

Now others came forward to tell their stories in the public forum of the hearings held by the Commission for the Study of the Ordination of Women as Rabbis in 1978.[118] These witnesses shed light on the growing circles of supporters for those who wanted to be rabbis. Those, who decades before would have become rabbis if they could, related how they were told to become *rebbetzins*. The teachers of the women who wanted to be rabbis described the fervor of their students and their despair as they were turned away from the place they wished to be. Women who wanted to be rabbis related how they were waiting, either outside the Seminary in jobs in the Jewish community or inside, at JTS or at its west coast affiliate, the University of Judaism, biding their time until the commission would reach what they hoped would be a favorable decision. Then they planned to find themselves among the very first female rabbinic students.[119] After all, so they charged, "[i]t was, everyone knew, only a matter of time."[120]

But others conveyed their resignation, or that of their daughters, who, unable to wait any longer were, even as they spoke, making application to the seminaries willing to ordain them.[121] For, not surprisingly, as the debate dragged on through the 1970s, some who wanted to be Conservative rabbis became frustrated. Their lives went on while the rabbis and scholars swiped at the question of ordaining them. They wanted to be rabbis and if they couldn't be Conservative rabbis, they would begin to look "for a new way of being a rabbi."[122] And so they turned to where women could become rabbis and were welcomed.[123]

After the commission's majority report encouraged their admission to rabbinical school in the class entering in the fall of 1979, the women who wanted to be Conservative rabbis were elated. Leslie Alexander told the press: "After all the waiting, the being in limbo, I can finally look forward to becoming a rabbi."[124] So, like Carol Glass and Debra Cantor, they resigned their jobs and turned up at the Seminary expecting to find themselves among the very first women in rabbinical school. But unexpectedly they found themselves waiting once more as the faculty, to them inexplicably, asked Cohen for yet more time to prepare yet more papers on the question of ordaining women rabbis.[125]

Delaying the vote at the Seminary coincided with Professor Saul Lieberman's written determination that women could not become rabbis. "[O]ne of the giant Talmudists of the age," Lieberman represented a link to the great academies of the Jewish past long gone, the heir to generations of Jewish scholars and scholarship, a towering figure at the Seminary and in the Jewish world at large. Former dean of the rabbinical school, rector of the Seminary, rabbi of its synagogue, he was deeply revered by the generations of Conservative rabbis, who, as his students, had had to pass his dreaded Talmud exams. A model of the disciplined scholar, Lieberman rarely ventured into contemporary rabbinical affairs. But once before, one of the strains caused by the *halachic* position of women had compelled him to try, in the 1950s, to resolve the problem of the *agunah*.[126] Now in the late 1970s, another of the strains caused by the status of women in Jewish law compelled him to step forward again, to affirm that *halachah* prohibited the ordination of women as rabbis.

At the first faculty debate on the question, Lieberman asserted Jewish law proscribed women's ordination. Yet, until the winter of 1979, he had "preferred not to deal with this question at all because of hidden reasons which I do not wish to disclose." But now as the Seminary faculty prepared to vote on the recommendations of the commission, he became "afraid that it is forbiden [*sic*] me to deny kindness to others, to evade and not respond." On "Rosh Hodesh Adar, 5739," corresponding to the evening of 27 February 1979, Professor Lieberman addressed a handwritten responsum to his Seminary colleagues Haim Zalman Dimitrovsky, David Weiss Halivni, Dov Zlotnick, Jose Faur, and Israel Francus.[127]

Now Lieberman joined the many who had probed the Jewish past to see "whether it is permitted to ordain a woman as a rabbi." He culled from rabbinic sources evidence to examine what he deemed the paramount issues of the question, a woman's capability to judge and "what is ordination in our day." Considering the statements not only of the Talmud, medieval sages, but even the "[p]ractice of the yeshivot of Lithuania," the great academies of the Jewish world that was no more, he resolved: "The end of the matter is that it is clear from the sources that being called by the title "rav" ("Rabbi he shall be called") reflects on the fitness to issue legal decisions and to judge.... Since a woman is not fit to judge, and she cannot become qualified for this, she cannot be ordained by this title." Then he issued a plea: "Let us not make ourselves objects of derision and jest."[128] Although his responsum was never published while the debate raged at the Seminary—some believed he had forbidden its publication[129]—it stoked the countermovement of those opposing women's ordination.

Even as those opposing women's ordination crafted new strategies to step up their pressure, the women who wanted to be rabbis decided to do the same. By now, for more than two years, "everyone at JTS knew there were six women in the graduate school who wanted to be rabbis." Back then, in 1977, they had decided not to "get together and talk strategy," not to "go public." Instead they had believed that it would be enough to show "that we're serious students, that we're here—first and foremost—to learn."[130]

But as the first of the women who had expected to find themselves in rabbinical school in the fall of 1979 found themselves still graduate students, they decided the "times had changed." Weeks before the Faculty Senate was to resume its debate, in late December 1979, the women who wanted to be rabbis, gathered together "to do something, to take action," to draft a letter to the faculty. As the seven signed their names, Debra S. Cantor, Nina Beth Cardin, Stephanie Dickstein, Nina Bieber Feinstein, Sharon Fliss, Carol Glass, and Beth Polebaum went public collectively for the first time.[131]

Each had reached on her own her decision to become a rabbi. Each was deeply committed to Jewish scholarship and Jewish texts and immersed in their study. Now, as they coalesced, they signaled publicly the existence of the "group—even a small group—of women students at the Seminary enrolled in a rabbinical course." Together they hoped to make women's ordination "a vital issue."[132] Sustaining one another, finding support in the solidarity of the group, they hoped they could press their case forward, that nothing, not even the "complicated halachic issues related to Jewish women ... [which] should be addressed carefully, directly, and within the scope of the halachic process," would "delay the admission of women to the Rabbinical School."

But, in December 1979, the collective of seven who wanted to be rabbis could not champion their cause over the powerful counter-movement fueled by the authority of the Seminary's leading rabbinical scholars. On December 18th, in a highly public Conference on Halachic Process, which included presentations by Seminary professors Francus, Zlotnick, Faur, and Dimitrovsky, some two hundred Conservative rabbis and scholars resolved to oppose the ordination of women as rabbis. As they did, they also announced that Professor Lieberman "had sent them a confidential message stating that women cannot lawfully be ordained."[133]

In the past, Conservative elites had managed to allow their synagogues and central institutions to follow different interpretations of Jewish law and yet to coexist comfortably. Most Conservative synagogues had mixed seating; the Seminary synagogue did not. Some Conservative synagogues counted women in the *minyan*; most then did not. But the issue of women's ordination disclosed the depth, to return to Cyrus Adler and David Aronson's words of half a century before, of "the prejudice against woman's equality in religious matters" and the sense that "[t]he entire fabric of Jewish law is opposed to women entering the rabbinate."[134] In 1979, Conservative leaders could not conceive how the different *halachic* determinations on the permissibility of the woman rabbi could coexist within the movement. And they had come to fear that were they to go forward with women's ordination, "irreparable damage" to the Seminary would occur.[135] "[S]everal very eminent professors might actually resign."[136]

Two days after the Conference on Halachic Process, certain that "the potential dismembering of the Seminary and the impoverishment of its faculty and their scholarship is too great a price to pay," the Seminary Senate set aside the question, tabling, according to Seminary professor Joel Roth, "the issue of the ordination of women for at least fifty years, if not forever."[137] Even as the faculty issued what Chancellor Cohen called "a defeat for women's ordination," the young women who had spent "years preparing for this day," whose futures were at stake, sat elsewhere at the Seminary, taking their Talmud exams.[138]

Now they asked: "Where do I go from here?" In the course of the debate Cohen had personally moved from preservation of the status quo to become a "passionate advocate of women's ordination."[139] He conceived of a new scheme to keep the women who could not be Conservative rabbis at the Seminary. He would immediately start a new academic program in religious ministry "to give women the same training that male students get in The Rabbinical School. . . . [C]omparable in duration, breadth, and depth to that of the rabbinical school," it would offer "a professional degree in divinity."[140] And he promised the disappointed that when the Seminary would, as one day it was bound to do, ordain women, those who had completed this course "could be retroactively ordained."[141]

To many, the tabling of the motion to admit women to the Seminary's rabbinical school and the proposals for the alternative program suggested that "the ordination debate was temporarily shelved."[142] But the debate continued as those who sought admission to Conservative rabbinical school, for themselves and those who supported them joined together to "form organizations, mobilize constituencies, and conduct 'illegitimate' actions" to keep the question alive.

Even as the women who wanted to be Conservative rabbis registered their disappointment, those who supported them registered anger. At a New Year's Eve party days after the faculty vote, supporters, including rabbis Simkha Weintraub and David Wolf Silverman, rabbinical student Lawrence Troster, and his wife Elaine Kahn, who never wanted to be a rabbi, decided they must "organize" something, not to let this issue die. Shortly thereafter, they stuffed a letter into faculty mailboxes, announcing the genesis of G.R.O.W., the Group for the Rabbinic Ordination of Women, to champion the "immediate admission of women to the Rabbinical School of the Jewish Theological Seminary of America."[143]

G.R.O.W. determined to build a wide base of support to carry forward the banner of women's ordination. They asked rabbis around the country to help them collect the names of 100,000 Conservative men and women who supported them. They planned to use the medium of the press to fan the flames.[144] In March, G.R.O.W. staged a rally on the steps of JTS, the very first time, so its organizers believed, in Seminary history that anyone had dared to demonstrate publicly. In April G.R.O.W. sponsored a public forum on women's ordination at the Conservative Synagogue of Riverdale, where commission member Francine Klagsbrun told her audience, "I'm angry . . . Conservative leaders are closing their eyes, hoping the whole thing will go away by shelving it. But of course it won't." Alongside her stood Rabbi Linda Holtzman, ordained at RRC and identified in G.R.O.W. publicity as "the only woman rabbi serving a Conservative pulpit in America." In May G.R.O.W. published a list of its supporters and lobbied at the Rabbinical Assembly annual convention.[145]

Enthusiasm for its activity astounded G.R.O.W. founders. They received letters from all over the country. Hillels asked for its resource packet and bibliography. Supporters sent checks. A Bethesda, Maryland, congregation created a G.R.O.W. branch. Years later, Rabbi Lawrence Troster and Elaine Kahn reminisced it "felt like we created a grassroots movement."

In addition, Troster and Kahn offered a highly personal contribution to the debate. They photographed their year-old twins, Sara and Rachel, wearing t-shirts blazoned "JTS Rabbinical School, Class 2001." Then they blew up the photo into a poster and sent it to Gerson Cohen.

But even as G.R.O.W. mobilized, the women who wanted to be rabbis continued to struggle with the question of "what next?" Those who had gone public but a few months before faced difficult decisions as Seminary administrators tried to court them, to keep them, arguing they should not turn away from the Conservative movement and what it permitted women to do. Ultimately, only one of the women who wanted to be a Conservative rabbi, Nina Bieber Feinstein, entered the alternative religious ministry program Cohen created to afford women "the same training that male students get in the Rabbinical School." As it evolved, it had become, in Debra Cantor's estimation, "a second-class program meant to train women who would serve as second-class synagogue functionaries."[146]

The others left the Seminary. Some, like Carol Glass, applied and won a place in the other rabbinical schools then letting women become rabbis. Stephanie Dickstein and Beth Polebaum turned away from their dream of becoming leaders in the Jewish community for careers in social work and law. Debra Cantor and Nina Cardin found alternative jobs in the Jewish world, believing that even if the Seminary would reverse its stance, "it is already 'too late' for [them] to plan on becoming a rabbi."[147] Their long struggle had exacted a personal toll. Debra Cantor wrote: "I don't know that I would be able to go back to rabbinical school now or in the near future. In any case, I'm not so sure, any longer, that I want to be a rabbi."[148]

Meanwhile, others contemplated a different kind of "illegitimate" action, private ordination. In this, by virtue of the authority of individual rabbis, not the completion of the course of study in a Seminary, one claims the title rabbi, teacher, and preacher in Israel. Earlier Regina Jonas had pursued this course. Now some of the women who wanted to be Conservative rabbis contemplated it. Ultimately, only one, Lynn Gottlieb, actually took it.[149] Meanwhile, others pursued yet another stratagem to push the question forward.

The Seminary was not the only institution appointing Conservative rabbis. Since 1901, as the alumni association of the Jewish Theological Seminary, the Rabbinical Assembly (RA) had served as the professional association of Conservative rabbis. The RA not only ruled on matters of Jewish law and guided rabbis' job placements, but it had also for decades welcomed those ordained elsewhere who wished to be Conservative rabbis. Some of these men wanted to leave behind the confines of Orthodoxy for Conservatism's unique blend of tradition and change. Others, ordained by the Reform seminaries, had personally become more traditional, observant of Jewish law, and wanted to lead Conservative congregants who shared their points of view. By 1957, 22 percent of the 619 men of the RA had been ordained at institutions other than JTS. Between 1950 and 1980 another 600 men ordained outside the Seminary asked to join them.[150]

Those championing women's ordination knew that with the question of the admission of women to the Seminary's rabbinical school closed for the moment, the Rabbinical Assembly offered a different, and perhaps more sympathetic, venue for raising the issue. Since the late 1960s, Cleveland rabbi Fishel Pearlmutter had spearheaded the campaign there. Even before the RA revised its constitution, in 1977, to open membership to all "upon whom the title of Rabbi has been duly and properly conferred,"[151] making the admission of women possible, he replied to the women who wrote him that they wanted to be Conservative rabbis, that ordination at another rabbinical school might possibly pave their way into the RA. Angered and frustrated after JTS tabled its decision, Pearlmutter wanted to continue the fight in the RA. Even as G.R.O.W. marshaled its efforts, he and his colleagues thought that the key lay in finding a female rabbi who wanted to join the RA.[152] Not long afterwards, Rabbi Beverly Magidson asked to do just that.

In 1972, as Brandeis student Beverly Weintraub, she had asked Gerson Cohen if the Seminary would admit her to rabbinical school. In 1979, HUC-JIR ordained her Rabbi Beverly Magidson. In 1972, she had wanted to be a Conservative rabbi. In 1979, she still wanted to be a Conservative rabbi. And so she began the careful course of preparing herself to make application for membership in the Rabbinical Assembly.

In May 1981, she submitted her application to the RA. She wrote of how she had studied at HUC-JIR only after the Seminary had turned her away, of how even then she had continued to maintain ties to the Conservative movement, of the time she had spent at Neve Schechter, JTS's campus in Israel. Since ordination she had worked as a Hillel rabbi, but were she to seek a pulpit, she wanted it in a Conservative synagogue. Now Pearlmutter began rallying supporters behind her cause.[153]

Over the course of the following year both the RA's membership committee and its executive council favorably reported on her request. But when the question of her membership came up at the RA convention in April 1983, it failed—only four votes short—of the necessary 75 percent majority required to "ordain" Beverly Magidson a Conservative rabbi.[154] Nevertheless, four months later, the press trumpeted: "Synagogue Hires Woman as Rabbi: Congregation is First to Pick for the Job a Woman Who is a Conservative Jew." With the behind-the-scenes help of Rabbi Wolfe Kelman, RA executive vice-president, and others, she had won access to the list of congregations looking for Conservative rabbis and had found herself a job.[155] Even as she did, those at the Seminary prepared to revisit the question tabled less than four years before.

The Rabbinical Assembly's preemptive strike, that it had almost accepted Magidson as a Conservative rabbi, compelled Gerson Cohen to move forward again. Determined to preserve "the strength, integrity, and institutional power of the Seminary within the Conservative movement," he adamantly refused to cede such a decision to the Rabbinical Assembly. This time he carefully orchestrated the timing of the issue, surprising the faculty, only after the close of the academic year, with the announcement that, in October 1983, the Seminary Senate would, at last, vote to open the rabbinical school to women.[156]

While the internal power struggles of Conservative elites forced Cohen to act, the death, in late March 1983, of the honored professor and staunch opponent of women's ordination, Professor Lieberman, eased his way. Those standing outside the Seminary's gates then understood this as decisive, asserting, literally within days of his death, that now women could be ordained Conservative rabbis.[157] Without the commanding figure of Lieberman, however much he had preferred to remain in the background, those leading the countermovement could no longer prevail.

On 24 October 1983, the mood at the Seminary, according to one student, "was subdued. . . . Teachers had declared a day of introspection and prayer, threats of walkouts circulated, and acrimonious charges were exchanged."[158] Many of the Talmud faculty boycotted the meeting. Talmud professor David Weiss Halivni wrote an impassioned letter to convey one last time to his colleagues the "personal tragedy" this step evoked.[159] Nevertheless, this time the "faculty voted 34-to-8 to allow the rabbinical school to go co-ed."[160]

Now the debate centered not around whether or not women would be admitted to the rabbinical school, but rather the conditions of their admission. Seminary professor Joel Roth argued that in order for female ordination to remain within the parameters of *halachah*, Jewish women wanting to be Conservative rabbis had to take on *hiyyuv*, to declare that they would accept the obligations of fulfilling the *mitzvot*, the commandments of Jewish law, even those traditionally incumbent only upon men.[161] Divided as to whether or not this would create two classes of women within Judaism, the faculty deferred the matter to those who would, at long last, find themselves beyond the debate over the ordination of women as Conservative rabbis, to those charged with admitting the first women to the Seminary's rabbinical school.[162]

Less than a year later, "23 women with pent-up frustration, ambition and hope" registered for the classes that would train them to become Conservative rabbis. Among them stood Debra Cantor, Nina Cardin, and Nina Bieber Feinstein, three of the seven, who, a long five years before, had pleaded with the faculty to reach this day.[163] Joining them was another, Amy Eilberg.

In the fall of 1984, Amy Eilberg appeared but one of the women enrolling in rabbinical school for the first time. By February 1985, it had become evident that a few months hence, she would become the first woman ordained by the Seminary and accepted into the Rabbinical Assembly.[164]

Like those who had made this journey with her, Eilberg had long prepared for this day. In high school she became deeply involved with USY and later was a counselor at Ramah. At Brandeis, at the "dawn of Jewish feminism," she had majored in Jewish studies. In college she learned how to read Torah, how to lay *tefillin*, and had, on her own, conceived of the possibility of taking on voluntarily the commandments required of men. She thought she would become a teacher. Her Hillel rabbi told her to become a rabbi. In 1976 she turned to JTS, not to the rabbinical school, but to do graduate work in Talmud, biding her time until the Seminary would ordain women. After earning her M.A., she continued her studies and taught at Midreshet Yerushalayim, the Seminary's intensive text study institute in Israel. When, in 1979, the Seminary tabled the question, she found herself deeply disappointed. She thought of an academic career, to complete a doctorate in Talmud, and took the essential course work. But that remained a second choice. A few years later she began studying social work, not at the Seminary but at Smith College, thinking this would help her, on her own, put together the components of a rabbinical education. Just as she was completing her M.S.W., the Seminary began interviewing the first women for the rabbinical school. Eilberg returned to JTS to find that her efforts to compile her own rabbinical curriculum had paid off. In the fall of 1984, she found herself but a year away from becoming a Conservative rabbi.[165]

In March 1985 she stood as the first woman to pass through the rabbinical school rite of passage, the senior sermon. Charged with exploring the implications of the weekly Torah reading, she did just what the women who wanted to be rabbis had always done, she used it to illuminate the roles of women in Judaism. Eilberg preached her senior sermon on the verses in Exodus, which described the gifts the ancient Israelites gave to decorate the sanctuary in the wilderness. But the men and the women had brought very different gifts for the Tent of Meeting. At one time, Eilberg professed, she would have liked to have agreed with the rabbinic authority who sought to obliterate the differences between their gifts. "But having waited a long time to be a rabbinical student," she had come to speak "today in a different era" and to "read Jewish texts through a different lens." In the 1970s Jewish feminists had sought "equal access ... obtaining for women that which had previously been exclusive to men." Now that most of those battles, so she thought, were won, the time had come to celebrate their difference. And so, she wondered, as she prepared to go forth, whether the gifts of the men who were rabbis and the gifts of the women who were about to become rabbis would also prove different. Would they now and in the future speak in different voices?[166]

In May 1985 Amy Eilberg became "Ha'Rav Chana Beyla," rabbi, teacher and preacher in Israel. With her admission into the Rabbinical Assembly assured, the RA began admitting the first of the women, including Rabbi Beverly Magidson, who, a long decade before, had first pressed for women to be Conservative rabbis.[167]

At last the question, which Seminary President Cyrus Adler had once contended the Jewish Theological Seminary would not consider, even "for a moment" had closed. The prospect of ordaining women rabbis had called forth responses from every Seminary president since Solomon Schechter. Since the 1970s the topic had both drained and electrified JTS scholars and students, Conservative rabbis, and the men and women of their congregations. In the end, the women who desperately wanted to become Conservative rabbis, with their supporters circled behind them, had proven that, even if they did not succeed, they were priming others to insist that Conservative leaders must finally accede to modernity. Even as the question of the woman rabbi drew to a close in Conservative Judaism, although the debate about the special gifts of women rabbis begun by Rabbi Amy Eilberg would continue, the first to challenge Orthodox Judaism to ordain women rabbis made their voices heard.

Epilogue

"Will there be Orthodox women rabbis?"

1984

Even as those within Conservatism closed their debate on the woman rabbi, the Orthodox launched theirs.[1] Earlier, one member of this wing had observed: "[T]he Orthodox community hardly took notice of the Reform ordination of women in 1973 or that of Reconstructionism in 1975."[2] She was right. The customs and practices of these liberal streams of modernizing Judaism, especially their understanding of Jewish law, differed so from Orthodoxy that the first women approaching ordination outside its boundaries did not propel the question into the Orthodox world. But one enterprising reporter in the 1970s stopped to ask an unnamed "Orthodox rabbi" what he thought. Learning that a few years hence Sally Priesand expected to become a rabbi, he pronounced, she "probably would not be recognized as a rabbi. It doesn't matter what they call her. And it would never be repeated. History would say that she was a star that blazed brilliantly and disappeared in one holy day."[3]

But in the mid-1980s, as those in the Conservative movement closed their debate, preparing to ordain as rabbis women whose patterns of text study and ritual observance closely approximated, even surpassed, what many Orthodox Jewish men and women had come to expect of their daughters, the question burst out in this sector of American Jewish life. As it did, learned Orthodox Jewish women, especially rabbis' wives, who broached it for others, and the first deeply committed young Jewish women who sought this for themselves, echoed the voices of the past, repeating—sometimes it seems verbatim—the lines of the arguments in favor of the woman rabbi which had swirled for more than a century.

They began by voicing their surprise, as so long ago Mary M. Cohen's fictional characters were stunned when one of them asked: "Could not—our *women*—be—ministers?"[4] One evening, an Orthodox rabbi's seven-year-old daughter, wondering what she would be when she grew up, mused: "... maybe I'll be a rabbi." Now her mother had to ask: "Where ever did she get the idea that she could be a rabbi? I silently wondered. Certainly not from her parents or siblings, who had not yet heard of women rabbis. Certainly not from her grandparents, all rabbis and wives. Certainly not from the several generations of male rabbinic models before them."[5]

And so the question emerged. Those confronting it for the first time looked about them to see what had launched it. In the late nineteenth century, their predecessors in the debate had observed women "physicians, preachers, dentists, lawyers, journalists, compositors, typewriters, bookkeepers, sales-women, telephone and telegraph operators." Those, at the end of twentieth century, recognized "women as Presidents and Prime Ministers and bankers, philosophers, scientists, professors, lawyers, [and] doctors."[6]

But if woman's entrance to the learned professions and to all avenues of political and social life had thrust forward the question from without, already it impinged upon the Orthodox from within. Some of the first Conservative female rabbis began sharing what they had learned in rabbinical school with their Orthodox "friend[s] and neighbor[s]," guaranteeing that "new ideas about women rabbis were surely replacing old diffidences."[7]

Now those asking for ordination for others began the process of turning to the sacred texts of the Jewish past, just as those who had preceded them had turned, to ask was this possible. In 1876, Isaac Mayer Wise had inferred from Genesis 1:27 that "God made man, male and female, and both in his own image, without any difference in regard to duties, rights, claims and hopes." A century later, the Orthodox writer and teacher and feminist Blu Greenberg, "[s]earching for a principle of sexual equality in Judaism," argued: "each person is created in the image of God. . . . Male and female, species specific, but each in the image of God. Distinctive, yet equal.[8]

She inferred "distinctive, yet equal" to signify "women were blessed with mental capacity and mental energy equal to that of men,"[9] capable of acquiring the learning signifying rabbi. For prooftexts, the new Orthodox champions of the woman rabbi pointed, as those before them had also pointed, to exemplary Jewish women of the past. Earlier champions of the woman rabbi had referred to Miriam and Deborah, Huldah and Beruriah. In the 1990s, new advocates did not have to stretch quite so far back in Jewish history. Instead they pointed to Henrietta Szold who, although "denied acceptance to rabbinical school at JTS earlier this century . . . plant[ed] the seed that would grow into a tree from which future generations would reap fruit"; and to "Judith Hauptman, perhaps the first woman to teach Talmudic law since the time of Beruriah." Again, they uncovered Hannah Rachel Werbemacher, the "maid of Ludomir," and "they called her rebbe."[10]

Moreover, proponents of the Orthodox female rabbi recognized they had little need to go beyond their own boundaries. As expectations for the educations of Jewish girls had risen sharply in all sectors of American Judaism, making their educations virtually equivalent to those of their brothers, leading Orthodox decision-makers had, over the course of several decades, allowed "the historically gender-restricted ideal of Torah study [to] become an egalitarian goal."[11] The resulting "explosion of women's learning within Orthodoxy" included "thousands of Orthodox women study[ing] Talmud."[12]

Erudite Orthodox female scholars had not only mastered Jewish texts but also taught them in a variety of settings, including new institutions offering Jewish girls and women the chance "to pursue parallel rabbinic studies."[13] On occasion, some of these thousands rose before assemblies to preach and to teach. As they wove their "way with ease through the rabbinic sources," they caused, at least one in the congregation—to reflect: "I find myself thinking [she] would make a splendid rabbi. And then I think: well, that's exactly what she is."[14] In demonstrating mastery of the texts, in teaching, these scholars began to stand as models, much like the proto-rabbis of the past, of the woman as rabbi.

Now the new champions of the woman rabbi had to wonder, since "dedicated *rebbeim* [and] learned teachers" had opened the "access route" of sacred text study to the rabbinate, could Orthodox women indeed be ordained? After all, ordination signified "the recognition of accomplishment, of accumulation of knowledge and ability to handle rabbinic texts." It was manifestly "a function of merit and not of gender."[15] And so they began another of the searches into the Jewish past to see if, indeed, there existed any "direct halakhic objection to the acts of training and ordaining a woman to be a rabbi, preacher, and teacher in Israel."[16] Now some in the Orthodox world became "convinced that I have the halachic backing to do so."[17] "[T]here is no formal ban to women's ordination."[18]

But until young Orthodox women who "love to learn," who wished to spend their lives "totally absorbed in Jewish texts," asked this for themselves, the question was never "practical." Then, in the spotlight of the press, they could proclaim to a wide audience "Why I'm Applying to Yeshiva U." In the fall of 1993, Haviva Krasner-Davidson mailed her rabbinical school application, which her husband had called for, to the Rabbi Isaac Elchanan Theological Seminary of Orthodoxy's Yeshiva University. As she did, she began unfolding to others what brought her to this day. She was: "someone who has been immersed in Jewish texts all her life, who hoped to grapple with the issues on a spiritual level; someone who sought the authority of the Orthodox movement rather than one of the more progressive branches of Judaism and who wanted the clout of the title 'rabbi.' "[19] As her mother admitted to the press: "It's our fault. . . . We raised her to feel she can accomplish whatever she wants."

Soon she learned, at Yeshiva University: "Say 'Haviva' " and those with the power to ordain "groan[ed]." Not long afterward, the "5-foot Talmudic scholar" found herself turned away from where she wished to be. Afterward, like her historic predecessors, she continued to raise the question, seeking out new strategies to prove herself worthy of that which she so desperately sought. As her journey lengthened, another, presumably but the first of those who in the years to come will follow her, already sat by her side.

As I write these words, in the early spring of 1998, the question of women's rabbinic ordination remains open in the world of Orthodoxy. Already the Jewish press has begun circling around the first women, hired by Orthodox congregations "to help the rabbi," who will teach and preach, counsel and visit the sick as "congregational intern[s]," not as "para-rabbi[s].[20] In the 1890s Hannah Solomon had displayed rising expectations for women's ordination: "should women desire to enter the ministry, there will be no obstacles thrown in their way."[21] A century later, Blu Greenberg echoed her optimism: "I believe the ordination of Orthodox women is close at hand."[22]

It took nearly a century to negotiate the path from the rising expectations for women in the rabbinate to the first of the women who became Reform, Reconstructionist, and Conservative rabbis. Those who envisioned women joining the rabbinate believed women could play a leading part in preserving Judaism as it adapted to the modern age. In the 1890s and early 1900s modernizing rabbis, their modern wives, heads of Jewish organizations, and editors of Jewish newspapers reflected abstractly on the prospect of the woman rabbi.

In the 1920s and 1930s five women who wanted to be rabbis spent enough time in rabbinical schools to compel their faculties, fellow students, and alumni to decide the question for their times. These five shared not only their ambitions to become a rabbi but also a common approach to blazing women's path to the rabbinate. Spurned for seeking to overturn that which, if they became rabbis, they would have had to uphold, these women all found themselves turning to Jewish tradition, to the Jewish women of the past. They read the classical texts of Jewish law, finding no statement specifically prohibiting women from assuming this title. They brought forward long lists of the learned women of Jewish history, who had engaged in sacred study, some who used their learning to teach and to rule. Arguing that these women, albeit without formal title, functioned much like rabbis, they asked to climb on their shoulders, to claim their places as rabbis, teachers, and preachers. Even as they advanced their arguments, those who opposed the woman rabbi read Jewish tradition to rule that this adaptation to modernity was one Judaism could never embrace.

These first aspirants, standing alone in times not propitious for women to enter new professions, failed to achieve their aims. But, in the second half of the twentieth century, others retraced their route. As new women turned to the history of Jewish women to justify that which they wished to achieve, some, catching glimmers of the women who before them had wanted to be rabbis, added their names to the historical record. Now, in times conducive to the expansion of women's roles in American life, more and more women joined this quest. As they did, supporters championing their ambition circled behind them. Together they rested their claims for women's right to seek the rabbinate on Jewish tradition. In so doing, they used the past to create a revolution. At last women became rabbis.[23]

This history of the debate on women rabbis thus has larger implications. It reveals the ways in which men and women drew upon the past to extend woman's sphere. It suggests a model for historians of women's changing role in religion and for those studying women in other professions. Finally, it proposes a project for the future, for others who need to climb on the shoulders of those who preceded them to create their own revolutions.

For now, the specific question of women rabbis remains unequivocally on the agenda of contemporary Orthodoxy. Covering a recent consultation on Orthodoxy and feminism, the press confirmed: "The question of women becoming Orthodox rabbis lingered throughout the conference."[24]

But how long before the debate is resolved, the historian cannot predict. What remains incontrovertible is that once the question of the woman rabbi is opened, it will not go away. As long as there are those who will, in the months and years ahead, come forward to ask this for themselves, or for their wives, daughters or sisters, they will compel their communities to join in the century-old debate. And if lessons from the past can indeed serve as prologue for the future, then they have ruled that this debate can end only when those women, superbly capable of leading, teaching, and preaching, will have, at long last, claimed their places as rabbis.

Notes

INTRODUCTION

1. AJA, Women Rabbis Nearprint: "Woman Rabbi Made to Feel Welcome," *Jewish Week*, 4 May 1974.

2. Sara Evans, *Personal Politics: The Roots of Women's Liberation in the Civil Rights Movement and the New Left* (New York: Vintage, 1979), 212.

3. Our collaboration produced several articles and book chapters: Rita J. Simon and PSN, "Teachers, Preachers, and Feminists in America: Women Rabbis," *Shofar* 10, 1 (Fall 1991): 2–10; Rita J. Simon, Angela J. Scanlan, and PSN, "Rabbis and Ministers: Women of the Book and the Cloth," *Sociology of Religion*, 54, 1 (Spring 1993): 115–22; rpt. in *Gender and Religion*, ed. William H. Swatos, Jr. (New Brunswick, NJ: Transaction Press, 1993); Rita J. Simon and PSN, "Lay Leaders' Views About Female Rabbis and Ministers," *Shofar* 13, 4 (Summer 1995): 52–58; Rita J. Simon and PSN, "In the Same Voice or is It Different?: Gender and the Clergy," *Sociology of Religion* 56, 1 (1995): 63–70; PSN and Rita J. Simon, "Ladies of the Sisterhood: Women in the American Reform Synagogue, 1900–1930," in *Active Voices: Women in Jewish Culture*, ed. Maurie Sacks (Urbana: University of Illinois Press, 1995), 63–75.

4. Sally Priesand, *Judaism and the New Woman* (New York: Behrman House, 1975), 62–67; Ellen Umansky, "Women in Judaism: From the Reform Movement to Contemporary Jewish Religious Feminism," in *Women of Spirit: Female Leadership in the Jewish and Christian Traditions*, ed. Rosemary Ruether and Eleanor McLaughlin (New York: Simon & Schuster, 1979), 339–42.

5. Anne Firor Scott, "On Seeing and Not Seeing: A Case of Historical Invisibility," rpt. in *Women and Women's Issues*, vol. 12, *Modern American Protestantism and Its World*, ed. Martin E. Marty (Munich: K. G. Saur, 1993), 30.

6. This is fully treated in Michael A. Meyer, *Response to Modernity: A History of the Reform Movement in Judaism* (New York: Oxford University Press, 1988); Quotation, Ludwig Philippson (1844), in David Philipson, *The Reform Movement in Judaism* (New York: Macmillan, 1931), 142.

7. Quotation, A. Adler (1844), in Philipson, *Reform Movement in Judaism*, 155.

8. Meyer, *Response to Modernity*, xi.

9. *Emet ve-Emunah: Statement of Principles of Conservative Judaism* (n.p.: Jewish Theological Seminary of America, 1988); Louis Finkelstein quoted in Abraham J. Karp, "A Century of Conservative Judaism in the United States," *AJYB* 86 (1986): 3.

10. Jeffrey S. Gurock, "Resisters and Accommodators: Varieties of Orthodox Rabbis in America, 1886–1983," *American Jewish Archives* 25, 2 (November 1983): 100–87.

11. For a fuller discussion, see Robert Gordis, "The Rabbinate: Its History, Functions, and Future," (1957), rpt. in his *Understanding Conservative Judaism*, ed. Max Gelb (New York: Rabbinical Assembly, 1978), 168–91. Questions come from Isaac Bashevis Singer, *In My Father's Court* (1962; rpt., New York: Fawcett Crest, 1983), quotation, 131. See also Mary Antin, "Malinke's Atonement," 1911, rpt. in *America and I: Short Stories by American Jewish Women Writers*, ed. Joyce Antler (Boston: Beacon Press, 1990), 27–56.

12. Gerda Lerner, *The Creation of Feminist Consciousness: From the Middle Ages to Eighteen-seventy* (New York: Oxford University Press, 1993), 166.

CHAPTER 1: RAISING THE QUESTION OF WOMEN'S RABBINIC ORDINATION, 1889

1. Mary M. Cohen, "A Problem for Purim," *JE*, 15 March 1889, 1. All emphases in original. All subsequent quotations from Cohen's story are from this same publication.

2. Karla Goldman has suggested that Cohen let the diffidence of Dora's character "bespeak the radical, fanciful nature of the proposal." Goldman, "Beyond the Gallery: The Place of Women in the Development of American Judaism" (Ph.D. diss., Harvard University, 1993), 256.

3. Note that Cohen did not raise *halachic* arguments.

4. On the lack of historical memory and its implications for the creation of feminist consciousness, see Gerda Lerner, *The Creation of Feminist Consciousness: From the Middle Ages to Eighteen-seventy* (New York: Oxford University Press, 1993).

5. Dianne Ashton, "Crossing Boundaries: The Career of Mary M. Cohen," *AJH* 83 (June 1995): 153–76, especially 154–55; quotation 159; see also, Dianne Ashton, "'Souls Have No Sex': Philadelphia Jewish Women and the American Challenge," in *When Philadelphia Was the Capital of Jewish America*, ed. Murray Friedman (Philadelphia: Balch Institute Press, 1993), 47–49; Dianne Lichtenstein, *Writing Their Nations: The Tradition of Nineteenth-Century American Jewish Women Writers* (Bloomington: Indiana University Press, 1992), 87–88, 112–13.

6. Ashton, "Crossing Boundaries," 155, 168, 175.

7. Ibid., 159–60; Barbara Welter, "The Cult of True Womanhood, 1820–1860," *American Quarterly* 178 (Summer 1966): 151–74.

8. Ashton, "Crossing Boundaries," 157, 161.

9. Ibid., 155, 157–58, 171–72. On Katharine M. Cohen, see the entry by Michele Siegel in *Jewish Women in America: An Historical Encyclopedia*, ed. Paula E. Hyman and Deborah Dash Moore (New York: Routledge, 1997): 245–46.

10. Mary M. Cohen, "Woman in the Synagogue," *RA*, 20 February 1897, 7.

11. Michael A. Meyer, *Response to Modernity: A History of the Reform Movement in Judaism* (New York: Oxford University Press, 1988), 251.

12. In *A Century of Judaism in New York: B'nai Jeshurun, 1825–1925, New York's Oldest Ashkenazic Congregation* (New York: Congregation B'nai Jeshurun, 1930), Israel Goldstein chronicled the pace of reforms—including the emergence of confirmation and mixed seating—introduced over the course of the nineteenth century in this synagogue, classified, as early as 1886, as Conservative; Leon Jick concluded: "The precise details of change varied from place to place, but the basic direction was universal. Respectability and Americanization were the goals; decorum, reform of ritual, and English were the means." Jick, *The Americanization of the Synagogue, 1820–1870* (Hanover, N.H.: Brandeis University Press, 1976), 183.

13. Moshe Davis, *The Emergence of Conservative Judaism: The Historical School in America* (Philadelphia: Jewish Publication Society, 1963), 119.

14. These are detailed in Goldman, "Beyond the Gallery."

15. Ibid., 115.

16. Barbara Welter, "The Feminization of American Religion: 1800–1860," in *Clio's Consciousness Raised: New Perspectives on the History of Women*, ed. Mary S. Hartman and Lois Banner (New York: Octagon Books, 1976), 138–41; Ann Douglas, *The Feminization of American Culture* (New York: Knopf, 1978), 97–98.

17. Marion A. Kaplan, *The Making of the Jewish Middle Class: Women, Family, and Identity in Imperial Germany* (New York: Oxford University Press, 1991), 68.

18. Quotation, Aaron Chorin, "The Service is for Women Also," 1842, in *The Rise of Reform Judaism: A Sourcebook of Its European Origins*, ed. W. Gunther Plaut (New York: World Union for Progressive Judaism, 1963), 252–53. Karla Goldman is correct that "the trend towards preponderant female presence in the synagogue was not an explicit part of any reform program" ("Beyond the Gallery," 115), for there is no indication that reformers had expected women to replace men as worshippers.

19. Davis, *Emergence of Conservative Judaism*, 119.

20. Isaac Leeser, 1844, cited in Davis, *Emergence of Conservative Judaism*, 123–24; Lance J. Sussman, "Isaac Leeser and the 'Philadelphia Pattern,'" in *When Philadelphia Was the Capital of Jewish America*, 27–28.

21. Goldman, "Beyond the Gallery," 126–46.

22. For a popular account of the scholarly debate on when Jewish women and men came to be separated in worship, see Bernadette Brooten, "Were Women and Men Segregated in Ancient Synagogues?" and Lawrence Schiffman, "When Women and Men Sat Together in American Orthodox Synagogues," *Moment* 14 (December 1989): 32–49. The debate continues in "Scholars Clash over Ancient Separation by Gender," *Moment* 15, 2 (April 1990): 6–11f.

23. Jonathan D. Sarna, "The Debate over Mixed Seating in the American Synagogue," *The American Synagogue: A Sanctuary Transformed*, ed. Jack Wertheimer (Cambridge, England: Cambridge University Press, 1987), 366–68.

24. Note that in the twentieth century, mixed seating comes to signify the divide between Conservatism and Orthodoxy.

25. Deborah Weissman, "Education of Jewish Women," *Encyclopedia Judaica Year Book 1988* (Jerusalem: Keter, 1988), 31. For twentieth-century examples of changing patterns of Orthodox Jewish female education, see Deborah Weissman, "Bais Yaakov: A Historical Model for Jewish Feminists," in *The Jewish Woman: New Perspectives*, ed. Elizabeth Koltun (New York: Schocken Books, 1976), 139–48; Norma Baumel Joseph, "Jewish Education for Women: Rabbi Moshe Feinstein's Map of America," *AJH* 83 (1995): 205–22; see also Shoshana Pantel Zolty, *"And All Your Children Shall Be Learned": Women and the Study of Torah in Jewish Law and History* (Northvale, N.J.: Jason Aronson, 1993).

26. Meyer, *Response to Modernity*, 140. On the negative consequences of German Jewish women lacking formal Jewish education, see Deborah Hertz, "Emancipation through Intermarriage in Old Berlin," in *Jewish Women in Historical Perspective*, ed. Judith Baskin (Detroit: Wayne State University Press, 1991), 185–86.

27. Stephan F. Brumberg, "Education of Jewish Girls in America," in Hyman and Moore, *Jewish Women in America*, 357–67.

28. Hyman B. Grinstein, "In the Course of the Nineteenth Century," in *A History of Jewish Education in the United States*, ed. Judah Pilch (New York: American Association for Jewish Education, 1969), 32–33.

29. Emily Fechheimer Seasongood, "Growing Up in America, 1851–1864," in *The American Jewish Woman: A Documentary History*, ed. Jacob R. Marcus (New York: Ktav, 1981), 173.

30. Dianne Ashton, "Rebecca Gratz," in *Jewish Women in America*, 547–50. There is very little material on the feminization of Jewish education; see also Rebecca Kobrin, "Teaching Profession," in *Jewish Women in America*, 1382–87.

31. Maimon Frankel, "For a Reform of Bar Mitzvah," 1810, in Plaut, ed., *Rise of Reform Judaism*, 172–73.

32. Isaac Asher Francolm, "Simplicity, Not Pomp," 1840, in Plaut, ed., *Rise of Reform Judaism*, 173–74.

33. Meyer, *Response to Modernity*, 34, 39–40, 50.

34. Ibid., 232, 237–38, 241.

35. Davis, *Emergence of Conservative Judaism*, 121–22.

36. W [Isaac Mayer Wise], "The Confirmation and the Bar Mitzvah," 1854, in Marcus, ed., *The American Jewish Woman*, 186–89, quotation, 188; Emily Fechheimer Seasongood, "Growing Up in America, 1851–1864," ibid., 176.

37. For example, in "Shevuoth Thoughts of Rabbis and Confirmands," *Jewish Tribune* (6 June 1924): 36–46, the author enumerated fifty-seven confirmation ceremonies. Forty of these listed confirmands' names. Only four confirmed more males than females.

38. Meyer examines the various conferences in depth in *Response to Modernity*.

39. Ibid., 65.

40. Ibid., xi.

41. "For Total Equality," Report to the Breslau Conference, 1846, in Plaut, ed., *Rise of Reform Judaism*, 253–54; Meyer, *Response to Modernity*, 139–40, 451, n. 75.

42. See Rachel Biale, *Women and Jewish Law: An Exploration of Women's Issues in Halakhic Sources* (New York: Schocken Books, 1984), 102–20.

43. Meyer, *Response to Modernity*, 89.

44. Ibid., 95, 140.

45. Ibid., 190.

46. Jacob Marcus argues that the synod at Augsburg had been influenced by the meeting in Philadelphia; "The Beginnings of the Religious Emancipation of Women in American Jewry: The Philadelphia Rabbinical Conference, 1869," in Marcus, ed., *The American Jewish Woman*, 286–88.

47. "The Beginnings of the Religious Emancipation," in Marcus, ed., *The American Jewish Woman*, 286–87; Meyer, *Response to Modernity*, 190, 255–58.

48. Meyer, *Response to Modernity*, 123; Michael A. Meyer, "The First Identical Ceremony for Giving a Hebrew Name to Girls and Boys," *Journal of Reform Judaism* (Winter 1985): 84–87.
Note that a ritual for naming a daughter and welcoming her into the Jewish community would emerge anew in America in the latter part of the twentieth century. When it would do so, it would come from the creative energies of the very first female rabbinical students seeking a Jewish ceremonial to bring infant girls as well as baby boys into the covenant of the Jewish people. Rabbi Sandy Eisenberg Sasso, the first woman ordained by the Reconstructionist Rabbinical College, claims to have created the first such ceremony for a baby girl while she was in rabbinical school; my interview with SES, 19 November 1991.

49. Abraham Geiger, "No Spiritual Minority," 1837, in Plaut, ed., *Rise of Reform Judaism*, 253.

50. David Philipson, *The Reform Movement in Judaism* (1907; rev. ed. New York: Macmillan, 1931), 183–84; Meyer, *Response to Modernity*, 140, 451, n. 75.

51. "For Total Equality," Report to the Breslau Conference, 1846, in Plaut, ed., *Rise of Reform Judaism*, 253–55.

52. Meyer, *Response to Modernity*, 140.

53. For example, see David Philipson, "Woman and the Congregation," *NFTSP* 1 (1913): 15–18.

54. Kaplan, *Making of the Jewish Middle Class*, 137.

55. Isaac Mayer Wise, "Woman in the Synagogue," *American Israelite* (8 September 1876): 4, in Marcus, ed., *The American Jewish Woman*, 293–95; subsequent quotations from Wise are from this same publication. Among Wise's other articles on Jewish women are "The Jewish Woman," *Die Deborah* (22 March 1867); "Does the Canon Law Permit Ladies to Sing in the Synagogue?" *The Israelite* 2:5 (10 August 1855): 36; 2:6 (17 August 1855): 44–45.

56. On Wise, see Sefton D. Temkin, *Isaac Mayer Wise: Shaping American Judaism* (Oxford: Littman Library, 1992).

57. Goldman makes this point; "Beyond the Gallery," 206–7.

58. On suffrage, see the classic work by Eleanor Flexner, *Century of Struggle: The Woman's Rights Movement in the United States* (Cambridge, Mass.: Harvard University Press, 1959).

59. Ellen Carol DuBois, *Feminism and Suffrage: The Emergence of an Independent Women's Movement in America, 1848–1869* (Ithaca: Cornell University Press, 1978), 15; Carl Degler, *At Odds: Women and the Family in America from the Revolution to the Present* (New York: Oxford University Press, 1980), 335, 358. See also Aileen S. Kraditor, *Ideas of the Woman Suffrage Movement* (New York: Columbia University Press, 1965). On Jewish women and suffrage, see Elinor Lerner, "Jewish Involvement in the New York City Woman Suffrage Movement," *AJH* 70 (June 1981): 442–61; Linda Gordon Kuzmack, *Woman's Cause: The Jewish Woman's Movement in England and the United States, 1881–1933* (Columbus: Ohio State University Press, 1990), 142–54.

60. In 1879 women won the right to vote at Congregation B'nai Jeshurun in New York City; see "1880, Woman Suffrage in the Synagogue," in Marcus, ed., *The American Jewish Woman*, 295; see also Goldman, "Beyond the Gallery," 248–53.

61. Ashton, "Crossing Boundaries," 175. In 1896, Rosa Sonneschein, editor of *The American Jewess*, thought Chicago's Temple Isaiah the "one Jewish congregation in the world where women have the unconditional right of membership; "Editorial, *AJ* 4, 3 (December 1896): 137–38.

62. Quoted in Ashton, "Crossing Boundaries," 175.

63. Ibid., 162.

64. Alice Kessler-Harris, *Out to Work: A History of Wage-Earning Women in the United States* (New York: Oxford University Press, 1982), 47, 53–54, 57; on nineteenth-century Jewish women writers, see Lichtenstein, *Writing Their Nations*.

65. "Declaration of Sentiments and Resolutions, Seneca Falls," in *Feminism: The Essential Historical Writings*, ed. Miriam Schneir (New York: Vintage, 1972), 76–82.

66. Nancy Cott, *The Grounding of Modern Feminism* (New Haven: Yale University Press, 1987), 215.

67. In 1915 the influential educator Abraham Flexner characterized a profession as a brotherhood; cited in Penina Migdal Glazer and Miriam Slater, *Unequal Colleagues: The Entrance of Women into the Professions, 1890–1940* (New Brunswick: Rutgers University Press, 1987), 175.

A partial listing of the historiography on professional women includes: Virginia Lieson Brereton and Christa Ressmeyer Klein, "American Women in Ministry: A History of Protestant Beginning Points," in *Women of Spirit: Female Leadership in the Jewish and Christian Traditions*, ed. Rosemary Ruether and Eleanor McLaughlin (New York: Simon and Schuster, 1979), 301–32; Mary Roth Walsh, *"Doctors Wanted: No Women Need Apply"—Sexual Barriers in the Medical Profession, 1835–1975* (New Haven: Yale University Press, 1977); Joan Jacobs Brumberg and Nancy Tomes, "Women in the Professions: A Research Agenda for American Historians," *Reviews in American History* 10 (June 1982): Margaret W. Rossiter, *Women Scientists in America* (Baltimore: Johns Hopkins University Press, 1982); Virginia G. Drachman, *Hospital with a Heart: Women Doctors and the Paradox of Separatism at the New England Hospital, 1862–1969* (Ithaca: Cornell University Press, 1984); Regina Markell Morantz-Sanchez, *Sympathy and Science: Women Physicians in American Medicine* (New York: Oxford University Press, 1985); Karen Berger Morello, *The Invisible Bar: The Woman Lawyer in America, 1638 to the Present* (New York: Random House, 1986); Lynn D. Gordon, *Gender and Higher Education in the Progressive Era* (New Haven: Yale University Press, 1990); Virginia G. Drachman, *Women Lawyers and the Origins of Professional Identity in America: The Letters of the Equity Club, 1887 to 1890* (Ann Arbor: University of Michigan Press, 1993).

68. Harriot Hunt cited in Walsh, *"Doctors Wanted,"* xiv–xvi, 27–28; see also Morantz-Sanchez, *Sympathy and Science*. Note Harvard Medical School admitted its first female students in 1945.

69. Cited in Walsh, *"Doctors Wanted,"* xiv–xvi, 1, 28.

70. Cited in Morello, *Invisible Bar,* 22, 44–45, 90, 96. Note, in 1927, Columbia University had its first female law students.

71. Morello, *Invisible Bar,* 14–21.

72. Carrie Kilgore, cited in Morello, *Invisible Bar,* 67–68, 90.

73. Barbara S. Spies, "Antoinette Brown Blackwell," in *Women Public Speakers in the United States, 1800–1925: A Bio-Critical Sourcebook*, ed. Karlyn Kohrs Campbell (Westport, Conn.: Greenwood Press, 1993), 63–75.

74. Wilmer A. Linkugel, "Anna Howard Shaw," in Campbell, ed., *Women Public Speakers,* 409–20.

75. John O. Foster, *Life and Labors of Maggie Newton Van Cott* (Cincinnati: Hitchcock and Walden, 1872).

76. For example, Ada C. Bowles, "Women in the Ministry," in *Woman's Work in America*, ed. Annie Nathan Meyer (New York: Henry Holt, 1891).

77. On the size of the WCTU, compare the General Federation of Women's Clubs which, in 1893, had 20,000 members, and the National American Women's Suffrage Association, which, in the same year, had 13,000 dues-paying members; Bonnie J. Dow, "Frances E. Willard," in Campbell, ed., *Women Public Speakers,* 476–89.

78. Frances E. Willard, *Woman in the Pulpit* (Chicago: Woman's Temperance Publishing Association, 1889; rpt. Washington, D.C.: Zenger Publishing Co., 1978), 65, 94, 97, 110–11. Among her other major works were *A Woman of the Century: Fourteen Hundred Seventy Biographical Sketches Accompanied by Portraits of Leading American Women in All Walks of Life*, ed. with Mary A. Livermore (Buffalo: Charles Wells Moulton, 1893); with Helen M. Winslow and Sallie Joy White, *Occupations for Women. A Book of Practical Suggestions, for the Maternal Advancement, the Mental and Physical Development, and the Moral and Spiritual Uplift of Women* (New York: Success, 1897).

79. Walsh, *"Doctors Wanted,"* xv.

80. Justice Joseph P. Bradley, cited in Morello, *Invisible Bar*, 20.

CHAPTER 2: RISING EXPECTATIONS
FOR WOMEN'S ORDINATION, THE 1890S

1. Jonathan D. Sarna, *A Great Awakening: The Transformation That Shaped Twentieth Century American Judaism and Its Implications for Today* (New York: Council for Initiatives in Jewish Education, 1995), quotation, 12.

2. Adolph Moses, "The Emancipation of Woman" (1892) in his *Yahvism and Other Discourses*, ed. H. G. Enelow (Louisville: Louisville Section of the Council of Jewish Women, 1903), 104. Cf. Isaiah 40:3–4.

3. Sarna, *Great Awakening*, 18–27.

4. Hannah G. Solomon, "Council of Women: Washington, D.C., February 1895," in Hannah G. Solomon, *A Sheaf of Leaves* (Chicago: printed privately, 1911), 131–32.

5. Hannah G. Solomon, *Fabric of My Life: The Autobiography of Hannah G. Solomon* (New York: Bloch, 1946), 42–43; quotation, *The Boston Transcript*, cited in Karen J. Blair, *The Clubwoman as Feminist: True Womanhood Redefined, 1868–1914* (New York: Holmes and Meier, 1980), 34, 56–57.

6. Anne Firor Scott, *Natural Allies: Women's Associations in American History* (Urbana: University of Illinois Press, 1991), 118, 120, 142.

7. Solomon, *Fabric of My Life*, 24–26.

8. Hannah G. Solomon, "Review of Spinoza's Theologico-Politicus" (1891), in Solomon, *Sheaf of Leaves*, 9–15. On Spinoza, see *EJ* 15: 275–84.

9. Solomon, *Fabric of My Life*, 43–44; Solomon, "Our Debt to Judaism" (1892), in *Sheaf of Leaves*, 16–30.

10. Scott, *Natural Allies*, 128–34, 140, 142.

11. Solomon, *Fabric of My Life*, 79–81; Faith Rogow, *Gone to Another Meeting: The National Council of Jewish Women, 1893–1993* (Tuscaloosa: University of Alabama Press, 1993), 9–10. Note that Solomon's version does not indicate that Henrotin first sought others to organize the Jewish Women's Committee.

There is no history of Jewish women and suffrage. The only article on the subject is Elinor Lerner's "Jewish Involvement in the New York City Woman Suffrage Movement," *AJH* (June 1981): 442–61. While Solomon was, according to Rogow, a "self-proclaimed suffragist," she, like many others, including Frances E. Willard, disassociated herself from the radical tactics of the suffrage movement and its negative public image; cf. Bonnie J. Dow, "Frances E. Willard," in *Women Public Speakers in the United States, 1800–1925: A Bio-Critical Sourcebook*, ed. Karlyn Kohrs Campbell (Westport, Conn.: Greenwood Press, 1993), 477. Note that the National Council of Jewish Women defeated a resolution endorsing woman's suffrage; Rogow, *Gone to Another Meeting*, 78–82.

12. Solomon, *Fabric of My Life*, 79–82; Rogow, *Gone to Another Meeting*, 13–14.

13. *Judaism at the World's Parliament of Religions: Comprising the Papers on Judaism Read at the Parliament, at the Jewish Denominational Congress, and at the Jewish Presentation* (Cincinnati: Union of American Hebrew Congregations, 1894), iii-vi. Note at least one contributor of two papers, Alexander Kohut, did not attend the conference.

14. Solomon, *Fabric of My Life*, 82–83. The date of the meeting is suggested by the report in *Judaism at the World's Parliament of Religions*, vi.

15. *RA*, 22 July 1893: 442, cited in Rogow, *Gone to Another Meeting*, 17.

16. The pioneering article, Deborah Grand Golomb's, "The 1893 Congress of Jewish Women: Evolution or Revolution in American Jewish Women's History," appeared in the first issue of *AJH* (70 [September 1980]: 52–67) devoted entirely to American Jewish women's history. In addition to Rogow's *Gone to Another Meeting*, see Ellen Sue Levi Elwell, "The Founding and Early Programs of the National Council of Jewish Women: Study and Practice as Jewish Women's Religious Expression" (Ph.D. diss., Indiana University, 1982), 49–82; Diane Lichtenstein, *Writing Their Nations: The Tradition of Nineteenth-Century American Jewish Women Writers* (Bloomington: Indiana University Press, 1992), 122–23.

17. Sadie American, "Organization," in *Papers of the Jewish Women's Congress* (Philadelphia: Jewish Publication Society, 1894), 245. Another sign of the unprecedented nature of the conference was the way presenters were listed in the program. The women were listed by first and last names, rather than by the traditional formula, e.g., Rebekah Kohut rather than Mrs. Alexander Kohut. Recognition of a woman's right to use her first name, rather than the title "Mrs." and her husband's first name, would remain on the agenda of women's rights advocates into the 1970s; see Elaine Showalter, "Only the Conception: Becoming a Feminist Critic," *Douglass Alumnae Bulletin* 66, 4 (Summer 1993): 2.

18. Gerda Lerner, *The Creation of Feminist Consciousness: From the Middle Ages to Eighteen-seventy* (New York: Oxford University Press, 1993), 10–11, 28, 113–14, 138–39, 159, 220.

19. Ibid., 113–14, 209. On Hannah Rachel Werbemacher, see H. Rabinowicz, *The World of Hasidism* (Hartford: Hartmore House, 1970), 202–10; Ada Rapoport-Albert, "On Women in Hasidism: S. A. Horodecky and the Maid of Ludomir Tradition," in *Jewish History: Essays in Honour of Chimen Abramasky*, ed. Ada Rapoport-Albert and Steven J. Zipperstein (London: Peter Halban, 1988): 495–525. By the early twentieth century, national meetings of Jewish women's organizations became established institutions,

providing forums for knowledgeable Jewish women to display their piety, learning, and religiosity.

20. Jonathan D. Sarna discusses several works JPS published to appeal to its "large number of women readers," part of the late nineteenth-century effort "to educate American Jewish women about their religion;" *JPS: The Americanization of Jewish Culture, 1888–1988* (Philadelphia: Jewish Publication Society, 1989), 43.

21. *Papers of the Jewish Women's Congress*, 6–7; Rebekah Kohut, *My Portion: An Auto-biography* (New York: Albert and Charles Boni, 1927), 180–82.

22. For a discussion of this theme in nineteenth-century American Jewish writing, see Lichtenstein, *Writing Their Nations*, 16–34.

23. Rogow, *Gone to Another Meeting*, 231–32; on Mannheimer's translation of *The Jewish Woman*, see Sarna, *JPS*, 307, n. 49.

24. Louise Mannheimer, "Jewish Women of Biblical and of Medieval Times," *Papers of the Jewish Women's Congress*, 17–19.

25. Henrietta G. Frank, "Discussion," *Papers of the Jewish Women's Congress*, 51.

26. Ray Frank, "Woman in the Synagogue," *Papers of the Jewish Women's Congress*, 65.

27. Hannah Solomon, "Address," in *Papers of the Jewish Women's Congress*, 166.

28. Ray Frank, "Prayer," in *Papers of the Jewish Women's Congress*, 8.

29. Mannheimer, "Jewish Women of Biblical Times," 17, 22, 24.

30. Ibid., 22, 24.

31. On female students at Hebrew Union College before 1900, see Samuel S. Cohon, "The History of the Hebrew Union College," *AJHQ* 40 (1950–51): 25–26; AJA, Nearprint: Women Rabbis, Jacob R. Marcus, "The First Woman Rabbi," Press Release (February 1972); Michael A. Meyer, "A Centennial History," in *Hebrew Union College-Jewish Institute of Religion at One Hundred Years*, ed. Samuel E. Karff (Cincinnati: HUC Press, 1976), 18, 46.

32. Rebecca J. Gradwohl, "The Jewess in San Francisco," *AJ* 4, 1 (October 1896): 12; "In Woman's Wake," *AJ* 4, 3 (December 1896): 142; see also, C. A. Danziger, "Ray Frank," *AJ* 7, 1 (April 1898): 19–21.

33. This account and what follows are constructed from Simon Litman, *Ray Frank Litman: A Memoir* (New York: American Jewish Historical Society, 1957); Reva Clar and William M. Kramer, "The Girl Rabbi of the Golden West: The Adventurous Life of Ray Frank in Nevada, California and the Northwest," *Western States Jewish History* 18 (1986): 99–111, 223–36, 336–51. For the various dates given for her birth, see Sarna, *Great Awakening*, 41, n. 46.

34. Ray Frank, "Letter to the Editor," *Jewish Messenger*, 23 May 1890, in *The American Jewish Woman: A Documentary History*, ed. Jacob Marcus (New York: Ktav, 1981): 380–83. Because she had "so ingeniously answered th[at] query," a month later she reflected upon pious Jewish woman's more customary role; Ray Frank, "If I Were a Rebitzin," *Jewish Times and Observer*, 20 June 1890, AJHS, Ray Frank Litman Papers, Box 1, F.F. Printed Material: Articles Written by R. F. Litman.

35. Cited in Litman, *Ray Frank Litman*, 10.

36. Clar and Kramer, "Girl Rabbi of the Golden West," chronicles the extensive press coverage of her career, especially that of the Anglo-Jewish press.

37. On the relevance of the West to her career, see my "A Land of Opportunities: Jewish Women Encounter America," in *What Is American about the American Jewish Experience?* ed. Marc Lee Raphael (Williamsburg, Va.: College of William and Mary, 1993), 78–80.

38. For example, Karlyn Kohrs Campbell's *Women Public Speakers in the United States, 1800–1925: A Bio-Critical Sourcebook* (Westport, Conn.: Greenwood Press, 1993) includes thirty-seven key orators; see also Gerda Lerner, *The Grimké Sisters from South Carolina: Pioneers for Women's Rights and Abolition* (New York: Schocken Books, 1966).

39. Cynthia Grant Tucker, *Prophetic Sisterhood: Liberal Women Ministers of the Frontier, 1800–1930* (Boston: Beacon Press, 1990), esp. 2, 39, 56. Note that only Pennsylvania's Meadville Theological School accepted women as students for the ministry. Harvard, which also ordained Unitarian ministers, refused admission to women. For a brief guide to theological and other distinctions among religious movements, see Leo Rosten, ed., *Religions of America: Ferment and Faith in an Age of Crisis* (1955; rev. ed. New York: Simon and Schuster, 1975).

40. On Ida C. Hultin, see Tucker, *Prophetic Sisterhood*, 31, 33, 34, 56, 97, 126–27, 198, 237. Hultin's "Woman in the Ministry" appeared in the Iowa franchise paper, *Woman's Standard* 3 (January 1889): 3.

41. AJHS, Ray Frank Litman Papers, Box 1, F.F. Letters from R. F. Litman re: Autobiography, Letter from Ray Frank to Rev. S. T. Willis, 15 December 1896. The date of her arrival in Cincinnati comes from Box 2, Scrapbook, *The Times-Star*, 11 January 1893. In her letter to Reverend Willis, Frank dates her arrival to 1892 and claims she stayed in Cincinnati a year.

42. Her Cincinnati experience is based on the following sources: AJHS, Ray Frank Litman Papers, Box 1, F.F. Published Biographical Material, *Israel*, no date; F.F. Letters from People Requesting Litman to Lecture, Letter from David Philipson, 12 March 1895; Reva Clar and William M. Kramer, "The Girl Rabbi of the Golden West," 109–10. Note there are no College records to confirm Ray Frank's attendance.

43. AJHS, Ray Frank Litman Papers, Box 2, Scrapbook, *The American Israelite*, 24 November 1892.

44. Frank, "Prayer," *Papers of the Jewish Women's Congress*, 8, 268.

45. The following quotations are from Frank, "Woman in the Synagogue," *Papers of the Jewish Women's Congress*, 52–65.

46. AJHS, Ray Frank Litman Papers, F.F. Letters from Ambrose Bierce to R. F. Litman, F.F. Letters from R. F. Litman to Stetson (Charlotte Perkins Gilman Stetson); F.F. Letter from Israel Zangwill, 1897; F.F. Letters from People Requesting Litman to Lecture, Letter from H. Landsberg, 26 August 1895. Box 2, Scrapbook contains press clippings, 1892–1901, especially *San Francisco Examiner*, 12 November 1893; F.F. Miscellaneous; see also Litman, *Ray Frank Litman*, 58.

47. Clar and Kramer, "Girl Rabbi of the Golden West," 345–50, base their argument on a single item in the press. The Ray Frank Litman papers suggest that subsequently a Mr. Sloss arranged her speaking engagements and publicity; AJHS, Ray Frank Litman Papers, Box 1, F.F. Letters from People Requesting Litman to Lecture, Letters from Bertha G. Sloss, 19 November 1897, 11 April 1898, 27 December 1898, 20 January 1901.

48. On receiving fees for lecturing, see Barbara S. Spies, "Antoinette Brown Blackwell," in Campbell, *Women Public Speakers in the United States,* 66; Lois W. Banner, *Elizabeth Cady Stanton: A Radical for Woman's Rights* (Boston: Little Brown and Co., 1980), 110–11.

49. AJHS, Ray Frank Litman Papers, Box 1, F.F. Letters from People Requesting Litman to Lecture, Letter from Joseph Stolz, 14 September 1893; Letter from Nathaniel Rubinkam, 15 September 1893; Box 2, Scrapbook, *San Francisco Chronicle,* 19 October 1893; Litman, *Ray Frank Litman,* 35.

50. Emil G. Hirsch, "Woman in the Pulpit," *RA,* 11 November 1893, 203. I am indebted to Professor Karla Goldman for bringing this to my attention. On Hirsch, see *Reform Judaism in America: A Biographical Dictionary and Sourcebook,* ed. Kerry M. Olitzky, Lance J. Sussman, and Malcolm H. Stern (Westport, Conn.: Greenwood Press, 1993), 88–90.

51. Emil G. Hirsch, "Woman in the Pulpit," *RA,* 11 November 1893, 203.

52. Solomon, *Fabric of My Life,* 107–8; Scott, *Natural Allies,* 127–28.

53. Bonnie J. Dow, "Frances E. Willard," in Campbell, *Women Public Speakers in the United States,* 479–80; Frances G. Willard, *Woman in the Pulpit* (1889; rpt. Washington, D.C.: Zenger Publishing Co., 1978); Hannah G. Solomon, "Council of Women," February 1895," in Solomon, *Sheaf of Leaves,* 131–32.

54. Hirsch, "Woman in the Synagogue," *RA,* 20 February 1897.

55. Rogow, *Gone to Another Meeting,* 16.

56. *Proceedings of the First Convention of the National Council of Jewish Women, November 15–19 1896* (Philadelphia: Jewish Publication Society, 1897): 15, 353–54. See also Karla Goldman, "The Ambivalence of Reform Judaism: Kaufmann Kohler and the Ideal Jewish Woman," *AJH* 79 (Summer 1990): 477–99.

57. Rogow, *Gone to Another Meeting,* 24–26; Elwell, "Founding and Early Programs of the National Council of Jewish Women," 109; Emil G. Hirsch, "Editorial: Signs of the Times," *RA,* 9 May 1896, 238.

58. "Sisterhoods of Personal Service," *The Jewish Encyclopedia* 11:398; Ronald B. Sobel, "A History of New York's Temple Emanu-El" (Ph.D. diss., New York University, 1980), 211–15; Israel Goldstein, *A Century of Judaism in New York: B'nai Jeshurun, 1825–1925* (New York: Congregation B'nai Jeshurun, 1930), 194–95; Sarna, *Great Awakening,* 25–26. See also Richard J. H. Gottheil, *The Life of Gustav Gottheil: Memoir of a Priest in Israel* (Williamsport, Penn.: Bayard Press, 1936), 179–80.

59. Synagogue and communal histories detail the names; see, for example, Irving Katz, *The Beth El Story* (Detroit: Wayne University Press, 1955), 89–92; Rosalind Mael

Bronsen, *B'nai Amoona for All Generations* (St. Louis: Congregation B'nai Amoona, 1984), 26–27; Abraham J. Feldman, *Remember the Days of Old: Congregation Beth Israel* (Hartford, Conn.: Congregation Beth Israel, 1943), 78; Rebekah Kohut, "Jewish Women's Organizations in the United States," *AJYB* 1931–1932, (1931), 165–201; see also Hasia R. Diner, *A Time for Gathering: The Second Migration, 1820–1880* (Baltimore: Johns Hopkins University Press, 1992), 103–4.

60. Sandra J. Berkowitz, "Rosa Fassel Sonneschein," in *Women Public Speakers in the United States*, 182–93; *Chicago Evening Journal*, 13 April 1895, cited in "Press Greetings," *AJ* 1, 3 (June 1895): 151.

61. *AH*, 5 April 1895, and *Cincinnati Times-Star*, 15 April 1895, in "Press Greetings," *AJ*, 1, 2 (May 1895): 99; Myrna Goldenberg, "Rosa Sonneschein and 'The American Jewess,'" *Proceedings of the Tenth World Congress of Jewish Studies*, Division B, Vol. II (Jerusalem: World Union of Jewish Studies, 1990): 331–38.

62. Dr. Adolph Moses, "The Position of Woman in America," *AJ* 1, 1 (April 1895): 15–20.

63. Henry Berkowitz, "Woman's Part in the Drama of Life," *AJ* 1, 2 (May 1895): 64.

64. "Editor's Desk," *AJ* 1, 3 (June 1895): 153–55; "Editorial," *AJ* 4, 3 (December 1896): 137–38; *AJ* 6, 3 (December 1897): 142. Similarly, she protested women's exclusion from voting at the First Zionist Congress, Rosa Sonneschein, "The Zionist Congress," *AJ* 6, 1 (October 1897): 20.

65. Rev. Ella E. Bartlett, "The New Woman," *AJ* 1, 4 (July 1895): 169–71; Editor, "A Word to Our Readers," *AJ* 7, 1 (April 1898): 45.

66. Rebecca J. Gradwohl, "The Jewess in San Francisco," *AJ* 4, 1 (October 1896): 12; "In Woman's Wake," *AJ* 4, 3 (December 1896): 142; see also C. A. Danziger, "Ray Frank," *AJ* 7, 1 (April 1898): 19–21.

67. Solomon, *Fabric of My Life*, 112. I am grateful to Peter Eisenstadt for the information about Susan B. Anthony in his letter of 26 December 1997; Max Heller, *Jubilee Souvenir of Temple Sinai 1872–1922* (New Orleans: Temple Sinai, 1922).

68. Hannah G. Solomon, "The Council of Jewish Women: Its Work and Possibilities," *RA*, 27 February 1897, 25–28; Solomon, *Fabric of My Life*, 111–12. The National Council of Jewish Women continues to assert incorrectly that Solomon was the first Jewish woman to act as rabbi; see its flyer, "Advocacy in Action, Washington Institute: Moments in History" (n.p., n.d.).

69. Mr. M. A. Marks claimed this for Cleveland's Wilson Street Temple; "Council of Jewish Women: Triennial Convention," *AH*, 9 March 1900, 549–52c.

70. *Proceedings of the First Convention of the National Council of Jewish Women*, 15, 353–54; Kaufmann Kohler, "Esther or Woman in the Synagogue," *AH*, 23 March 1900, 605–7; Goldman, "Ambivalence of Reform Judaism," 477–99.

71. Hirsch, "Woman in the Synagogue," 1, 7.

72. All in *RA*, 20 February 1897, 7–8.

73. *RA*, 20 February 1897, 7–10; 27 February 1897, 24–25. Those voicing opposition to

female rabbis included Minnie D. Louis, Mrs. Emanuel Mandel, Miriam Landsberg, Ellen E. De Castro, Lottie T. Sloman, Esther J. Ruskay, Mrs. Bettie J. Gusdofer, Flora Schwab, and Katherine De Sola.

74. *RA*, 20 February 1897, 7–10; 27 February 1897, 24–25. Those in favor, albeit with qualifications, of female rabbis included Estelle Sinsheimer, Mary M. Cohen, Ray Frank, Hannah G. Solomon, Mrs. Frederick Nathan, Julia I. Felsenthal, Henriette G. Frank, Henrietta Szold, Julia Richman, Aurelia Rice, Mrs. Louise Mannheimer, Mrs. Sadie T. Wald, Rose Sommerfeld, Ruth Ward Kahn, Sadie American, Mrs. J. Beer, and Etta L. Nussbaum.

75. Mrs. J. Beer, *RA*, 27 February 1897, 25; Estelle Sinsheimer, *RA*, 20 February 1897, 7; Julia I. Felsenthal, *RA*, 20 February 1897, 10.

76. Hannah Solomon, *RA*, 20 February 1897, 8; Henrietta Szold, *RA*, 20 February 1897, 9.

77. She presented "The Outlook of Judaism;" *Judaism at the World's Parliament of Religions*, 295–303. Note that Max Landsberg presented "The Position of Woman Among the Jews" there; 241–54. On Josephine Lazarus, see the entry by Sue Levi Elwell, in *Jewish Women in America*, ed. Paula E. Hyman and Deborah Dash Moore (New York: Routledge, 1997), 809–10; see also Diane Lichtenstein, *Writing Their Nations*, 90–93. Note she was the sister of the famed poet Emma Lazarus.

78. See the responses by PSN and June Sochen in "The Greatest American Jewish Leaders," and Benny Kraut, "American Jewish Leaders: The Great, Greater, and Greatest," *AJH* 78 (December 1988): 184–90, 195–98, 201–36.

79. On Szold, see Joan Dash, *Summoned to Jerusalem: The Life of Henrietta Szold* (New York: Harper and Row, 1979). On her work at the Jewish Publication Society, see Sarna, *JPS*, 47–94.

80. Henrietta Szold, "The Jewish Publication Society of America," 327–33; "What Has Judaism Done for Woman?" 304–10, *Judaism at the World's Parliament of Religions*.
It is not clear whether Szold spoke about the Jewish Publication Society at the Jewish Denominational Congress held 28–30 August 1893 (in which case she was the only woman on this program) or whether she discussed its work in the Jewish Presentation to the Parliament of Religions some two weeks later. According to the "Programme" of the *Papers of the Jewish Women's Congress*, Szold gave "What Judaism has done for Woman" [*sic*] on 21 September 1893.
While the Congress of Jewish Women was a landmark event within American Jewish women's history, its audience was largely Jewish women. Only a few men participated in its program, and, according to one news report, few men were actually in its audience; *Papers of the Jewish Women's Congress*, 6–7; *The American Israelite*, 7 September 1893, 6, cited in Golomb, "The 1893 Congress of Jewish Women," 52.

81. I am relying upon the typescript manuscript at the JMMD, MS 38 - Henrietta Szold Papers; formerly in Box BS28 Henrietta Szold: School Books, Printed Material, Writings, Articles About. Henrietta Szold, "The World's Congress of Religions, The Addresses and Papers Delivered Before the Parliament," "What Judaism Has Done for Women [*sic*]." This was published in *The World's Congress of Religions*, ed. J. W. Hanson

(Vancouver: J. M. MacGregor Publishing Co., 1894), 587–93. The following quotations are from this typescript.

There are apparently two versions of "What Judaism Has Done for Women." The typescript manuscript differs in a number of lengthy passages from "What Has Judaism Done for Woman?" in *Judaism at the World's Parliament of Religions*, 305–10. The latter omits entirely Szold's envisioning women free to enter the professions. Consequently, my reading of this text differs significantly from that of scholars who relied on this edition of the text; see, for example, Lichtenstein, *Writing Their Nations*, 83.

82. Szold's erudition also underscored the disparity in the ascribed status of the men and that of the women speaking for Judaism at the Columbian World's Exposition. While many of the women who spoke for Christianity at the World's Parliament of Religions were ordained ministers, the women who spoke for Judaism, including Szold, obviously held no such formal credentials. Instead the majority of them came to this task avocationally. Only a handful—among them Mary M. Cohen and Henrietta Szold—had won reputations for their writing and their "professional" service to the Jewish community. In sharp contrast the men who represented Judaism to the world did so by virtue of the authority conferred by vocation. They were ordained rabbis and scholars. Of the twenty-nine men who stood for Judaism at the Exposition, no more than two were laymen. The rest wore the mantle of rabbi, doctor, professor, or reverend; "Contents," *Judaism at the World's Parliament of Religions*, xiii–xviii. This juxtaposition of largely leisured, middle-class women displaying their informally acquired knowledge of Judaism versus the representatives of the learned Jewish profession pointed subtly, but surely, to the question of women in the rabbinate.

83. Dash, *Summoned to Jerusalem*, 41–43; A. P. Mendes, 1886, quoted in Robert E. Fierstien, "From Foundation to Reorganization: The Jewish Theological Seminary of America, 1886–1902" (D. H. L. diss., Jewish Theological Seminary, 1986), 67.

84. See, for example, Susan Dworkin, "Henrietta Szold," *Response* 18 (Summer 1973): 43; Charlotte Baum, Paula Hyman, and Sonya Michel, *The Jewish Woman in America* (New York: New American Library, 1976), 43; Anne Lapidus Lerner, "On the Rabbinic Ordination of Women," in *The Ordination of Women as Rabbis: Studies and Responsa*, ed. Simon Greenberg (New York: Jewish Theological Seminary of America, 1988), 93; Susan Grossman and Rivka Haut, "Introduction," to their *Daughters of the King: Women and the Synagogue* (Philadelphia: Jewish Publication Society, 1992), 8.

85. Letty Cottin Pogrebin, *Deborah, Golda, and Me: Being Female and Jewish in America* (New York: Crown Publishers, 1991), 53.

86. Mel Scult, "The Rabbi," *Hadassah Magazine* (June/July 1990): 23–24.

87. Hadassah, RG #7 Special Collections Henrietta Szold, Box 6, Associates Correspondence Series S-Z, Folder 48: Emily Solis-Cohen and Family, 1897–1939, Henrietta Szold to Miss E. N. Solis, 13 February 1897.

88. JMMD, MS 38 - Henrietta Szold Papers; Box, 1, Folder 20 -Correspondence 1903: Letter from Henrietta Szold to Judge Mayer Sulzberger, 14 February 1903.

89. JMMD, MS 38 - Henrietta Szold Papers; Box 1, Folder 20 -Correspondence, 1903: Letter to Henrietta Szold from Cyrus Adler, 22 February 1903.

90. Letter from Henrietta Szold to Haym Peretz, 16 September 1916, in *Henrietta Szold: Life and Letters*, ed. Marvin Lowenthal (1942; rpt. Westport, Conn.: Greenwood Press, 1975), 92. Later, in Palestine, on the anniversary of a family death, she was so dismayed at being closeted in the women's room where, cut off from the main service, she could not hear the *kaddish*, that she helped organize a congregation more to her liking, where men and women took part in the service, even in the reading of the law; JMMD, MS 38 - Henrietta Szold Papers, Box 4, Folder # 5, Clippings: "Our Own Women: Henrietta Szold," *United Synagogue Recorder* (June ?, 1923): 17.

91. Sarna, *Great Awakening*, 16.

92. *AH*, 5 March 1897, 484–85.

93. AJA, Microfilm #3/1 Hebrew College, Letters from Henrietta Szold, 1866–1944; originals in Israel: Letter from Henrietta Szold to her mother, 2 December 1904.

94. AJHS, Ray Frank Litman Papers, Box 1, F.F. Published Biographical Material, *Israel* (n.d.); F.F. Letters Addressed Mainly to Prof. S. Litman convey her activities.

Note also that by the turn of the century the "prophetic sisterhood" of the liberal Unitarian female ministers began its decline. After 1906, it was not until 1917 that another woman was ordained. Meanwhile, the graying women of the sisterhood found themselves without pulpits or diverted to "ministries" of social and municipal work; Tucker, *Prophetic Sisterhood*, 171–95, 225–26.

95. For example, a search of the *NYT* for articles on women and clergy reveals nothing between 16 November 1896: 2 and 25 May 1921: 17.

96. In the 1890s rather than reporting on women ministers, *NYT* had covered the more newsworthy items of "Man and Wife Pastors"; 30 January 1896, 9; 14 February 1896, 10; 18 February 1896, 14.

97. *AH*, 1 November 1912, 13.

CHAPTER 3: ''[W]OMAN CANNOT JUSTLY BE DENIED
THE PRIVILEGE OF ORDINATION'': 1922

The quotation that forms the title for chapter 3 is from *CCARY* 32 (1922): 51.

1. AJA, Rabbis, F.F. Correspondence . . . re admission of women to the College for the Purpose of Ordination, 1921–1922, Miscellaneous File: J. Lauterbach and Oscar Berman, "Minority Report of the Committee on the Question of Graduating Women as Rabbis," 20 June 1921.

2. Surprisingly, David Neumark's biographical entry, by Anthony D. Holz, in *Reform Judaism in America: A Biographical Dictionary and Sourcebook*, fails to include Martha among his children; ed. Kerry M. Olitzky, Lance J. Sussman, and Malcolm H. Stern (Westport, Conn.: Greenwood Press, 1993), 153–54. On David Neumark, see AJA, Biographies File: Martha Neumark Montor, "Papa Was a Philosopher," Reminiscences of Dr. David Neumark by his daughter, December 1966.

3. AJA, Nearprint File—Martha Neumark Montor: Martha Neumark, "The Woman

Rabbi: An Autobiographical Sketch of the First Woman Rabbinical Candidate," *The Jewish Tribune and Hebrew Standard*, 10 April 1925: 1.

4. AJA, HUC Academic Records, Cincinnati, OH, 1914–1953, Microfilm no. 118; Personal communication from Mrs. Montor to Ida Cohen Selavan, 6 December 1979 in Ida Cohen Selavan, "Women Rabbis: A Short List," in *The Jewish Almanac*, ed. Richard Siegel and Carl Rheins (New York: Bantam, 1980), 49.

5. AJA, Nearprint File—Martha Neumark Montor: Martha Neumark, "The Woman Rabbi: Difficulties that Beset Path of First Woman Rabbi Outlined in Brief Autobiographical Sketch," *The Jewish Tribune*, 17 April 1925: 5. Part of this was reprinted; Ann D. Braude, "Jewish Women in the Twentieth Century: Building a Life in America," in *Women and Religion in America*, vol. 3, ed. Rosemary Radford Ruether and Rosemary Skinner Keller (San Francisco: Harper and Row, 1981–86), 161–65.

6. AJA, Nearprint File—Martha Neumark Montor: Martha Neumark, "The Woman Rabbi: An Autobiographical Sketch."

7. AJA, Ms. Col. #5, C-1/4 Board of Governors, 1920–1930: Report of Dr. Kohler to Board of Governors, 31 May 1921.

8. AJA, Ms. Col. #5, C-1/4 Board of Governors, 1920–1930: Report of Dr. Kohler to Board of Governors, 31 May 1921; Ellen M. Umansky first pieced together much of the choreography of the debate; "Women in Judaism: From the Reform Movement to Contemporary Jewish Religious Feminism," in *Women of Spirit: Female Leadership in the Jewish and Christian Traditions*, ed. Rosemary Ruether and Eleanor McLaughlin (New York: Simon and Schuster, 1979), 339–40.

9. See chap. 5.

10. AJA, Rabbis, F.F. Correspondence between Faculty and Board of Governors of HUC regarding admission of women to the College for the Purpose of Ordination, 1921–1922, Miscellaneous File: David Philipson to the Board of Governors, 29 June 1921.

11. Unless noted otherwise, the following paragraphs are based on AJA, Rabbis, F.F. Correspondence . . . re admission of women to the College for the Purpose of Ordination, 1921–1922, Miscellaneous File: J. Lauterbach and Oscar Berman, "Minority Report of the Committee on the Question of Graduating Women as Rabbis," 20 June 1921.

12. Jacob Z. Lauterbach, "Responsum on Question, 'Shall Women Be Ordained Rabbis?'" *CCARY* (1922): 161.

13. AJA, Rabbis, F.F. Correspondence . . . re admission of women to the College for the Purpose of Ordination, 1921–1922, Miscellaneous File: Bloom to Englander, 7 July 1921.

14. On Lauterbach and *halachah*, see Michael A. Meyer, "A Centennial History," 69, and Lewis M. Barth, "Rabbinics," 330, both in *Hebrew Union College-Jewish Institute of Religion: At One Hundred Years*, ed. Samuel E. Karff (Cincinnati: HUC Press, 1976); Mark E. Washofsky, "Jacob Z. Lauterbach" in *Reform Judaism in America*, 119–20; Michael M. Meyer, *Response to Modernity: A History of Reform Judaism* (New York: Oxford University Press, 1988), 312.

15. AJA, Rabbis, F.F. Correspondence . . . re admission of women to the College for the

Purpose of Ordination, 1921–1922, Miscellaneous File: J. Lauterbach to the President and Faculty of HUC, 12 December 1921; HUC Faculty Minutes, 21 December 1921.

16. AJA, Biographies: Martha Neumark Montor, "Papa Was a Philosopher."

17. AJA, HUC Faculty Minutes, 12 December 1921, p. 27; AJA, Rabbis, F.F. Correspondence ... re admission of women to the College for the Purpose of Ordination, 1921–1922, Miscellaneous File: David Neumark to HUC Faculty, 26 January 1922.

18. AJA, HUC Faculty Minutes, 24 January 1922, 32.

19. AJA, HUC Faculty Minutes, 30 January 1922, 33; February 1922, 35.

20. AJA, HUC Faculty Minutes, 22 March 1922, 37.

21. These and the following paragraphs are from Lauterbach, "Responsum on Question," 156–62.

22. On the commandments incumbent upon women, see Rachel Biale, *Women and Jewish Law: An Exploration of Women's Issues in Halakhic Sources* (New York: Schocken Books, 1984), 10–43.

23. This and what follows are from *CCARY* (1922): 163–77; quotations 163, 168, 173.

24. Rabbis Levinger, Barnett Brickner, Joseph L. Baron, mentioned the Christian denominations; *CCARY* (1922): 163, 164–65, 168–69. On Anna Howard Shaw, see above, chap. 1.

25. Mark Chaves provides dates of Christian women's ordination; *Ordaining Women: Culture and Conflict in Religious Organizations* (Cambridge: Harvard University Press, 1997), table 2.1; The American Association of Women Ministers, cited in E. Wilbur Bock, "The Female Clergy: A Case of Professional Marginality," *American Journal of Sociology* 72 (1967): 531. On women's ordination in Christianity in these years, see Emily C. Hewitt and Suzanne R. Hiatt, *Women Priests: Yes or No* (New York: Seabury Press, 1973), 102; "Woman's Progress Toward the Pulpit," *Literary Digest* (23 October 1920): 34.

26. Rabbi Rauch in *CCARY* (1922): 165–66. In the summer of 1920, the same summer Martha Neumark led services in Michigan, NFTS issued a call to its members to take charge of summer services in the absence of vacationing rabbis; "Report of the National Committee on Religion," 31 October 1920 in *NFTSP* (1921): 58; see also, PSN and Rita J. Simon, "Ladies of the Sisterhood: Women in the American Reform Synagogue, 1900–1930," in *Active Voices: Women in Jewish Culture,* ed. Maurie Sacks (Urbana: University of Illinois Press, 1995): 63–75, esp. p. 68.

27. Rabbi Stern in *CCARY* (1922): 171.

28. Rabbis Englander, James G. Heller, Frisch, in *CCARY* (1922): 166, 169, 170.

29. Rabbis Joseph L. Baron and Joseph Leiser, in *CCARY* (1922): 169, 173–74.

30. Rabbi Joseph Leiser and Prof. David Neumark, in *CCARY* (1922): 173, 177.

31. AJA, Martha Neumark to Maurice Schapiro, 25 May 1975.

32. *CCARY* (1922): 156–60, 175–77.

33. *CCARY* (1922): 171–72. Mrs. Frisch's opinion was changed by the men's debate.

34. Mrs. Abram Simon, "What Can the Women Do for Judaism?" *The Union Bulletin* (October 1921): 12ff. I am indebted to Denise Meringolo of the Jewish Historical Society of Greater Washington for sending this to me. An original typescript of this, not credited to Carrie Simon, is in the AJA, MS #267, 1/3, Abram Simon Collection, Sermons and Addresses, O-Y, Untitled; see also PSN and Rita J. Simon, "Sisterhood Ladies and Rabbis," esp. 74, n. 21. In her welcome to the women of NFTS in January 1923, Mrs. Daniel P. Hays echoed Simon in calling for women in the ministry; AJA, NFTS, Box 2, F.F. 2/1, Proceedings of Fifth Assembly, 1923, vol. 1, p. 89.

35. AJA, Nearprint File—Martha Neumark Montor: Martha Neumark, "The Woman Rabbi: An Autobiographiocal Sketch."

36. Cited in Meyer, "A Centennial History," 99; AJA, Nearprint File—Martha Neumark, "The Woman Rabbi: Difficulties that Beset the Path."

37. AJA, Nearprint File—Martha Neumark Montor: Martha Neumark, "The Woman Rabbi: An Autobiographical Sketch."

38. Rae Montor, *Origins: How I Got Here and What's in My Baggage* (typescript, p. 7). I am indebted to Martha Neumark Montor's daughter for sharing this with me. She indicated the phrase was her mother's.

39. AJA, Nearprint File—Martha Neumark Montor: Martha Neumark, "The Woman Rabbi: Difficulties that Beset the Path."

40. Because Neumark had studied privately with her father, she entered the rabbinical program in the second year. She was to have completed the course with the Class of 1926; AJA, Martha Neumark Montor to Maurice Schapiro, 25 May 1975. On the rabbinical curriculum, see Meyer, "A Centennial History," 58.

41. AJA, Ms. Col. #5, C-2/17, N, General: Letter from Registrar to Whom It May Concern re Martha Neumark, 17 February 1925. The HUC School for Teachers was established in New York City in 1923, part of a wave of Hebrew teachers colleges founded in the 1910s and 1920s. They included the Mizrachi Teachers Institute (1917), Hebrew Teachers College in Baltimore (1919), Hebrew Teachers College in Boston (1920), and the College of Jewish Studies in Chicago (1924). The Hebrew Union College School for Teachers closed in 1931. See Leo L. Honor, *Selected Writings of Leo L. Honor*, ed. Abraham P. Gannes (New York: Reconstructionist Press, 1965), 49–50, 87, n. 11.

42. AJA, New York World's Fair, 1964; Letters to and from Mrs. Martha Neumark Montor protesting the anti-Israel mural in the Jordan Pavilion, May 29–June 28, 1964; Miscellaneous: Martha Montor to Jacob Rader Marcus, 28 June 1964.

43. Meyer, "A Centennial History," 137–69. The JIR merged with HUC in 1950.

44. Irma L. Lindheim, *Parallel Quest: A Search of a Person and a People* (New York: Thomas Yoseloff, 1962), 106.

45. This and what follows are taken from Lindheim, *Parallel Quest*; pages 106–14 cover her years at the Jewish Institute of Religion.

46. Lindheim, *Parallel Quest*, 91–92.

47. The details are in AJA, Irma L. Lindheim, Nearprint.

48. Lindheim, *Parallel Quest*, 8; AJA, Irma L. Lindheim, Nearprint: *Jewish Daily Bulletin*, 28 September 1934.

49. Lindheim, *Parallel Quest*, 107, 111.

50. Lindheim, *Parallel Quest*, 112. Wise's biographer, Melvin I. Urofsky, confirms her assessment; *A Voice That Spoke for Justice: The Life and Times of Stephen S. Wise* (Albany: State University of New York Press, 1982), 101.

51. AJA, Ms. Col., #19, 9/7, Faculty Meetings, Minutes 1922–1951, 2 February 1923.

52. AJA, Ms. Col. #19, 9/7, Faculty Meetings, Minutes 1922–1951, 7 March 1923, 4 May 1923; *Jewish Institute of Religion Preliminary Announcement, 1923–1924*, 6; *Jewish Institute of Religion Catalogue 1946–47, 1947–48*, 24.

53. AJA, Ms. Col. #19, JIR 1921–50, S. General (I) 1923–48, 32/4: Letter from Stephen Wise to Rabbi Lee Levinger, 16 November 1925.

54. Irma L. Lindheim, *The Immortal Adventure* (New York: Macaulay Co., 1928).

55. AJHS, Stephen S. Wise Papers, Box 113: Zionism—Correspondence, Letter from Stephen S. Wise to Irma, 10 July 1925.

56. Lindheim, *Parallel Quest*, 184.

57. Ibid., 112.

58. On Askowith, see *Universal Jewish Encyclopedia* 1:552; *Who's Who in American Jewry* (1938–39); *NYT*, 25 October 1958; I have located materials on Askowith in a number of archives. The largest collection is at HC, School of General Studies Collection, currently unprocessed, File—Dora Askowith.

Among her publications are: "The Purchase of Louisiana," *Menorah* 34, 6 (June 1903; rpt. Chicago: Denoyer-Geppert, 1953); *The Toleration of the Jews Under Julius Caesar and Augustus* (New York: Columbia University, 1915); "Prolegomena to Legal Fictions or Evasions of the Law," in *Jewish Studies in Memory of Israel Abrahams* (New York: Jewish Institute of Religion, 1927); "Preface," to Luigi Luzzatti, *God in Freedom* (New York: Macmillan, 1930); *Three Outstanding Women: Mary Fels, Rebekah Kohut, Annie Nathan Meyer* (New York: Bloch Publishing, 1941). In 1956 she claimed to have written 104 articles, the majority for the Anglo-Jewish press; AJHS, Papers of the American Association of Jewish Education, Letter from Dora Askowith to Judah Pilch, 13 August 1956. I am especially grateful to Dr. Peggy Pearlstein of the Library of Congress for bringing Askowith materials to my attention and to family member Dennis S. Askwith [*sic*] of Gaithersburg, Md.

59. See, for example, her "Outline of the Course in the History Sources for the Major Religious Systems," (New York Public Library, n.d.). On the Hunter College Menorah, see *Menorah* 3, 1 (February 1917): 57; 3, 2 (April 1917): 118.

60. HC, School of General Studies … Dora Askowith: Letter from D.A. to Professor Cohen, 5 September 1944. On the percentage of Jews at Barnard College, see Susanne Klingenstein, *Jews in the American Academy, 1900–1940: The Dynamics of Intellectual Assimilation* (New Haven: Yale University Press, 1991), 210, n. 14.

61. Dora Askowith, "Miscellany: The First Zionist Flag," *Jewish Social Studies* (January 1944): 55–57; A. Bein, "The First Zionist Flag," *Jewish Social Studies* (April 1944): 150.

62. Hadassah, RG #4, Zionist Organizations and Zionist Institutional History, Box #1, F.F. #6.

63. The Women's Organization for an American Jewish Congress, "A Call to the Jewish Women of America: The Women's Organization for an American Jewish Congress," (New York: American Jewish Congress?, 1917), 8. The only extant copy I found is in the New York Public Library.

64. The Women's Organization for an American Jewish Congress, "A Call to the Jewish Women of America"; Gerald Sorin, *A Time for Building: The Third Migration, 1880–1920* (Baltimore: Johns Hopkins University Press, 1992), 211–12; American Jewish Congress, *Report of the Proceedings of the American Jewish Congress* (Philadelphia: December 1918) (New York: American Jewish Congress, n.d.).

65. Dora Askowith, "The Call of the Jewish Woman to the American Jewish Congress," *The Maccabaean* (April 1917): 26–28.

66. *The Bulletin of the Associate Alumnae of Barnard College*, vol. 14, no. 1 (December 1924); *NYT*, 25 October 1958, 21. For publications, see above.

67. Dora Askowith, "The Jewish Woman Claims Her Place," *The Jewish Ledger* (New Orleans, La.), 14 September 1928: 35–39ff. Since this was distributed through the Jewish Telegraphic Agency, it may have appeared elsewhere.

68. AJA, Ms. Col. #19, JIR, 1921–50. Askowith, Dora. Correspondence 1948. 2/8, Letter from Dora Askowith to Stephen Wise, 2 August 1948.

69. On Askowith at JIR, see JIR Faculty Meeting Minutes, vol. I, 15 April 1924; vol. II, 27 February 1929; 13 June 1929; 30 January 1930; 27 February 1930; 10 April 1930; 9 October 1930; 3 February 1931; 19 February 1931; 11 June 1931; 19 November 1931; 24 March 1932; 19 October 1936; 27 January 1937; 4 October 1937. See also AJA, Ms. Col. #19, JIR 1921–50, Dora Askowith Correspondence, 1948, 2/8: Letter from Dora Askowith to Stephen S. Wise, 2 August 1948; AJA, Ms. Col. #49, Stephen S. Wise, 1/6 Gertrude Adelstein: Letter from Gertrude Adelstein to Stephen S. Wise, 10 October 1930.

70. Askowith claimed to have published her student sermon, but I have not located this. Instead this is drawn from Dora Askowith, "The Role of Women in the Field of Higher Jewish Education," where she discussed her research for that sermon; *Judaism* 5 (1956): 169–72.

71. Cf. Meyer, "A Centennial History," 154.

72. JIR Faculty Minutes, 3 February 1931.

73. AJA, Ms. Col. #19, JIR 1921–50, Dora Askowith Correspondence, 1948, 2/8: Letter from Dora Askowith to Stephen S. Wise, 2 August 1948.

74. Deborah Dash Moore, "A Synagogue Center Grows in Brooklyn," in *The American Synagogue: A Sanctuary Transformed*, ed. Jack Wertheimer (Cambridge, England: Cambridge University Press, 1987), 297–326; David I. Cederbaum, "Extent and Cost of Jewish Education in the United States," *JE* 1 (1929): 53–54.

75. I am grateful to Jay Lueger for bringing to my attention early material on Helen Levinthal; *NYT*, 29 November 1932, 16. AJA, Ms. Col. #19, JIR 1921–50, F.F. Students, General Correspondence, Minutes, Lists 1931–41, 36/4.

76. JIR, Faculty Meeting Minutes, 23 April 1931; 7 June 1931; 23 September 1931; 22 October 1931; 29 October 1935; AJA, Ms. Col. #19 JIR 1921–50, Students, General Correspondence, Minutes, Lists 1931–41, 36/4. Other female students in these years included Dr. Trude Weiss Rosmarin, later editor of *The Jewish Spectator*; Tamar de Sola Pool, who would become national president of Hadassah; and Judith Kaplan Eisenstein, former Bat Mitzvah girl and composer of Jewish music.

Note that in 1931, Lily Montagu, the religious organizer, leader, and preacher of Liberal Judaism in England, toured the United States on behalf of the World Union for Progressive Judaism. She spoke at JIR and also received an honorary doctorate from HUC. There is no indication that her model of religious leadership influenced the female rabbinical aspirants of this era. On her 1931 tour, see AJA, Ms. Col. #19, JIR 1921–50, Lilian Helen Montagu, 27/6; on Montagu, see Ellen M. Umansky, *Lily Montagu and the Advancement of Liberal Judaism: From Vision to Vocation* (New York: Edwin Mellen Press, 1983).

77. AJA, Ms. Col. #19, JIR 1921–50, Students, General Correspondence, Minutes, Lists 1931–41, 36/4: Helen Levinthal admitted as Helen L. Sukloff; AJA, Ms. Col. #19, Stephen S. Wise, 4/19 JIR 1922–48: Report of Activities for 1937–38, 1938–39; *Jewish Institute of Religion Catalogue*, 1937–38, 1938–39.

78. "Girl Completes Rabbinic Study; 9 Men Ordained," *Herald Tribune*, 19 May 1939; JIR, Faculty Minutes, 29 October 1935.

79. LLC, "Woman Passes Test, but She is Barred from Becoming a Rabbi Because Talmud Doesn't Recognize Her Sex in Synagogues," *New York World-Telegram*, 29 May 1939. I am deeply indebted to Lester Lyons, husband of the late Hadassah Levinthal Lyons, who shared his files with me.

80. For example, when the class of 1939 received letters enclosing the regulations for the thesis the students were required to submit to get their M.H.L. degrees and ordination, Helen Levinthal's name was pencilled in at the bottom; AJA, Ms. #19, JIR 1921–50, Students: Thesis, Correspondence, Lists, 36/8.

81. Cited in LLC, Letter from Alfred Gottschalk to Earl Stone, 24 July 1985.

82. RC, Rabbi Israel H. Levinthal Material: correspondence, RG 32, Box 12, F.F. Levinthal Correspondence, 1936–40, Letter from Boaz Cohen to Israel Levinthal, 17 October 1939. On Boaz Cohen, see PSN, *Conservative Judaism in America: A Biographical Dictionary and Sourcebook* (Westport, Conn.: Greenwood Press, 1988), 53–55.

83. AJA; Helen Hadassah Levinthal, "Correspondence re her completion of all rabbinic courses," 1971–72. Correspondence File: Letter from Israel Levinthal to Jacob Marcus, 14 April 1972; Letter from Helen Levinthal Lyons to Earl Stone, 18 May 1971.

84. JIR, Faculty Minutes, vol. II, 19 June 1930, described Benderly's proposal. Meyer, "A Centennial History," 155. Re her classmates' sense that she completed the same curriculum they did, see LLC, Letter from Earl Stone to Helen Levinthal Lyons, 25 May 1971. Isaac Levitats earned an M.H.L. in 1933; *Jewish Institute of Religion Catalogue*, 1935–36.

85. Moore, "A Synagogue Center Grows in Brooklyn," 314.

86. Helen Hadassah Levinthal, "Women Suffrage from the Halachic Aspect," JIR Department of Talmud (HUC-JIR, New York), esp. 23, 86.

87. Levinthal, "Women Suffrage from the Halachic Aspect," 19.

88. AJA, Ms. Col. #19, JIR 1921–50, Box 37, F.F. 9 (37/9): Chaim Tchernowitz Correspondence.

89. AJA, Ms. Col. #19, JIR 1921–50, Students: Thesis, Correspondence, Lists, 36/8: Faculty Meeting, 31 March 1939.

90. RC, Rabbi Israel H. Levinthal Material: RG 32, Box 6, Sermons and Addresses 1935–39, F.F. 1939, 3 March 1939. Lester Lyons has reported that his wife did not keep copies of her sermons and speeches; interview with Lester Lyons, 7 June 1993.

91. AJA, Ms. Col. #19, JIR 1921–50, Commencement 1938, 1939, 5/18: Petition, 12 May 1938.

92. AJA, Ms. Col. #19, JIR 1921–50, Commencement 1938, 1939, 5/18: Letter from Stephen Wise to the Junior Class, 25 May 1938.

93. LLC, Yoffe, "Portraits of Yiddish Women," *Der Tag* (23 May 1940); I am grateful to Mr. Lyons for the translation; AJA, Ms. Col. #19, JIR 1921–50, Commencement 1938, 1939, 5/18: Letter from Gertrude Adelstein to Stephen Wise, 4 May 1939. Meyer explains that during most of the school's history, Wise avoided the word "ordination" in conferring the rabbinical degree and that he never used the traditional formulation of *semikha* in the Hebrew certificate awarded JIR graduates; "A Centennial History," 159, 273, n. 50.

94. JIR Faculty Minutes, Vol. III, 24 January 1938; AJA, Helen Hadassah Levinthal Lyons, "Correspondence re her completion of all rabbinic courses," 1971–72 Correspondence File, Letter from Israel Levinthal to Jacob Marcus, 14 April 1972; LLC, Letter from Israel Levinthal to Alfred Gottschalk, 25 April 1972.

95. This and what follows are based on LLC, "Girl Completes Rabbinic Study; 9 Men Ordained," *Herald Tribune*, 29 May 1939; "Religious History in the Making," typescript from B'nai Sholaum re 1939 High Holidays; *Brooklyn Jewish Center Review* (June 1939): 11ff; "Religion," *Time* (2 October 1939): 48; "Woman Passes Tests, but She Is Barred from Becoming a Rabbi because Talmud Doesn't Recognize Her Sex in Synagogues," *New York World-Telegram*, 29 May 1939.

96. I recognize that historical arguments from silent sources are extremely problematic. Yet, none of the sources on Helen Levinthal or by Dora Askowith then or later indicate awareness of Jonas's accomplishment. For example, in "Women in the Ministry," Dora Askowith's letter to the editor of *NYT* (7 March 1947, 24), she does not mention Jonas. Similarly, in 1956 in listing women she saw as *rabbinim*, Jonas does not appear; "The Role of Women in the Field of Higher Jewish Education." The news accounts describing Helen Levinthal's graduation from JIR in 1939 do not mention Jonas's precedent. For example, the *Herald Tribune* claimed: "Miss Levinthal is believed to be the first woman ever to complete a scholastic course leading to the rabbinate" (29 May 1939). Finally, in a letter written in April 1972, Rabbi Israel Levinthal mentions that only now has he learned from the press of Regina Jonas; AJA, Helen Ha-

dassah Levinthal, Correspondence re her completion of all rabbinic courses, Correspondence File 1971–72: Letter from Israel Levinthal to Jacob Marcus, 14 April 1972.

97. Unless otherwise noted, what follows is from Katharina von Kellenbach, " 'God Does Not Oppress Any Human Being': The Life and Thought of Rabbi Regina Jonas," *Leo Baeck Institute Year Book* 39 (1994): 213–25; citation, 213. See also Alexander Guttman, "Hochschule Retrospective," *CCARJ* (Autumn 1972): 74, 79; Alexander Guttman, "The Woman Rabbi: An Historical Perspective," *Journal of Reform Judaism* (Summer 1982): 21–25.

98. Meyer, *Response to Modernity,* 191; *EJ* (Jerusalem: Keter, 1972) 8:799–801.

99. Citations, von Kellenbach, "Regina Jonas," 215–19. I wish to thank Prof. von Kellenbach for going over Jonas's thesis with me.

100. On Baneth, see *EJ* 4:161.

101. Professor Israel Lehman confirmed this in an interview, 9 February 1989.

102. Citations, von Kellenbach, "Regina Jonas," 215.

103. "Max Dienemann," *EJ* 6:25.

104. On the various forms of rabbinic ordination, see "Semikhah," *EJ* 14: 1140–47.

105. Citation, von Kellenbach, "Regina Jonas," 219–20 (emphasis in original).

106. PSN and Simon, "Ladies of the Sisterhood," 68.

107. AJA, Ms. Col. #72, UAHC, Box 44, F.F. /8: 1921–22. Executive Secretary Correspondence: Letter from Benno Lewinson to George Zepin, 23 February 1921.

108. Conservative Jewish women organized the National Women's League of the United Synagogue of America in 1918. The Women's Branch of the Union of Orthodox Jewish Congregations was founded in 1923. On Orthodox women in New York City in these years, see Jenna Weissman Joselit, *New York's Jewish Jews: The Orthodox Community in the Interwar Years* (Bloomington: Indiana University Press, 1990), 97–122.

109. "The Advance of Womanhood—New Social Trails," *AH,* 18 November 1927: 1.

110. Alice Kessler-Harris, *Out to Work: A History of Wage-Earning Women in the United States* (New York: Oxford University Press, 1982), 116, 226–27; Rosalind Rosenberg, *Divided Lives: American Women in the Twentieth Century* (New York: Hill and Wang, 1992), 94.

111. Barbara Miller Solomon, *In the Company of Educated Women: A History of Women and Higher Education in America* (New Haven: Yale University Press, 1985), table 2. See also Patricia Albjerg Graham, "Expansion and Exclusion: A History of Women in American Higher Education," *Signs: Journal of Women in Culture and Society* (Summer 1978): 764.

112. Rosenberg, *Divided Lives,* 94; Solomon, *In the Company of Educated Women,* 172; Kessler-Harris, *Out to Work,* 227.

113. Marjorie Nicolson, quoted in Graham, "Expansion and Exclusion," 765.

114. Penina Migdal Glazer and Miriam Slater, *Unequal Colleagues: The Entrance of*

Women into the Professions, 1890–1940 (New Brunswick: Rutgers University Press, 1986), 22.

115. Solomon, *In the Company of Educated Women*, 119–21; Rosenberg, *Divided Lives*, 94–95; Graham, "Expansion and Exclusion": 771; Lynn D. Gordon, *Gender and Higher Education in the Progressive Era* (New Haven: Yale University Press, 1990), 5.

116. Gordon, *Gender and Higher Education in the Progressive Era*, 5; Ruth Sapinsky, "The Jewish Girl at College," *Menorah Journal* 2, 5 (December 1916): 294–300.

117. William H. Chafe, *The Paradox of Change: American Women in the 20th Century* (New York: Oxford University Press, 1991), 111; Rosenberg, *Divided Lives*, 94–95.

118. Solomon, *In the Company of Educated Women*, 185.

119. On career aspirations of Jewish college men and women, see "Professional Tendencies Among Jewish Students in Colleges, Universities, and Professional Schools," *AJYB 5681* 22 [1920–21] (Philadelphia: Jewish Publication Society, 1920), 383–93.

120. My interview with Lester Lyons, 7 June 1993.

121. Montor, *Origins: How I Got Here and What's in My Baggage*, 7.

122. See chap. 2.

123. Lindheim, *Parallel Quest*, 81; AJHS, Stephen S. Wise Papers, Box 113: Zionism—Correspondence: Letter from Stephen S. Wise to Irma Lindheim, 4 November 1935.

124. AJA, Nearprint File—Martha Neumark Montor: Martha Neumark, "The Woman Rabbi: Difficulties that Beset the Path."

125. Rosemary Skinner Keller, "Patterns of Laywomen's Leadership in Twentieth-Century Protestantism," in *Women and Religion in America*, vol. 3, 271–73, 299–303.

126. Chaves, *Ordaining Women*, table 2.1.

127. "Woman's Progress Toward the Pulpit," *Literary Digest* (23 October 1920): 34; "Favors Women As Rabbis," *NYT*, 6 October 1922, 25; "Women in Pulpits Debated in Temple," *NYT*, 21 March 1924, 7; "Methodists Accept Woman As Preacher," *NYT*, 27 March 1925, 9; "Protest Woman in Pulpit," *NYT*, 30 June 1925, 44; "2 More Women Ordained," *NYT*, 26 April 1926, 23; "German Synod Admits Women to Clergy, but Only Celibates," *NYT*, 10 May 1927, 10.

128. Bock, "The Female Clergy": 534, table 1.

129. Libbian Benedict, "Jewish Women Headliners—XLVIII: Clarice M. Baright—Magistrate," *AH*, 1 January 1926. See also "Business Women in Industry," *AH*, 5 November 1926; Elsa Weihl, "Jewish Women Headliners—LVII: Elsa Weihl, Writer," *AH*, 5 November 1926: 844; Virginia Gildersleve, "Women and Careers," *AH*, 2 November 1928: 827ff.

130. AJA, Nearprint File—Martha Neumark Montor: Martha Neumark, "The Woman Rabbi: Difficulties that Beset the Path." See for example, AJA, Ms. Col. #5, C-1/4, Board of Governors, 1920–1930, 3 March 1921, 31 March 1921: when the Board considered Dora Landau's letter querying whether women qualified for scholarships; see also the discussion of Adeline Seltzer's application; JIR Faculty Minutes, Vol. II, 23 April 1931, 7 June 1931.

131. Lucile Helene Uhry, *The Guardian*, June 1919. I am deeply grateful to my American University colleague, Professor Saul Newman, and to his father, the late Jeremy Newman, for bringing these to my attention.

132. Letter from Stephen S. Wise to "My dear Lucille," 31 May 1919, courtesy of Jeremy U. Newman.

133. "Profile Mrs. Louis I. Newman," *Rodeph Sholom Chronicle* (New York, 1972), courtesy of Jeremy Newman.

134. On Wise's political intervention for Norvin Lindheim, including correspondence with the president of the United States and others, see AJHS, Stephen S. Wise Papers, Box 113, Zionism—Correspondence: Letters to and from Stephen S. Wise, dated 7 May 1919 through 4 June 1925 discuss the matter. On Stephen Lindheim, see Lindheim, *Parallel Quest*, 209.

135. Ralph Marcus, "In Memoriam: Norvin R. Lindheim," *Jewish Institute Quarterly* 4, 2 (January 1929; misdated January 1928). AJHS, Stephen S. Wise Papers, Box 113, Zionism—Correspondence: Letter from Stephen S. Wise to Norvin Lindheim, 16 March 1925.

136. JIR, Faculty Minutes, Vol. I (September 1922–July 1928); II (September 1928–July 1932); III (1933–43). Askowith, who entered the Institute in its first year, is discussed in a number of meetings. The faculty concluded that Lindheim's lack of a bachelor's degree was more than made up for by her "background of information and culture" and her work at JIR which warranted admitting her as a regular student; 11 December 1924.

137. I am grateful to Dianne Ashton for suggesting this term.

138. JIR Faculty Minutes, Vol. II, 23 April 1931, 7 June 1931 re Adeline Seltzer's application. Note the historian Michael Meyer writes of Martha Neumark: "Her grades generally were at best mediocre"; "A Centennial History," 263, n. 26.

139. Chafe, *Paradox of Change*, 100; Nancy Cott, *The Grounding of Modern Feminism*, (New Haven: Yale University Press, 1987), 217–18; Solomon, *In the Company of Educated Women*, table 5.

140. Chaves, *Ordaining Women*, 27.

141. Bock, "The Female Clergy": 534, table 1. Bock gives the following figures for employed female clergy: 1900: 3,405; 1910: 685; 1920: 1,787; 1930: 3,276; 1940: 3,148; 1950: 6,777; 1960: 4,695.

142. Israel S. Chipkin, "The Jewish Teacher in New York City and the Remuneration for His Services," *JED* 2 (1930): 166–67.

143. Samuel Dinin and Israel L. Eisenberg, "Professional Prospects in Jewish Education," *JED* 5 (1933): 53; "Members of the National Council for Jewish Education," *JED* 2 (1930): 176–77.

144. RC, Brooklyn Jewish Center, Box 10, F.F.—Correspondence with L Names: Letter from Israel Levinthal to Annie Linick, 11 March 1940. On the Academy, see Moore, "A Synagogue Center Grows in Brooklyn," 315–20.

145. Chafe, *Paradox of Change*, 100, 44.

146. AJA Ms. Col. #5, B-3/6, From Songs and Yells of the H.U.C. Student Body, 1923–24 #23. Rae Montor described Mannie Neumark as brilliant; *Origins: How I Got Here and What's in My Baggage*, 6.

147. Chafe, *Paradox of Change*, 111; Solomon, *In the Company of Educated Women*, 176.

148. Chipkin, "The Jewish Teacher in New York City," 166–67.

149. Cott, *Grounding of Modern Feminism*, 179, 182–83.

150. Cott, *Grounding of Modern Feminism*, 221; Chafe, *Paradox of Change*, 101.

151. Cott, *Grounding of Modern Feminism*, 221.

152. The *AH* observed that in 1920 HUC had failed to fill thirty-four vacant pulpits and had only graduated ten new rabbis; "Editorial," 18 June 1920: 117.

153. PSN, *Conservative Judaism in America*, 302.

154. LLC, *Brooklyn Jewish Center Review* (June 1939): 11ff.

155. On morality as the "practical operative principle of the Reform movement," see Meyer, *Response to Modernity*, 65.

156. AJA, HUC Board of Governors Meetings, 21 January 1922: 162.

157. Urofsky, *A Voice That Spoke for Justice*, 101.

158. Urofsky, *A Voice That Spoke for Justice*, 101; James Waterman Wise, *Legend of Louise: The Life Story of Mrs. Stephen S. Wise* (New York: Jewish Opinion Publishing Corp., 1949).

159. Justine Wise Polier, "The Rabbi's Daughter as Judge and Humanist," in *Creators and Disturbers: Reminiscences by Jewish Intellectuals of New York*, ed. Bernard Rosenberg and Ernest Goldstein (New York: Columbia University Press, 1982), 336; Karen Berger Morello, *The Invisible Bar: The Woman Lawyer in America: 1638 to the Present* (New York: Random House, 1986), 93. I am grateful to my colleague, Professor Richard Breitman, for suggesting Justine Wise Polier to me.

160. *Who's Who in American Jewry 1928*, 2d ed. (New York: The Jewish Biographical Bureau, 1928). I wish to thank American University student Andrea Becker Herman who assisted in compiling this data. Note the category of "volunteer, social, welfare or civic work[er]" surely encompassed some women, although I think relatively few, who were professional social workers. The 1928 *Who's Who* uses these categories interchangeably and does not indicate who engaged in social work as a profession. On women in the profession of psychiatric social work, see Glazer and Slater, *Unequal Colleagues*, 165–208.

161. Mordecai M. Kaplan, "What the American Jewish Woman Can Do for Adult Jewish Education," *JED* 4, 3 (October-December 1932), 144; see also Carole S. Kessner, "Kaplan and the Role of Women in Judaism," in *The American Judaism of Mordecai M. Kaplan*, ed. Emanuel Goldsmith, Mel Scult, and Robert Seltzer (New York: New York University Press, 1990), 335–56.

162. AJHS, Stephen S. Wise Papers, Box 113, Zionism—Correspondence, Letter from Stephen S. Wise to Irma Lindheim, 18 May 1925.

163. On Henry Montor, see "Henry Montor," *EJ* 12:281; *AJYB 1984* vol. 84 (New York: American Jewish Committee, 1983): 337; Abraham J. Karp, *Haven and Home: A History of the Jews in America* (New York: Schocken Books, 1985): 290–91.

164. Interview with Professor Karel Montor, 20 December 1995; Montor, *Origins: How I Got Here and What's in My Baggage.*

165. Montor, *Origins: How I Got Here and What's in My Baggage.*

166. AJA, Martha Neumark Montor—Nearprint File: Memo to Paul M. Steinberg, from Martha Neumark Montor, 26 March 1962.

167. Interview with Professor Karel Montor, 20 December 1995. Martha Neumark Montor's feminist legacy extended to her son. A professor at the United States Naval Academy, Karel Montor was the faculty member commanded to plan, in the summer of 1976, for the integration of its first female midshipmen.

168. Montor, *Origins: How I Got Here and What's in My Baggage*, 15.

169. AJA, New York World's Fair, 1964, Letters to and from Mrs. Martha Neumark Montor; AJA, Martha Neumark Montor to Maurice Schapiro, 25 May 1975.

170. Kessler-Harris, *Out to Work*, chap. 11.

171. AJA, New York World's Fair, 1964, Letters to and from Mrs. Martha Neumark Montor, F.F. Miscellaneous: Letter from Martha Neumark Montor to Jacob Rader Marcus, 28 June 1964. AJA, Nearprint File—Martha Neumark Montor: Martha Neumark, "The Woman Rabbi: Difficulties."

172. AJA, Martha Neumark Montor—Nearprint File: Memo to Paul M. Steinberg, from Martha Neumark Montor, 26 March 1962. AJA, New York World's Fair, 1964, Letters to and from Mrs. Martha Neumark Montor, Letter from Martha Neumark Montor to Jacob Rader Marcus, 28 June 1964. AJA, Biographies File: Martha Neumark Montor, "Papa Was a Philosopher."

173. Lindheim, *The Immortal Adventure*, 74, 104.

174. Lindheim, *Parallel Quest*, 201–3. Here Lindheim quoted from letters she wrote to and received from Szold at the time.

175. Lindheim, *Parallel Quest*, 226, 253. On the controversy with Lipsky, see Hadassah, RG #4 Zionist Organizations and Zionist Institutional History, Box #1, Folders #3, 4, 7.

176. AJHS, Stephen S. Wise Papers, Box 113, Zionism—Correspondence: Irma Lindheim, "Palestine Challenges: To an Immortal Adventure," typescript of address at Carnegie Hall on 17 March 1935.

177. On Lindheim's later activities, see Hadassah, Microfilm Reel #16 Zionist Political History, Hadassah President's Correspondence Series, RG #7 Irma Lindheim Correspondence, 26 July 1943–1 August 1963, 16 January 1964–10 February 1977.

178. AJHS, Stephen S. Wise Papers, Box 113, Zionism—Correspondence: Letter from Irma Lindheim to Stephen S. Wise, 5 July 1939.

179. HC, School of General Studies . . . Dora Askowith: Letter from Dora Askowith to ?, n.d. (follows letter dated 2 April 1956).

180. "Outline of the Course in the History Sources for the Major Religious Systems," (New York Public Library, n.d.). For very different evaluations of Askowith as a professor, see HC, School of General Studies . . . Dora Askowith: Josephine Rosenzweig, "Minutes of Interview Held in Prof. A. Broderick Cohen's office," 5 March 1941, when a student committee petitioned to have Askowith tenured. See AJA, Ms. Col. #19, JIR 1921–50, Dora Askowith Correspondence: Letter from H. Slonimsky to Rabbi Bertram W. Korn, 16 August 1948: "I would merely say that in spite of the formidable and impressive character of the curriculum vitae which she gives Dr. Glueck in her letter, she is an utterly ungifted person who, in the course of more than twenty or twenty-five years of teaching at Hunter has never been advanced beyond night courses and extension courses."

181. See, for example, HC, School of General Studies . . . Dora Askowith: Letter from Dora Askowith to Professor Cohen, 24 July 1941; Letter from Dora Askowith to Dr. Patterson, 20 December 1941. Askowith's professional marginality and her devotion appear typical of other female historians, who, in these years, "were not well integrated into the academic marketplace"; Kathryn Kish Sklar, "American Female Historians in Context, 1770–1920," *Feminist Studies* 3, 1–2 (Fall 1975): 179, 181.

182. HC, School of General Studies . . . Dora Askowith: Dora Askowith, "The Thirty-Fifth Anniversary of the Founding of the Hunter College Menorah Society" (December 1947). AJHS, Stephen S. Wise Papers, Box 136: Personal Correspondence, Folder 18: Dora Askowith: Letter from Dora Askowith to Stephen S. Wise, 14 May 1943.

183. See, for example, HC, School of General Studies . . . Dora Askowith: Memo from A.?.?. to Dr. Colligan, 1 October 1937; Letter from Dora Askowith to President Shuster, 8 February 1942. See also AJHS, Stephen S. Wise Papers, Box 112: Zionism, Correspondence, Folder 11: Kohut, Rebekah, 1895–1949. The correspondence indicates that both Stephen Wise and Rebekah Kohut tried to improve both Askowith's position at Hunter and her material circumstances. (Letter from Stephen S. Wise to Rebekah Kohut, 2 October 1934). Here, too, Wise reported that Hunter College President Shuster criticized Askowith: "she doesn't really teach History but only Jewish History, no matter what the subject is that she is supposed to teach." (Letter from Stephen S. Wise to Rebekah Kohut, 2 May 1942).

184. Askowith's papers at HC and at AJHS (in the Stephen S. Wise Papers) refer to other articles she published.

185. Dora Askowith, "Letter to the Editor: Women in the Ministry," *NYT*, 7 March 1947, 24.

186. AJA, Ms. Col. #19, JIR, 1921–50. Askowith, Dora. Correspondence 1948. 2/8, Letter from Dora Askowith to Stephen Wise, 2 August 1948. Askowith, "The Role of Women in the Field of Higher Jewish Education," 169–72.

187. "Dora Askowith, Teacher, Author," *NYT*, 25 October 1958, 21. Apparently, only a short story excerpted from this remains: see Dora Askowith, "Three Classmates," *The Jewish Advocate*, 4 December 1947. Askowith claimed that this was from the autobiography; AJHS, Stephen S. Wise Papers, Box 136: Personal Correspondence, Folder 18: Dora Askowith: Letter from Dora Askowith to Stephen S. Wise, 4 February 1948.

188. She wore an academic gown to preach; "First," *Time* (2 October 1939): 48.

189. LLC, "Religious History in the Making," typescript.

190. LLC, "The First Woman to Complete a Rabbinical Course," *Brooklyn Jewish Center Review* (June 1939), 11ff.

191. LLC, "Helen Levinthal Lyons to Occupy Pulpit Tonight," *The Jewish Center Bulletin* (12 January 1940): 1.

192. LLC, Jewish Center Lecture Bureau, Programs 1946–47; "Helen Levinthal Lyons: Lecturer," (New York: Jewish Center Lecture Bureau).

193. LLC, Jean Yoffe, "Portraits of Yiddish Women," *Der Tog*, 23 May 1940.

194. LLC, Helen Levinthal curriculum vitae; Simchat Torah Program, Beth El Synagogue, 19 October 1984; Program for a reception honoring Lester and Helen Lyons, held on behalf of the JTSA, 18 June 1986.

195. In all there are nineteen letters, to and from, among others, Rabbi Earl Stone, Helen Levinthal Lyons, Rabbi Israel Levinthal, and HUC-JIR President Alfred Gottschalk, dated 10 May 1971 to 23 October 1985, tracing the discussion. LLC, Earl S. Stone to Alfred Gottschalk, 10 May 1971; Helen Levinthal Lyons to Earl S. Stone, 18 May 1971.

196. LLC, Letter from Alfred Gottschalk to Israel Levinthal, 2 May 1972.

197. LLC, Letter from Earl Stone to Mrs. Lester Lyons, 22 September 1975, 30 May 1979.

198. LLC, Joshua Peck and K. J. White, "Ordination decision applauded by woman who trained as rabbi," *Gannett Westchester Newspapers*, 19 February 1985; Letter from Earl S. Stone to Mrs. Lester Lyons, 9 April 1985.

199. LLC, Letter from Earl Stone to Mrs. Lester Lyons, 23 May 1985; Letter from Lester Lyons to Eugene P. Edwinn, 28 May 1985; Letter from Eugene P. Edwinn to Alexander Schindler, 4 June 1985.

200. LLC, Letter from Alfred Gottschalk to Earl Stone, 24 July 1985.

201. LLC, Letter from Earl Stone to Mrs. Lester Lyons, 6 August 1985.

202. LLC, HUC-JIR, "A Special Citation of Recognition to Helen Levinthal Lyons," 11 November 1988.

203. Adrienne Rich, *Of Woman Born* (New York: W. W. Norton, 1976), 43–45.

204. Marion A. Kaplan, *The Making of the Jewish Middle Class: Women, Family, and Identity in Imperial Germany* (New York: Oxford University Press, 1991): 68. See also Meyer, *Response to Modernity,* 379. See chap. 1 of this book.

205. Kaplan, *Making of the Jewish Middle Class,* 168–69, 173, 281, n. 69.

206. von Kellenbach, " 'God Does Not Oppress Any Human Being,' " 221; Marion A. Kaplan, *The Jewish Feminist Movement in Germany: The Campaigns of the Jüdischer Frauenbund, 1904–1938* (Westport, Conn.: Greenwood Press, 1979), 167, n. 35; Kaplan, *Making of the Jewish Middle Class,* 169. For example, Kaplan suggests that one-third of the female doctors at the end of the Imperial Era were Jews.

207. Kaplan, *Jewish Feminist Movement in Germany*, 93.

208. Ibid., 81, 93, 162–64, 168, n. 60; on *agunot*, see chap. 1.

209. Note that Montagu had come to Germany on behalf of the World Union for Progressive Judaism; Umansky, *Lily Montagu and the Advancement of Liberal Judaism*, 177; see n. 76.

210. Kaplan, *Jewish Feminist Movement in Germany*, 81, 93, 162–64, 168, n. 60.

211. My interview with Israel Lehman, 9 February 1989.

212. Mary Lowenthal Felstiner, *To Paint Her Life: Charlotte Salomon in the Nazi Era* (New York: HarperCollins, 1994), 55; Marion A. Kaplan, "Jewish Women in Nazi Germany: Daily Life, Daily Struggles, 1933–39," in *Different Voices: Women and the Holocaust*, ed. Carol Rittner and John K. Roth (New York: Paragon, 1993), 187–212.

213. Alexander Guttman, "Hochschule Retrospective," *CCAR Journal* (Autumn 1972) indicated that in 1932 of the 155 students at the Hochschule, 27 were women.

214. von Kellenbach, " 'God Does Not Oppress Any Human Being,' " 220.

215. Ibid., 220–22.

216. Ibid., 221–25.

217. Gratz College Holocaust Archive, Interviews of Hardy Kupferberg and Susan Neulander Faulkner. I wish to thank Prof. Reena Sigman Friedman for bringing this to my attention.

218. Sally Priesand, *Judaism and the New Woman* (New York: Behrman House, 1975), 67. This is the published version, with minimal revisions, of Priesand's rabbinic thesis (Klau Library, Hebrew Union College, 1972).

219. AJA, Ms. Col. #19, JIR 1921–50, Admissions and Registration, 1/6: Letter from Henry Slonimsky to Mrs. Nettie Stolper, 23 September 1947.

220. AJA, Henry Slonimsky, Essay with Bibliography Discussion Changes in the Status of Women and Marriage (France 1948), Small Collections, unpaged.

221. Anna Quindlen, *Living Out Loud* (New York: Random House, 1988), xvii.

CHAPTER 4: "AN IDEA WHOSE TIME HAS COME": 1972

The quotation that forms the title for chapter 4 is taken from AJA, HUC-JIR Board of Governors Reports and Minutes of Meetings, 1971–73: "Report of the President of the Board of Governors," 1 June 1972, 3–4.

1. "Report on the Ordination of Women," *CCARY* 66 (1956): 92.

2. Rosalind Rosenberg, *Divided Lives: American Women in the Twentieth Century* (New York: Hill and Wang, 1992), 147; Barbara Miller Solomon, *In the Company of Educated Women: A History of Women and Higher Education in America* (New Haven: Yale University Press, 1985), 63, table 2.

3. Alice Kessler-Harris, *Out to Work: A History of Wage-Earning Women in the United*

States (New York: Oxford University Press, 1982), 300–3; Rosenberg, *Divided Lives*, 157–62.

4. Solomon, *In the Company of Educated Women*, 133, table 6; 190–91, 198.

5. Sara M. Evans, *Born for Liberty: A History of Women in America* (New York: Free Press, 1989), 261; Leila J. Rupp and Verta Taylor, *Survival in the Doldrums: The American Women's Rights Movement, 1945 to the 1960s* (New York: Oxford University Press, 1987), 21, Eugenia Kaledin cited, 18. See also William H. Chafe, *The Paradox of Change: American Women in the 20th Century* (New York: Oxford University Press, 1991), 163, 188.

6. Edward Shapiro, *A Time for Healing: American Jewry since World War II* (Baltimore: Johns Hopkins University Press, 1992), 143, 149. See also Deborah Dash Moore, *To the Golden Cities: Pursuing the American Jewish Dream in Miami and L.A.* (New York: Free Press, 1994), 38–39, 49–50.

7. Rosenberg, *Divided Lives*, 167.

8. Unless otherwise noted, this and what follows are from: AJA, Microfilm 2041, Meridian, Mississippi, Temple Beth Israel Minutes and Miscellaneous Material Relating to the Activities of Rabbi and Mrs. William Ackerman. AJA, Paula Ackerman, Correspondence File, including Letter to Jacob Marcus, 24 April 1979. Ellen Umansky, "Paula Ackerman: Reform's Lost Woman Rabbi," (interview) *Genesis 2* 17, 3 (June/July 1986): 18–20. See also Ellen Umansky, "Paula Ackerman," in *Reform Judaism in America: A Biographical Dictionary and Sourcebook*, ed. Kerry M. Olitzky, Lance J. Sussman, and Malcolm H. Stern (Westport, Conn.: Greenwood Press, 1993), 1–2. Note that this erroneously includes Ackerman as her maiden name and gives the wrong concluding date for her spiritual leadership. See instead, *Four Centuries of Jewish Women's Spirituality: A Sourcebook*, ed. Ellen M. Umansky and Dianne Ashton (Boston: Beacon Press, 1992), 122–23, 184–86.

9. On this theme, see Shuly Rubin Schwartz, " 'We Married What We Wanted to Be': The *Rebbetzin* in Twentieth-Century America," *AJH* 83 (June 1995): 229.

10. Mrs. William Ackerman, "Participation of Small Sisterhoods: House of Living Judaism Campaign," *NFTSP* (1948): 217–18.

11. On Carrie Simon, see chap. 3.

12. Paula H. Ackerman, "Report of the National Committee on Religious Schools," *NFTSP* 4 (18 December 1944): 74–75; (22 December 1945): 136–37.

13. Ackerman, "Participation of Small Sisterhoods," 217–18.

14. AJA, Paula Ackerman, Correspondence File, Letter from Paula Ackerman to "Friend," (likely Jacob D. Schwarz), 12 December 1950.

15. AJA, Paula Ackerman, Correspondence File, Letter from JDS (Jacob D. Schwarz) to Mrs. William Ackerman, 20 December 1950. On Jacob D. Schwarz, see the unsigned entry in *Reform Judaism in America*, 187–88.

16. AJA, Paula Ackerman, Correspondence File, Letter from JDS (Jacob D. Schwarz) to Mrs. William Ackerman, 20 December 1950.

17. AJA, Paula Ackerman, Correspondence File, Letter from Paula Ackerman to "Friend" (Jacob D. Schwarz), 9 January 1951. For a discussion of the possibility opening to Paula Ackerman because she lived on the frontier of Jewish life, see PSN, "A Land of Opportunities: Jewish Women Encounter America," in *What Is American about the American Jewish Experience?*, ed. Marc Lee Raphael (Williamsburg, Va.: College of William and Mary, 1993), 81–82.

18. AJA, Microfilm 2041, Jane Evans to Paula Ackerman, 18 December 1950; quotations, "The Silent Sex," *Time*, 22 January 1951, 48.

19. AJA, Paula Ackerman, Correspondence File, Letter from Maurice N. Eisendrath to Sidney Kay, 12 December 1950; Letter from Sidney Kay to Maurice N. Eisendrath, 11 January 1951; UAHC News Release, 15 January 1951; Letter from Paula Ackerman to Jake (Jacob D. Schwarz), 23 January 1951; Eisendrath quoted in *Time*, 22 January 1951, 48.

20. AJA, Paula Ackerman, Correspondence File, Letter from Paula Ackerman to Jake (Jacob D. Schwarz), 23 January 1951; Letter from S.H.G. (Samuel H. Goldenson) to Sidney Kay, 30 January 1951.

21. AJA, Paula Ackerman, Correspondence File, Letter from Mrs. William Ackerman to "Friend" (Jacob D. Schwarz), 9 January 1951.

22. AJA, Microfilm 2041 includes her reports to the congregation, 11 November 1951, 26 October 1952, 25 October 1953; AJA, Paula Ackerman File, Letter to Jacob Marcus, 24 April, 1979.

23. AJA, Microfilm 2041, Paula Ackerman's report to the congregation, 25 October 1953.

24. Umansky, "Paula Ackerman: Reform's Lost Woman Rabbi"; AJA, Paula Ackerman, Nearprint: *CCAR Newsletter*, 35, 5 (February 1989).

25. AJA, Microfilm 2041, Jane Evans to Paula Ackerman, 18 December 1950.

26. Ellen M. Umansky, *Lily Montagu and the Advancement of Liberal Judaism: From Vision to Vocation* (New York: Edwin Mellen Press, 1983), esp. 39–40, 176–79. On Montagu not influencing the debate in an earlier era, see chap. 3.

27. An exception to this is Dora Askowith who first referred to Montagu in 1956; "The Role of Women in the Field of Higher Jewish Education," *Judaism* 6 (1956): 169–72.

28. Ellen M. Umanksy, "Tehilla Lichtenstein," in *Jewish Women in America: An Historical Encyclopedia*, ed. Paula E. Hyman and Deborah Dash Moore (New York: Routledge, 1997), 850–51.

29. Umansky, "Tehilla Lichtenstein"; Rebecca T. Alpert, "Tehilla Lichtenstein," in *Reform Judaism in America*, 126–27; *Four Centuries of Jewish Women's Spirituality*, 121–22.

30. AJA, Ms. Col. #340, 1/2, Beatrice Sanders Papers 1951–1986, *Pueblo Chieftain* (3 October 1984): 5A. I am indebted to the late Professor Jacob Marcus for suggesting Beatrice Sanders to me. See also William Toll, "The Domestic Basis of Community: Trinidad, Colorado's Jewish Women, 1889–1910," in his *Women, Men and Ethnicity: Essays*

on the Structure and Thought of American Jewry (Lanham, Md.: University Press of America, 1991), 63.

31. Scholars of Christian religious educators make the same argument; cf. Dorothy Jean Furnish, "Women in Religious Education: Pioneers for Women in the Professional Ministry," in *Women and Religion in America,* ed. Rosemary Radford Ruether and Rosemary Skinner Keller, vol. 3 (San Francisco: Harper and Row, 1981–86), 310–38. Furnish highlights Sophia Lyon Fahs who began studying for her B.D. in 1923, so that as a religious educator she would "have the advantage of an equal standing with the pastor in the church." In 1959, Fahs, an educator who had argued that "all ministers are educators, and all religious educators are preachers and priests," was ordained; 322–26.

32. Biographical material comes from Libbie L. Braverman, *Libbie: Teacher, Counselor, Lecturer, Author, Education Director, Consultant, and What Happens Along the Way* (New York: Bloch, 1986) and the obituary in *AJYB 1992* 92 (New York: American Jewish Committee, 1992), 592. In addition to her book, see also Libbie L. Braverman, "Hebrew in a Reform Temple School," *JED* 5 (1933): 40–44.

33. Braverman, *Libbie,* 139–45.

34. Michael Meyer calls Jewish Science "a fringe phenomenon," *Response to Modernity* (New York: Oxford University Press, 1988), 314. In 1954, there were 235 Jews in Meridian, Mississippi, less than 100 Jews in Trinidad, Colorado, and 6,500 Jews in Akron, Ohio; "Jewish Population of the United States, 1954," *AJYB* 56 (1955): table 1: Communities with Jewish Populations of 100 or More (Estimated).

35. Trude Weiss-Rosmarin, "Women Rabbis," *JS* (March 1951): 6.

36. Carole S. Kessner, "Introduction," in *The "Other" New York Jewish Intellectuals,* ed. Carole S. Kessner (New York: New York University Press, 1994), 12.

37. Deborah Dash Moore provides biographical material and discusses some major themes of Weiss-Rosmarin's writing in "Trude Weiss-Rosmarin and the *Jewish Spectator,*" in Kessner, *"Other" New York Jewish Intellectuals,* 101–21. On the ages of the students, see Trude Weiss Rosmarin, "The Growing Movement of Jewish Adult Education," *JS* 2, 8 (January 1937): 13–15ff. (Note that, in print, the hyphen in Weiss-Rosmarin was sometimes omitted.)

Weiss-Rosmarin may also have studied at the JIR. Faculty minutes indicate that she applied to its Institute for Advanced Studies in the fall of 1931 and that she was admitted as an auditor to prepare in "subjects in which she is deficient." Whether or not she attended its classes is not clear; JIR, Faculty Meeting Minutes, vol. 2, 23 September 1931; 22 October 1931.

38. Kessner, "Introduction," 12; Moore, "Trude Weiss-Rosmarin," 102.

39. AJA, Ms. Col. #12, Trude Weiss-Rosmarin 6/14, Articles, Brochures Concerning the School of the Jewish Woman, New York, 1934–39.

40. On the *JS*'s readership, see Moore, "Trude Weiss-Rosmarin," 109. Trude Weiss Rosmarin, *Jewish Women Through the Ages* (New York: Jewish Book Club, 1940) collected articles previously published in *JS.* This work corresponds to histories of "women worthies," a term coined by Natalie Zemon Davis. For a discussion of this and other

conceptual frameworks for the writing of women's history, see Gerda Lerner, "Placing Women in History: Definitions and Challenges," in her *The Majority Finds Its Past: Placing Women in History* (New York: Oxford University Press, 1970), 145–59.

41. Moore, "Trude Weiss-Rosmarin," 102; Trude Weiss Rosmarin, "Jewish Women in a Man's World," *JS* (May 1950): 12.

42. Moore, "Trude Weiss-Rosmarin," 118.

43. Kessner, "Introduction," 12.

44. Weiss-Rosmarin, "Women Rabbis," 6.

45. On Jeanette Weinberg, I interviewed Rita Simon Gordon, 14 August 1989; on Natalie Lansing Hodes, Gerard W. Kaye, "Women at the Top: A Movement Status Report," *Reform Judaism* (Fall 1992): 25; on Dalsheimer, see Trude Weiss-Rosmarin, "Women in the Synagogue," *JS* (March 1956): 6–7. Note that Helen Dalsheimer succeeded her husband as president of Baltimore Hebrew Congregation. In the 1930s, the Reform synagogue in Johnstown, Pennsylvania had a female president; Ewa Morawska, *Insecure Prosperity: Small-Town Jews in Industrial America, 1890–1940* (Princeton: Princeton University Press, 1996), 146–47. Linnell Ammerman, president of Temple Sinai (Washington, D.C.) from 1965 to 1967, believes she was the first woman elected in her own right to head a large Reform temple; my interview with Linnell Ammerman, 20 September 1991. According to Gerard Kaye, in 1971, only seven Reform temples had female presidents.

46. Rev. Lyman Richard Hartley, "Women as Ministers: The Pros and Cons," *NYT Magazine*, 13 April 1947, 19ff.

47. "Women in Church," *Time*, 6 June 1955, 65; "Women and the Pulpit," *Newsweek*, 6 June 1955, 50; "A First Lady Minister in Robes of a New Role," *Life*, 12 November 1956, 151–52.

48. Citation in Mark Chaves, *Ordaining Women: Culture and Conflict in Religious Organizations* (Cambridge: Harvard University Press, 1997), 74, 82.

49. Virginia Lieson Brereton and Christa Ressmeyer Klein, "American Women in Ministry: A History of Protestant Beginning Points," in *Women of Spirit: Female Leadership in the Jewish and Christian Traditions*, ed. Rosemary Ruether and Eleanor McLaughlin (New York: Simon and Schuster, 1979), 301–32; "Women in Church," *Time*, 6 June 1955, 65; "Breakthrough for the Woman Minister," *Christian Century* 74 (23 January 1957); Wilbur Bock, "The Female Clergy: A Case of Professional Marginality," *American Journal of Sociology* 72 (1967): 534.

50. Chaves, *Ordaining Women*, 15, table 2.1.

51. *CCARY* 32 (1922): 51, 164–65.

52. Barnett Brickner, "President's Message," *CCARY* 65 (1955): 13–14. On the influence of the Protestant debate in the 1950s, see also Jonathan D. Sarna, "Women in the Rabbinate: How Did We Reach this Anniversary? The American Story," *The Chronicle (HUC-JIR)* 53 (Summer 1993): 8–9ff.

53. This and the following citations are from Weiss-Rosmarin, "Women Rabbis," *JS* (September 1955), 5–6ff. All emphases are in the original.

54. UAHC president Alexander Schindler called her this; "Jane Evans: A Builder of Reform Judaism," *Reform Judaism* (Fall 1983): 30–31.

55. *Bulletin of Union Temple of Brooklyn* (13 October 1955); my interview with Jane Evans, 1 August 1989. For a fuller discussion of Trude Weiss-Rosmarin's views on feminism, see "Jewish Women in a Man's World," *The Gates of Zion* 6, 2–3 (April 1952): 12–16; "Jewish Women in a Man's Land," *The Gates of Zion* 6, 4 (July 1952): 5–11. I am grateful to Dr. Peggy Pearlstein for bringing this to my attention.

56. On the early NFTS, see PSN and Rita J. Simon, "Ladies of the Sisterhood: Women in the American Reform Synagogue, 1900–1930," in *Active Voices: Women in Jewish Culture*, ed. Maurie Sacks (Urbana: University of Illinois Press, 1995), 63–75. On Jane Evans, see Ellen M. Umansky, "Jane Evans," in *Reform Judaism in America*, 50–51. See also the following at the AJA: Jane Evans, "Oral History Interview" by Abraham J. Peck, 4 November 1985, c-721, c-722; Jane Evans, Biographies File, Oral History Interview, 21 August 1985. On the expanding vision of NFTS, see Women of Reform Judaism, *Index of Resolutions: Adopted by the NFTS, 1913–1985* (New York: Women of Reform Judaism, 1988).

57. On Evans's crediting Simon as "an inspiration," see NFTS, *Pre-Convention Meeting of the NFTS Board of Directors*, November 1961 (typescript; used by permission of Women of Reform Judaism, The Federation of Temple Sisterhoods): 54.

58. My interview with Jane Evans, 1 August 1989. Evans has no copies of any speeches, since she preferred not to speak from a prepared text.

59. AJA, Microfilm 2041, Meridian, Mississippi, Temple Beth Israel: Letter from Jane Evans to Paula Ackerman, 18 December 1950.

60. Irving Spiegel, "Women as Rabbis Urged at Parley," *NYT*, 30 April 1957, 60.

61. This and what follows are from "Report on the Ordination of Women": 90–93.

62. On the connections between the civil rights movement and the emergence of the women's liberation movement, see Sara Evans, *Personal Politics: The Roots of Women's Liberation in the Civil Rights Movement and the New Left* (New York: Vintage Books, 1979).

63. *CCARY* 66 (1956): 93.

64. NFTS, *Pre-Convention Meeting of the NFTS Board of Directors* (November 1961): 62.

65. Rupp and Taylor, *Survival in the Doldrums*, 166–67, 134.

66. Unless otherwise noted, this and what follows are from NFTS, *Pre-Convention Meeting of NFTS Board*: 54–64.

67. For a list of Benderly's protégées, see Alexander M. Dushkin, *Living Bridges: Memoirs of an Educator* (Jerusalem: Keter, 1975), 9–10. For an evaluation of how Samson Benderly opened the field of Hebrew teaching to women, see Jenna Weissman Joselit, *New York's Jewish Jews: The Orthodox Community in the Interwar Years* (Bloomington: Indiana University Press, 1990), 130–31.

68. Samuel H. Silver, *Portrait of a Rabbi: An Affectionate Memoir on the Life of Barnett*

R. Brickner (Cleveland: Barnett R. Brickner Memorial Foundation, 1959), 13, 22, 26. New York Public Library, American Jewish Committee Oral History Collection, Interview with Rebecca Ena Aaronson Brickner, 23–24 February 1983.

69. Silver, *Portrait of a Rabbi*, 26. New York Public Library, American Jewish Committee Oral History Collection, Interview with Rebecca Ena Aaronson Brickner, 23–24 February 1983. Her curriculum vitae is at the Western Reserve Historical Society, Cleveland, Ohio; "Mrs. Barnett R. Brickner, Biographical Material for Publicity Purposes," n.d. I am grateful to librarian Merrily F. Hart for locating this.

70. Silver, *Portrait of a Rabbi*, 104–5.

71. "If you will it, it is no fairytale," from Theodor Herzl's *Altneuland* (1902), became the motto of the Zionist movement; "Theodor Herzl," *EJ* 8 (Jerusalem: Keter, 1972): 420.

72. On Simon's first recorded reference to the woman rabbi, in 1921, see above, chap. 3. For other occasions in which she referred to women entering the rabbinate, see "Report of the National Committee on Religion," *NFTSP* 3 (31 October 1930): 33–36 (Carrie Simon was vice-chairman of this committee); AJA, NFTS Nearprint: Mrs. Abram Simon, "Four Presidents on the N.F.T.S. Silver Jubilee," *Topics and Trends* (January-February 1938): 3.

73. AJA, Ms. Col. #73, NFTS, Box 5, F.F. 3, Resolutions at 23rd Biennial, 1961, 6; Box 29, F.F. 2, 23rd Biennial Assembly, 1961.

74. AJA, Ms. Col. #73 NFTS, Box 5, F.F. 5, 1963 Transcript of the 24th Biennial Meeting, 5–9. See also Irving Spiegel, "Jewish Group to Debate Right of Women to Serve as Rabbis," *NYT*, 20 November 1963, 38; "Women Endorsed as Reform Rabbis," *NYT*, 21 November 1963.

75. Avis Clamitz Shulman, "Ordaining Women as Ministers" (typescript, n.d; internal evidence suggests either 1955 or 1956).

76. I am indebted to Rabbi Gary Zola for bringing my work to the attention of Avis Clamitz Shulman shortly before her death. I wish to thank HUC-JIR Registrar, Rosalind Chaiken, for her letter of 9 November 1992 and a copy of Avis Clamitz's HUC transcript. I am especially grateful to Avis Clamitz Shulman's daughter, Deborah Shulman Sherman, of Rishon le Zion, Israel, for locating critical information about her mother. These sources include: United Jewish Appeal interview with Avis Clamitz Shulman, interviewers: Menahem Kaufman and Lauren Deutsch, 29 June 1977; Avis Clamitz Shulman, "Ordaining Women as Ministers" (typescript, n.d; internal evidence suggests either 1955 or 1956); Deborah Shulman Sherman, "A Short Biography of Avis Shulman" (typescript, July 1994); a bibliography of Avis Clamitz Shulman's publications compiled by Deborah Shulman Sherman, and Avis Clamitz Shulman's scrapbook for the years 1929–48.

77. On Emil Hirsch and women rabbis, see chap. 2. United Jewish Appeal Interview with Avis Clamitz Shulman, 1–2.

78. Shulman, "Ordaining Women as Ministers," 4–5. She also told her daughter this; Letter from Deborah Shulman Sherman to PSN, 20 July 1993.

79. United Jewish Appeal Interview with Avis Clamitz Shulman, 4.

80. Cf. Schwartz, "'We Married What We Wanted to Be'": 223–46.

81. ACSS: Alvin Arends, "Avis Clamitz Shulman Speaks Today on Return of the Jews to England." This and the quotations that follow are from her scrapbook. Most of the clippings do not provide full bibliographic information.

82. ACSS: Avis Clamitz Shulman Scrapbook: "Lecturer Says Business Woman Also Can Be Success As Housewife," Canton, Ohio, 4 February 1931; Letter from Richard E. Gutstadt to Mrs. H. L. Maza, 2 January 1935.

83. ACSS: "Temple Sisterhood Open Meeting," 11 February 1936; Part of the time Clamitz Shulman, like Ray Frank, used a booking agency for her talks; Letters to Ricklie Boasberg Lecture Bureau, 13 October 1941, 14 October 1941 in her scrapbook.

84. ACSS: "Six Faiths in Fellowship: Shall Man or Money—Be Master" (Chicago, Handbill); "Lynchings—How to Prevent Them?" (Handbill). Her address, "Lynchings—How to Prevent Them," appeared in the *Chicago Sunday Bee*, 21 February 1932.

85. ACSS: "Forum Brings Four Ladies in Thrilling Symposium," *Covenant Club News* (Chicago), 9 March 1938; "Program of Conference of Jewish Women's Organizations," (Chicago), 23 December 1935.

86. For one of many examples, see ACSS: "To Speak for Hadassah," *Peoria Journal* 1935.

87. ACSS: "Jewish Women to Hear Mrs. Shulman," Minneapolis 1932; "Jewish Women Will Celebrate Feast of Lights," *Chicago Daily News*, November 1937; "Lecturer Says Business Woman Also Can Be Success As Housewife," Canton, Ohio: 4 February 1931; "An Interesting Subject by a Charming Speaker," 1937.

88. Rabbi Margaret Meyer, ordained at HUC-JIR (Cincinnati) in 1986, has indicated to me that in her work among congregations in small towns in Ohio, she met Jews who claim that they had met a woman rabbi decades before.

89. Shulman, "Ordaining Women as Ministers," 5.

90. Shulman, "Ordaining Women as Ministers," 5.

91. Cf. AJA, HUC Academic Records, Cincinnati, Ohio, 1914–1953, Microfilm #118. I counted sixteen women in these years. Most, with the exceptions of Martha Neumark and Goldie Barstein, took only a course or two. Rabbi Irwin Blank, Barstein's classmate, related to me in a conversation that he remembers Barstein wanted to be a rabbi. NFTS Executive Director emerita Eleanor Schwartz recalled the names of other women who studied at HUC in the 1940s and 1950s with the hopes of becoming a rabbi; PSN interview, 2 January 1990.

Cf. the recent admission of women to the state-supported, formerly all-male military college, The Citadel. In 1995, the first, and then only, woman cadet, Shannon Faulkner, dropped out after less than a week. In reporting on the admission of two women for 1996, *NYT* (5 August 1996, A10) wrote: "Officials at the institution have said the women will be roommates, which many believe will help them survive the crucial first year. When Ms. Faulkner left . . . she said the isolation had been excruciating."

92. For example, note that Betty Friedan's *The Feminine Mystique* was published in 1963, the Equal Pay Act passed in 1963, and Title VII of the Civil Rights Act, banning discrimination in employment on the basis of sex as well as race, passed in 1964.

93. William H. Chafe, *The Unfinished Journey: America Since World War II* (New York: Oxford University Press, 1991), 320. He writes: "In 1940, only 15 percent of young people from the ages 18 to 22 attended college. By 1965, that figure had mushroomed to 44 percent."

For background on the collegiate education of American Jews surpassing the levels of other white Americans, see Sidney Goldstein, "Profile of American Jewry: Insights from the 1990 National Jewish Population Survey," *AJYB 1992* 92 (New York: American Jewish Committee, 1992), 110–11; Sylvia Barack Fishman, *A Breath of Life: Feminism in the American Jewish Community* (New York: Free Press, 1993), 70–71.

94. AJA, Ms. Col. #135, HUC-JIR Board of Governors (1891–1972), HUC Faculty Minutes, December 1955–June 1962, "Report on Preparatory Department," 5 April 1957; Michael A. Meyer, "A Centennial History," in *Hebrew Union College-Jewish Institute of Religion: At One Hundred Years*, ed. Samuel E. Karff (Cincinnati: Hebrew Union College Press, 1976), 179–80.

95. The names of its programs suggest the parallels. Inspired by the Peace Corps, NFTY had a Torah Corps and Mitzvah Corps. Jeffrey K. Salkin suggests that its Friendship Circle was borrowed from the Freedom Riders of the South; "NFTY at Fifty: An Assessment," *Journal of Reform Judaism* (Fall 1989): 22. And if, as William Chafe argues (*The Unfinished Journey*, 326), "[m]usic constituted perhaps the most important 'sacrament' for the young," the NFTY songsters of these years contain Reform Jewish youth's sacraments.

96. The most useful sources on NFTY are the articles in "NFTY After Fifty Years: A Symposium," *Journal of Reform Judaism* (Fall 1989); quotations, Salkin, "NFTY at Fifty: An Assessment": 23; Edwin Cole Goldberg, "The Beginnings of Educational Camping in the Reform Movement": 8. See also Michael A. Meyer, *Response to Modernity*, 307, 377–78; *Women of Reform Judaism Salute Youth of Reform Judaism: NFTY at Fifty* (New York: NFTS, 1989).

97. AJA, Ms. Col. #135, HUC-JIR Board of Governors (1891–1972), Faculty HUC Minutes, Cincinnati, 25 October 1957.

98. I am grateful to Rabbi Margaret J. Meyer for bringing Toby Fink Laping and the women of the Undergraduate Program to my attention. And I am indebted to Professor Marc Lee Raphael and Judith Pilzer Rudolph for helping me locate a number of the women who studied in the program. The records of the undergraduate department are from AJA, HUC-JIR Academic Records 1971–78, Microfilm 2034. Approximately a dozen women took courses in the department.

99. Letter from Roberta Sholin Statman to PSN, 14 November 1989. The third female student was Xandra Riga Kaden.

100. This and the following paragraphs are based on my interview with Toby F. Laping, 10 December 1989.

101. According to HUC-JIR Registrar Rosalind Chaiken, none of the "student admission records for the joint UC/HUC program" were retained by HUC; Memo to author, 10 May 1989. Apparently, for many, the admission process was highly informal.

102. AJA, HUC-JIR Academic Records 1971–78, Microfilm 2034.

103. My interview with Norma Kirschner Skolnik, 15 November 1989.

104. My interview with Norma Kirschner Skolnik, 15 November 1989; AJA, HUC-JIR Academic Records 1971–78, Microfilm 2034; HUC-JIR, *Rabbinic Alumni Directory* (n.p.: HUC-JIR, 1988), 48.

105. *Who's Who in World Jewry 1955: A Biographical Dictionary of Outstanding Jews, 1955*, ed. Harry Schneiderman and Itzhak J. Carmin (New York: Who's Who in World Jewry, 1955). I wish to thank American University student Andrea Becker Herman who assisted in compiling this data. Note the category of communal, social, and welfare workers, organization executives and leaders surely encompassed some women, although I think relatively few, who were professional social workers. Like the 1928 *Who's Who* (see chap. 3), *Who's Who in World Jewry 1955* uses these categories interchangeably and does not indicate those engaged in social work as a profession.

106. Schneiderman and Carmin, *Who's Who in World Jewry 1955*. Note that in *Who's Who in American Jewry 1928*, 2d ed. (New York: The Jewish Biographical Bureau, 1928), less than 15 percent of American Jewish women could be found in such professions.

107. Cf. the lists of professional women in *Jewish Women in America*, 1625–1632.

108. My interview with Judith Pilzer Rudolph, 4 October 1989; my interview with Georgia Sperber Davis, 3 January 1990.

109. My interview with Ann Blitzstein Folb, 21 November 1989.

110. Rupp and Taylor, *Survival in the Doldrums*, 166–67.

111. My interview with Ann Blitzstein Folb, 21 November 1989.

112. My interview with Ann Blitzstein Folb, 21 November 1989; my interview with Georgia Sperber Davis, 3 January 1990.

113. Rabbi Sally J. Priesand Scrapbook, undated, unpaged: Letter from Ann Blitzstein to SJP, 15 April 1964; Jack Hume, "Girl Sets Her Goal to be 1st Woman Rabbi," newspaper clipping, undated, but most likely *Cleveland Plain Dealer* March–early April 1964. I am deeply grateful to Rabbi Sally J. Priesand for sharing this with me.

114. SJPS: "My Autobiography," typescript, undated, written for admission to the undergraduate department of HUC-JIR; my interview with SJP, 1 February 1993.

115. SJPS: "My Autobiography;" "The sermon for April 18, 1961, Beth Israel-The West Temple," manuscript; certificate from the Union Camp Institute, June-July 1961.

116. SJPS: six handwritten notes, undated (on the same page as the Union Camp Institute certificate for June-July 1961), emphasis in original.

117. Todd Gitlin, *The Sixties: Years of Hope, Days of Rage* (New York: Bantam Books, 1987), 20.

118. Toby Fink Laping and Ann Blitzstein Folb earned M.S.W. degrees. Norma Kirschner Skolnik earned an M.L.S. Roberta Sholin Statman earned a master's in elementary education.

119. Kessler-Harris, *Out to Work*, 311. Note that by 1970 women still made up but 4.7 percent of all lawyers (compared to 3.5 percent in 1950 and 1960) and but 8.9 percent of all physicians (compared to 6.1 percent in 1950 and 6.8 percent in 1960); Solomon, *In the Company of Educated Women*, 127, table 5.

120. SJPS: "My Autobiography"; "Diploma, high school department of Beth Israel-The West Temple," 22 May 1964; "NFTY Pilgrimage schedule, May 4–6, 1962"; SJP, "The Significance of Friday Night Services," *West Temple Bulletin* 10, 3 (November 1961).

121. SJPS: Letter from Joseph Karasick to SJP, 17 June 1963.

122. SJPS: Letter from Miriam O. Weiss to SJP, 20 June 1963.

123. SJPS: Letter from Samuel Sandmel to SJP, 5 February 1964; Letter from Joseph Karasick to SJP, 18 February 1964.

124. SJPS. Jack Hume, "Girl Sets Her Goal to be 1st Woman Rabbi."

125. SJPS: Letter from Ann Blitzstein to SJP, 15 April 1964; Letter from Ann Blitzstein to SJP, 25 May 1964.

126. In *The Sixties*, Todd Gitlin observes that freshman enrollments rose 37 percent that fall (163–64).

127. My interview with Sherry Levy-Reiner, 20 October 1989; my interview with Georgia Sperber Davis, 3 January 1990.

128. By the time Priesand was ordained in 1972, Michal (Marcia) Bernstein (ordained 1975) and Laura Geller (ordained 1976) were already in the rabbinical departments at other of the HUC-JIR campuses. Sandy Eisenberg Sasso entered the Reconstructionist Rabbinical College in 1969; my interview with SES, November 19, 1991. Rebecca Alpert enrolled there in 1971 after reading about SJP in *Newsweek*; Rita Simon interview with Rebecca Alpert, n.d.

129. On the triumph of the women's movement in raising the consciousness of the press, see Sheila Tobias, *Faces of Feminism: An Activist's Reflections on the Women's Movement* (Boulder, Colo.: Westview Press, 1997), 87.

130. Edward B. Fiske, "Women's 'Lib' on the March in the Churches," *NYT*, 17 May 1970, sec. 4, 15; "The Holy War of the Reverend Trudie Trimm: Lady Pastor Battles Male Bias Against Women Ministers," *Ebony* 24 (September 1969): 70–74; "An Awakening of Black Nun Power," *Ebony* 23 (October 1968): 44–46; George Dugan, "Lutherans Vote to Ordain Women," *NYT*, 25 October 1970, 36.

131. "New Challenge to Jewish Seminaries," *NYT*, 1 June 1969, E9; the symposium appears as "The Future of Rabbinic Training in America: A Symposium," *Judaism* 18 (Fall 1969): 387–420; Silver's challenge appears on p. 398.

132. "Rabbi Sally," *Newsweek*, 23 February 1970, 89; "Women at the Altar," *Time*, 2 November 1970, 71ff. In addition to the many clippings in SJPS, the AJA Nearprint File

on women rabbis has many of the local, national, and international articles covering the phenomenon of the first women who became rabbis.

133. The following are from SJPS: Synagogue bulletins from Rodeph Shalom (Philadelphia), 9 March 1970, and Temple Israel Messenger (Detroit), 27 February 1970. Jewish papers included the *Intermountain Jewish Jews*, 27 February 1970; "Sally Will Be Rabbi," *Ha-aretz*, 11 March 1970; "Women: the 'Rabbi,'" *Maariv*, 27 February 1970; and "Rabbi Sally," *Yiddishe Zeitung* (Johannesburg, South Africa), 13 March 1970. National papers reprinting the story included "Oy Vey! A Woman Rabbi!" *Chicago Sentinel*, 26 February 1970.

134. SJPS: Irving Spiegel, "Women as Rabbis Urged at Parley," *NYT*, 30 April 1957, 60; "Sisterhood Topics: Women Rabbis in Britain?" *American Judaism* (?), Passover 5727, Spring 1967.

135. SJPS: Letter from George ? to SJP, 17 March 1970? (emphasis in original).

136. SJP, Address to the Temple Israel Sisterhood, Dayton, Ohio (Cassette tape, 19 October 1971). I am grateful to Rabbi Sally J. Priesand for sharing this with me.

137. SJPS: Letter from Rev. John A. Schultehise to SJP, 18 January 1965; Notecard from Rabbi Dan Litt to SJP, 11 March 1965.

138. SJPS: The titles appear in announcement of Adath Israel Men's Club for 14 January 1970; Letter from Julius Nodel to Sally Priesand, 3 February 1970; her address to the B'nai B'rith Women's convention in Miami Beach was reported in the *Cleveland Jewish News*, 10 July 1970.

139. Norman B. Mirsky, *Unorthodox Judaism* (Columbus: Ohio State University Press, 1978), 68–75.

140. AJA, Nearprint: Women Rabbis, *Council Woman*, June 1974; my interview with Sherry Levy-Reiner, 20 October 1989.

141. That sustenance was figurative and literal. Because she received honoraria for speaking, Priesand had planned, during her last year in rabbinical school, to take speaking engagements instead of a student pulpit. However, she changed her mind when given the opportunity to work at Cincinnati's historic Plum Street Temple; SJP, Address to Temple Israel Sisterhood.

142. Sheila Tobias identifies three stages of feminist issues. The second, advocating "role change," as Priesand did, was likely to win feminist support but to be opposed by men and women who are not feminist; *Faces of Feminism*, 93–96.

143. See, for example, "Rabbi Sally," *Newsweek*, 2 November 1970, 81; George Vecsey, "Her Ambition is to Become a Rabbi—and a Housewife," *NYT*, 13 April 1971, 32. On the nineteenth-century professionals, see chap. 1.

144. SJP, Address to Temple Israel Sisterhood. See also George Vecsey, "Her Ambition is to Become a Rabbi—and a Housewife," *NYT*, 13 April 1971, 32.

145. SJP, Address to Temple Israel Sisterhood. Quotation, SJPS: *Congregation B'nai Israel Bulletin* (April, May, June, presumably 1970).

146. HUC-JIR Dean Kenneth Roseman affirmed the perception: "[SJP] is a rather un-

usual gal in that she is quite impervious to the Women's Lib nonsense. She has her own 'thing' to do, but this is not it, and I think she is a little bit upset about the number of people who think that she is some kind of a crusader for women's rights. She just wants to be a rabbi!"; (HUC-JIR SJP Registrar File, Letter from Kenneth D. Roseman to Robert S. Adler, 30 November 1970). I am grateful to Rabbi Sally J. Priesand for granting consent and to HUC-JIR registrar Rosalind Chaikin for giving me access to these materials.

147. SJP, Address to Temple Israel Sisterhood. Note that Michal Bernstein also recalled that College officials assumed she was in rabbinical school to find a husband, even though, as she asserted, the majority of the men in her class were already married; my interview with Michal Bernstein Mendelssohn, 11 March 1997.

148. SJP, Address to Temple Israel Sisterhood.

149. SJP, Address to Temple Israel Sisterhood; SJPS: The following correspondence discusses this: Letter from Kenneth Roseman to Joseph Forman, 23 July 1968; Letter from Jehiel Novick to SJP, 2 August 1968; Letter from Kenneth Roseman to SJP, 9 August 1968.

150. SJP, Address to Temple Israel Sisterhood; SJPS: Letter from Arthur A. Robinson to Kenneth D. Roseman, 8 December 1968.

151. SJP, Address to Temple Israel Sisterhood; SJPS: "Sally Priesand: She Could Become World's Very First Female Rabbi," *Hattiesburg American*, 19 September 1969. Note that Congregation B'nai Israel, the only synagogue in Hattiesburg, Mississippi, included Reform and Orthodox Jews. Its Orthodox members refused to count Priesand in their separate *minyan* and preferred to call her *rebbitzen*.

152. SJP, Address to Temple Israel Sisterhood.

153. AJA, HUC-JIR Board of Governors Reports and Minutes of Meetings, 1971–73: "Report of the President of the Board of Governors, 1 June 1972: 3–4; Presumably, this was implicit in the letter which informed her that she was "officially . . . admitted to the Rabbinic School of Hebrew Union College-Jewish Institute of Religion"; SJPS: Letter from Kenneth D. Roseman to SJP, 14 May 1968. Note also that Gottschalk's deliberate language surely reflected his awareness that Rabbi Earl Stone and others were then championing that Helen Levinthal receive the ordination she had been denied in 1939; see chap. 3.

154. Gitlin, *The Sixties*, esp. 242–43, 342–43.

155. Meyer, "A Centennial History," 231–32; SJPS: typescript of conclusion of her talk at Golden Square Lodge, no date, but surely May 1970.

156. Meyer, "A Centennial History," 231.

157. On this point, see Mark Chaves, *Ordaining Women*, 64–83.

158. AJA, Ms. Col. #167, Maurice N. Eisendrath Papers, Box 2/6 Sermons and Papers: "Report to UAHC Board of Trustees," 3 December 1966.

159. AJA, Ms. Col. #167, Maurice N. Eisendrath Papers, Box 2/6 Sermons and Papers: "Report of Maurice N. Eisendrath to Board of Trustees, UAHC, NY," 13 December 1970.

Eisendrath's 1970 reference to "snide jokes" may have referred to the remarks of his UAHC colleague, Rabbi Albert Vorspan, director of the UAHC's Commission on Social Action, and later its senior vice-president. In 1969, Vorspan wrote in his satirical *My Rabbi Doesn't Make House Calls* (Garden City, N.Y.: Doubleday, 1969), of the daring proposal of hiring a woman rabbi.

[I]t is the women who really run the congregation anyway—and they certainly run our homes. Jewish life is matriarchal, and a male rabbi merely confuses the roles. Can we persuade our parent body and seminary to ordain women? It's worth a try. A luscious rabbi, with a quiet but nice-looking husband, would get us into *Time* Magazine and put us on the map (pp. 66–67).

Eleanor R. Schwartz, Executive Director Emerita of the Women of Reform Judaism: Federation of Temple Sisterhoods recalled another snide joke. At the concluding banquet of one CCAR convention (likely 1956), the master of ceremonies "broke up the entire assembly" with "I dreamed I preached a sermon in my Maidenform Bra"; Letter from Eleanor R. Schwartz to PSN, 3 August 1989.

160. Gary P. Zola, "JTS, HUC, and Women Rabbis," *Journal of Reform Judaism* (Fall 1984): 39–45.

161. The symposium was prompted by Charles Liebman's critique, "The Training of American Rabbis," *AJYB* 69 (1968): 3–114. Respondents included Ira Eisenstein, president of the Reconstructionist Rabbinical College; Seymour Siegel, professor at the Jewish Theological Seminary; Emanuel Rackman, assistant to the president of Yeshiva University; and Arthur Green, described then as the head of Chavurat Shalom Community Seminary. On Green's short-lived plans to make Chavurat Shalom an alternative seminary, see Riv-Ellen Prell, *Prayer and Community: The Havurah in American Judaism* (Detroit: Wayne State University Press, 1989), 92–93.

162. Daniel Jeremy Silver, "Presentation" in "The Future of Rabbinic Training": 398. What prompted Silver to raise the question is unknown as is whether or not he was aware from his hometown *Cleveland Plain Dealer* that Priesand was then in rabbinical school. After reading about his proposal, SJP wrote Silver; SJPS: Letter from SJP, to Rabbi Daniel Silver, 24 June 1969; Letter from Daniel Silver to SJP, n.d. Note that another Cleveland rabbi, Fishel Perlmutter, proved pivotal in raising women's ordination in Conservative Judaism.

163. Silver refers specifically to the Fair Employment Practices Act, which I am unable to locate. Instead I suggest that by this title, he is referring to the legislation and presidential decrees, which, in these years, opened new possibilities for employment to women. On an earlier Fair Employment Practices Committee, established in 1941 by the federal government to meet wartime exigencies, see Chafe, *The Unfinished Journey*, 18–19.

164. The story of Congressman Howard Smith's proposal to add the word sex and derail the Civil Rights Act has often been recounted; see, among others, Rupp and Taylor, *Survival in the Doldrums*, 176–79.

165. Tobias, *Faces of Feminism*, 102–6; Rosenberg, *Divided Lives*, 209.

166. On the legacy of Title IX of the 1972 Educational Act, see Amy Shipley, "Most College Funding Going to Men's Sports," *Washington Post*, 29 April 1997: E1ff.

167. On the American Association of Women Ministers, see M. P. Harrington, "Women Ministers Celebrate Jubilee," *Christian Century* 86 (8 October 1969): 1295. For percentage, see Chaves, *Ordaining Women*, 15, fig. 2.1. See also, Mark Chaves, "Ordaining Women: The Diffusion of an Organizational Innovation," *American Journal of Sociology* 101, 4 (January 1996): 840–73. On liberal feminism, see Chafe, *The Paradox of Change*, 203, 211.

Note that at the same time, in England, John D. Raynor, senior minister of the London Liberal Jewish Synagogue and honorary director of Leo Baeck College, which trained rabbis for Great Britain's Reform and Progressive synagogues, announced that this seminary would accept women for rabbinical training; AJA, Women Rabbis, Nearprint: "Female Rabbis Frowned Upon," *Globe*, 2 February 1967.

168. Emily C. Hewitt and Suzanne R. Hiatt, *Women Priests: Yes or No?* (New York: Seabury Press, 1973), 80; Brereton and Klein, "American Women in Ministry," 301–32; HUC-JIR Sally Priesand Registrar File: "Bishop Betty? Rabbi Sally? Two Seek End to Age-Old Sex Barriers in Ministry," *The National Observer*, 30 March 1970, 9.

169. In Alfred Gottschalk's *Your Future as a Rabbi: A Calling that Counts*, a manual written for students considering the rabbinate, he posed the question "Should a Woman be a Rabbi?" and traced some of its history in the CCAR (New York: Richards Rosen Press, 1967), 40–43.

170. SJPS: Note from Alfred Gottschalk to SJP, undated; Letter from Malcolm H. Stern to SJP, 3 March 1970; Letter from Mark A. Golub to SJP, 9 March 1970; Letter from Leo Turitz to SJP, undated.

171. On Nelson Glueck and his college presidency, see Meyer, "A Centennial History," 171–243. Quotation, "Life at the Crossroads," *Time*, 27 July 1959, 39–40.

172. My interview with SJP, 1 February 1993.

173. AJA, Microfilm 2041, Letter from Nelson Glueck to Paula Ackerman, 19 January 1951; "Report on the Ordination of Women," *CCARY* 66 (1956): 90–93; my conversation with Rabbi Margaret J. Meyer, 4 April 1989. This and what follows are from my interview with Helen Iglauer Glueck, 2 November 1993. On Helen Glueck, see *American Men and Women of Science 1995–96*, 19th ed., vol. 3 (New Providence, N.J.: R.R. Bowker, 1996), 207.

174. Silver, *Portrait of a Rabbi*, 104–5.

175. On the difficulties encountered by women in science, see Margaret W. Rossiter, *Women Scientists in America: Struggles and Strategies to 1940* (Baltimore: Johns Hopkins University Press, 1982). I first argued that Helen Glueck served as a model for her husband in " 'Top Down' or 'Bottom Up': Two Movements for Women's Rabbinic Ordination," in *An Inventory of Promises: Essays on American Jewish History in Honor of Moses Rischin*, ed. J. Gurock, M. L. Raphael (Brooklyn: Carlson Publishing, 1995), 201–2.

176. Note I have not argued that President Glueck championed female ordination as a way to solve a shortage of rabbis, a problem Glueck raised in remarks made in 1966;

AJA, HUC-JIR Board of Governors Reports and Minutes of Meetings 1966–68, Box #215: Los Angeles School-Administrative Board Meeting, 10 June 1966. Mark Chaves's "event-history analysis" of this factor in the timing of women's ordination concludes that denominations did not ordain women to solve "internal personnel supply problems"; "Ordaining Women": 858.

177. Nelson Glueck's report to the Board of Governors (30 January 1964) cited in Morris W. Graff, "Rebitzen: An Old Title with a New Meaning," *CCARJ* (October 1965): 52.

178. AJA, HUC-JIR Office of the President, General Correspondence 1969–1970, P-Si, Box 162: Letter from Nelson Glueck to Mrs. Hyman C. Weisman, 9 September 1970.

179. The dedication appears in SJP, "Toward a Course of Study for Reform High School Youth Dealing with the Historic and Changing Role of the Jewish Woman" (Rabbinic Thesis: HUC-JIR, 1972).

180. HUC-JIR SJP Registrar File: Rabbinic Thesis Proposal, 14 December 1970; Memo to SJP from Kenneth Roseman, 8 February 1971; handwritten note approving change of direction, signed by Jacob Petuchowski.

181. SJP, "Toward a Course of Study for Reform High School Youth."

182. SJPS: p. 48 (my page numbering). This copy of the resolution appeared on the page with a note from Harry Hachen, a Reform lay leader in Cincinnati who sold insurance to students at HUC, who wrote to say how much he had enjoyed reading about her; form letter from Harry Hachen to HUC-JIR student body, November 1969, with handwritten note to SJP. Information on Harry Hachen from my conversations with Rabbi Debra Hachen, 25 March 1997 and Rabbi David Hachen, 27 March 1977. I have no way of knowing how SJP came by her copy of this text.

183. I have drawn this from the more accessible published revision of her thesis: SJP, *Judaism and the New Woman* (New York: Behrman House, 1975), 62–67. Note that Priesand knew the *Hochschule* Talmud professor refused to ordain Jonas. Jacob Petuchowski, also a professor of rabbinics, whom Priesand initially asked to guide her thesis, never did sign her ordination. However, hers was not the only one he refused to sign. On Petuchowski, see *Reform Judaism in America*, 161–62. On his refusing to sign others' ordination certificates; my conversation with Rabbi Jonathan Rosenbaum, 2 June 1994.

184. HUC-JIR SJP Registrar File: Sylvan D. Schwartzman, "Report on the Rabbinic Thesis by SJP," 12 May 1972. The points of her feminist critique were listed in Schwartzman's report.

185. Evans, *Born for Liberty*, 278–79.

186. SJP, *Judaism and the New Woman*, 62, 67.

187. HUC-JIR Sally Priesand Registrar File: Letter from SJP to Sir, 14 June 1963; "1st Woman Rabbi in U.S. Ordained," *NYT*, 4 June 1972, 76; "For Total Equality," Report to the Breslau Conference, 1846, in W. Gunther Plaut, *The Rise of Reform Judaism* (New York: World Union for Progressive Judaism, 1963), 253–55.

188. SJP, "Preparation for the Rabbinate—Yesterday, Tomorrow," *CCARY* 85 (1975): 162–64.

Unfortunately, I cannot, in the context of this book, discuss Priesand's rabbinical career. Her first position was assistant rabbi at New York City's Stephen Wise Free Synagogue. In 1979, she left the congregation when she was not promised that she would succeed its ailing senior rabbi.

In the next years, unable to secure a position commensurate with her experience, she took part-time jobs. In 1981 she came to her current congregation, Monmouth Reform Temple in Tinton Falls, New Jersey.

Priesand well understood that opening the rabbinate to women had by no means fulfilled Reform's historic commitment to equality of the sexes. Throughout her career she has continued to call upon Reform leaders and institutions to incorporate women and their perspectives in contemporary Judaism. See my entry on Sally Priesand in *Jewish Women in America*, 1102–4.

CHAPTER 5: THE DEBATE IN CONSERVATIVE JUDAISM

The quotation that forms the title for chapter 5 is taken from Gerson D. Cohen, "Women in the Conservative Movement," *Outlook* (Winter 1973): 6.

1. *Ezrat Nashim* refers to "the help of women" and also to the women's court in the Jerusalem Temple.

2. Ezrat Nashim, "Jewish Women Call for Change, 1972," in *The American Jewish Woman: A Documentary History*, ed. Jacob R. Marcus (New York: Ktav, 1981), 894–96. Reading the text carefully, Marcus noted that Ezrat Nashim "did, however, stop short of demanding the ordination of women as Conservative rabbis." Nevertheless, both the press and its spokeswomen saw this event as calling "for the acceptance of women as rabbis and cantors;" Paula E. Hyman, "Feminism in the Conservative Movement," in *The Seminary At 100: Reflections on the Jewish Theological Seminary and the Conservative Movement*, ed. Nina Beth Cardin and David Wolf Silverman (New York: Rabbinical Assembly, 1987), 374. See also Barbara Trecker, "10 Religious Feminists to Confront the Rabbis," *New York Post*, 14 March 1972, 71; Enid Nemy, "Young Women Challenging Their '2d-Class Status' in Judaism," *NYT*, 12 June 1972, 43; Alan Silverstein, "The Evolution of Ezrat Nashim," *CJ* 30 (Fall 1975): 41–51.

3. In 1990 I presented "The Beginnings of the Religious Emancipation of American Jewish Women" at the Berkshire Conference of Women Historians. There I noted that Carrie Simon had called for women's ordination. In responding to my paper, Professor Paula Hyman, a founding member of Ezrat Nashim, remarked that its members would have liked to have known of such precedents.

4. The phrase comes from Michael A. Meyer, *Response to Modernity: A History of the Reform Movement in Judaism* (New York: Oxford University Press, 1988), xi.

5. Simon Greenberg, "In Honor of Louis Finkelstein," *PRA (1965)*: 80–81.

6. Abraham J. Karp, "A Century of Conservative Judaism in the United States," *AJYB* 86 (1986): 3.

7. For a fuller discussion of this theme, see PSN, *Conservative Judaism in America: A*

Biographical Dictionary and Sourcebook (Westport, Conn.: Greenwood Press, 1988), 1–24.

8. Brief histories of these appear in PSN, *Conservative Judaism in America.*

9. Some of these are detailed in PSN, *Conservative Judaism in America*, esp. 4–5, 6–7, 13–15. For Reform's reactions to some of the same issues, see chap. 1.

10. Ezrat Nashim, "Jewish Women Call for Change, 1972," 896.

11. Note that members of Ezrat Nashim and others not only recalled the example of Szold but helped perpetuate it as an early example of the question at the seminary; Susan Dworkin, "Henrietta Szold," *Hadassah Magazine* (February 1972), rpt. in "The Jewish Woman: An Anthology," ed. Liz Koltun, a special issue of *Response* 18 (Summer 1973): 43. Several of the contributors—as well as the editor—belonged to Ezrat Nashim. A revised version of the anthology appeared as *The Jewish Woman: New Perspectives*, ed. Elizabeth Koltun (New York: Schocken Books, 1976). Note that the same account about Szold would appear in Charlotte Baum, Paula Hyman, and Sonya Michel, *The Jewish Woman in America* (New York: New American Library, 1975), 43.

12. On Adler, see *Selected Letters of Cyrus Adler*, ed. Ira Robinson, 2 vols. (Philadelphia: Jewish Publications Society, 1985); Cyrus Adler, *I Have Considered the Days* (Philadelphia: Jewish Publication Society, 1941).

13. Gerald Sorin observed that many aspects of Conservative synagogues, including their services, were then "not distinguishable from what Jews were doing in the Orthodox Young People's Synagogues, the American Orthodox synagogues, or after 1912, in the Orthodox synagogues associated with the Young Israel movement;" *Tradition Transformed: The Jewish Experience in America* (Baltimore: Johns Hopkins University Press, 1997), 136.

14. AJA, Cyrus Adler Papers, Microfilm 517: Addresses, articles, biographical sketches, tributes, and miscellaneous items, 1909–34: "On the Woman Rabbi," typescript, n.d. but given as an interview, possibly to Leon Spitz of the *Day* and likely in the early 1920s.

15. AJA, Cyrus Adler Papers, Microfilm 517: Leon Spitz interview with Cyrus Adler, "A Jewishly Educated Laiety [*sic*] is Our Fundamental Need," n.d.

16. AJA, Cyrus Adler Papers, Microfilm 517: "On the Woman Rabbi."

17. This and what follows are from David Aronson, "Woman's Position in Israel," *The Jewish Forum* (August and October 1922): 260–64, 376–81. See also Joshua 17:3–4. On Aronson, see PSN, *Conservative Judaism in America*, 35–37.

18. JTSA, Library-Archives, Arch. 42, Louis Ginzberg Collection, Box 18, F.F. "Address to the United Synagogue of America by Louis Ginzberg," 16 June 1918. On Ginzberg, see Eli Ginzberg, *Keeper of the Law: Louis Ginzberg* (Philadelphia: Jewish Publication Society, 1966).

19. A full discussion of women's role in Conservative Judaism in the first half of the twentieth century is not possible here. This is drawn from the following sources: Rose B. Goldstein, "Women's Share in the Responsibility for the Future of Judaism," *Outlook* 8, 4 (May 1938): 7; "Jewish Home-Making Work of the Women's League," *The United*

Synagogue Recorder 1, 1 (July 1920): 1; Deborah M. Melamed, *The Three Pillars: Thought, Worship, and Practice for the Jewish Woman* (New York: Women's League of the United Synagogue of America, 1927), esp. pp. 25–26, 34–35, 53, 146; Jonathan D. Sarna, "The Debate over Mixed Seating in the American Synagogue," in *The American Synagogue: A Sanctuary Transformed*, ed. Jack Wertheimer (Cambridge, England: Cambridge University Press, 1987), 363–94. See also Emily Solis-Cohen, Jr., *Woman in Jewish Law and Life: An Inquiry and a Guide to Literary Sources of Information Concerning the Nature of Jewish law, and the Status Accorded Woman* (n.p.: Jewish Publication Society for the New York City Jewish Welfare Board, 1932); *They Dared to Dream: A History of National Women's League* (New York: National Women's League of the United Synagogue of America, 1967).

20. Louis Finkelstein, "Jewish Education for Women," *Outlook* 8, 4 (May 1938): 7; "Notes and News," *JED* 9 (1937): 108.

21. Adler, "On the Woman Rabbi."

22. Although I viewed HUC-JIR student records at the AJA, which was key to uncovering the women who had studied in the rabbinical department, I was denied access to such files at JTSA. Therefore, this argument is built on the assumption that had such women tried to attend rabbinical school, the existing faculty minutes would reflect discussion of their application.

23. Rose B. Goldstein, "Women's Share in the Responsibility for the Future of Judaism," *Outlook* 8, 4 (May 1938): 7.

24. Mrs. David (Bertha Friedman) Aronson, "Today's Challenge to the Jewish Woman," *Outlook* 7, 1 (September 1936): 6. A survey of the first nine volumes of *Outlook* (1930–38) discloses that Seminary professors' wives, like Carrie (Dreyfuss) Davidson and Mrs. Alexander (Hanna Hoffman) Marx, and rabbis' wives were its most frequent contributors.

25. Sarna, "Mixed Seating in the American Synagogue," 379–86; Mordecai Waxman, ed., *Tradition and Change* (New York: Burning Bush Press, 1958). Only in September 1984, as the first female rabbinic students entered, did the Seminary offer two daily services, an egalitarian one and one which retained separate seating for men and women.

26. Mordecai M. Kaplan, "The Teachers Institute and Its Affiliated Departments," in *The Jewish Theological Seminary of America: Semi-Centennial Volume*, ed. Cyrus Adler (New York: Jewish Theological Seminary of America, 1939), 121–43.

27. Ibid., 121–22.

28. RC, Records of JTSA, 1a-13-45: "Doctor Joffe's Report, 1905–1906." I am grateful to archivist Julie Miller for bringing this to my attention and to Professor Mel Scult for the biographical information; *JTSA Register, 1907–1908.*

29. From the academic year 1904–5 until the year 1932–33, the *JTSA Register* listed the students in the various courses. I found no other women in the rabbinical department in these years.

30. *JTSA Register, 1934–35*, 49; Kaplan "The Teachers Institute," 125, 131, 139; Israel S.

Chipkin observed that 80 percent of the students in the Teachers Institute's extension courses, adult education for those who lacked the background to enter the other departments, were female; "The Israel Friedlaender Classes, *PRA 1931*: 167–78.

31. Kaplan, "The Teachers Institute," 138–39. In 1948, a survey of the graduates of eight Hebrew teachers colleges, like the Teachers Institute, concluded that most of the women "raised families and left their positions, and most of the men chose the rabbinate as a profession"; Judah Pilch, "From the Early Forties to the Mid-Sixties," in *A History of Jewish Education in the United States*, ed. Judah Pilch (New York: American Association for Jewish Education, 1969), 149–51. For her experiences as a student and faculty member at the Teachers Institute, see Judith Kaplan Eisenstein, "Looking Back: A Career in Jewish Music," (typescript, n.d.). Part of this appeared in *The Reconstructionist* (Jan.-Feb. 1987).

32. I am indebted to Professor Ira Robinson for communicating this to me (e-mail, 13 July 1994). It comes from Cyrus Adler's Report to the Board of Directors of JTSA, 11 March 1923.

33. RC, RG 3, Faculty Records, Series A: Faculty Meeting Minutes, 1929–1977, Box 2, 1940–41, Faculty Meeting III, 8 January 1941, p. 16; 6 February 1941, p. 26.

34. Note that from 1912 to 1914 Rose Abramson Maximon taught Hebrew in the Seminary's college program; Shulamith Reich Elster, "Hebrew Teachers Colleges," in *Jewish Women in America: An Historical Encyclopedia*, eds. Paula E. Hyman and Deborah Dash Moore (New York: Routledge, 1997), 608.

35. "Religion," *Time* (2 October 1939): 48.

36. There are numerous sources on Kaplan. See, among others, Mel Scult, *Judaism Faces the Twentieth Century: A Biography of Mordecai M. Kaplan* (Detroit: Wayne State University Press, 1993).

37. Scult, *Judaism Faces the Twentieth Century*, 351, also 170–172, 356, 396, n.8.

38. Cited in Carole S. Kessner, "Kaplan and the Role of Women in Judaism," in *The American Judaism of Mordecai M. Kaplan*, ed. Emanuel Goldsmith, Mel Scult, and Robert Seltzer (New York: New York University Press, 1990), 347–48, 354.

39. Scult, *Judaism Faces the Twentieth Century*, 301–2. See also the memoir, "Judith Kaplan Eisenstein Becomes the First Bas Mitzvah 1921 [*sic*]," in *Eyewitnesses to American Jewish History, Part IV, The American Jew 1915–1969*, ed. Azriel Eisenberg (New York: Union of American Hebrew Congregations, 1976), 29–32; Felicia Lamport writes of her joint bat mitzvah with another of Kaplan's daughters; *Mink on Weekdays (Ermine on Sundays)* (Boston: Houghton Mifflin, 1950), 126–29. On bat mitzvah, see Paula E. Hyman, "The Introduction of Bat Mitzvah in Conservative Judaism in Postwar America," *YIVO Annual* 19 (1990): 133–46.

40. Scult, *Judaism Faces the Twentieth Century*, 302. I follow Scult's analysis of Judith Kaplan's bat mitzvah and not that of Kessner, "Kaplan and the Role of Women in Judaism," 351. Ira Eisenstein describes the early bat mitzvah; "Sex Equality in the Synagogue," *The Reconstructionist* (6 March 1953): 18–20. See also Leon S. Lang, "What Have We Done with Confirmation?," *PRA 1936*: 291.

41. Mordecai M. Kaplan, "What the American Jewish Woman Can Do For Adult Jewish Education," *JED* 4 (1932): 144.

42. Ira Eisenstein, "President's Message," *PRA 1954*: 152.

43. "Equalization of Status of Women," *PRA 1954*: 143. See also Robert Gordis, "Responsum on the Sabbath," *PRA 1950*: 155.

44. Theodore Friedman, "Discussion," *PRA 1955*: 34; Sanders Tofield, "Woman's Place in the Rites of the Synagogue with Special Reference to Aliyah," *PRA 1955*: 182–90; Aaron H. Blumenthal, "An Aliyah for Women," 1955, rpt. in *And Bring Them Closer to Torah: The Life and Work of Rabbi Aaron H. Blumenthal*, ed. David R. Blumenthal (Hoboken: Ktav, 1986), 11–24.

45. Rabbi Gershon Winer, "Discussion," *PRA 1955*: 34–35.

46. In 1962, only 8 out of 254 rabbis actually granted women *aliyot* with no restrictions. Ten years later, but 7 percent of 142 rabbis reported women regularly receiving *aliyot* in their synagogues; another 17 percent permitted them on special occasions; Daniel J. Elazar and Rela Geffen Monson, "Women in the Synagogue Today," *Midstream* 27, 4 (April 1981): 25–26. For congregational reaction to this in the mid-1950s, see Deborah Dash Moore, *To the Golden Cities: Pursuing the American Jewish Dream in Miami and L.A.* (New York: Free Press, 1994), 121.

47. Winer, "Discussion": 34–35.

48. Marshall Sklare, *Conservative Judaism: An American Religious Movement* (1955, 1972; rpt. Lanham, Md.: University Press of America, 1985), 86–90.

49. See, for example, "Resolutions," *NWLP 1954* (November 1954, n.p.).

50. Irving Spiegel, "Women as Rabbis Urged at Parley," *NYT*, 30 April 1957: 60; see chap. 4.

51. Note that Judith Berlin Lieberman was dean of the Shulamith School for Girls. Her husband was Saul Lieberman, Seminary professor of Talmud and, at one time, dean of the rabbinical school. In these years, the girls' school was only an elementary one.

52. RC, JTSA Records, RG 1M, Box 153: Letter from Gladys Citrin to Dr. Finkelstein, 20 May 1957. Note she had originally written "final" in front of "goal," but she crossed it out.

53. In these years more than half the students attending the Seminary still came from such Orthodox backgrounds. Moreover, Miss Citrin's years of Jewish education certainly equalled, if not exceeded, their norm which, in 1955, was 7.8 years of preliminary education and 2.6 years of teachers' college (i.e., Midrasha); Arthur Hertzberg, "The Conservative Rabbinate: A Sociological Study," in *Essays on Jewish Life and Thought: Presented in Honor of Salo Wittmayer Baron*, ed. Joseph Blau et al. (New York: Columbia University Press, 1959), 311, 328–29.

54. RC, JTSA Records, RG 1M, Box 153: Letter from Louis Finkelstein to Gladys Citrin, 28 May 1957.

55. My interview with Elaine Mann, 2 October 1991.

56. RC, JTSA Records, RG 30, Commission for the Study of the Ordination of Women,

Box 4, F.F. 3, Letter from Barbara Meltzer Cash to Rabbi Nelson and Ritual Committee, n.d. JWRC: Transcripts of Commission Hearings on Women in the Rabbinate, JTSA, Washington, DC, 17 August 1978, pp. 57–58.

57. My interview with Sandy Eisenberg Sasso, 19 November 1991; RC, JTSA Records, RG 30, Commission for the Study of the Ordination of Women, Box 4, F.F. 3: Letter from Eileen G. Leiderman to Rabbi S. Cohen, 14 September 1978; my interview with Rabbi Jan Kaufman, 8 November 1989. Note also that Donna Berman decided she wanted to be a rabbi, in 1965, when she was nine; my interview with her, 29 March 1989. Karyn Kedar made a similar announcement in 1965 at the age of eight; my interview with her, 28 March 1989.

58. Scult, *Judaism Faces the Twentieth Century*, 362.

59. I found in *The Reconstructionist* only a single reference to the woman rabbi before the late 1960s; Sylvia A. Barras, "Wraps Off the Rebbetzin," (15 June 1956): 20–24. See also Ruth F. Brin, "Can A Woman Be A Jew?" *The Reconstructionist* (25 October 1968): 7–14.

60. Phone conversation with Rabbi Ira Eisenstein, 20 June 1997; Ira Eisenstein, *Reconstructing Judaism* (New York: Reconstructionist Press, 1986), 224–31. I wish to thank RRC president David A. Teutsch who confirmed that college records from these years reveal no discussion of the question; Letter to me, 8 November 1994.

61. I am deeply grateful to Rabbi Sandy Eisenberg Sasso for sharing with me her press clippings and selected speeches from the 1970s. This and what follows, unless otherwise noted, are based on these files; my interview with her, 19–20 November 1991; and Betsy Covington Smith, *Breakthrough Women in Religion* (New York: Walker and Co., 1978), 38–58.

62. SES Files: "Between Man and Man: A Creative Service," 6 June 1969.

63. SES Files: *Youth* 21, 16, 13 September 1970.

64. SES Files: "2 Rabbinical Students Are Wed: Ceremony Is 'Historic' in Judaism, *Bulletin*, n.d. They wed 25 June 1970.

65. SES Files: Agnes Palazzetti, "Husband-Wife Rabbis in Residence at Chautauqua," *Buffalo Evening News*, 10 August 1973; "RP Youth, Wife First Rabbi Team," *Star & Herald* (Panama, R.P.), 14 May 1974; Nancy Livingston, "Woman Rabbi Zeroes in on Subtle Opposition," *St. Paul Dispatch*, 5 November 1973.

66. Quoted in SES, "Woman in the Pulpit," *Outlook* (Spring 1984): 6ff.

67. My interview with SES, 19–20 November 1991. Note that she never finished her dissertation. Years later she reflected that she failed to do so because she had not written on women as—although she did not know this at the time she was a student—had the other women who wanted to be rabbis.

68. SES, "B'rit B'not Israel: Observations on Women and Reconstructionism," *Response* 18 (Summer 1973): 101–5.

69. SES Files: "Presentation to American Jewish Committee," May 1972. The press viewed her presentation as feminist; see SES: George Dungan [*sic*], "Female Rabbinical

Student Asks Increased 'Feminity' [*sic*] in Judaism," *NYT*, 7 May 1972; Louis Cassels, "Fem Lib in Judaism: Women Rabbis Emerging," *Record*, 23 June 1972; "Women's Role in Judaism," *JE*, 16 June 1972. Also note that at the same time she was asked, at the suggestion of Dr. Eisenstein, to write an article for *YWCA World* on woman's position in Judaism. Apparently, the feminist critique she crafted was not published. A draft of the article is in these files.

70. It is not possible to discuss her subsequent career. Note she has written prize-winning children's books, including *In God's Name* and *A Prayer for the Earth—The Story of Naamah, Noah's Wife*.

71. Anne Lapidus Lerner, " 'Who Hast Not Made Me a Man': The Movement for Equal Rights for Women in American Jewry," *AJYB 1977* 77 (1976): 3–38.

72. See, for example, Reena Sigman Friedman, "The Jewish Feminist Movement," in *Jewish American Voluntary Organizations*, ed. Michael N. Dobkowski (New York: Greenwood Press, 1986), 575–601; Sylvia Barack Fishman, *A Breath of Life: Feminism in the American Jewish Community* (New York: Free Press, 1993), 1–15. Note these accounts fail to consider that an old guard, like Jane Evans and Trude Weiss-Rosmarin, had been raising "feminist issues" for decades; cf. Leila J. Rupp and Verta Taylor, *Survival in the Doldrums: The American Women's Rights Movement, 1945 to the 1960s* (New York: Oxford University Press, 1987).

73. *NWLP 1970*: 37–51. Rabbi Aaron Blumenthal referred to the Sigal responsum in the symposium, "Resolved, That the Woman in Judaism Should Have More Rights," *NWLP 1972*: 51–52; RC, Rabbi Fishel Pearlmutter Papers, Box 2, F.F. 4: Letter from Fishel Pearlmutter to Susan Weidman Schneider, 25 January 1980. He claimed he had been raising the admission of women to the Rabbinical Assembly for almost a dozen years, first as a question to the membership committee chair from the convention floor. Note that Rabbi Pearlmutter was from Cleveland and would likely, by 1968, have read about Sally Priesand in the local press (see chap. 4).

See also *CJ* 26, 4 (Summer 1972) which included articles by Ezrat Nashim members, Paula E. Hyman ("The Other Half: Women in the Jewish Tradition") and Judith Hauptman ("Women's Liberation in the Talmudic Period: An Assessment") as well as David M. Feldman, "Woman's Role and Jewish Law": 14–21, 22–28, 29–39. *CJ* 29, 1 (Fall 1974) published the symposium, "Women and Change in Jewish Law": 3–24. Here editor Stephen C. Lerner acknowledged that "[t]he impetus for the rediscovery of the inequalities Jewish women experience came from without"; "The Editor's Page": 3.

74. Cf. Seminary professor Joel Roth: "I have made it quite clear, I hope, that I would be opposed to any argument for women's ritual rights which was predicated on an *a priori* claim that men and women *must* be equal"; "On the Ordination of Women as Rabbis," in *The Ordination of Women as Rabbis: Studies and Responsa*, ed. Simon Greenberg (New York: Jewish Theological Seminary of America, 1988), 170–71.

75. "Women's Lib," *Newsweek*, 17 September 1973, 63. The *NYT* considered this front-page news; "Conservative Jews Vote for Women in Minyan," 11 September 1973, 1ff. See also RC, Rabbi Fishel Pearlmutter Papers, Box 1, Folder 4: Letter from Seymour Siegel to Colleague, 5 October 1973.

76. Aaron H. Blumenthal, "The Status of Women in Jewish Law," 1974; rpt. in *And Bring Them Closer to Torah*, 25–41. He used the word "gesture" in "An Aliyah for Women."

77. Judah Nadich, "Presidential Address," *PRA 1974*: 25.

78. Mark Chaves, "Ordaining Women: The Diffusion of an Organizational Innovation," *American Journal of Sociology* 101, 4 (January 1996): 866–67. For the current struggle in Roman Catholicism, see Peter Steinfels, "Catholic Theologians Urge Discussion on Female Priests," *NYT*, 8 June 1977, 32.

79. Note I argued this first in "'Top Down' or 'Bottom Up': Two Movements for Women's Rabbinic Ordination," in *An Inventory of Promises: Essays on American Jewish History in Honor of Moses Rischin*, ed. Jeffrey S. Gurock and Marc Lee Raphael (Brooklyn: Carlson Publishing, 1995), 197–208.

80. See, for example, Beth Wenger, "The Politics of Women's Ordination: Jewish Law, Institutional Power, and the Debate over Women in the Rabbinate," in *Tradition Renewed: A History of the Jewish Theological Seminary*, ed. Jack Wertheimer (New York: Jewish Theological Seminary, 1997), 485–523. Note I was refused permission to examine many of the RC archival sources she used, including much of the correspondence of the Commission for the Study of the Ordination of Women as Rabbis [RG 30] and the relevant faculty senate minutes.

81. Many of these events were reported in the press: Eleanor Blau, "Role for Women in Jewish Ritual Backed by Conservative Group," *NYT*, 14 November 1973, 35; Irving Spiegel, "Conservative Seminary Is Urged to Train Women as Rabbis," *NYT*, 7 May 1974, 23; Irving Spiegel, "Conservative Rabbi Sees Women in the Pulpit Soon," *NYT*, 21 April 1975, 32. Others appeared in Judah Nadich, "Presidential Address," *PRA 1974*: 25; Blumenthal, "The Status of Women in Jewish Law," 38–39; "Resolutions," *PRA 1975*: 278; "Resolutions," *PRA 1976*: 322–23; "Resolutions," *PRA 1976*: 321–22; "Resolutions," *PRA 1977*: 139.

82. Some, but not all of the commission's papers, were published in Greenberg, *The Ordination of Women as Rabbis;* quotations, Gordon Tucker, "Final Report of the Commission for the Study of the Ordination of Women as Rabbis," 20–21 (emphasis in original), 27–28, 29–30. The JWRC has papers not appearing here: David Weiss Halivni, "On Ordination of Women"; Gershon C. Bacon, "On the Ordination of Women"; and David A. Resnick, "A Response to the 'Final Report of the Commission for the Study of the Ordination of Women as Rabbis.'"

83. "Conservative Jewry to Vote on the Ordaining of Women," *NYT*, 13 January 1979, 23–24; George Vecsey, "Conservative Rabbis to Vote Today on Question of Ordaining Women," *NYT*, 20 December 1979, sec. II, 8; George Vecsey, "Plan to Ordain Jewish Women Put Off in Vote," *NYT*, 21 December 1979, sec. II, 1; Charles Austin, "Conservative Rabbis Reject Admission of a Woman to Their Group," *NYT*, 13 April 1983, sec. I, 23. See also "Resolutions Adopted," *PRA 1980*: 299.

84. Charles Austin, "Conservative Group Votes to Admit Women as Rabbis," *NYT*, 25 October 1983; "Women Begin Studies to be Conservative Rabbis," *NYT*, 9 September

1984, sec. I, 50; Ari L. Goldman, "Conservative Jews Ordain a Woman," *NYT*, 13 May 1985, sec. II, 3.

85. For press coverage of the political debates, see, for example, Amy Stone, "Gentlemen's Agreement at the Seminary," *Lilith* 1, 3 (Spring-Summer 1977): 13–18; Reena Sigman Friedman, "The Politics of Women's Ordination," *Lilith* 6 (1979): 9–15; JWRC: Nina Cardin, "Women as Conservative Rabbis—Where We Are Now," *Spectrum*, 8 (March 1979): 4. There were literally hundreds, if not thousands, of articles in the national, international and Jewish presses.

86. See the list in David Golinkin, *An Index of Conservative Responsa and Practical Halakhic Studies: 1917–1990* (n.p.: Rabbinical Assembly, 1992), 76–77. Only some of these were published in Greenberg, *The Ordination of Women as Rabbis.*

87. Mayer E. Rabinowitz explained: "The halakhic objections raised relate exclusively to functions that a rabbi is commonly but not necessarily expected to perform." These included woman's ability to, among others, officiate at weddings (*mesadder kiddushin*), represent the congregation in prayer (*sheliah tzibbur*) and serve as a witness; "An Advocate's Halakhic Responses on the Ordination of Women," in Greenberg, *The Ordination of Women as Rabbis*, 107. Note that a full discussion of these *halachic* issues lies outside the scope of this book.

88. Greenberg, "On the Question of Women as Rabbis," by the Jewish Theological Seminary of America, in *The Ordination of Women as Rabbis*, 71ff.

89. Robert Gordis, "The Ordination of Women," in Greenberg, *The Ordination of Women as Rabbis*, 48.

90. Anne Lapidus Lerner, "On the Rabbinic Ordination of Women," in Greenberg, *The Ordination of Women as Rabbis*, 93–94; Gordis, "The Ordination of Women," 50.

91. Greenberg, "On the Question of Women As Rabbis," 85. Gordis, "The Ordination of Women," 53. Robert Gordis observed that none of the women he met at Sabbath services in his Orthodox synagogue ever refrained from shaking hands with a man, as they must if they observed the prohibitions surrounding a woman's menstrual cycle; Gordis, "The Ordination of Women," 51–52.

92. Lerner, "On the Rabbinic Ordination of Women," 97.

93. Beverly Weintraub and Nancy Forse to Rabbi Gerson D. Cohen, 7 June 1972. I am grateful to Rabbi Beverly Magidson who shared this letter with me.

94. My interview with Susannah Heschel, 30 May 1990; see also her interview in Diana Bletter and Lori Grinker, *The Invisible Thread: A Portrait of American Jewish Women* (Philadelphia: Jewish Publication Society, 1989), 22–24; "Toppling a Jewish Tradition: A Conservative seminary votes to ordain women rabbis," *Time*, 7 November 1983, 83.

95. Cited in Gerson D. Cohen, "Women in the Conservative Movement: 1973," *Outlook* (Winter 1973): 5–6ff. So far, I have not discovered who wrote this letter. It is not that of Beverly Weintraub and Nancy Forse, nor Susannah Heschel, nor Kinneret Shiryon (Sandy Levine).

96. Unless otherwise noted, this and what follows are constructed from a series of inter-

views I conducted with Rabbi Joan Friedman, n.d.; Rabbi Carol Glass, 16 November 1988 and her lecture to my class, 9 April 1987; Rabbi Amy Eilberg, 26 March 1989; Rabbi Beverly Weintraub Magidson, 26 March 1989; Rabbi Leslie Alexander, 10 April 1989; Rabbi Jan Kaufman, 8 November 1989; and Professor Judith Hauptman, 17 December 1990. Additional materials came from Rabbi Kinneret Shiryon including copies of her correspondence as Sandy Levine with Conservative leaders dated 1973–77; Amy Stone, "Gentlemen's Agreement at the Seminary," 13; JWRC: Alan Silverstein, untitled history of Ezrat Nashim, typescript, note 7A; JWRC: Pamela Mendels, "Ms. Rabbi: What's Life Like for the 20 Women in the Conservative Movement's First Co-ed Rabbinical Class?" *Baltimore Jewish Times* (n.d., likely fall 1984); Elaine Shizgal Cohen, "Women Rabbinical Students Reflect on Their Calling," *Melton Journal* (Fall 1987): 6–9.

97. Letter from Sandy Levine to JTS, 23 October 1973. I am grateful to Rabbi Kinneret Shiryon for sharing her files with me.

98. Letter from Sandy Levine to Gerson Cohen, 7 April 1975. "Ellington's Debra Cantor Joins First Women in Seminary's Rabbinical College," *Connecticut Jewish Ledger*, 13 September 1984, 2.

99. On Ramah, see Shuly Rubin Schwartz, "Ramah—The Early Years, 1947–52," (M.A. Thesis, Jewish Theological Seminary of America, 1976); *The Ramah Experience: Community and Commitment*, ed. Sylvia C. Ettenberg and Geraldine Rosenfield (New York: Jewish Theological Seminary of America, 1989). Several contributors to *The Ramah Experience* traced the trajectory of its decisions on women's ritual participation; see, for example, pp. 8–10, 43–45, 67–68; See also RC, Rabbi Fishel Pearlmutter Papers, Box 1, Folder 6: "Policy on Participation of Girls in Religious Services and Ceremonials at Ramah Camps," May 1977.

100. Nina Cardin, "Let Me In; Let Me Out," *Outlook* (Spring 1984): 5ff.

101. Letter from Gerson D. Cohen to Misses Beverly Weintraub and Nancy Forse, 14 July 1972, courtesy of Rabbi Beverly Magidson.

102. Enid Nemy, "Young Women Challenging Their '2nd-Class Status' in Judaism," *NYT*, 12 June 1972, 43.

103. This and what follows are from RC, JTSA Records, RG 3A Faculty Minutes, Box 5, 1972–73, 3 January 1973.

104. RC, RG 3A Faculty Minutes, Box 5, 1972–73, 3 January 1973, 53–55; 7 February 1973, 60–66; includes brief papers, David Weiss, "The Ordination of Women as Rabbis" and Seymour Siegel, "The Question of Women Rabbis."

105. Gerson D. Cohen to Sandra Faye Levine, 25 April 1975; Amy Stone, "Gentlemen's Agreement at the Seminary," 13; JWRC: Pamela Mendels, "Ms. Rabbi." Beverly Weintraub Magidson used the term the Teachers Institute, although, under Cohen, that became the Department of Education in the Graduate School.

106. Cohen, "Women in the Conservative Movement": 6, 34.

107. By 1977, Sandy Levine had been attempting to apply to the rabbinical school for four years; Stone, "Gentlemen's Agreement at the Seminary."

108. Friedman, "The Politics of Women's Ordination," 9.

109. Letter from Gerson D. Cohen to Sandy Levine, 25 April 1975, courtesy of Rabbi Kinneret Shiryon.

110. By the time he became chancellor, Cohen had recognized that the proliferation of university Jewish Studies programs, including those training scholars for the professorate, had made the Seminary but one among many institutions competing for students in academe. Accordingly, he restructured the Seminary to model it on the university and created a graduate school, open to men and to women, to train scholars in Jewish history, philosophy, literature, and rabbinics. The rabbinical school, while remaining the "first-born son," was now "but one child of many"; Gerson D. Cohen, "The Conservative Jewish Mission in Our Tenth Decade," *PRA 1977: 37–43.*

111. Judith Hauptman quoted in Stone, "Gentlemen's Agreement at the Seminary." On Helen Levinthal Lyons, see chap. 3.

112. Susannah Heschel and others observed that there was always "a lot of talk" about Hauptman. See, for example, Rachel Susan Frielich, "A Sociological Analysis of the Ordination of Women as Conservative Rabbis" (B.A. thesis, Barnard, 1984), 30. Hauptman was also mentioned by Beverly Magidson; Papers of the CCAR Task Force on Women Rabbis: "From Beverly Magidson; concerning her application for membership in the RA."

113. This and the following paragraphs are based on my interview with Professor Judith Hauptman, 17 December 1990 and Judith Hauptman, "Talmud Pioneer," *Outlook* (Spring 1984): 7ff.; Bletter and Grinker, *The Invisible Thread*, 198–201. Note Hauptman had to ask each member of the rabbinical school Talmud faculty individually.

114. Cf. the religious leadership of Georgia Harkness. Harkness earned a Ph.D. in 1923 and was appointed professor of applied theology at Garrett Biblical Institute in 1939. She thus "became the first woman to teach in a major theological seminary in the United States in a field other than Christian education." She was an advocate for women's ordination in the Methodist Church from the 1920s until its successful resolution in 1956; Rosemary Skinner Keller, "Patterns of Laywomen's Leadership in Twentieth-Century Protestantism," in *Women and Religion in America*, ed. Rosemary Radford Ruether and Rosemary Skinner Keller, vol. 3 (San Francisco: Harper and Row, 1981–86), 271–73, 299–303.

115. Judith Hauptman, "Talmud Pioneer."

116. For example, Rabbi Jan Kaufman earned an M.A. in Jewish history in 1975. Rabbi Amy Eilberg began her graduate work in Talmud in 1976. See also Debra Cantor, "Get Ready, Get Set . . . Wait," *Moment* (October 1983): 38–42.

117. Lynn Gottlieb was "rabbi for Temple Beth Or," a congregation for the deaf in New York City; "It's Called a Calling: An Interview with Lynn Gottlieb," *Moment* (May 1979): 32–38. Carol Glass was "an unordained associate" at Adath Jeshurun Congregation in Minneapolis; "Conservative Jewry to Vote on the Ordaining of Women," *NYT*, 13 January 1979, 23–24. Debra Cantor was "assistant rabbi/cantor for High Holidays"; "Ellington's Debra Cantor Joins First Women in Seminary's Rabbinical College."

118. This and what follows are based on JWRC: Transcripts of Commission Hearings on Women in the Rabbinate, Jewish Theological Seminary. Commission hearings were held in Washington, D.C., 17 August 1978; in Los Angeles, 6 September 1978; in Minneapolis, 13 September 1978; in Chicago, 14 September 1978; in New York at JTS, 1–2 November 1978 and 3 December 1978; in Toronto, 22 November 1978. The overwhelming majority of those who testified favored women's ordination. Excerpts from the hearings in Minneapolis were published by Judy Aronson, Steven Foldes, Carol Glass, and Riv-Ellen Prell-Foldes, "To Change a Tradition: One City's Views," *Sh'ma* 9, 164 (22 December 1978): 25–28.

119. Judy Aronson was told to be a *rebbetzin* (13 September 1978); Sandy Winters taught Jan Kaufman (17 August 1978); female staff at Hillel were lobbying from the outside (6 September 1978); Leslie Alexander was waiting at the University of Judaism; my interview with her, 10 April 1989. Susan Grossman was studying for an M.A. in Judaic studies at Brooklyn College; *Four Centuries of Jewish Women's Spirituality: A Sourcebook*, ed. Ellen M. Umansky and Dianne Ashton (Boston: Beacon Press, 1992), 204. By my count, at least nine of the women who spoke, wished, either then or before, to be rabbis.

120. Cantor, "Get Ready, Get Set . . . Wait."

121. Tracy Klirs informed the commission that she was then applying to HUC-JIR and RRC (14 September 1978); Sandy Koppel related that her daughter was then at RRC (2 November 1978).

122. My interview with Rabbi Carol Glass, 16 November 1988.

123. As early as 1976, those at HUC-JIR took note that "the number and quality of applicants to the College-Institute has increased considerably" in recent years. College Dean Lawrence Raphael understood: "The growth of the feminist movement among Jewish women and the publicity which surrounded Sally Priesand's ordination in 1972 (and Sandy Sasso's ordination from the Reconstructionist Rabbinic School in 1974) has accomplished more than any recruiter could hope to achieve" (Lawrence W. Raphael, "Who Wants to be a Rabbi and Why?" *CCARJ* [Spring 1976]: 63–64).

What he did not have to tell his colleagues was that some of the women becoming Reform and Reconstructionist rabbis had been turned away at the Seminary. Among them at HUC-JIR were rabbis Beverly Weintraub Magidson and Jan Kaufman and at RRC, Rabbi Joy Levitt; American Jewish Committee, *Consultation: The Role of Women in Jewish Religious Life: A Decade of Change, 1972–1982; Papers and Summary of Proceedings* (New York: American Jewish Committee, 1982), 12.

By now the very first women to seek ordination at the Academy for Jewish Religion were studying there. The Academy for Jewish Religion, the only non-denominational rabbinical seminary in the U.S., was founded, in 1955, in opposition to the merger of HUC and JIR. Its founder was Louis Newman, whose wife, so long ago had wanted to be rabbi. Emily Korzenik was ordained there in 1981; Michael A. Meyer, "A Centennial History," *Hebrew Union College-Jewish Institute of Religion at One Hundred Years*, ed. Samuel E. Karff (n.p.: Hebrew Union College Press, 1976), 188–90; see chapter 3 above; Emily Faust Korzenik, "On Being a Rabbi," in *Daughters of the King*, 250–53.

124. Leslie Alexander, quoted in Joel Kotkin, "Women Backed as Conservative Rabbis," *Washington Post*, 1 February 1979.

125. Letter from Gerson D. Cohen to Colleague, 27 April 1979 (courtesy of Rabbi Carol Glass).

126. On Lieberman, see the entry in PSN, *Conservative Judaism in America*. The phrase comes from Robert Gordis, "The Ordination of Women—A History of the Question," *Judaism* 129, 33 (Winter 1984): 11.

127. Saul Lieberman, "Ordaining Women as Rabbis," in *Tomeikh KeHalakhah: Responsa of the Panel of Halakhic Inquiry*, vol. 1, ed. Wayne R. Allen (Mount Vernon, N.Y.: Union for Traditional Conservative Judaism, 1986), 14–19, Eng. trans. by Wayne Allen, 20–22. All quotations are from this translation. Note that Wenger erred in asserting that Lieberman "never wrote a formal responsum on the question of women's ordination"; Wenger, "The Politics of Women's Ordination," 507.

128. Lieberman, "Ordaining Women as Rabbis," 20–22.

129. Gordis, "The Ordination of Women—A History of the Question": 11.

130. Unless otherwise noted, this and what follows are based on Cantor, "Get Ready, Get Set . . . Wait."

131. This and what follows are from the letter from Debra S. Cantor, Nina Beth Cardin, Stephanie Dickstein, Nina Bieber Feinstein, Sharon Fliss, Carol Glass, and Beth Polebaum to Seminary Faculty; 6 December 1979. Courtesy of Rabbi Carol Glass.

132. See chap. 4, Avis Clamitz Shulman, "Ordaining Women as Ministers" (typescript, n.d.).

133. Rochelle Saidel Wolk, "The Bitter Letter of the Law," *Moment* 5, 2 (January–February 1980): 63.

134. Cf. Mortimer Ostow, chairman of the Seminary's Department of Pastoral Psychiatry. He cautioned: "a woman appearing as a central figure in a religious service is likely to distract some of the male worshippers from a reverent attitude and encourage erotic fantasies. . . . When a woman comes to represent divinity, there appears a psychologic problem"; "Women and Change in Jewish Law," *CJ* 29, 1 (Fall 1974): 6–7.

135. JWRC: Joel Roth, "Statement to the Faculty Senate, 20 December 1979," *Ikka d-Amrei: A Journal of the Students of the Jewish Theological Seminary of America*, 2, 1 (January 1980): 58–60.

136. Fishel A. Pearlmutter, "Will Egalitarianism Compel the R.A.?" *Sh'ma* 13, 250 (18 March 1983): 77.

137. Joel Roth, "Statement to the Faculty Senate, 20 December 1979"; Ismar Schorsch drafted the "Motion for Senate Consideration on December 20, 1979."

138. Quotations from George Vecsey, "Plan to Ordain Jewish Women Put Off in Vote," *NYT*, 21 December 1979, sec. II, 1; my interview with Carol Glass.

139. Sharon Fliss and Gerson Cohen quoted in Vecsey, "Plan to Ordain Jewish Women Put Off in Vote."

140. Letter from Gerson D. Cohen to Colleague, 26 March 1980; Quotations from Richard Yaffe, "To Give Women Equal Training without the Title," *Jewish Week-Examiner*, 6 April 1980 (courtesy of Rabbi Carol Glass).

141. Cantor, "Get Ready, Get Set . . . Wait": 41. Also, my interview with Carol Glass.

142. Cf. Wenger, "The Politics of Women's Ordination," 509.

143. This and what follows, unless otherwise noted, are from my interview with Rabbi Lawrence Troster and Elaine Kahn, 19 January 1998. I am deeply grateful to them for sharing their G.R.O.W. files; Letter from Elaine B. Kahn for G.R.O.W., undated.

144. See, for example, Robert Blair Kaiser, "Drive Pressed for Ordaining Female Rabbis," *NYT*, 23 March 1980, 40. Other reporters helped continue the debate. See, for example, "Our Readers Speak: Women as Rabbis," *Moment* 5, 5 (May 1980): 34–37.

145. These are reflected in the G.R.O.W. files: convention committee as of March 5; anonymous, "Rally Speech"; Elaine Kahn, "Introductory Remarks at G.R.O.W. Rally, JTS, Tuesday, March 18, 1980"; "Tip Sheet"; "Francine Klagsbrun's speech," typescript; Letter from Lawrence Troster to G.R.O.W. supporter; G.R.O.W. Supporters, as of May 1980; Letter from Lawrence Troster and Elaine B. Kahn to G.R.O.W. supporter, May 1980.

146. JWRC: "Religious Ministry Program Begins: Communal Structures to be Strengthened," *Bulletin of the Jewish Theological Seminary of America* (February 1982); Cantor, "Get Ready, Get Set . . . Wait": 42.

147. Carol Glass conveyed some of this information to me; JWRC: Nina Cardin, "Women as Conservative Rabbis."

148. Cantor, "Get Ready, Get Set . . . Wait": 42.

149. Carol Glass reported considering private ordination but questioned its legitimacy; lecture to my class, 9 April 1987. Lynn Gottlieb was privately ordained by Rabbis Zalman Schacter-Shalomi and Everett Gendler; my interview with Rabbi Lynn Gottlieb, 15 August 1997. There is some confusion about the date of her ordination. In her introduction to Lynn Gottlieb's *She Who Dwells Within: A Feminist Vision of Renewed Judaism*, Ellen Umansky dates the ordination to 1980 (San Francisco: Harper, 1995). In our conversation Gottlieb thought it was 1981. On the role of Rabbinical Assembly executive Wolfe Kelman and issue of private ordination, see Stone, "Gentleman's Agreement at the Seminary": 17–18; "Conservative Jewry to Vote on the Ordination of Women," *NYT*, 13 January 1979, 23–24.

150. See "Conservative Rabbis in America: The RA" in PSN, *Conservative Judaism in America*, esp. 304.

151. "The Revised Constitution of the Rabbinical Assembly," *PRA 1977*: 153. On Pearlmutter's role in this, see RC, Rabbi Fishel Pearlmutter Papers, Box 1.

152. RC, Rabbi Fishel Pearlmutter Papers, Box 1, Folder 1: Letter from Fishel Pearlmutter to Carol Glass, 16 March 1977; Box 2, Folder 4: Letter from Fishel Pearlmutter to Harold Schulweis, 11 January 1980; Letter from Aaron Blumenthal to Fishel Pearlmutter, 12 March 1980.

153. RC, Rabbi Fishel Pearlmutter Papers: Box 2, Folder 5: application essay of Beverly Magidson; Letter from Beverly Weintraub Magidson to Fishel Pearlmutter, 12 December 1982. Note, for example, that in June 1982, "on the occasion of the tenth anniversary of the ordination by Hebrew Union College of the first woman rabbi, Sally Preisand [*sic*]," those at the American Jewish Committee's *Consultation: The Role of Women in Jewish Religious Life* raised the possibility of achieving female Conservative rabbis through the Rabbinical Assembly; 1, 22.

154. This was widely covered in the press; see, for example, Charles Austin, "Conservative Rabbis Reject Admission of a Woman to Their Group," *NYT*, 13 April 1983.

155. Charles Austin, "Synagogue Hires Woman as Rabbi," *NYT*, 9 August 1983, A24; my interview with Rabbi Beverly Weintraub Magidson, 26 March 1989.

156. Wenger, "The Politics of Women's Ordination," 511. Cf. Amy Eilberg: "the admission of women to the rabbinical school at JTS is now imminent; if there are conservative women rabbis," *Sh'ma* 13, 259 (14 October 1983): 128–29.

157. In March 1983, I was working on a book on Conservative Judaism. Within days of Lieberman's death, Conservative rabbis and others outside the JTS environs, who knew of my project, were telling me now women could be ordained at the Seminary. Cf. Frielich, "A Sociological Analysis of the Ordination of Women as Conservative Rabbis," 47.

Note that Beth Wenger argues that Lieberman's death did not influence Cohen's tactical move; "The Politics of Women's Ordination, 512. Since I was denied access to the sources she used, I cannot comment. I would, however, suggest that, given the psychological barriers of voicing this, it should not be surprising that the written record is silent.

158. Leonard Gordon, "A Woman in the Mirror: Conservative Judaism Faces Feminism," in *The Seminary at 100: Reflections on the Jewish Theological Seminary and the Conservative Movement*, ed. Nina Beth Cardin and David Wolf Silverman (n.p.: Rabbinical Assembly, 1987), 361.

159. AJA, David Weiss Halivni, Letter Stating His View Concerning the Ordination of Women, 1983.

160. JWRC: Pamela Mendels, "Ms. Rabbi."

161. Roth, "On the Ordination of Women as Rabbis," 127–87.

162. In fact, Seminary publications would declare "[w]omen are expected to accept equality of obligation in the performance of *mitzvot*" for those applying to rabbinical school; JTSA, *Academic Bulletin, 1986–1987, 5747* (New York: JTSA, n.d.), 33. But many considered and consider this issue "unresolved"; Amy Eilberg, "Kol Isha: A New Voice in Conservative Judaism," in *The Seminary at 100*, 351. See also, *Sh'ma*, 15, 295 (31 May 1985): 113–15: Carolyn Braun, "Equality of obligation for women at jts?"; Lori Forman, "Under a *tallit* a woman is invisible"; and Pamela Hoffman, "Why I wear *tallis* and *tefillin*."

163. "Women Begin Studies to Be Conservative Rabbis," *NYT*, 9 September 1984, 50.

164. Ari L. Goldman, "Conservative Assembly Votes to Admit Women as Rabbis," *NYT*, 14 February 1985, I1.

165. My interview with Rabbi Amy Eilberg, 26 March 1989; See also Ari L. Goldman, "10-Year Dream of Being a Rabbi Coming True for a Woman," *NYT*, 17 February 1985, 40; Aviva Cantor, "Rabbi Eilberg," *Ms.* (December 1985): 45–46.

166. JWRC: Amy Eilberg, "Senior Sermon: March 16, 1985—Parashat Vayakhel Peku-dey" (Exodus 35:1–38:20), typescript. Note that she referred to Carol Gilligan's influential work, *In a Different Voice: Psychological Theory and Women's Development* (Cambridge: Harvard University Press, 1982). Her sermon was based on Exodus 35:22–29.

167. Rabbi Beverly Weintraub Magidson's application to the RA failed again in May 1984, in part because some preferred that its first female member be ordained at JTS; Kenneth A. Briggs, "Rabbinic Group Rejects Woman for Membership," *NYT*, 17 May 1984, sec. II, 11; Ari L. Goldman, "A Woman Finds Bias As a Rabbi," *NYT*, 22 June 1984, sec. II, 2. Magidson was accepted by the RA in March 1985 along with Rabbi Jan Kaufman; "Assembly Admits Women Rabbis," *Washington Post*, 12 March 1985, B4.

EPILOGUE: "WILL THERE BE ORTHODOX WOMEN RABBIS?"

The quotation that forms the title of the epilogue is taken from Blu Greenberg, "Will There Be Orthodox Women Rabbis?" *Judaism* 33, 1 (Winter 1984): 23–33.

1. Note that Orthodoxy encompasses a broad spectrum from the ultra-Orthodox and Hasidic Jews to those deemed, at various historical points, Neo-, Modern, and most recently Centrist Orthodox. The debate about women's ordination has engaged only the latter. All references to the Orthodox refer to this sector.

The classic typology of the Orthodox and their institutional frameworks, is Charles S. Liebman, "Orthodoxy in American Jewish Life," *AJYB* 66 (1965): 21–98. Samuel Heilman has shown how, despite efforts to ignore modernity, ultra-Orthodox Jews have encountered and absorbed certain of its ideas and accoutrements; *Defenders of the Faith: Inside Ultra-Orthodox Jewry* (New York: Schocken Books, 1992).

2. Greenberg, "Will There Be Orthodox Women Rabbis?": 23. The correct dates are 1972 and 1974.

3. Unnamed Orthodox rabbi quoted in Terence Shea, "Bishop Betty? Rabbi Sally? Two Seek End to Age-Old Sex Barriers in Ministry," *National Observer*, 30 March 1970, 9.

4. Mary M. Cohen, "A Problem for Purim," *JE* (15 March 1889): 1.

5. Greenberg, "Will There Be Orthodox Women Rabbis?": 25.

6. Henry Berkowitz, "Woman's Part in the Drama of Life," *AJ* 1, 2 (May 1895): 64. Greenberg, "Will There Be Orthodox Women Rabbis?": 25, 33.

7. Blu Greenberg, "Is Now the Time for Orthodox Women Rabbis?" *Moment* (December 1993): 52.

8. Isaac Mayer Wise, "Woman in the Synagogue," 1876, in *The American Jewish Woman: A Documentary History*, ed. Jacob R. Marcus (New York: Ktav, 1981), 293–95; Greenberg, "Will There Be Orthodox Women Rabbis?": 26.

9. Greenberg, "Will There Be Orthodox Women Rabbis?": 28.

10. Haviva Krasner-Davidson, "Why I'm Applying to Yeshiva U.," *Moment* (December 1993): 97; Greenberg, "Will There Be Orthodox Women Rabbis?": 26; Gershon Winkler, "They Called Her Rebbe," *Moment* (December 1993): 56–57ff.

11. Norma Baumel Joseph, "Jewish Education for Women: Rabbi Moshe Feinstein's Map of America," *AJH* 83 (June 1995): 222.

12. Greenberg, "Is Now the Time for Orthodox Women Rabbis?": 51.

13. Blu Greenberg listed the following: "Nechama Leibowitz, Naomi Cohen, Chanah Beilinson, Oshra Enker, Aviva Zornberg, Menucha Chwat, Tamar Ross, Chanah Henkin, Devora Steinmentz, Dena Weiner, Malka Bina, Esther Krauss, Rivka Haut, Beruriah David, Maidy Katz"; "Is Now the Time for Orthodox Women Rabbis?": 52. Note that she is not referring to the distinguished historian of American Jewry, Naomi Wiener Cohen, widow of Gerson Cohen, but rather to Naomi G. Cohen, professor of Jewish thought and philosophy at Haifa University and author of *Philo Judaeus: His Universe of Discourse* (Frankfurt am Main: Peter Lang, 1995). Blu Greenberg saw New York City's Drisha as offering women "parallel rabbinic studies"; "Will There Be Orthodox Women Rabbis": 32.

14. Greenberg, "Is Now the Time for Orthodox Women Rabbis?": 50.

15. Greenberg, "Will There Be Orthodox Women Rabbis?": 29.

16. Gordon Tucker, "Final Report of the Commission for the Study of the Ordination of Women as Rabbis," in *The Ordination of Women as Rabbis: Studies and Responsa* (New York: JTSA, 1988), 20–21 (original italicized).

17. Krasner-Davidson, "Why I'm Applying to Yeshiva U.": 54–55.

18. Rabbi Irving Greenberg according to Laura Blumenfeld, "A Most Unorthodox Idea: She Wants to Be a Rabbi, but the Men Say It's Just Not Kosher," *Washington Post*, 11 December 1993, C4.

19. This and what follows are based on Krasner-Davidson, "Why I'm Applying to Yeshiva U."; Haviva Krasner, "Politics: Issues on the Cutting Edge," *Jewish Women's Resource Center Newsletter* (Winter/Spring 1990): 11; Laura Blumenfeld, "A Most Unorthodox Idea: She Wants to Be a Rabbi, but the Men Say It's Just Not Kosher," *Washington Post*, 11 December 1993, C1ff. (quotation C4); Haviva Ner-David to Pamela Nadell, e-mail: 16 June 1997, 17 June 1997. Note that since making *aliyah*, she has shortened her last name. She continues to study and hopes for private ordination from a rabbi who believes that *halachah* does not bar women's ordination. She has also reported that in Jerusalem another woman has joined her quest.

20. See, for example, Debra Nussbaum Cohen, "New Role Reveals New Reality: Woman Hired at Orthodox Shul for Pastoral Counseling," *Washington Jewish Week*, 1 January 1998; Nancy Zuckerbrod, "Women's Work? Jobs in Orthodox Shuls Spur Debate," *Washington Jewish Week*, 15 January 1998, 1ff.

21. Hannah G. Solomon, "Council of Women: Washington, D.C., February 1895," in Hannah G. Solomon, *Sheaf of Leaves* (Chicago: printed privately, 1991), 131–32.

22. Greenberg, "Is Now the Time for Orthodox Women Rabbis?": 52. Note that she ex-

pected that obstacles would prevent these women from taking on congregational posts in the immediate future.

23. Between 1972 and 1997, Hebrew Union College-Jewish Institute of Religion ordained 262 women rabbis. (HUC-JIR web page, [huc.edu]). Between 1974 and June 1997, 85 of the 200 rabbis ordained at the Reconstructionist Rabbinical College were female (e-mail from the Reconstructionist Rabbinical College, 12 March 1997). Rabbi Shohama Wiener, president of the Academy for Jewish Religion, reported 17 women ordained since 1981 (19 August 1997). Rica Ziman, administrator of the Jewish Theological Seminary's Rabbinical School, reported 79 women ordained since 1985 (19 August 1997). Great Britain's Leo Baeck College has ordained 22 women. One, Rabbi Lynn Gottlieb, holds private ordination. In the early 1990s both HUC-JIR and JTS ordained the first women at their Jerusalem campuses.

24. Debra Nussbaum Cohen, " 'Orthodox feminist' no longer an oxymoron," *Washington Jewish Week*, 27 February 1997, 22. See also "Orthodox feminism," *Washington Jewish Week*, 15 August 1996, 5.

Abbreviations

ACSS	Avis Clamitz Shulman Scrapbook
AH	*The American Hebrew*
AJ	*The American Jewess*
AJA	American Jewish Archives, Cincinnati, Ohio
AJH	*American Jewish History*
AJHQ	*American Jewish Historical Quarterly*
AJHS	Courtesy, American Jewish Historical Society, Waltham, MA
AJYB	*American Jewish Year Book*
CCARJ	*Central Conference of American Rabbis Journal*
CCARY	*Central Conference of American Rabbis Yearbook*
CJ	*Conservative Judaism*
EJ	*Encyclopedia Judaica*
Hadassah	Archives of Hadassah, The Women's Zionist Organization of America, Inc.
HC	Archives and Special Collections of Hunter College
HUC	Hebrew Union College
HUC-JIR	Hebrew Union College-Jewish Institute of Religion
JIR	Jewish Institute of Religion
JE	*Jewish Exponent*
JED	*Jewish Education*
JS	*The Jewish Spectator*
JMMD	Jewish Museum of Maryland
JTSA	Jewish Theological Seminary of America
JTSA Register	*Jewish Theological Seminary of America Register*
JWRC	Jewish Women's Resource Center, New York
LLC	Lester Lyons Collection

NFTS	Women of Reform Judaism: Federation of Temple Sisterhoods: formerly National Federation of Temple Sisterhoods
NFTSP	*Proceedings of the National Federation of Temple Sisterhoods*
NWLP	*Proceedings of the National Women's League of the United Synagogue of America*
NYT	*New York Times*
Outlook	*Women's League Outlook*
PRA	*Proceedings of the Rabbinical Assembly (of America)*
PSN	Pamela S. Nadell
RA	*Reform Advocate*
RC	Courtesy of the Ratner Center for the Study of Conservative Judaism, The Jewish Theological Seminary of America
SJP	Rabbi Sally J. Priesand
SJPS	Rabbi Sally J. Priesand Scrapbook
SES	Sandy Eisenberg Sasso, Rabbi, Congregation Beth El Zedeck
Response	*Response: A Contemporary Jewish Review*
UAHC	Union of American Hebrew Congregations

Acknowledgments

In the decade I have worked on this book, I have accumulated a long list of those I not only must, but wish to, thank. First among them is my colleague and friend, Rita Simon, who, with great grace, realized that I found myself compelled to write this book and not the one that we had originally planned.

Several institutions advanced this project in material ways. I began what became this history under the auspices of a Marguerite R. Jacobs Memorial Fellowship at the American Jewish Archives. Their staff, especially Abraham J. Peck, Fannie Zelcer, and Kevin Proffitt, who understands this researcher's oblivion to the weather, guided me through the Archives' rich holdings and answered my many requests expeditiously and with good cheer. American University generously supported this project, funding research assistants, travel, a course-release, and most importantly, one sabbatical during which I began my research and another during which I wrote a good portion of the manuscript. In addition, a fellowship from the Memorial Foundation for Jewish Culture enabled me to complete this book.

Archivists and staff at many institutions graciously answered my queries, often surprising both of us with what lay on their shelves and lurked in their closets. I wish to acknowledge Michelle Feller-Kopman, Gina Hsin, and Holly Snyder of the American Jewish Historical Society; the staff of American University's Interlibrary Loan; Jane Lowenthal of the Wollman Library at Barnard College; Joseph Glaser and Rosalind Gold of the Central Conference of American Rabbis Task Force on Women in the Rabbinate; Merrily F. Hart of the Cleveland College of Jewish Studies and Jean Lettofsky of the Western Reserve Historical Society; Josey Fisher and Marion Salkind of the Gratz College Holocaust Oral History Archive; Rosalind Chaiken, Norman J. Cohen, Alfred Gottschalk, Phillip Miller, and Gary Zola of Hebrew Union College-Jewish Institute of Religion; Ira Daly and Susan Woodland of the Archives of Hadassah, the Women's Zionist Organization of America; Lee Sellers and Julio Hernandez-Delgado of the Archives and Special Collections of Hunter College; Virginia North of the Jewish Museum of Maryland; Denise Meringolo of the Jewish Historical Society of Greater Washington; Mayer Rabinowitz and Gerry Schwartzbart of the Library and Rare Book Room and Julie Miller of the Ratner Center for the Study of Conservative Judaism at the Jewish Theological Seminary of America; the Jewish Women's Resource Center; Peggy Pearlstein and Sharon Horowitz of the Library of Congress Hebraica Division; the New York Public Library Judaica Division; Lily Schwartz of the Philadelphia Jewish Archives Center at the Balch Institute; Lois England of the Archives of Washington Hebrew Congregation; Shelley Buxbaum of the Women's League for Conservative Judaism; the Women's Rabbinic Network; Jane Evans, Eleanor Schwartz, and Ellen Rosenberg of Women of Reform Judaism, The Federation of Temple Sisterhoods.

Not only institutions but many individuals helped ferret out buried sources. I wish to thank those who agreed to interviews, brought to my attention materials only they knew existed, shared their insights, and commented upon my public presentations. They include Leslie Alexander, Linnell Ammerman, Dianne Ashton, Michal Bernstein, Irwin Blank, Georgia Sperber Davis, Amy Eilberg, Peter Eisenstadt, Ira Eisenstein, Ann Blitzstein Folb, Joan Friedman, Reena Sigman Friedman, Carol Glass, the late Helen Glueck, Karla Goldman, David Golinkin, Rita Simon Gordon, Lynn Gottlieb, Judith Hauptman, Susannah Heschel, Paula Hyman, Jan Kaufman, Elaine Kahn, Toby Fink Laping, Israel Lehman, Carolyn Gray LeMaster, Sherry

Levy-Reiner, Jay Lueger, Beverly Magidson, Elaine Mann, Margaret J. Meyer, the late Jeremy Newman, Saul Newman, Haviva Ner-David, Mindy Portnoy, Riv-Ellen Prell, Stanley Rabinowitz, Marc Lee Raphael, Ira Robinson, Jonathan Rosenbaum, Judith Pilzer Rudolph, Jonathan D. Sarna, Shuly Rubin Schwartz, Mel Scult, Ida Selavan, Nancy Forse Shloush, Norma Kirschner Skolnik, David Teutsch, Lawrence Troster, and Beth Wenger. American University students, Jodie Fields, Andrea Becker Herman, Vanessa Slifer, and Michelle Terry, facilitated my research, always in the best of spirits, by Xeroxing, reading microfilm, and culling from imposing biographical dictionaries the data I sought.

The relatives of the women who would have been rabbis and the pioneers themselves spent hours poking around dusty attics and leafing through old albums to find the documents I guessed they possessed. They shared their files, their clippings, their scrapbooks, their photos, even cassettes of old speeches, a wealth of documents without which I would have had to write a very different book. Sally Jane Priesand trusted her original documents to me and to UPS and maintained a deep interest in this history. Sandy Eisenberg Sasso gave graciously of her time and her papers. From half a world away Deborah Shulman Sherman dug out the scrapbooks of her mother, Avis Clamitz Shulman, and Kinneret Shiryon unearthed correspondence written when she was Sandy Levine. In New York, Lester Lyons painstakingly sorted through the clippings and letters of his late wife, Helen Levinthal Lyons. Rae Montor and Karel Montor kindly recalled for me what they knew of the attempt of their mother, Martha Neumark Montor, to become a rabbi. Dennis Askwith shared memories of his aunt, Dora Askowith.

Numerous individuals took time out of their busy schedules to critique this work-in-progress. Colleagues Deborah Cohen, Katharina Kellenbach, and Marc Lee Raphael gave valued comments. Beacon Press's readers and editors Deborah Chasman, Tisha Hooks, Lydia Howarth, and Susan Worst helped shape this book. For over a decade Hasia Diner has surely heard more than she ever cared to know about this subject. Her critique enabled me to write a much better book than I would have. Of course, I remain responsible for what lies herein.

Saving the most important for last, I thank my family. My husband, Edward Farber, has shared this project with me as we have shared our lives for more than twenty-five years. Our children, Yoni and Orly, came into the world in the years in which this task absorbed me. I dedicate it to them with love and the hope that by the time they are old enough to read this, they will find it surprising that ever there was a time women could not be anything they wished to be.

Rockville, Maryland
March 1998

Index